CENTRAL B
about 1922

W9-BVX-615

Bijou Palace

DIRKSENSTRASSE

NEUE FRIEDRICH STRASSE

Busch Circus

National Gallery

New Museum

Stock Exchange

NEUER MARKT

Church of St. Mary

Old Museum

KAISER wil-HELM STRASSE

Academie

Cathedral

LUSTGARTEN

Post Office

KÖNIGSTRASSE

City Hall

SUBWAY

Tomb of Unknown Soldier

Armory

Imperial Palace

University

Opera

Crown Prince's Palace

Church of St. Nicholas

SCHLOSSPLATZ

Church of St. Hedwig

Dresdener Bank

Marstall

Spree Canal

MÜHLDAMM

Spree River

Reichsbank

GERTRAUDTEN STRASSE

SUBWAY

JERUSALEMER STRASSE

SPITTEL MARKT

LEIPZIGER STRASSE

| 0 | 100 | 200 | 300 | 400 YARDS |

| 0 | 100 | 200 | 300 | 400 METERS |

Tietz Department Store

ENSTRASSE

Mosse Publishing Company

BEFORE THE DELUGE

BEFORE

THE DELUGE

A Portrait of Berlin in the 1920's

by Otto Friedrich

HARPER & ROW, PUBLISHERS

1817

NEW YORK
EVANSTON
SAN FRANCISCO
LONDON

Portions of this book have previously appeared elsewhere in somewhat different form: Chapter I, "The Birds of Berlin," in *Esquire* magazine; Chapter XV, "I Couldn't Control Myself," in *Works in Progress*.

Acknowledgment is gratefully made to reprint passages from the following:

Memoirs 1921—1941 by Ilya Ehrenburg. Translated by Tatania Shebunina and Yvonne Kapp. English translation copyright © 1963 by MacGibbon & Kee Ltd. Reprinted by permission of the World Publishing Company.

In the Twenties: The Diaries of Harry Kessler by Harry Kessler, with an introduction by Otto Friedrich. Translated by Charles Kessler. Copyright © 1971 by Weidenfeld & Nicolson Ltd. Reprinted by permission of Holt, Rinehart and Winston, Inc.

Fun in a Chinese Laundry by Josef von Sternberg. Copyright © 1965 by Josef von Sternberg. Reprinted by permission of the Macmillan Company.

Maps by Jean Paul Tremblay

Photo Research by Yvonne Freund

FIRST EDITION

STANDARD BOOK NUMBER: 06-011372-3

LIBRARY OF CONGRESS CATALOG CARD NUMBER: 70-156522

To Priscilla

Contents

Illustrations

"All free men, wherever they may live,
are citizens of Berlin. And therefore, as
a free man, I take pride in the words:
Ich bin ein Berliner."

—JOHN F. KENNEDY

BEFORE THE DELUGE

The Birds of Berlin PROLOGUE

> Therefore let us found a city here
> And call it "Mahagonny,"
> Which means "city of nets." . . .
> It should be like a net
> Stretched out for edible birds.
> Everywhere there is toil and trouble
> But here we'll have fun. . . .
> Gin and whiskey,
> Girls and boys . . .
> And the big typhoons don't come as far as here.
>
> BERTOLT BRECHT

"WOULD YOU LIKE ME TO SHOW YOU?" the old man asks. Professor Edwin Redslob is more than old; he is ancient, a survivor of almost a century of violence. He was already in his mid-thirties when Germany's broken armies came straggling home from the First World War, and now he is eighty-six, tall and smiling and white-haired. He can hardly see through the thick lenses that fortify his eyes, but he totters across his dusk-darkened studio, past the window that opens onto the white-blossoming apple trees in the garden, and then he bends over a wooden cabinet that contains his treasures.

As an art expert, he joined the Interior Ministry more than fifty years ago to help the nascent Weimar government create a new image for the new Germany, and he began by commissioning a young Expressionist painter named Karl Schmidt-Rotluff to redesign the most fundamental image, the German eagle. Now he bends over

3

a shallow drawer, grunts and fumbles through a sheaf of pictures, and finally pulls forth the one he wants: the Weimar eagle. He holds it high, gazing at it with affection. The eagle boasts all the pride and dignity of its imperial ancestors, black wings spread wide, beak hungrily open, but it has other qualities as well. It seems less grim than the traditional eagle; indeed, it seems almost cheerful, a friendly eagle. "A marvelous thing," says Dr. Redslob. "But the number of insults that this picture provoked—you wouldn't believe it."

It is a mistake, perhaps, to attach too much importance to symbols. In the Berlin Zoo, there is a real eagle—two of them, in fact— and we can stand outside the cage and regard the imprisoned beast that we consider the German symbol, and our own. At the base of an artificial tree, there lies a pool of rather dirty water, and one of the eagles slowly lowers its claw-feet into the pool and begins picking at the bloody carcass of a rabbit that has been left there to satisfy its appetite for carrion.

In the tranquillity of the Zoo, there are cages for every variety of giant bird—huge hawks wheeling restlessly within the limits of their confinement, flamingos folding and unfolding themselves, and even some mournful marabous, which stand in stoic silence and stare back at their visitors. Wandering loose in the Zoo, ignoring the elephants and the rhinoceroses, there are dozens of mallards, always two by two, the green-headed male trailed by his speckled brown and white mate. Nor do they remain in the Zoo. They float among the swans in the canals outside the Charlottenburg Palace. They roam among the chestnut trees in the Tiergarten. They nibble at weeds in the Havel River. "You don't have ducks like that in American cities?" a Berliner asks in surprise. "Here they are everywhere."

Berlin, more than almost any other great city, is a city of birds. One hears not only sparrows chirping in the midst of the traffic on the Kurfürstendamm but wood thrushes singing in the Glienicker Park. One sees species one never expects to find in cities—magpies and nightingales and a black-feathered, yellow-beaked diving grebe known as a "water chicken." Even at the Hilton Hotel, the traveling businessman wakes to the sound of peacocks screeching in the night.

One reason for this variety of birds is that Berlin has always been what Jean Giraudoux called "no city of gardens [but] a garden itself." Though it is still the largest metropolis between Paris and

Moscow, it also has 835 farms, and almost 200 waterways, and more than half of its land is devoted to parks, forests, and gardens. There are wild boars roaming in the woods of Berlin, and herds of deer, and there are flocks of sheep grazing on the outer runways of Tempelhof airport. The air is clear and cool, a little sharp.

Another reason for the birds of Berlin is that the Berliners care for them, feed them and watch over them. In the southern district of Lichterfelde, in the shadow of a gigantic white research hospital that has been heavily financed by the Rockefeller Foundation, a pink-cheeked old gentleman welcomes a visitor by leading the way out into the back yard so that one can watch him take a shovelful of sunflower seeds from a metal box and spray it on the lawn. One of the green-headed mallards rushes forward to snap up the seeds, and the old man points to a linden tree where a dozen long-tailed doves sit cooing in anticipation. "Turkish doves," he says. "They come from the Himalayas, and they always stop here for their food."

The birds represent, generation after generation, a kind of permanence in a city that has never known the century-old traditions of a Paris or a London. Born in the thirteenth century in the mud and swamps at the junction of the Spree and Havel rivers, Berlin remained a minor crossroads during the grand reigns of Venice and Amsterdam and even, for that matter, Hamburg. As late as 1860, Henry Adams described it as "a poor, keen-witted provincial town, simple, dirty, uncivilized, and in most respects disgusting." Only in the latter part of the nineteenth century, with industrialization and the coming of the railroads, and then the political triumphs of Bismarck, did Berlin grow into the great metropolis of Central Europe (its population, which was 198,000 in 1815, soared to 826,000 by the time the Empire was founded in 1871, and to 2,529,000 in 1900). It was during this period that Mark Twain called Berlin "the German Chicago" and illustrated the taste of his times by writing rhapsodic descriptions of the Kaiser's capital. "It is a new city; the newest I have ever seen. Chicago would seem venerable beside it. . . . The next feature that strikes one is the spaciousness, the roominess of the city. There is no other city, in any country, whose streets are so generally wide. . . . Only parts of Chicago are stately and beautiful, whereas all of Berlin is stately and substantial, and it is not merely in parts but uniformly beautiful."

This imperial city of broad boulevards and massive stone

façades, of neo-Grecian pillars and neo-Roman arches, crumbled to its death under the fearful Allied bombardments that ended World War II. As early as 1943, when the clock of the Kaiser Wilhelm Memorial Church stopped forever at the hour of 7:30, about one thousand acres were laid waste in a single night. In the last months of the war, armadas of American bombers roared over the city every day, and the RAF returned to the battlefield every night. The bombings—363 raids in all—destroyed about ten square miles of central Berlin, wrecked about one-third of the city's 1.5 million buildings, killed or seriously injured about 150,000 people. It was probably the most crushing attack ever inflicted on a major capital, and when the air raids ended in April of 1945, the encircling Russians moved up masses of artillery, a total of 22,000 guns, and began a systematic shelling of everything that remained. In the governmental headquarters around the Wilhelmstrasse, the Russian shells landed at a rate of one every five seconds. The Royal Palace burst into flames, the dome of the Reichstag collapsed in a shower of splintered steel, and when one salvo landed on a riding stable in the Tiergarten, a herd of screaming horses went stampeding down the Kurfürstendamm, their manes and tails aflame.

But the Berliners survived, and with them the indefinable spirit that they call, simply, *"Berlinisch."* Berliners are not at all like other Germans. They are the New Yorkers of Central Europe. They speak in an odd dialect of their own, and, like New Yorkers, they often were born somewhere else. It has been said that the typical Berliner comes from Silesia; it has also been said that every Hungarian can recognize Berlin as his capital. Other Germans, particularly from the south, dislike the Berliners. They consider them raucous, cynical, and generally undignified. The Berliners return the dislike. They regard other Germans as stodgy provincials, and quite likely to be Nazi sympathizers. (They themselves have voted for the left in every election in this century.) What others consider cynicism, the Berliners call wit; what others call brashness, they call pride. They take immense pride in their city, in its breezy sophistication, its air, its trees, its zoo, its remarkable number of slim and beautiful blondes, and they even take a perverse pride in their miseries—their ruined buildings and their wall. This pride is based largely on Berlin's great past, however, and today it contains a strong element of self-delusion.

In the twenty-five years since the war, Berlin has lived through a number of reincarnations: from the defeated enemy capital to the besieged fortress under Soviet blockade, to the showcase of Western democracy, to the isolated and insulated anomaly of today. The thirty-mile-long wall that the East Germans finally built around West Berlin, in order to stop the westward flow of refugees, seemed at first a damning confession of Communist failure, but the ten years since the erection of the wall have weathered the raw concrete blocks, and the barbed wire has rusted from silver to brown, and the "death strips" of mines and machine-gun nests have served their purpose. Berlin today (West Berlin, specifically) has become a sad and stoical city. Its neon lights no longer look so brightly attractive as they once did; its economy depends on outside subsidies; its population is old and growing older; its suicide rate is the highest in Germany, and there is a pervading smell of sewers overflowing beneath the esplanades.

Berliners take solace not only in their birds and trees but in their memories. The oldest ones still talk of the *Kaiserzeit,* those years before 1914, when, as one of them says, "There was peace and order, and a respect for traditional values—*eine cristliche Weltanschauung.*" There are also some, undeniably, who cherish pleasant memories of the Hitler years, when a perverted sort of order reigned, and a shrill voice on the radio summoned all Germans to struggle for the greater glory of the Fatherland. To many Berliners, however, there is another era that seems, in retrospect, to have been the one marvelous season in the sun. A kind of local industry has sprung up, in fact, to satisfy the desire for books, pictures, records, and television shows on what Berliners call *Die goldenen zwanziger Jahre,* the golden twenties.

The twenties were not golden for everyone, of course, for these were the years of the great inflation, of strikes and riots, unemployment and bankruptcy, and Nazis and Communists battling in the streets. Still, the magic names keep recurring—Marlene Dietrich, Greta Garbo, Josephine Baker, the grandiose productions of Max Reinhardt's "Theatre of the 5,000," three opera companies running simultaneously under Bruno Walter, Otto Klemperer, and Erich Kleiber, the opening night of *Wozzeck,* and *The Threepenny Opera.* . . . Almost overnight, the somewhat staid capital of Kaiser Wilhelm had become the center of Europe, attracting scientists like Einstein and von Neumann, writers like Auden and Isherwood, the builders and designers of the Bauhaus School, and a turbulent colony of more than fifty thousand Russian refugees. Vladimir Nabokov gave tennis lessons here, and young daredevils forced their cars to more than a hundred miles an hour on the new Avus speedway, and ladies in evening dress would proceed directly from the theatre to the pandemonium of the six-day bicycle races. Berlin's nightclubs were the most uninhibited in Europe; its booted and umbrella-waving streetwalkers the most bizarre. Above all, Berlin in the 1920's represented a state of mind, a sense of freedom and exhilaration. And because it was so utterly destroyed after a flowering of less than fifteen years, it has become a kind of mythical city, a lost paradise.

There are physical remnants of this lost city everywhere, but it requires a kind of historical imagination to reconstruct the way things were. On one desolate corner of the Wilhelmstrasse, for instance, stands a large segment of a yellow brick wall, an entry to a building that no longer exists. The entry has three arched doorways, and on its roof two headless goddesses face the traffic rumbling along the Anhalter Strasse. This was once the Anhalter Bahnhof, the terminus for all the trains from Austria, Bavaria, and the southeastern cities like Dresden and Leipzig. Some forty thousand people once passed through these arches every day, but there are no trains from the south any more, and the front wall of the station stands alone in an empty field of weeds. Some birds have made a nest in one of its four upper windows. A few blocks to the north, just across the Communist wall, that bomb-scarred building is where the Prussian State Legislature used to sit, when there was a Prussia, and it had a legislature. The last man to make good use of the place was an East German engineer who strung a cable one night from the upper windows to the giant wall and slid to freedom. The building has been closed since then.

Berlin evolved, over the years, along an east-west axis. At the center of this axis, there was, and still is, the Brandenburg Gate, a gigantic neo-Grecian portal, supported by twelve Doric columns, sixty-five feet high, and surmounted by a sculpture of four horses drawing the chariot of the Goddess of Victory. To the east of this gate, along the broad expanse of Unter den Linden, the Kaisers built the solemn buildings of official Berlin—the square, massive, pillared edifices of the Reichschancellery, the Opera, the state library, the university, the arsenal, the cathedral, and finally the Royal Palace. Beyond that lay the cluttered alleys of the old city, that original island in the middle of the Spree River, and then row on row of the glum stucco tenements that housed the city's workers. To the west of the Brandenburg Gate, Unter den Linden turned into the Charlottenburger Chaussee, which swept through the Tiergarten, past the Zoo and the commercial district around the Kurfürstendamm, and out to the new villas of the rich in Grunewald. Even now, when the wall has slashed its way across the front of the Brandenburg Gate, the social geography remains much the same—slums and official buildings in the Communist East, parks and department stores in the West—but, to misquote the old saying, the more things remain the same, the more they change.

The Russians, after World War II, seem to have felt a passionate desire to eradicate the citadels of their enemies. The Communists rebuilt the bombed Opera House, exactly as it was, but they demolished the entire Royal Palace and renamed the vacant space Marx-Engels Platz. Only one fragment has been preserved. On the south side of the square, one oddly old-fashioned balcony has been literally embedded in the long, new State Council Building. It is the balcony where Karl Liebknecht, having marched into the abandoned palace during the chaos of 1918, proclaimed the German Revolution. At the other end of Unter den Linden, the Russians had no sentimental feelings whatever about the Reichschancellery. There is nothing there now but an empty field, and the underground bunker where Hitler and Goebbels committed suicide is just a mysterious hump in the field, covered by grass.

In the West, too, the past lies everywhere, half-buried or half-hidden. On the Steinplatz, just north of the Kurfürstendamm, there is a six-foot stone memorial to the victims of Nazism, and the plaque states that the stones in the memorial came from the ruins of the city's main synagogue, wrecked by Storm Troopers in 1938 during the orgy of window-smashing known as *Kristallnacht*. Around the corner, on the Fasanenstrasse, where the synagogue used to stand, one mosquelike doorway and one pillar from the vanished temple have been embedded, like Liebknecht's balcony, in the bleakly modern gray building that now houses the Jewish Community Center. Berlin has very few Jews nowadays, about 6,000, as compared to 200,000 during the twenties.

Rebuilding has become a German obsession, and so Berlin is full of new skyscrapers, bright, shiny slabs of steel and glass, and some of the city's most famous old institutions have moved into new quarters, keeping only the old names. The Bristol, for example, was once a famous hotel on Unter den Linden, and Kempinski's was a noted restaurant nearby; today, with Unter den Linden ablaze with Red flags, the Bristol-Kempinski has reopened as the most luxurious establishment on the Kurfürstendamm. Other landmarks of the old Berlin still stand in their old places, but deprived of their former functions. Just north of the Brandenburg Gate, the gigantic Reichstag building still shows the bullet holes of 1945, still bears the slightly ironic inscription over its lofty entrance: *"Dem Deutschen Volk"* ("To the German People"). Except for a symbolic visitation from Bonn every year, no legislators meet here at all any more. Here, where Karl Liebknecht first spoke out against Germany's mistakes in World War I; here, where the body of the murdered Walther Rathenau lay in state; here, where Gustav Stresemann gave his famous orations for a reconciliation between Germany and France; here, where the frightened deputies voted emergency powers to Adolf Hitler—here they are installing air-conditioning to make the old building suitable for offices for bureaucrats.

And just a little to the south, where the chestnut trees bloom white along the banks of the Landwehr Canal, the famous Bendlerblock has been converted to offices too. (One of them, in fact, provides the headquarters for a cosmetics company.) This ugly concrete compound was once the German War Ministry, and the Bendlerstrasse was one of those names like Whitehall or the Quai d'Orsay, synonymous with German power. It was in a second-story office on the Bendlerstrasse, a beautiful office with French windows and parquet floors, that Count von Stauffenberg plotted the attempt to assassinate Hitler on July 20, 1944; it was in a small courtyard at the back of the Bendlerblock that Stauffenberg and four other conspirators were lined up against a wall and shot. There is a plaque marking the spot, and a few students wander in to look at it. The Bendlerstrasse has been renamed the Stauffenbergstrasse. The German Army has its headquarters elsewhere.

The old Berlin survives partly in its ruins, as ancient Rome survives in the Forum, but these are dead fragments. Unlike Rome, though, the lost city still lives in the memories of the people who once were there. They are scattered all over the world nowadays, these old Berliners, for the real destruction of Berlin came not from Allied bombers but from the tyranny of Adolf Hitler. On the day he came to power, in January of 1933, the Berliners' diaspora began. Many have died since then, and among the survivors, there is no great desire to return to the hollowed-out, filled-in relic of the city they once knew. But as Hemingway said of Paris, the Berlin of the 1920's remains, for those who remember it, a moveable feast, and in their cities of age and exile, they still delight in savoring the faint, salty taste of their youth.

"It was a renaissance," says Sol Hurok, the impresario, eighty-one years of age, stocky and ruddy, with just a fringe of white hair. There is a grand piano in his Fifth Avenue office, and photographs of ballerinas on the walls, and the old man is recalling how he made his headquarters at the Eden Hotel every summer, and how he signed up Artur Schnabel, and Rudolf Serkin, "and all the great artists." "A renaissance," he says again, in his almost impenetrable Russian accent. "The greatest renaissance in this century. Now how would you translate that into words?"

"If I could choose a time to live in, any time, any place, I'd choose the 1920's, in Berlin," says Rabbi Joachim Prinz. A friendly, sardonic man in a somewhat baggy blue suit, he has been president of the American Jewish Congress, and he takes pride in his auto-graphed portraits of the Kennedys, but now, amid the heavy volumes of the Torah in his library in Orange, New Jersey, he talks about his days as a young student, and about the theatre, and the concerts and the night life. "The Romanische Café was the center of everything. There is even a book about it—here, I give it to you. It was a big, ugly place, across from the Kaiser Wilhelm Memorial Church, but everybody went there, the writers, the actors, every-body." How often did he himself go there? "Every night!" the rabbi answers promptly. How long did he stay? "Until two o'clock in the morning." Is that when it closed? "I don't know when it ever closed," says Rabbi Prinz.

"I loved Berlin," says Yehudi Menuhin, who gave a famous debut there, playing concerti of Bach, Beethoven, and Brahms, when he was thirteen. He is fifty-four now, and living in London, but he is still strikingly boyish, with gray-blond hair and bright blue eyes and a red turtleneck sweater. "Berlin had a most advanced and neurotic society," says Menuhin. "Not the authentic society but a new society based on new money, and on extravagance, brashness, show. The neurosis was the clash of values, between the old and the new. Everything became possible. Everything became Experience, with a capital E—and a capital X."

"I came to Berlin in 1926, and everything I had ever heard about it turned out to be true," says Abram Chasins, the pianist, a small, fragile figure with large ears and a quick smile. We are sitting in his study on the upper East Side of Manhattan, and it is getting dark outside, and as he talks, Chasins gets up from his chair and begins pacing up and down, trying to explain. "Everything was so elegant, so clean, so full of life. It was not in Paris but in Berlin that I saw the most beautiful girls in the world. They were *luscious*."

"Listen to this, listen to this—'so long as your panties are hanging on the chandelier, I'll know that you still—love—me.' " Kenneth Tynan, the theatre critic who created *Oh! Calcutta!,* guffaws as he puts a collection of old Berlin nightclub songs on the record player. Behind him on the wall of his elegant London apartment hangs a rosy painting of a lady's behind. Tynan was never in Berlin during the 1920's, but he has sensed a certain pattern connecting those years to our own. "I enjoy decadence, and I also enjoy democracy. Germany then was about as decadent as it's humanly possible to be, but it was also fairly democratic. It even seemed to be moving toward Socialism, and that would have been ideal—Socialism and self-gratification at the same time."

It would be a mistake to portray the Berlin of the 1920's as one long whirl of half-naked ladies dancing the Charleston. There were all kinds of serious and sober men at work here too—a theologian like Dietrich Bonhoeffer, who was to be executed by the Nazis, and a rocket engineer like Wernher von Braun, who was to achieve high office in Washington. But Berlin was not simply a city of intellectuals either, for most of its people lived the way most people live in other times and other cities, going to work in the morning and returning home at night, worrying about taxes or not worrying about taxes, eating and drinking and marrying and dying. And it is in the ordinariness of life, less than in its surprises, that we can see the common destinies that unite us.

Still, Berlin in the 1920's was a city unlike any other, we tell ourselves, not only because of what it was but because of the fate that lay before it. In retrospect, we may believe we can see the violence of Nazism inherent in the violence of Berlin, but we know that the rise of Fascism was not inevitable, that it could have been prevented up to the very day on which Hitler took power. Yet because it all did happen, we know that Berlin was a doomed city—as doomed as Pompeii—even at the height of its flowering under the benevolent glare of the Weimar eagle. And now only the birds in the parks remain always, more or less, the same.

CHAPTER II

"The Kaiser Has Abdicated" 1918

There died a myriad,
And of the best, among them,
For an old bitch gone in the teeth,
For a botched civilization. . . .

EZRA POUND

HERMANN ULLSTEIN, one of the five brothers who ran the largest press empire in Germany, remembered many years later that the message had come in a telephone call from the office of the Imperial Chancellor, Prince Max of Baden. "News of the greatest importance will soon be announced," the caller said. At the other end of the line, in the editorial office of Berlin's biggest tabloid paper, the *Berliner Zeitung am Mittag*, Dr. Emil Leimdörfer ordered the printers to stop the presses. Within a few minutes, the familiar rumbling in the basement came to a sudden halt. In the eerie silence that followed, a number of editors got up from their desks and gathered in clusters, asking one another in low voices what might happen next. It was just before noon on November 9, 1918.

The door burst open, and the manager of the printing department bustled in to protest against Leimdörfer's order.

"Herr Doktor!" he shouted. "What on earth is all this about stopping the machines? The public's got to have its paper! Better print less news than keep them waiting!"

The editor, Count Max von Montgelas, who had once worked for the Hearst newspapers in the United States, answered with great

14

solemnity: "This is a moment that occurs only once in a century. Try to hold on just another minute or two!"

The phone rang again, and the frantic voice of a privy councilor at the Chancellery shouted the news: "Herr Doktor! His Majesty the Kaiser has abdicated!"

Leimdörfer promptly sent the news bulletin whistling down a pneumatic tube to the composing room, where the managing editor was waiting next to a printer at a linotype machine. The managing editor dictated the story directly to the printer, who took it down and then ran with the hot lead slugs of type to the stone table where the page form was waiting. It took just five minutes for new plates to be fitted into seven printing presses. "And within a quarter of an hour after the call from the Chancellery," Ullstein said proudly, "hundreds of thousands of our newspapers are the first to announce to the world the end of the German Empire. Outside we hear the news vendors shouting: 'The Kaiser abdicates! Ebert made Chancellor! Armistice imminent!' The shouting is taken up by the people pouring out into the streets. . . . The papers are torn from the sellers' hands. While one and all are wild with joy at the prospect of the war's end, they nevertheless feel shocked at *this* end."

Scarcely four years had passed since the euphoric days of August, 1914, when Kaiser Wilhelm II, that pompous figure with the hooked mustache and the withered arm, had reviewed his legions as they passed through the Brandenburg Gate on their way to war. The Germans had genuinely believed, whatever the facts might be, that they were going to war to defend the Fatherland against the aggressive threats of the envious and encircling Allies. Even so rational and humane an observer as the historian Friedrich Meinecke looked back on those days with pride because of their "exaltation of spirit . . . one of the most precious, unforgettable memories. . . . It seemed once more that a kind angel might lead the German people back to the right path."

In the four years of "exaltation," no less than 1,773,000 Germans had been killed (the greatest loss by any one nation in a war that killed a total of at least 8.5 million), and more than 4 million more had been wounded. And even among the survivors, there were occasions when, as Nikita Khrushchev said, the living would envy the dead. Bertolt Brecht, who spent those years as an orderly in a military hospital, recalled the treatment of the wounded as a surrealistic kind of assembly line: "If the doctor ordered me: 'Amputate a leg, Brecht!' I would answer, 'Yes, Your Excellency!' and cut off the leg. If I was told: 'Make a trepanning!' I opened the man's skull and tinkered with his brains. I saw how they patched people up in order to ship them back to the front as soon as possible." There is some evidence that the poet was exaggerating, or indulging in a morbid joke—one scholarly account insists that he spent the war years working in a clinic for venereal disease—but perhaps he was simply expressing, in another form, the truth of his own poetry. For one of Brecht's earliest and most celebrated works, which he often sang to his own music, was "The Legend of the Dead Soldier." This soldier had already "died a hero's death," but "because the war . . . was still far from done," a band of medics dug up the corpse and pronounced him fit for combat. They then "filled him up with a fiery schnapps," and waved some incense to drive away the smell of the graveyard, and a band played, and the soldier marched off, once again, to "a hero's death."

Although the Allied blockade reduced the German people to scrounging for turnips to avoid starvation, and although many of them had become utterly sick of war, the vast majority clung to the belief that their hardships would end in victory. The invading mass of Russians had already given up, after all. The campaigns of Verdun and the Somme and the Marne had taken a ghastly toll, but the Germans had carried those campaigns into the heart of France. The only question was how long the French could hold out before Marshal Hindenburg and General Ludendorff swept triumphantly into Paris. Early in 1918, Hindenburg had actually promised the Kaiser that he would capture the French capital by April 1, and the third of Ludendorff's great spring offensives crashed through five French defense lines, reaching a point only thirty-seven miles from Paris—but there, at a small town called Château-Thierry, the German advance was battled to a standstill by two fledgling regiments of United States Marines. Then, with more than two million fresh American troops pouring into France, the Allied counteroffensive began. British troops, supported by a new weapon called the tank, attacked the Hindenburg Line; French and Americans pushed forward near the Argonne. And the swaggering General Erich Ludendorff, who had run out of troops to be sacrificed, suddenly snapped. On the afternoon of September 28, he raged around his office, cursing the Kaiser and the politicians back in Berlin. The next day, the two commanders summoned the Kaiser and his chief ministers to military headquarters and informed them that the war was lost. An armistice must be signed immediately.

It is profoundly difficult, as we have learned in recent years, for a nation to accept the fact that a war cannot be won, and that all those who died, died in vain. "I . . . cry out to the mourners: he died for nothing," wrote Kurt Tucholsky, the brilliantly caustic social commentator in Berlin, "for madness, for nothing, for nothing, for nothing." The generals, who were responsible, subsequently preferred to blame their loss on defeatism and sabotage at home, on those amorphous forces that they blamed for what they liked to call "the stab in the back," the forces that Adolf Hitler later took to denouncing as "the November criminals." And to many Germans, any accusation seemed plausible because the defeat itself was so shattering, so sudden, and so inexplicable.

Once General Ludendorff made his announcement to the Kaiser, however, there was no choice but to accept it. In response to Allied declarations that there could be no negotiations with what Woodrow Wilson had called "the military masters and monarchial autocrats of Germany," the Kaiser agreed to the formation of a reasonably democratic new coalition, headed by the urbane and liberal Prince Max of Baden, and bringing into the government the Social Democratic opposition. On hearing the High Command's plea for an armistice, the Socialist leader, Friedrich Ebert, turned white, and Prince Max asked for a week's delay before making his appeal to the enemy. "The Supreme Command requests it," the Kaiser answered, "and you have not been brought here to make difficulties for the Supreme Command."

On October 3, 1918, the German government, through the good offices of the Swiss Minister in Washington, formally asked for an armistice based on President Wilson's celebrated "Fourteen Points." And so the negotiations began. Ludendorff apparently thought, though, that the armistice would be precisely that, a temporary halt in the fighting while both sides regathered their strength. The Allies, of course, had no such idea. In a proclamation to the German Army, Ludendorff announced that the enemy was demanding an unconditional surrender, which was "unacceptable to us soldiers." At that point, Prince Max demanded Ludendorff's resignation, and got it.

The proud general had to spend the last month of the war in a Berlin boardinghouse before fleeing to Sweden in dark glasses and false whiskers.

If the generals had given up, the war-weary mass of ordinary Germans certainly had no overwhelming desire to fight on for nothing. As early as April of 1917, and again in January of 1918, when the food ration was cut to an average of one thousand calories per day, there had been riotous strikes by Berlin's metal and munitions workers. They demanded not only more food but "the speedy bringing about of peace." Lacking leadership, however, the strike lasted only a few days and apparently inspired Ludendorff to launch his ill-fated offensives. The lack of radical leadership was not entirely accidental, for the man who claimed that leadership was now working as a shoemaker in Luckau Prison.

In retrospect, Karl Liebknecht seems a most implausible figure to act as the firebrand of the German Revolution. A contemporary photograph shows him striding along a Berlin street with a huge sheaf of papers under his arm—a short, slender man, with pince-nez and a rather military black mustache. He wears a broad-brimmed black hat and one of those stiff white collars that pokes upward into the chin rather than folding down over the necktie. He looks the very model of an accountant on his way to the Reichsbank.

Liebknecht, by then in his forties, had always been a lonely, high-strung, and essentially unlikable man. His father was one of the founders of German Socialism, a friend of Karl Marx, and the old-line party leaders accepted the newcomer less as a comrade than as a comrade's son. What made Liebknecht different from those old-line leaders was a quality that might be called, depending on one's point of view, either passion or fanaticism. As early as 1907, he had published a fierce attack on Germany's military system, and served an eighteen-month sentence for treason. In the crisis of 1914, when the Socialists abandoned their traditional internationalism to vote for the financial credits to wage war, Liebknecht reluctantly bowed to the party's demand for a unanimous vote, but he broke away at the end of that year and became the first Reichstag deputy to vote against new war credits. The military retaliated by calling him to active service in the reserves, and even putting him in a "punishment battalion." As a Reichstag deputy, however, Liebknecht had the right to attend each session, and he repeatedly rose to ask embarrassing questions about the shooting of Belgian hostages, and about the specific causes of the war itself—questions that the other deputies regularly greeted with cries of "Nonsense!" and "Madness!"

When the Socialists finally expelled him in 1916 (not until the following year did a group of like-minded deputies rebel against the war and form the Independent Socialist Party), Liebknecht began publishing a radical newsletter under the name of Spartakus and recruiting other leftists into a group called the Spartakusbund. The Spartakus letters were a small affair—only five hundred copies were printed—and Liebknecht determined to take more drastic action. On May 1, 1916, he called a public meeting at the Potsdamer Platz and began to deliver a harangue: "Down with the war! Down with the government!" At that point, mounted police charged the crowd and seized Liebknecht. For "attempted treason" and "contumacy to the authority of the state," the lonely radical received a four-year prison term.

But now, at the end of October, 1918, the old order was crumbling, and the authorities issued a general amnesty that enabled Karl Liebknecht to return to the increasingly feverish city of Berlin. He had left it as an isolated dissenter; he returned as a prophet vindicated, and with the full support of Lenin's new regime in Russia. Huge crowds welcomed Liebknecht and even carted him through the streets in a flower-bedecked carriage. "Liebknecht has been carried shoulder-high by soldiers who have been decorated with the Iron Cross," one of the government's chief ministers marveled. "Who could have dreamt of such a thing happening three weeks ago?"

The German Army had fought to a point of imminent defeat, but the navy had scarcely fought at all. Ever since the Battle of Jutland in 1916, the British blockade had confined the fleet of twenty-four battleships and cruisers to the harbors of Kiel, Wilhelmshaven, and Hamburg. It is not certain to this day who actually decided to attempt a suicidal break through that blockade—Prince Max, the Imperial Chancellor, was not even informed—but on October 28, the order came from Berlin to steam out into the North Sea for one last grand battle with the British Navy. In Kiel, Admiral Franz von Hipper promptly passed the order along to his men, and the men just as promptly refused to obey. In the boiler rooms of the battleships *Thüringen* and *Helgoland,* stokers quenched the fires by turning hoses on them. The mutinous sailors started by singing revolutionary songs, then raised the red flag of revolt over their idled ships, and finally marched into Kiel and seized control of the city.

In ordinary times, the mutiny would not have lasted much more than a day, but these were times of disintegration, when a revolt succeeds not because of its own strength but because of the weakness, the loss of nerve, of the ruling authorities. In four years of war, the Kaiser's Reich had rotted so badly that the sailors' ill-organized uprising spread without resistance to the rest of the North Sea ports, and within a week, to Berlin.

The Kaiser had left Berlin at the end of October to join his generals at Supreme Headquarters in the Belgian resort of Spa. There, if nowhere else, he could confidently wear his field marshal's uniform and imagine himself still worthy of the title of *allerhöchsten Kriegsherr* (all-highest warlord). But if the Kaiser could not face the increasing turbulence of Berlin, Ludendorff's successor, General Wilhelm Gröner, could. In a meeting with Prince Max and Ebert, at which Gröner announced that the army could not hold out beyond Saturday, November 9, the general learned that the government itself could not hold out unless the Kaiser abdicated. Both Max and Ebert hoped that the Crown Prince might succeed to the throne under a regency, but when General Gröner got back to Spa, he found the Kaiser totally unwilling to give up his crown. Prince Max had equally little success in getting the Kaiser back to Berlin, or in discussing the crisis by telephone, and so he resolved to go to Spa himself.

"If I should succeed in persuading the Kaiser," Prince Max said to Ebert, "do I have you on my side in the struggle against the social revolution?"

Ebert agreed, but with a warning.

"If the Kaiser does not abdicate, the social revolution is inevitable. I do not want it—in fact, I hate it like sin."

Later that same day, however, the Social Democrats confronted Prince Max with a series of new demands and threatened to withdraw from the government unless both the Kaiser and the Crown Prince abdicated by noon of November 8. Prince Max canceled his trip to Spa and struggled to hold his disintegrating cabinet together until an armistice could be concluded. But the cabinet itself had very little control over the nation. Within the course of a few days, an uprising in Munich deposed the Bavarian monarchy, insurgents calling themselves the Workers' and Soldiers' Councils seized control of Frankfurt, Leipzig, Stuttgart, and Düsseldorf, and trainloads of mutinous sailors from Kiel and the North Sea ports began streaming into Berlin. Crowds of truculent soldiers stopped officers in the streets and tore the epaulets from their shoulders. The cabinet ordered the commandant of Berlin to cut off the railroad lines from Hamburg, to occupy the gas and electric plants, and to patrol the main avenues—but the commandant's own troops were in revolt. And Prince Max was still trying to convince the Kaiser by telephone to give up his throne.

"Your abdication has become necessary to save Germany from civil war," Prince Max said on the night of November 8. "The troops are not to be depended upon. . . . This is the last possible moment. Unless the abdication takes place today, I can do no more."

The Kaiser refused to give in. He threatened to reconquer his own Reich by force, and he blamed Prince Max for the government's collapse. "You sent out the armistice offer, you will have to accept the conditions," said the Kaiser. With that, he hung up and went to bed.

Perhaps the most realistic account of Waterloo is not that of a Napoleon or a Wellington but that of Stendhal's Fabrizio, who spent most of the famous day in wandering around the Belgian countryside, trying to find a new horse, losing his musket, falling into ditches, and asking various equally bewildered soldiers, "Is this a real battle?" So it was on the day of the German Revolution.

Artur Schnabel, for one, was in the Rhineland on November 8, giving a series of piano recitals, when he heard that revolution had broken out in Berlin, so he telephoned his wife to see if she was safe. "She had promised our two little boys that they would see *Hansel and Gretel* in the afternoon at the opera house," Schnabel recalled later. "Then she was warned not to go out but to stay at home; but when she saw how unhappy the children were she did not have the heart to deprive them of the expected pleasure; so they went and saw *Hansel and Gretel* on the day of the revolution. Many other children were there and they enjoyed it just as much as they could."

On that same day, the executives of UFA, Germany's biggest movie company, organized a press reception in Berlin for a preview of their newest film, *Carmen*, directed by Ernst Lubitsch and starring the beautiful young Pola Negri. "That evening, my lamé gown was a shimmering triumph," Miss Negri said not long ago. "The champagne was chilled to absolute perfection. . . . The studio orchestra played selections from *Carmen* to get us in the mood. . . . We sat down in the projection room, and the film began. There was applause at my first appearance. Over it and lingering for just a moment after, I heard a faint sound in the distance . . . gunfire." Nobody else paid any attention, but as the noise got louder, Miss Negri turned to Lubitsch and asked if he heard it too. "Yes, shh!" Lubitsch said. "There's nothing anybody can do. Watch the picture."

When the movie ended, everyone applauded enthusiastically and then lingered in the projection room to offer congratulations, and to avoid the unknown dangers of the streets. Until then, the industrious movie-makers had apparently forgotten that their whole country was collapsing. "When the newspapers are shouting daily of disaster, you soon cease to listen," Miss Negri observed. She herself decided that night to make a run for the subways, which were still operating. "The streets were completely deserted," she said. "The only sound was the gunfire directly overhead which crashed through the air with a deafening din. In order not to be hit by a stray bullet, I walked in short steps with my back pressed against the walls of the building. . . . By the time I arrived [at the subway station], I was wringing wet."

The general strike began at 9 A.M. on the cold, gray morning of November 9. It had been called by the Independent Socialists, prodded by Karl Liebknecht and the Spartakists, and its goal was simple: The Kaiser must abdicate. As the crowds began gathering in the streets, the Social Democrats had to decide whether to join in the strike or to cling to their posts in the tottering regime of Prince Max.

Early on that November morning, the Social Democrats' deputy leader, Philipp Scheidemann, telephoned the Chancellery to find out whether the Kaiser had given up. Not yet, was the answer. Scheidemann said the Socialists could wait only until the strike officially began at nine o'clock, and then they would resign. At nine,

Scheidemann called the Chancellery again, found that there was no news from Spa, and announced that the Socialists were abandoning the government forthwith. Officials inside the Chancellery were still trying desperately to reach the Kaiser, but there were only two telephones at the Kaiser's villa. His courtiers had taken one phone off the hook, and they kept the other one busy so that no calls from Berlin could get through. Outside Prince Max's Chancellery, meanwhile, the crowds of striking workers had grown to tens of thousands, waving red flags and shouting for the government to resign. Isolated and desperate, Prince Max simply decided on his own authority to announce the Kaiser's abdication. His aides began telephoning the newspapers.

But the Kaiser had not abdicated. He was still sitting by the fireplace in his fog-shrouded villa outside Spa, occasionally wandering out for walks in the garden, then returning to argue with his generals. Marshal Hindenburg, the seventy-one-year-old commander, was silent and evasive, leaving it to General Gröner to argue the case for realism. When fanatical subordinates claimed that the army could reconquer the rebellious cities of Germany, Gröner was the one who finally said, "Sire, you no longer have an army." They then took a poll of regimental commanders—to this, the Imperial Army had been reduced, to taking polls of its officers. When the poll showed that the army wanted nothing but peace, the Kaiser railed at his officers' abandonment of their oath to their warlord. "Oath to the colors? Warlord?" asked General Gröner. "Today, these are only words." In the stalemate, the Kaiser decided to go to lunch. "After a good lunch and a good cigar, things will look better," said the Crown Prince. After that good lunch, however, the word came that Prince Max had announced the abdication. "Treason, gentlemen!" cried the Kaiser, "bare-faced, outrageous treason!" Only after a long argument with his generals did he agree, finally, to board a special train to his last refuge in Holland.

Philipp Scheidemann, too, was having a good lunch that day. A round, stolid Social Democrat of the old school, Scheidemann had made his way through the tumultuous city to the relative haven of the Reichstag, and there he settled down and ordered a bowl of potato soup. "The Reichstag was like an armed camp," Scheidemann recalled later. "I sat hungry in the dining hall. . . . Then a crowd of workers and soldiers rushed into the hall and made straight for our table. Fifty of them yelled out at the same time, 'Scheidemann, come

along with us at once. Philipp, you must come out and speak. . . .
Liebknecht is already speaking from the balcony of the palace. . . .
Liebknecht intends to proclaim the Soviet Republic.' Now I clearly
saw what was afoot. I knew his slogan—supreme authority for the
Workers' and Soldiers' Councils. Germany to be therefore a Russian
province, a branch of the Soviet. No, no, a thousand times no! . . . I
[went to the window of the Reichstag and] said a few words, which
were received with tremendous cheering. 'Workers and soldiers . . .
the cursed war is at an end. . . . The Emperor has abdicated. . . .
Long live the new! Long live the German Republic!' "

In actual fact, just as the Kaiser had not abdicated when Prince
Max announced the abdication, neither had Liebknecht reached the
Royal Palace—he was still driving around Berlin and haranguing
the strikers at various street corners—but the capital was in such a
state of confusion that Scheidemann's impromptu declaration from
a window of the Reichstag was accepted by the cheering crowd
below as the promulgation of a new law. Almost by accident, Germany had suddenly become a republic, while Scheidemann placidly
returned to his bowl of potato soup. He did not even realize that
his own party leader, Friedrich Ebert, was still hoping to form
a regency. "Ebert's face turned livid with wrath when he heard what
I had done," Scheidemann said later. "He banged his fist on the table
and yelled at me. . . . 'You have no right to proclaim the Republic!' "

But this was no time for rights and technicalities. The shouting
crowds surged eastward from the Reichstag toward the Kaiser's
abandoned palace, eager to see who would gain control of the ugly
stone building that had symbolized for so long the power of the
Hohenzollern emperors. When the general strike began on that
morning of November 9, the empty palace was heavily guarded,
and the barricaded garrison had orders to shoot to kill, but when
the word came that the Kaiser had abdicated, the Berlin commandant issued new orders: "Don't shoot at the people under any
circumstances. Withdraw all troops from the neighborhood of the
palace." At about 2:30 in the afternoon, as the crowds milled about
in the square outside the palace, a shopkeeper named Schlesinger
pleaded with people not to ransack the building, since it was now
public property. To prove his point, he hoisted a red blanket to the
main balcony from which the Kaiser had once reviewed his loyal
troops.

At about four that afternoon, with snow beginning to fall, Karl Liebknecht finally reached the palace, accompanied by a small band of rebel sailors. "A cheer sounded," said Ben Hecht, who had just arrived in Berlin as a twenty-four-year-old reporter for the Chicago *Daily News.* "I watched a black-eyed, quick-moving little man get out of [a] taxi and walk through the snow to the palace entrance. The tall, rosy-cheeked marines stood at salute as he passed." The little man marched on into the palace, followed by about a hundred marines. "There were no orders given," Hecht reported. "It looked like a revolution in which anybody could do what he wanted. . . . I asked no questions and followed Liebknecht. The tall palace rooms were deserted except for a bewildered elderly fellow in a leather apron." From the main balcony of the palace, Liebknecht began making a speech. "The day of liberty has dawned," he said. "A Hohenzollern will never again stand at this place. . . . I proclaim the free socialist Republic of Germany. . . . We want to build the new order of the proletariat, an order of peace and happiness, with liberty for all our German brothers and for our brothers throughout the world. We extend our hands to them. . . ."

Ben Hecht did not understand German very well, and so he missed most of the speech, but, like a good reporter, he followed the speaker into the vanished Emperor's bedroom. "Liebknecht started undressing himself. There was a fierce, lyric look in his black eyes. . . . After several minutes, Liebknecht stood barefoot in a suit of long winter underwear. Some of its buttons were missing and the flap of the seat was baggy from too much laundering. He picked up his briefcase and four large books. With these under his arms, he approached the Kaiser's bed. . . . The marines had stiffened. They stood watching. . . . Liebknecht . . . placed his bulging briefcase and four reference books on the small bedside table and crawled in between the cold royal sheets. The room had become heavily silent. I heard the royal bedsprings creak as Liebknecht stretched out his legs. Then, as he turned to reach for a book, there was a sudden sharp noise. The spindly-legged bedside table, an antique, had collapsed under the unaccustomed weight of revolutionary literature. The lamp hit the floor and one of its bulbs exploded. And the Soldiers of the Revolution fled . . . routed by more ghosts than I had been able to imagine."

For a day of revolution, there was surprisingly little violence.

Shooting broke out sporadically, but the huge crowds remained relatively peaceful—the number of dead totaled only about fifteen. Liebknecht, after the scene at the Royal Palace, returned to the streets and moved on to the offices of a conservative newspaper, the *Lokal-Anzeiger*, which he took as the headquarters for a new radical paper, *Die Rote Fahne* (*The Red Flag*). At police headquarters in the Alexanderplatz, which had been barricaded by the crowds, a left-wing Independent Socialist named Emil Eichhorn simply walked up to the door and announced: "I am the new police president." There was no opposition whatever from the terrified police, not even when Eichhorn marched through the cellblocks and released 650 prisoners who had been arrested during the past few days of demonstrations.

By nightfall of that day, November 9, it had become clear that, although nobody quite knew who ruled Berlin, the old regime of the banished Kaiser had fallen. Prince Max met Friedrich Ebert in the Chancellery and simply handed over to him whatever powers of government were left to be handed over. Ebert pleaded with the Prince to stay on in Berlin as an "administrator" for the affairs of the Hohenzollern monarchy, but Max politely declined.

"Herr Ebert," said Prince Max, "I commit the German Empire to your keeping."

"I have lost two sons for this Empire," said the distracted Ebert.

But there was no empire any more. There was only Friedrich Ebert—all alone in the Chancellor's private office on the second floor of the abandoned building on the Wilhelmstrasse—and shaken by the events that had suddenly made him the highest official in Germany. He had been born to poverty, the son of a tailor in Heidelberg. He had spent his early years as a saddle-maker, and later as a bartender. He had worked on a Socialist newspaper, then become a professional party functionary in Berlin. He brought to the organization such novelties as accounting and filing (the elderly conspirators who had preceded him traditionally burned all their correspondence), and the membership rapidly began to grow. Ebert was forty-eight now, somewhat stout, with hooded eyes and a rather adventurous goatee. Despite the goatee, though, he was a thoroughly conventional man, respected for his decency and good sense rather than for intellect or passion. To him, Socialism meant better wages and working conditions, under a benevolent monarchy—and here he found himself thrust, not quite legally, into the position once held by Bismarck.

Suddenly one of the office telephones, numbered 988, began to ring. Ebert picked it up with some bewilderment and found that it was a secret private line, installed by Ludendorff, to military head-quarters in Spa.

"Gröner speaking," said the voice of Ludendorff's successor.

Ebert warily asked the general how the army planned to deal with the crisis. The answer was reassuring. The Kaiser, now asleep on his private train, had agreed to flee to Holland. Hindenburg was in complete command of the front-line armies and expected to march them back to Germany.

"What do you expect from us?" Ebert asked.

"The field marshal expects the government to support the officer corps in maintaining discipline and strict order in the army. . . ."

"What else?" Ebert asked.

"The officer corps expects," said Gröner, "that the government will fight against Bolshevism and places itself at the disposal of the government for such a purpose."

"Convey the thanks of the government to the field marshal," said Ebert.

And so General Gröner committed the remnants of the Imperial Army to the fight for the new Republic, while Friedrich Ebert committed that Republic to the maintenance of the old officer corps; together, they agreed to suppress by force the Revolution that they both "hated like sin." In later years, when the secret of the private telephone line became known, Ebert was fiercely attacked for his compact with General Gröner. "The German Army was saved," wrote one of the more extreme critics, "but the Republic, on the very day of its birth, was lost." Friedrich Ebert undoubtedly felt quite dif-ferently. Until that same day, the Kaiser had been talking of using the army to reconquer the rebellious cities of Germany. For the new Republic to gain the support of the army, Ebert believed, meant not the destruction but the salvation of democracy in Germany.

"The really important thing during any crisis," says one Berliner who remembers the days of the Revolution, "is whether the street-cars are running. If the streetcars keep running, then life is bearable." And so it should be recorded that on November 9, the day the German Empire fell, the streetcars of Berlin continued running. Telephones functioned, too, and so did the systems that provided gas, water, and electricity.

Friedrich Ebert's idea of a revolution was obviously quite different from Karl Liebknecht's idea of a revolution, but that does not mean that it was no revolution at all. The downfall of a governing monarchy is a rather substantial political change, after all, and Ebert followed the abdication by rapidly enacting a series of social reforms that had been no more than dreams a year earlier. "The government created by the Revolution . . . is setting itself the task of carrying out the Socialist program," began the decree of November 10 from Ebert's regime of six Social Democratic and Independent "commissioners."

The decree forthwith proclaimed an amnesty for political prisoners and announced complete freedom of speech, press, and assembly. All public groups were to be elected by the free, equal, and secret ballots of everyone over the age of nineteen. The decree also promised that the Ebert government would do its best to provide food, jobs, and housing—and, eventually, the socialization of basic industries. This last objective was never carried out, to be sure, but Ebert's objectives seem, in retrospect, far more admirable than his left-wing critics ever admitted. ("We have not had a revolution in Germany, but we've had a counterrevolution," cried Kurt Tucholsky.) Ebert's actions also represented, in their limited way, the limited goals of an essentially conservative population. Even on the day of the Revolution, when firing broke out around the Royal Palace, it has been said that the crowds scurrying for cover in the adjacent park scurried only along the pathways. That was because the signs at the edge of the paths gave a firm order: "DON'T WALK ON THE GRASS."

There remained the bleak necessity of formally ending the war. Until the last moment, the civilian leadership found it hard to believe that their mighty armies had collapsed so completely. As late as October 7, Walther Rathenau, the brilliant industrialist who had organized Germany's raw materials for the war effort, published an impassioned appeal for a *levée en masse*. "The people must be ready to rise in defense of their nation. . . . There is not a day to lose. . . . There will be enough men to be found who are yet sound, full of patriotic fervor. . . . All men capable of bearing arms must be combed out of the offices, the guard-rooms and depots. . . . Our front is worn out; restore it, and we shall be offered better terms."

Prince Max had taken Rathenau's proposal seriously enough to ask the High Command whether such a mobilization might have any hope of success. The High Command promptly answered that it would not. But the High Command itself, while unable to fight on, was also unwilling to surrender. Prince Max, solicitous of the army's sensitivity, therefore had called on a civilian cabinet official, Matthias Erzberger, to head a three-man German commission to sign the armistice. This was fitting, in a way, since Erzberger had been one of the earliest critics of the war, but it also imposed on Erzberger the responsibility that the army itself should have borne—that of surrendering.

En route from Berlin, Erzberger stopped in at Supreme Headquarters in Spa to see if there was any last message from Hindenburg. One can imagine the loathing with which the old field marshal regarded his visitor. Erzberger was a rather pudgy and ill-mannered politician, able and intelligent but widely regarded as a schemer and a "defeatist." But Hindenburg's greatest anxiety, apparently, was that Erzberger might demand that the General Staff join in signing the surrender. With tears in his eyes, Hindenburg clutched Erzberger's hand and urged him to do his patriotic duty.

In a car bedecked with white flags, with a trumpeter standing on the running board and blowing his bugle, Erzberger and his two commissioners drove westward into the Forest of Compiègne. A light rain was falling, and the leaves were beginning to drift down from the silver birch trees as the Germans arrived at the lonely railroad siding where Marshal Foch was awaiting them. His terms were harsh: the evacuation of all German forces behind the Rhine, the surrender of the fleet and all heavy armaments. There were to be no negotiations. The Germans had seventy-two hours to sign. And so, on the morning of November 11, Erzberger signed.

General Gröner was as good as his word. It took him less than a month after the armistice to perform the difficult feat of marching two million soldiers home from France to Germany. By early December, therefore, he was ready to "restore order" in Berlin.

During that first month of peace, Friedrich Ebert's writ had scarcely extended beyond the Chancellery, for the Berlin garrison had virtually disintegrated, and a half-dozen different military or pseudo-military groups roamed the streets more or less at will. The whole city, wrote Tucholsky, resembled "a fourth class waiting room full of misfortune. . . . Our Berliners . . . no longer work, instead they hold meetings and run around." On December 11, then, Ebert felt cheered to see the vanguard of nine army divisions marching up Unter den Linden. The sky was lead-gray, and the marching infantry-men looked weary, but General von Lequis and his cavalrymen made an impressive show as they rode into the city with their lance pennants fluttering and their band playing "*Deutschland über Alles.*" "I salute you," Ebert declared to the defeated army as he welcomed the troops at the Brandenburg Gate, "who return un-vanquished from the field of battle."

No sooner had the army arrived, however, than most of it dis-integrated. Soldiers either drifted into the streets or simply packed up and went home. And so the crisis of governmental authority con-tinued. Five days after the army's entry into Berlin, a National Con-gress of Workers' and Soldiers' Councils convened in the capital and claimed full sovereignty for itself as the representative of the Ger-man people. Although the Congress was numerically dominated by Ebert's Social Democrats, it passed a resolution demanding the election of all officers by their soldiers, the abolition of all insignia, and the eventual replacement of the regular army by a People's Army (Volkswehr). General Gröner and his chief aide, Major Kurt von Schleicher, promptly rode to Berlin in full-dress uniforms and told Ebert that the resolution was intolerable. "If you complicate [my task] by nonsense of this sort," said General Gröner, "I must say that this is the end!" Ebert's response to the Congress' militant resolu-tions was, characteristically, more diplomatic. He simply ignored them. It was much more important that the Congress had ratified his own leadership and had joined in calling elections for a new National Assembly. This Assembly, presumably, would represent not just the radicals but all of the people.

General Gröner was not alone in his defense of the old system, and the bitterness of the professional officers was mild compared to that of the officers who were now being demobilized. At a military rally in the Berlin Philharmonic Hall during that first postwar month, a government spokesman pleaded for support of the new Republic, but a twenty-five-year-old air force captain named Hermann Goering rose to protest. Climbing to the platform in his full uniform, decorated with silver epaulets and Germany's highest medal, *Pour le Mérite*, the former commander of the Richthofen Squadron declared: "We officers did our duty for four long years . . . and we risked our bodies for the Fatherland. Now we come home—and how do they treat us? They spit on us. . . . And therefore I implore you to cherish hatred—a profound, abiding hatred of those animals who have outraged the German people. . . . But the day will come when we will drive them out of our Germany."

One man who had already dedicated himself to that hatred had only been a corporal, but he felt presentiments of higher things. Adolf Hitler, then twenty-nine, half-blinded during a gas attack, was confined to a hospital in Pasewalk, eighty miles north of Berlin, when a pastor told him of "the greatest villainy of the century," the Revolution and armistice. "Everything went black before my eyes," Hitler later wrote in *Mein Kampf*. "I tottered and groped my way back to the dormitory, threw myself on my bunk and dug my burning head into my blanket and pillow. . . . So it had all been in vain. In vain all the sacrifices . . . in vain the death of two millions. . . . There followed terrible days and even worse nights. . . . In these nights hatred grew in me, hatred for those responsible for this deed. In the days that followed, my own fate became known to me. . . . I, for my part, decided to go into politics."

It was not given to Friedrich Ebert to know the consequences of these hatreds. His most immediate problem in these closing days of 1918 was the insurrection of the People's Naval Division. An ill-disciplined assemblage of mutinous sailors from the various North Sea ports, the People's Naval Division numbered some three thousand men, the largest left-wing force in Berlin. With the fall of the Royal Palace on November 9, the sailors had taken possession of the building, which they proceeded to pillage. (One observer noted that even the handles of the Kaiser's walking sticks had been unscrewed and stolen.) Ebert did not want them in the palace, but he had no way of forcing them out, so he agreed in mid-December to pay them 125,000 marks for "guarding" the palace, if they, in turn, would reduce their force to six hundred men and move out of the palace into the adjoining Marstall, a large stone building that had once served as the royal stables. Five days later, the sailors had neither reduced their force nor moved out of the palace but they now demanded another eighty thousand marks as a Christmas bonus. When they tried to collect the money, nervous guards opened fire on them. Ebert finally agreed to pay, but only if the keys to the palace were surrendered, whereupon the sailors invaded the Chancellery and marched into the office of Ebert's civilian military governor of Berlin, Otto Wels. After smashing up the office, they seized Wels and two of his subordinates and took them back to the palace. There, they beat their captives with rifle butts and threw them into a rat-infested coal cellar to serve as hostages until the money was paid. The rest of the invaders remained at the Chancellery, where they locked the gates, seized the telephone switchboard, and refused to let anyone leave or enter. Once again, Ebert relied on his secret telephone line to military headquarters, now located at Kassel, about two hundred miles southwest of Berlin. General Gröner's aide, Major von Schleicher, answered at the other end.

"The government is made prisoner, Major," said Ebert. "You have always said that if such an event took place you would come to our assistance. Now is the time to act."

"I will take the necessary measures at once," said Major von Schleicher. "General von Lequis' troops in Potsdam will march on Berlin to set you free."

Ebert continued negotiating with the sailors, however. Late in the evening, he got them to withdraw from the Chancellery in exchange for his promise of unconditional payment of the eighty-thousand-mark Christmas bonus. But as soon as the sailors heard that eight hundred Imperial Horse Guards were marching into Berlin from the suburban garrison of Potsdam, they rushed back to the Chancellery and demanded that Ebert call them off. Now that Ebert thought he could settle the crisis by negotiations, he again called military headquarters and said he wanted the troops recalled. General Gröner had other ideas. "The field marshal and I are at the end of our patience," he said. "Your persistence in this eternal negotiation is breaking down the fighting spirit of the last troops faithful to the officers. . . . The field marshal and I are determined to hold to the plan of liquidation of the Naval Division, and we shall see to it that it is carried out."

At about midnight, the Imperial Horse Guards clattered into the square in front of the palace. Reinforced by another thousand troops who had been bivouacked in the Tiergarten, they methodically went about setting up their artillery and machine guns. All night, the sailors waited with increasing fear for the attack that would come at dawn. They tried several times to parley with the Horse Guards, but with no success. At five in the morning, a leader of the Independent Socialists entered the palace and persuaded the sailors to release the battered Otto Wels and his two assistants from the coal cellar, but the Horse Guards still had their orders. At seven o'clock, a captain of the guards marched up to the palace gate and demanded that the sailors surrender within ten minutes or the army would begin firing. The sailors, who had won a promise of reinforcements from other naval units on the North Sea, did not answer. The first artillery barrage blasted open the main entrance to the palace. The iron doors swung ajar, crazily tilted on their hinges. One pillar fell with a crash, and an arm broke off one of the female statues supporting the main balcony. From the shattered windows, the sailors responded with sporadic rifle fire, but when a vanguard of a hundred guardsmen charged the doorway, they found the palace virtually abandoned. The sailors had fled through an underground passage to the nearby Marstall.

The guardsmen now concentrated their artillery fire on the royal stables, and at 9:30, the sailors finally waved a white flag and asked for a twenty-minute truce. The trapped sailors were ready to surrender. The shelling had already killed thirty of them and wounded more than a hundred. The survivors had little ammunition and no food. But what neither side realized was that Karl Liebknecht's Spartakists had been cruising the city since early morning, appealing for everyone to save the palace from a monarchist counterrevolution. Thousands of people answered the call, and soon they packed all the streets leading to the palace—held back only by the roar of artillery. As soon as the twenty-minute truce was called, they swarmed into the square and began haranguing and harassing the beleaguered guardsmen. The effect was overwhelming. Soldiers who might willingly fire at a distant abstraction called "the enemy" found themselves helpless when confronted by throngs of argumentative students and reproachful old women. Some of the guardsmen threw down their weapons in disgust, others began to fall back, and ultimately the officers had to march their remaining troops out of the palace square, leaving it in the possession of the triumphant crowd.

It was a shattering defeat for the proud generals, the last defeat of the Imperial Army. But this was also Christmas Eve, and to many Berliners, Christmas was more important. Count Harry Kessler, a protean figure who drifted through the 1920's as diplomat, publisher, art patron, and man-about-town, observed the shambles outside the Royal Palace but also noted in his diary that "throughout the blood-letting, hurdy-gurdies played in the Friedrichstrasse while street vendors sold indoor fireworks, gingerbread, and silver tinsel. Jewellers' shops in Unter den Linden remained unconcernedly open, their windows brightly lit and glittering. In the Leipziger Strasse the usual Christmas crowds thronged the big stores. In thousands of homes the Christmas tree was lit and the children played around it with their presents. . . . In the Imperial Stables lay the dead, and the wounds freshly inflicted on the Palace and on Germany gaped into the Christmas night."

The next day, Christmas itself, the Spartakists called for another huge demonstration, and the crowd marched from the Tiergarten to the Royal Palace and then on to the headquarters of the Socialists' own newspaper, *Vorwärts* (*Forward*). The Spartakists seized the building and began printing leaflets entitled *The Red Vorwärts*: "All power to the workers and soldiers! Down with the Ebert-Scheidemann government!" Poor Ebert by this time had very little government left. The Independent Socialists quit his coalition on December 29, blaming him for the "bloodbath" at the Marstall. One of the Independents, Emil Eichhorn, clung to his post as police chief, however, and as Ebert surveyed the armed forces still loyal to his command, he could count on no more than about 150 men in all of Berlin.

Inexorably, it seemed, the power to rule the streets of Berlin was drifting into the hands of Karl Liebknecht's Spartakists. By now, Liebknecht's leadership of the left had been strengthened by the reappearance of one of his earliest and most brilliant associates, Rosa Luxemburg. A small, stout woman, then forty-five, afflicted with a hip injury that made her limp, Rosa Luxemburg had come from Poland, where she had been one of the leaders of the Socialist movement, a gifted orator and writer, a rival even of Lenin. Jailed during the war for her support of Liebknecht, she had written an influential series of prison letters that attempted to formulate the Spartakus doctrine—militant but democratic Socialism, internationalism and peace at almost any price. Despite her "radical" beliefs, however, Rosa Luxemburg was a cautious tactician. She argued repeatedly that there must be no revolution until the forces of the left were united, and the working class was ready to rise.

Now, in the last week of 1918, that time seemed near. Liebknecht's Spartakusbund summoned a convention to extend its power by merging with the left wing of the Independent Socialists and a labor group called the Revolutionary Shop Stewards. The three formed a new party: the Communist Party of Germany. From day to day, Berlin was full of rumors that Liebknecht was about to stage a putsch, and the weary Friedrich Ebert could think of no response except flight. "I shall go away," he said to General Gröner over the now-useless telephone line. "I shall disappear utterly from the Chancellor's palace and go to sleep. . . . Only a porter will be left. If the Liebknecht crowd takes this opportunity to seize power, there will be nobody here. . . . And then we shall be in a position to set up our government somewhere else. . . ."

CHAPTER III

"Some Shots Were Fired. Nobody Knew Why" 1919

We [in the Freikorps] were a band of fighters drunk with all the passions of the world. . . . What we wanted, we did not know; what we knew, we did not want.

ERNST VON SALOMON

BERLIN IN THE WINTER is never a very cheerful place. The sky hangs gray and low over the city for days on end, and the stone buildings that line the broad boulevards look massively bleak and forbidding. As the new year of 1919 began, the people of the defeated city, swarming with embittered ex-soldiers and refugees from the east, knew every form of cold and hunger and misery. An epidemic of influenza killed thousands; more than seventeen hundred died in a single day. And the armistice was not a peace. While the Allied diplomats in Paris conjured over their terms for a settlement, the Allied navies continued to blockade the German coast.

"Germany lay prostrate," wrote Count Kessler. "France gave open vent to her desire for our extermination, expressing it monumentally in her Prime Minister's words: 'There are twenty million Germans too many.' The continuation of the blockade after the armistice was rapidly fulfilling this wish; within six months from the armistice it had achieved a casualty list of 700,000 children, old people and women. . . . The German people, starved and dying by the hundred thousand, were reeling deliriously between blank despair, frenzied revelry, and revolution. Berlin had become a nightmare, a carnival of jazz bands and rattling machine guns. . . . On the very day [of one battle in the center of the city] the streets were placarded with a poster 'Who has the prettiest legs in Berlin? Visit the Caviare-flapper dance at such and such a cabaret at 8:30 P.M.' Profiteers and their girls, the scum and riffraff of half Europe—types preserved like flies in amber in the caricatures of George Grosz— could be seen growing fat and sleek and flaunting their new cars and ostentatious jewelry in the faces of the pale children and starving women shivering in their rags before the empty bakers' and butchers' shops."

George Grosz himself had enlisted in the army during what he later called "the mass intoxication" of 1914, but he had soon found the war to be a matter of "filth, lice, idiocy, disease, and deformity." Discharged for what was then called "brain fever," he returned to "dark, gloomy" Berlin and started to set down on paper the horrors that he had seen. Recalled to service again in 1917, he went into a kind of amnesic fit. "One night, I was found semi-conscious, partially buried in a dung pit," he said later. "I was regarded as a deserter and was told that I was to be shot." Count Kessler knew of the young artist, however, and got him transferred to a mental institution until he could return to Berlin and resume his work. "My drawings expressed my despair, hate and disillusionment," Grosz said. "I drew drunkards; puking men; men with clenched fists cursing at the moon. . . . I drew a man, face filled with fright, washing blood from his hands. . . . I drew lonely little men fleeing madly through empty streets. I drew a cross-section of a tenement house: through one window could be seen a man attacking his wife; through another, two people making love; from a third hung a suicide with body covered by swarming flies. I drew soldiers without noses; war cripples with crustacean-like steel arms; two medical soldiers putting a violent infantryman into a strait-jacket made of a horse blanket. . . . I drew a skeleton dressed as a recruit being examined for military duty. I also wrote poetry. . . ."

In his time of despair, Friedrich Ebert suddenly found a major ally, Gustav Noske, a stocky man of fifty-one, with rimless glasses and a cavalryman's mustache. Noske had spent the first days of the revolution as Ebert's emissary to the naval mutineers in Kiel, and when the Independents' withdrawal from the government left the War Ministry vacant, General Gröner suggested that Noske might be worth consulting. The army had good reason to put its confidence in Noske, for he had been reared in the parochial kind of Socialism where, as he put it, "no one ever talked of Marx or Marxism." He had once hoped to be a forester, but his parents were too poor for him to get the necessary training, and so he became an apprentice to a basket weaver. For him, as for Ebert, Socialism meant rising from poverty and sharing in the glories of the Kaiser's Reich. He dismissed Rosa Luxemburg and the other Socialist intellectuals from beyond the Elbe with the contemptuous term, *"Ostleute"* ("East people"). Even before the war, he had argued strenuously for Germany's right to acquire colonies in Africa, and his nationalism was so militant that one newspaper made fun of him with a poem that ran:

> Noske straps his saber on,
> Noske goes all out,
> Noske fires, boom, boom, boom,
> Noske storms the redoubt.

Now, returning from Kiel, Noske found Ebert's office filled with politicians arguing chaotically about candidates for the War Ministry. Noske demanded a decision, and when somebody turned and asked him if he himself wanted the post, he answered: "Of course. Someone must become the bloodhound. I won't shirk the responsibility."

Noske was an energetic organizer, and, as Ebert's new bloodhound, he promptly set to work to organize the forces available to the government. In doing so, he soon learned of a secret plan that Major Kurt von Schleicher had devised to combat the disintegration of the old regiments. As early as mid-December, the Supreme Command had approved Schleicher's plan and assigned a relatively obscure infantry commander named General Ludwig von Maercker to organize an entirely new kind of volunteer force known as the Freikorps. Schleicher wanted only the most loyal and disciplined veterans, who could be organized into highly mobile "storm battalions," each with its own trucks and artillery. To maintain high morale, Maercker figured out a compromise between the blind obedience of the old Imperial Army and the surly insubordination of the new "Soldiers' Councils." Each Freikorps recruit would sign on for only a short term, renewable each month, and he would have the right to vote for "deputies," who would speak for the enlisted men on such matters as pay, leave, and any complaints against the officers.

On January 4, in the midst of another one of the Spartakists' daily demonstrations, Noske took the demoralized Friedrich Ebert for a drive out to the suburban town of Zossen, thirty-five miles southwest of Berlin. There was a parade ground there, covered with snow, and when the two Socialist ministers arrived at the edge of the field, a military band suddenly began to play. Then the men of "Maercker's Volunteer Rifles" started marching briskly across the field. There were artillerymen and machine-gunners too—four thousand troops in all—all in neat formations, all marching with the flawless precision of the prewar army. "Real soldiers," said the astonished Ebert. And every single one of these troops, General Maercker told the two ministers, had signed a personal pledge of loyalty to "the provisional government of Chancellor Ebert." As the two enheartened ministers drove back to Berlin, Noske slapped Ebert on the back and said, "Don't worry. Everything is going to turn out all right now."

Maercker's Volunteer Rifle Corps was only one of about a dozen Freikorps units that the army had already formed—the navy provided the Ehrhardt Brigade and the Löwenfeld Corps—and the movement was spreading. Originally, the Freikorps represented the professional officers' passionate desire to rebuild an effective armed force; within a rather short time, they were to become a collection of some two hundred piratical bands, merciless in their attacks on civilians and loyal to nobody but their own unit commanders. In that first week of January, though, Ebert inevitably saw the new Freikorps as the only force that could stand between his own government and a Communist putsch. Within forty-eight hours of Ebert's drive to Zossen, the test came.

Emil Eichhorn, the Independent Socialist who had taken over police headquarters on November 9, had refused to leave when the Independents quit the government at the end of December. On the contrary, he continued to install his own supporters in the top ranks of the Berlin police and to ignore the depredations of leftist groups like the People's Naval Division (Eichhorn had declared the police neutral during the battle of the Marstall). On January 4, the government told Eichhorn that he was dismissed, but Eichhorn promptly went to the headquarters of his party, the Independents, who thereupon joined with the Communists in calling for a mass protest demonstration.

The next day was a Sunday, and the restless Berliners mobilized by the thousands outside police headquarters in the Alexanderplatz. When Eichhorn's successor drove up to police headquarters, the crowd blocked him from the entrance and roughed him up as well. Eichhorn himself appeared on a balcony and told the crowd that he would never give up his post. Inside the police headquarters, the left-wing leaders, apparently intoxicated by the turbulence outside, decided that the time for a real revolution had finally come.

Only two of the seventy-one left-wing leaders were Communists —Liebknecht and Wilhelm Pieck—and the official Communist line argued that the revolution should be delayed until the workers were solidly behind it—but Liebknecht, never the most tranquil of men, could not resist the temptation to become the Lenin of Germany. In the euphoric mood of the Alexanderplatz, he carried all opposition before him. At twilight, Liebknecht went out on the balcony and told the crowd of his great plans. "He speaks with unctuous solemnity like a parson," said one observer at the scene, "intoning his words slowly and expressively. . . . Only part of his words were intelligible, but his sing-song inflexion carried . . . right across the square. When he ended, there was a roar of approval, red flags were flourished, and thousands of hands and hats rose in the air." As night fell, the left-wing leaders inside police headquarters formed a fifty-three-member "Revolutionary Committee" and proclaimed a general strike to begin the next morning. They declared that they had "deposed" the Ebert government, and they decided to start handing out the arms they had been collecting ever since the armistice.

So began "Spartakus Week." The strike on Monday morning succeeded in closing most of Berlin's factories, stores, transport, and electricity. Some 200,000 demonstrators surged through the streets, and bands of them seized most of the main railroad stations, the newspapers, and even, for a time, the Brandenburg Gate, where riflemen could fire down on anyone moving in Unter den Linden. It is difficult now, looking back with the hindsight of more than fifty years, to tell whether these roving bands really represented the militant proletariat or whether many of them were simply wanderers, bystanders, the crowds who gather around any sign of action in any large city. At this point, Berlin had some 250,000 unemployed, and many of them were hungry and desperate, ready for anything. And when we look at photographs of the Spartakist troops on the march, we see nothing more formidable than a band of workmen, most of them in baggy suits and half-buttoned coats, in galoshes and berets and old fedoras, all of them walking out of step, with their rifles swinging crazily at every angle.

Bertolt Brecht, in his first-produced play, *Drums in the Night*, portrayed the whole scene as one of utter confusion. The hero, Kragler, wandering toward the battle around the *Vorwärts* building, ends up in Glubb's Gin Mill. "He says he wants to go down to the newspaper district, that's where things are happening," one of the bar girls remarks. "But what *is* happening in the newspaper district?" ". . . Just control yourselves," says Glubb, the bartender. ". . . Sure you feel offended, they slaughtered you with cannon and sabres, and swindled you, and spat on you a little. So what?" And from one corner, a drunk bursts into song:

> All my brothers now are dead, yes, dead.
> I've come through alive, I don't know how.
> In November I was Red, yes Red.
> But it's January now.

Throughout the confusion, the ubiquitous Count Kessler wandered the streets, constantly noting down what he saw:

"*January 6*: Eleven o'clock, corner of Siegesallee and Viktoriastrasse. Two processions meet, the one is going in the direction of Siegesallee, the other in that of Wilhelmstrasse. They are made up of the same sort of people, artisans and factory girls, dressed in the same sort of clothes, waving the same red flags, and moving in the same sort of shambling step. But they carry slogans, jeer at each other as they pass, and perhaps will be shooting one another down before the day is out. . . .

"When I reach Brandenburger Tor, vast masses of [Spartakists] are coming down Unter den Linden from the east. At Wilhelmstrasse they encounter just as immense a throng of Social Democrats. . . . Suddenly, shortly after one, a tremendous uproar: 'Liebknecht, Liebknecht! Liebknecht is here!' I see a slender, fair-haired youth running away from the mob. They catch up with him, strike him. He keeps on running. . . . From all sides there are shouts of 'The Young Liebknecht! Liebknecht's son!' He stumbles, disappears under the seething mob. . . . Suddenly he is visible again, his face mangled and blood-stained, exhausted but supported by Spartakists who have rushed in and now drag him away.

"Meanwhile a hansom cab is surrounded by the mob, which tries to drag out the occupants. One of them is supposed to be Liebknecht himself, but I can see pretty clearly that he is just an elderly man with spectacles and a soft hat. The crowd nevertheless rocks the cab from side to side. The old nag staggers from one side to the other as though drunk. But rescue arrives here too in the shape of Spartakists who punch their way through the throng and run off in triumph with the wearily trotting chestnut bay and its rickety cab. . . .

"Going back through Leipziger Strasse, I meet a crowd of armed civilians lined up in front of a department-store. Impossible to tell whether they are on the Government or Spartakus side. A strong detachment of government troops moves across Potsdamer Platz at the double. There is shouting all the time. . . . Shortly after four (it was still reasonably light) I looked for a moment into the Ministry of Foreign Affairs. Empty. No clerks, no attendants, let alone senior officials; just soldiers at the windows. As I left, some shots were fired. Nobody knew why. . . .

"I went to the Kaiserhof [Hotel] and, to anticipate all eventualities, took a room. Service was normal, though guests were few and far between. . . . I heard soldiers in the street below shouting to each other, then saw them running across the wet, glistening pavement and taking cover. Silence followed. At half past five violent shooting, the rat-tat-tat of machine-guns, the pounding of artillery or trench mortars, the blast of grenades. . . . Soldiers were in the hotel, waiting for Spartakus to launch an attack. Government troops, they said, still held the key central points. . . .

"*January 7:* At eleven o'clock I watched a big Spartakus parade in the Siegesallee. Shots were being fired in the Königgrätzer Strasse. On the Brandenburger Tor were Government troops with a machine-gun. The Wilhelmstrasse was again choked with people, Government sympathizers. The windows of all Ministries were crowded with soldiers.

"At four in the afternoon I was passing the Brandenburger Tor when there was an outburst of rifle-fire and tossing of hand-grenades. Panic. Hundreds of people rushed in the direction of the Tiergarten. I remained where I was and could see that Spartakus was trying to push forward from Unter den Linden to Wilhelmstrasse. Someone said that a group of Spartakists had climbed Brandenburger Tor and captured the section of Government troops. At any rate the machine-gun up there was not firing any more. . . .

"At nine o'clock, at home, I could hear machine-gun fire in front of the door. Towards one in the morning, a hot exchange of shots in the street. At two, more rifle fire.

"*January 8:* The Wilhelmstrasse is impassable. A gun has been mounted in front of the Chancellery. At intervals a machine-gun fires from the balcony of the Ministry of Interior to prevent Spartakists from bringing a machine-gun into position on the roof of a house at the corner. . . . I made my way to the upper part of Unter den Linden. To the rat-tat-tat of distant machine-guns life proceeded almost normally. A fair amount of traffic, some shops and cafés open, street-vendors peddling their wares, and barrel-organs grinding away as usual."

What makes Count Kessler's chronicle so interesting is not simply his description of the anarchy in the streets but his total unawareness of the grand strategies in the rival headquarters. The newspapers published inconclusive reports of inconclusive negotiations between Ebert and the Independent leaders, but most Berliners, like Kessler and various characters in Brecht's plays, experienced Spartakus Week only as a bewildering series of clashes, of shouting crowds and armed men rushing across streets, of intermittent gunfire from unidentified snipers at unknown targets. Among the leftist leaders, too, there was confusion. When Rosa Luxemburg learned that Liebknecht had started the revolution without any real preparation, she cried in protest, "How could you? What about our program?" The "Revolutionary committee" met and argued for hour after hour about that program, and the Communist newspaper, *Die Rote Fahne,* complained bitterly about the lack of leadership: "The masses were standing from nine in the morning in the cold and fog. Somewhere their leaders were sitting and conferring. The fog lifted and the masses were still standing. . . . But nobody knew what to say because the leaders were still conferring."

The one man who knew what he wanted to do was War Minister Gustav Noske, the bloodhound. On the first morning of the general strike, January 6, he abandoned the threatened Chancellery and walked through the Brandenburg Gate to the red-stone building that housed the army General Staff. Finding that building also threatened by a crowd, he summoned a car and drove to the southwestern suburb of Dahlem, where he set up his headquarters in a classroom of a girls' boarding school. Ably supported by his Berlin commandant, General Walther von Lüttwitz, Noske spent the first day organizing radio communications and summoning every available unit of both regular and Freikorps troops. By January 9, he was able to send a force of twelve hundred men to one of the main Spartakist outposts in the headquarters of the Social Democratic newspaper, *Vorwärts*. Some 350 defenders armed with rifles had barricaded themselves behind rolls of newsprint, but the government forces quickly blew open the doorway with two howitzers. Clearing out the building, despite the white flag flown by the defenders, the troops seized three hundred prisoners and summarily executed a number of them.

On the night of January 11, Noske himself marched from Dahlem into the center of Berlin at the head of a force of about three thousand Freikorps troops, including Maercker's Rifles. Up the Potsdamer Strasse, and then to the Wilhelmstrasse, where the Chancellery lay in silence, they met no opposition whatever. Even the once-powerful People's Naval Division remained in the Marstall, cowed into neutrality. Noske promptly sent one unit marching eastward to recapture the police headquarters on the Alexanderplatz. The Freikorps blasted open the front of the building, and then the invaders swept in, shooting down anyone who fought back, as well as a good many who didn't. The rest of Noske's force moved on to establish headquarters in the Moabit barracks just north of the Tiergarten.

The next day, the bloodhound's troops spread out from Moabit to both east and west, clearing out any building that offered any resistance, breaking up any street demonstrations with armored cars and machine guns. "Today," Count Kessler wrote on January 14, "the band . . . stood playing *Lohengrin* among the splintered glass in the courtyard behind the badly battered main gate of Police Headquarters. A large crowd collected in the street, partly to see the damage and partly to hear *Lohengrin*. Nonetheless shooting continues." The strike lasted only two more days, the last Spartakist resistance only two more days beyond that. The toll of dead, mostly among the insurgents, came to more than a thousand.

Then the Freikorps began hunting for Karl Liebknecht. In the last days of Spartakus Week, the Communist leader slipped away from the battleground in disguise and went into hiding. He found sanctuary with a worker's family in the slum district of Neukölln, in the southeast of the city. Ignoring the ruin of the revolt he had launched, Liebknecht peacefully spent his time reading fairy tales to the young daughter of the household that was sheltering him. He heard that his own wife and son had been captured, but he made no effort to do anything about it. He seemed in a kind of trance.

Neukölln was an obvious target for the Freikorps manhunt, and each day, the street patrols came dangerously close to capturing the fugitive. On the night of January 14, Liebknecht decided to flee to the middle-class district of Wilmersdorf, about four miles to the west. There he found a haven in the apartment of a relative named Frau Markussohn, and there he was joined by two other fugitives—Rosa Luxemburg, exhausted, her cheeks sunken, and plagued by crippling headaches, and Wilhelm Pieck, a relatively minor Communist functionary who had come to bring false identity papers. Even here, Liebknecht continued to issue manifestoes: "Hold hard. We have not fled. We are not beaten. . . ." And Rosa Luxemburg wrote a last attack against the government's claim that order had been restored: " 'Order rules in Berlin.' You stupid lackeys! Your 'order' is built on sand. Tomorrow the revolution will rear ahead once more and announce to your horror amid the brass of trumpets: 'I was, I am, I always will be!' "

This sanctuary lasted only one day. A neighbor informed the police of the strangers in the building, and at 9 P.M. on January 15, a squad of Horse Guards marched into the apartment and arrested them. The Horse Guards had made their headquarters in the Eden Hotel, next to the Zoo, and there they brought the three prisoners for questioning. After being pushed through a cordon of taunting soldiers, Liebknecht and Luxemburg disappeared into a second-floor suite, while Pieck waited outside in the corridor. The questioning by Captain Waldemar Pabst began formally enough, but, as might be expected, the formality did not continue for long. "I shall never forget," one of the hotel maids said later, "how they knocked the poor woman down and dragged her around." (Pieck, curiously enough, was not mistreated at all, and there is some reason to believe that he saved himself by informing on other rebel leaders—an interesting be-

ginning for the man who ultimately became the first President of
Communist East Germany.)

When the interrogation of Liebknecht and Luxemburg ended,
Captain Pabst made a show of having them driven off into custody
at Moabit Prison, where a number of other insurgent leaders were
being detained. But Pabst and the Horse Guards had already
planned quite a different end to the affair. Troopers led the two battered prisoners, separately, to a side entrance of the Eden Hotel,
where a burly private named Otto Runge was waiting with his rifle.
Liebknecht came out the door first, and Runge promptly clubbed
him over the head with the butt of his rifle. The guards bundled
Liebknecht into a waiting car and drove off toward the Tiergarten.
Then came Rosa Luxemburg, limping and dazed from the beating
she had already received. Once again, Runge swung his rifle butt,
and a second band of guards thrust the dying woman into a second
waiting car.

The first car, carrying Liebknecht and six officers, stopped in one
of the dark byways of the Tiergarten. The officers said the car had
broken down. They pushed Liebknecht out into the street, and then
an officer named Captain Horst von Pflugk-Hartung shot him to
death. The six officers dragged the body back into the car and delivered it to a nearby mortuary, explaining that they had found the
corpse of this unknown man at the side of the road. Back at the Eden
Hotel, they officially reported to Pabst that they had been forced to
shoot the prisoner "while trying to escape."

Rosa Luxemburg was too badly beaten for the officers in the
second car to attempt such a masquerade, and so a lieutenant named
Kurt Vogel simply put a pistol to her head and blew her brains out.
The troopers then drove to the Liechtenstein Bridge and threw Rosa
Luxemburg's body into the Landwehr Canal. They, too, returned to
the Eden Hotel with an extraordinary tale to tell. They said that their
car had been stopped by an angry crowd of citizens who had demanded vengeance on the notorious Communist leader. They had
surrendered their prisoner to the crowd, they said, and they had no
idea what might have happened to her. For a time after this story
was made public, there were rumors that Rosa Luxemburg was still
alive, in hiding, awaiting the propitious moment to return to the
battle for Berlin. Not until four months later, at the end of May, did
the bloated and unrecognizable corpse wash up at one of the locks
of the Landwehr Canal.

Friedrich Ebert was genuinely horrified at the murders. He ordered a judicial investigation, but, as so often happens, nobody was quite sure who was actually responsible, and the investigating judge was not excessively determined to find out. The lowest man, Private Runge, the one who had swung the rifle butt, was naturally the only one who went to prison. He served a term of several months for attempted murder. Lieutenant Vogel, who had shot Rosa Luxemburg, was convicted of illegally disposing of a corpse, but he fled to Holland and was eventually amnestied. Captain Pabst, who lived on until 1970, admitted that he had ordered the murders but insisted to the end that they were "an execution in accordance with martial law," and that the Freikorps in general had "the full support of Noske." Nobody has ever proved that Noske was actually involved, but Noske never succeeded in clearing his reputation either. That was part of the price of being the bloodhound.

As for Ebert, he was determined to invoke the verdict of the entire German people on all the successes and failures of his brief regime. He had good reasons for this strategy, since the Social Democrats had won at least a quarter of the votes in every election since the turn of the century. Now, on January 19, the very week after the smashing of the Spartakus uprising, thirty million Germans went to the polls, and the results were a solid triumph for Ebert. The much-abused Social Democrats won almost 11.5 million votes, 38 percent of the total, and 163 of the Reichstag's 421 seats. Next came the Catholic Center Party, with 89 seats, and then the liberal Democratic Party with 74. The right-wing Nationalists, who still accused Ebert of betraying the Kaiser, won only 42 seats, and the Independent Socialists, who had seemed so powerful during the street fighting in Berlin, got only 22. The Communists, still hoping to gain power through the disintegrating Workers' and Soldiers' Councils, boycotted the election and got nothing.

The Social Democrats' victory was clearly a vindication of Ebert's disputed rule (which had originally been based on nothing more substantial than Prince Max's weariness of conflict). More important, it was a vindication of Ebert's belief that the national sovereignty, which had rested for so long in the hands of the Hohenzollern emperors, could not be inherited by self-appointed revolutionary groups in Berlin but only by the German people as a whole. With this mandate, Ebert now proposed to create a legitimate parliamentary government, and to write a new constitution for the nation. Berlin itself was still an unsafe place to carry out this plan, however, and so Ebert decided to convene his Constituent Assembly in the famous old town of Weimar, 150 miles southwest of the capital. Weimar had a great tradition of culture and humanism—Goethe and Schiller had lived here, under the benevolent patronage of the grand duke—but there were also practical reasons for the decision. Maercker's Volunteer Rifles could and did provide an atmosphere of tranquillity by digging in just outside the little town and maintaining strong patrols at the railway station, the post office, and the national theatre.

It was in this theatre, where Franz Liszt had once conducted the premiere of Wagner's *Lohengrin*, that Ebert and his five commissioners now sat on the stage, decorated with pots of tulips and carnations. Ebert, in a black frock coat, gave the opening address on February 6 and appealed for a new era of peace and conciliation. He blamed Germany's miseries on "Kaiserism" and promised that the Socialists would do their best to renew the nation. There were sporadic interruptions from both the Nationalists and the Independent Socialists, but the overwhelming majority of the delegates responded by electing Ebert as the first President of the German Republic. Ebert, in turn, named Philipp Scheidemann as Chancellor, to head the so-called "Weimar Coalition" of Social Democratic, Center, and Democratic parties, and then the delegates settled down to considering the new Constitution.

It had been drafted by Hugo Preuss, a professor of law at the University of Berlin, a liberal, and a Jew. Since Germany had had little experience with constitutional government—neither had most other nations, for that matter—Preuss had pieced together what he considered the best features of all functioning systems. Like America, the new "Weimar Republic" would have a strong President, elected by the whole people; like Britain, it would have a Chancellor responsible to the legislature; like France, it would protect minority interests through proportional representation; like Imperial Germany, it would retain, though on a limited scale, the autonomy of the provincial state governments. In retrospect, we know that the Weimar Constitution had dangerous weaknesses. Provincial autonomy permitted the Nazis to flourish in Bavaria under the protection of compliant state authorities; proportional representation caused such a proliferation of small parties (at the end there were forty different groups in the Reichstag) that representative government came to a standstill; and the famous Article 48, which empowered the President to rule by decree, eventually led to the installation of Adolf Hitler in the Chancellery.

All this lay beyond the prophetic powers of the delegates in Weimar, however, as they argued for weeks over the protection of local interests and the colors of the new republican flag. But what Preuss had drafted was essentially a sound and democratic Constitution, and after a series of minor compromises, the draft was officially approved. The troubles that were to come stemmed not from the Constitution, which, like all constitutions, was simply a piece of paper, but from the society that the Constitution was supposed to represent. It was a society fiercely divided against itself, divided not only between extremes of radical and conservative ideology but between classes, regions, and religions. It was a society shattered by both the psychological and economic consequences of military defeat, and still facing the crises of reparations, inflation, foreign invasion, and intellectual demoralization. "The history of the world's democratic constitutions had, up to this time, been largely a story of people searching for a rational political document under which they could live," as one historian, Richard Watts, has observed. "The constitution . . . drafted at Weimar . . . began and would end as a document in search of a people."

While the Assembly was lumbering along in Weimar, under the guns of the Freikorps, the battered Communist leadership in Berlin decided on one last attempt to seize power by force. "Workers! Proletarians!" cried the front page of *Die Rote Fahne* on March 3. "The hour has come again. The dead arise once more. . . . Let all work cease. . . . Gather in the factories! . . . On to the general strike!" The Communist chairman, Leo Jogiches, a Polish intellectual who had been the lover of Rosa Luxemburg, argued that there must be no violence, no provocation that would enable Noske's increasingly powerful Freikorps to repeat the massacres of January. But, as before, the Communist leaders had very little control over the turbulent rebels. Large numbers of workers already had weapons, and they promptly attacked several police stations. The People's Naval Division abandoned its previous neutrality and marched out of the palace to besiege the police headquarters in the Alexanderplatz. This time, however, Noske and his Freikorps commanders were not only ready but eager to suppress the uprising. Ebert's cabinet authorized Noske to use dictatorial powers in Berlin, and Freikorps troops began pouring into the city by the tens of thousands, armed with tanks, artillery, and flame throwers.

Once again, Count Kessler was watching and recording:

"*March 6:* In the morning . . . severe skirmishes . . . Barricades and wire entanglements have been erected all over the city, partly by Spartakists, partly by Government troops. There were no papers this morning, so I went to see for myself the state of things. . . . The Rathaus [City Hall] is in the hands of armed patrols of the Republican Security Guard. The latter and a People's Naval Division are attacking the Police Headquarters, where Reinhardt [Brigade] Government troops are lodged. At the corner of Königstrasse . . . a fairly phlegmatic crowd stands behind a barrier . . . and listens to the shooting; there is nothing to be seen. Bullets are whizzing across the Alexanderplatz and from time to time the dull thud of a mortar can be heard. . . .

"*March 8:* The last two days have seen more bloodshed in Berlin than any since the start of the revolution . . . five to six hundred dead. . . . For the moment the strike has been suspended. . . . At the Chancellery they are drunk with victory. . . . In the northern parts of the city, seething hatred . . . is said to be the preponderant mood. Reinhardt [Brigade] soldiers who go through the streets alone there are torn to pieces by the mob. . . .

"About a quarter to five I was passing down the Wilhelmstrasse when a lorry stationed in the courtyard of the Chancellery was being loaded with prisoners, both civilians and soldiers. . . . Suddenly a soldier with a whip jumped on the lorry and several times struck one of the prisoners just before the lorry drove out into the street. . . .

"I went inside the Chancellery. . . . I reported . . . the incident of the prisoner being struck, demanded an inquiry, and had my testimony recorded. The lieutenant expressed his regret at the incident, but explained . . . that the prisoner was found to have on him the papers of three officers who have disappeared. . . . The bitterness of the Reinhardt troops is boundless. Last night a sergeant was stopped in the street by Spartakists and shot out of hand. Two soldiers have been thrown into the canal by Spartakists and others have had their throats cut. All the abominations of a merciless civil war are being perpetrated on both sides. . . .

"The electricity is on again. Business as usual in the cabarets, bars, theatres, and dance halls. . . .

"*March 9:* Today the struggle is for the Frankfurter Allee. This is being kept under machine-gun fire by the Spartakists and . . . howitzer shelling by the Government. Flyers are participating in the struggle. It is a proper battle. . . .

"In the afternoon took a walk through the center of the city to inspect the damage. . . . There is a lot of glass lying about in the streets and in some parts it is covered with a thick layer of pulverized brick. Police Headquarters has some fresh scars to add to its old ones. Every single window of Tietz [department store] is smashed. On the pavement in front of the store is a pool of blood. The house opposite, at the corner of Prenzlauer Strasse, is wrecked from the roof to two floors down, either through aerial bombing or shelling. . . . Barbed wire and barricades manned by Government forces everywhere. A good deal of shooting still, though not quite clear by whom or what for . . .

"*March 10:* Yesterday Noske proclaimed martial law in Berlin: 'The cruelty and bestiality of the Spartakists fighting against us compel me to issue the following order: Every individual caught in the act of armed conflict against the Government forces is to be shot immediately. Noske.' . . .

"This evening the Government announces that executions have begun. A batch of thirty, for a start. Noske is ensconced in the Ministry of War behind barbed wire . . . just like Nicholas II or the tyrant Dionysus.

"*March 13:* Soldiers went to arrest George Grosz in his studio. He managed to escape on the strength of some false papers he had on him and is now a fugitive, sleeping in a different place each night.

"The White Terror proceeds without restraint. The execution of twenty-four sailors by Government troops in the courtyard of a house in Französische Strasse appears to have been sheer gruesome murder: the sailors simply came to collect money from the paymaster's office. . . .

"*March 14:* I cannot get out of my head the memory of the execution of the twenty-four sailors in the Französische Strasse. . . . This evening I tried, but failed, to find distraction in Reinhardt's production of *As You Like It*. I am haunted by these murders and shootings which are the order of the day in Berlin. . . .

"*March 16:* In the morning to George Grosz's studio. . . . He told me something of what he has seen during the past few days. . . . In the vicinity of the Hotel Eden, a lieutenant shot a soldier . . . who did not have his identity papers on him and gave an impertinent answer. The man's comrades, whether from grief or fury, wept. Grosz now professes himself to be a Spartakist. Force, he argued, is essential to implement its idea because there is no other way to overcome middle class inertia."

The story is generally told in political terms, with each side blaming the other, but the suffering reached a state far beyond any political differences. John Maynard Keynes, for example, cited the testimony of an observer who accompanied Herbert Hoover's mission to help the starving: "You think [this] is a kindergarten for the little ones. No, these are children of seven and eight years. Tiny faces, with large dull eyes, overshadowed by huge puffed, rickety fore-heads, their small arms just skin and bones, and above the crooked legs with their dislocated joints the swollen pointed stomachs of the hunger edema. . . . 'You see this child here,' the physician in charge explained; 'it consumed an incredible amount of bread, and yet it did not get any stronger. I found out that it hid all the bread it re-ceived underneath its straw mattress. The fear of hunger was so deeply rooted in the child that it collected the stores instead of eating the food: a misguided animal instinct made the dread of hunger worse than the actual pangs.'"

And at the end of the battles, the women had to collect the bodies. Käthe Kollwitz, the artist, went to the central morgue in Berlin and recorded the scene: "A dense crowd of people filing by the glass windows, behind which the naked bodies lie. Each has its clothing in a bundle lying upon the abdomen. On top is the number. I read up to number 244. Behind the glass windows lay some twenty or thirty dead. . . . Now and then some of the people waiting would be led out past me to the other room, and I heard loud wailing from that room. Oh, what a dismal, dismal place the morgue is."

So Noske had won this third and last test of strength between the Social Democrats and the left. Central Berlin was a shambles, and another two thousand people had been killed, but Ebert's govern-ment finally stood triumphant behind the guns of the reborn army. Among the executed prisoners was Communist Chairman Leo Jo-giches, and with his death, the Communists went into a period of retrenchment and reorganization. The Spartakus movement was dead. But so were Ebert's promises of a republic based on social justice.

The armistice of 1918 had been only an armistice, and nothing had been settled, not even Germany's frontiers in the east and west. But the Allies could still fight on, if necessary, which the Germans could not. The Allies were drafting a peace treaty accordingly.

Despite Germany's obvious helplessness, Foreign Minister Count Ulrich von Brockdorff-Rantzau went to the Versailles peace conference in April of 1919 with a set of proposals that now seem remarkably ingenuous. Germany would agree to disarm to the same degree that her neighbors disarmed. She was prepared to give up a few border territories—Alsace-Lorraine to France, northern Schleswig to Denmark, and a small area around Posen to the newly independent state of Poland—but only after plebiscites proved that the inhabitants wanted the change. Germany would pay reparations, but only for damage to civilians and their property. She demanded the return of her African colonies and her captured merchant fleet.

Brockdorff-Rantzau was a professional diplomat, a thin, bloodless Prussian with a monocle, and the French gave him a reception that must have filled him with dread. They forced his special train, loaded with 180 diplomats and experts all preparing to argue the German case, to creep along at ten miles an hour so that the Germans could get an impressive view of the devastated countryside of northern France. In Versailles itself, the French led the Germans to an isolated hotel, surrounded by barbed wire, and told them to carry their own baggage upstairs. Only after a week of confinement in the hotel was Brockdorff-Rantzau finally summoned to the Hall of Mirrors, where French Premier Georges Clemenceau welcomed him by announcing, "The hour has struck for the weighty settlement of our account." There were to be no negotiations; the Germans were simply to receive the terms that the Allies had agreed on.

The terms were stunning. France was to get Alsace-Lorraine outright, she would occupy all German territory west of the Rhine for fifteen years, and she would take possession of the rich coal mines of the Saar district, which was to be governed by the League of Nations. Poland would get the important industrial region of Upper Silesia, most of Posen province, and West Prussia (thus establishing a Polish "corridor" to the sea and cutting off East Prussia from the rest of Germany). Denmark and Belgium would slice off several border regions, and the League would take charge of Germany's African colonies. And disarmament would apply to Germany alone. Her military forces would be cut to 100,000 long-term volunteers, her General Staff would be abolished, and, since the army was to be purely for internal use, Germany would be forbidden to possess any warplanes, tanks, or armored cars. The Weimar Republic would have to admit formally that it was responsible for "causing all the loss and damage to which the [Allies] have been subjected as a consequence of the war imposed on them by the aggression of Germany." A Reparations Commission would be established to assess the amount Germany must pay (preliminary estimates ran as high as $120 billion). And finally, Kaiser Wilhelm and all other "war criminals" would have to be turned over for prosecution by the Allies.

Brockdorff-Rantzau made a futile effort to submit German counterproposals and then brought the peace treaty back to Berlin. He recommended that it be rejected. With all parties uniting to halloo their opposition to the treaty, Chancellor Scheidemann not only rejected it but resigned, crying out in the Reichstag, "What hand would not wither that binds itself and us in these fetters?" The Allies were not greatly concerned about German protests, however. Their answer was simple. Either the German government would sign the treaty or the Allied armies would invade Germany. In fact, the Allies gave the Germans exactly one week—until 7 P.M. on June 23 —to comply.

Scheidemann's resignation on June 19 left Germany without any government at all. While Ebert hunted for someone willing to take over the Chancellery, he also had to ponder whether his generals would try to fight on, or accept defeat—or attempt a coup against him. The army still had some 350,000 men, after all, and the Freikorps officers were of uncertain loyalty. At headquarters, General Gröner had already asked Hindenburg to decide the army's future, and to put his answer in writing. Hindenburg, as usual, was evasive.

"Ought we not to appeal to the officers and . . . our citizens to sacrifice themselves to save our national honor?" he asked.

"The significance of such a gesture would escape the German people," Gröner dryly answered.

Hindenburg retired to his quarters to brood over his answer. After a restless night, he said to Gröner, "I agree with you . . . but I cannot and will not give up those views which have guided me all my life." He handed Gröner a note for the government, in which he admitted that "we cannot . . . count on repelling successfully a determined attack of our enemies . . . but as a soldier I would rather perish in honor than sign a humiliating peace."

Two days before the Allied deadline—the same day on which the German Navy contributed its share by scuttling fifty of its sixty-eight ships in captivity at Scapa Flow—Ebert finally put together a cabinet that was willing to sign the peace treaty. Its Chancellor was a relatively obscure Social Democratic labor leader, Gustav Bauer. Its dominant member was its Deputy Chancellor and Finance Minister, Matthias Erzberger, leader of the Catholic Center Party, who had taken the responsibility of signing the original armistice. Since then, Erzberger had engaged in private discussions with various Allied diplomats, and he now argued that if Germany would sign the treaty, as it must, the Allies might agree to drop the galling clauses about war guilt and war criminals. After a violent debate, the Reichstag voted to accept the treaty on these conditions. The Allies promptly rejected the proposal, replying that "the time for discussion is past," and warning that the Germans had only twenty-four hours left before the Allied invasion would begin. At this, the Bauer government began coming apart. General Maercker called on War Minister Noske and urged him not to sign but to take over as dictator.

"For you, Herr Minister, I would let myself be cut to pieces," said the general, "and so would my infantrymen."

"General, now I, too, have had enough of this rotten mess," said Noske.

Threatened with Noske's resignation, Ebert once again telephoned Hindenburg, and Hindenburg once again evaded the responsibility. "You know as well as I that armed resistance is impossible," the field marshal said to General Gröner, but when it came time to report that decision to Ebert, Hindenburg said, "You can give the answer to the President as well as I." As soon as Gröner had given the answer, then, Hindenburg clapped a hand on his shoulder and said, "You have taken a heavy burden on yourself."

The High Command's acceptance of defeat ended Noske's dream of dictatorship, and Ebert persuaded him to stay in office. Then the government sent the Allies its answer. Germany still viewed the treaty as an "unheard-of injustice," the message said, but it was "yielding to overwhelming force," and it was "ready to sign." The message reached Paris just an hour and a half before the new invasion was scheduled to start.

In looking back across time, we occasionally see that the political crises of a given period were not necessarily its most important events. We forget even the names of the once-powerful princes who commissioned Michelangelo's David or Bach's Brandenburg Concerti. And in this spring of 1919, when the Freikorps forces were battling their way through Berlin, and the German government was trying to negotiate for a treaty to end the war, the scientists who worked at the Kaiser Wilhelm Institutes in the peaceful western suburb of Dahlem were concerned with something more fundamental, an imminent eclipse of the sun.

The reason for this concern was that it would provide the first opportunity to obtain scientific proof for the revolutionary theories of the young director of the Astrophysical Institute, Albert Einstein. The first elements of his theory, dealing mainly with time and motion, had been published as early as 1905—when Einstein was still a twenty-six-year-old examiner at the Swiss Patent Office in Berne—and a subsequent series of papers led to the General Theory of Relativity in 1915. Two years before that, the great physicist, Max Planck, had voyaged to Switzerland and promised the émigré every honor the Berlin scientific community could offer, if he would return to Germany and make his headquarters in the capital. He was, even in his appearance, a most remarkable figure—"still a young man," according to the diaries of the French novelist Romain Rolland, "not very tall, with a wide and long face, and a great mane of crisp, frizzled, and very black hair, sprinkled with gray and rising from a lofty brow." So at the age of thirty-four, Einstein returned to Germany and became not only a director of the Kaiser Wilhelm Institutes but a professor at the University of Berlin and a member of the Prussian Academy of Sciences. He had, however, no fixed duties of any kind. He moved into a large and handsomely furnished apartment in the suburb of Dahlem, gave one seminar a week for his fellow scientists, played his violin, and worked at his theory.

Physicists were fascinated by the computations by which Einstein showed, among other things, that mass and energy are the same, that the speed of light is a constant, and that the energy of a mass can be computed in terms of the square of the speed of light. But if the theory was difficult to comprehend, it was even more difficult to prove. In March of 1917, however, Britain's Astronomer Royal, Sir Frank Dyson, suggested that an eclipse on March 29, 1919, would provide an excellent chance for such a proof, since the darkened sun would pass through an exceptionally bright group of stars, the Hyades. At that moment, the light rays from the stars could be measured as they passed close to the sun. According to one key argument of Einstein's theory, light has mass and therefore must be subject to the influence of gravity. Thus the light rays from the Hyades must bend as they passed the sun during the eclipse.

The major difficulty at the time was that Britain and Germany were at war, but wars play only a limited part in the plans of astronomers. As soon as the armistice was signed, Britain's Royal Astronomical Society announced that, with four months still to go, it would send two expeditions to photograph the eclipse at the points where it could best be observed, the town of Sobral in northern Brazil and the island of Príncipe in the Gulf of Guinea. When Einstein was asked how much the light rays of the Hyades should be deflected by the sun's gravity, he computed the answer to be 1.75 seconds of an arc. In due course, the royal astronomers journeyed to the tropics, worried over the cloudbursts that threatened the view of the eclipse, and aimed their primitive cameras at the sun. The team sent to Brazil never got any clear pictures at all, and the African group got only sixteen. It took eight months for the scientists to return to London and study the comparative photographs of the Hyades during an eclipse and during an ordinary evening. When they measured the results, they found that the light rays during the eclipse had indeed been bent out of their normal path by the sun's gravity, and that the degree of deflection was almost exactly what Einstein had prophesied: 1.64 seconds. Alfred North Whitehead, who was present when these events were disclosed at a meeting of the Royal Astronomical Society, felt that "the whole atmosphere of tense interest was exactly that of the Greek Drama. We were the chorus commenting on the decree of destiny as disclosed in the development of a supreme incident." The next day's *Times* of London was more succinct. "Revolution in Science," said the headline. "Newtonian Ideas Overthrown."

"How Long Will I Live?" 1920

It is impossible to think of a number, or even of a name, of one's own free will. If one investigates the seeming voluntary formation, let us say, of a number of many digits, uttered in unrestrained mirth, it always proves to be strictly . . . determined.

SIGMUND FREUD

GENERAL LUDENDORFF DID NOT REMAIN in exile for more than a few months. Indeed, when the Swedish Social Democrats protested against his taking refuge in Stockholm, the general surveyed the growing Freikorps strength back in Germany and returned forthwith to Berlin. Under the name of "Karl Neumann" ("New Man"), he acquired a free suite at the Adlon Hotel, and since the Allied Disarmament Commission met in the same hotel, and since the Allies theoretically wanted Ludendorff as a war criminal, the Adlon's owners provided their pseudonymous guest with a private exit onto the Wilhelmstrasse.

Even with such protection, though, the Adlon was too public a headquarters for the conspiracy that Ludendorff was planning. "If I ever come to power again, there will be no pardon," the general had said. "I would have Ebert, Scheidemann and company hanged and watch them dangle." With the help of some friends, Ludendorff therefore moved to an apartment on the Viktoriastrasse, overlooking the Tiergarten, and here he began welcoming an unusual number of visitors. There came, for example, Baron von Lüttwitz, who had helped Defense Minister Noske suppress the Spartakists; and Captain Pabst, who had arranged the murder of Liebknecht and Rosa Luxemburg; and Wolfgang Kapp, the co-founder of the short-lived

58

Fatherland Party; and various minor intriguers like an unemployed journalist named Handke, who insisted on calling himself "Dr. Schnitzler."

The conspirators' goal, obviously, was to overthrow the government, but they seemed, for a time, to have neither a clear plan of attack nor the armed force to carry it out. The man who provided both was a spade-bearded naval captain by the name of Hermann Ehrhardt. At the time of the mutiny in Kiel, Ehrhardt had begun mobilizing antirevolutionary soldiers into a five-thousand-man "Ehrhardt Brigade," which one impartial expert later called the best combat unit he had ever seen. Ehrhardt fought ruthlessly against a Spartakist uprising in Brunswick in the spring of 1919, then marched on Munich to lead the suppression of the Communist government of Bavaria, then roved through Silesia in search of Polish guerrillas. But as soon as the Versailles Treaty came into effect, limiting Germany to 100,000 troops, the War Ministry issued orders that the Ehrhardt Brigade was to be disbanded.

Ehrhardt's troopers, by now stationed in the garrison at Döberitz, some fifteen miles west of Berlin, became openly mutinous. They talked of invading the capital and overthrowing the Ebert regime. Captain Ehrhardt went to the Berlin commandant, General Lüttwitz, and asked what he was supposed to do about the angry rebels in his brigade.

"Don't do a thing and keep quiet," said Lüttwitz. "I will not permit the troops to be disbanded."

"But the order has already gone out," said Ehrhardt.

"That is my worry," said Lüttwitz.

On March 1, Lüttwitz repeated his promise in public when he reviewed a parade by the Ehrhardt Brigade and declared: "I will never permit such an elite troop to be taken away from me in such tempestuous times."

Lüttwitz had no sense of discretion whatever, and his pronouncements naturally led to rumors that he was planning a coup against the Ebert government. Lüttwitz did not seem to care. He was a small, fierce Prussian aristocrat whose political views consisted mainly of a yearning for the Hohenzollern Empire and a contempt for all republican politicians. When two right-wing leaders came to ask him what his plans were, since they themselves had plans to demand a new election, Lüttwitz was scornful of political maneuvers. "I prefer," he said, "to rely on my battalions."

If anything could have made Matthias Erzberger more hated than his signing of the armistice, it was his energetic imposition of new taxes to rescue the Republic from bankruptcy. Now that we have become accustomed to paying a large share of our incomes to support a permanent war economy, it seems hard to believe that wars were ever financed in other ways, but the incredible fact is that Imperial Germany's conservative finance officials never levied a single mark in extra taxes to pay the gigantic costs of World War I. The total cost had been 164 billion marks (the mark was then worth 4.20 to the dollar). Of this, 93 billion had been raised by war loans, and 29 billion by Treasury bills. The government had produced the rest simply by printing more money on the government printing presses. (The other great powers were scarcely more prudent. "Lenin is said to have declared that the best way to destroy the Capitalist System was to debauch its currency," John Maynard Keynes observed. "In the latter stages of the war all the belligerent governments practiced, from necessity or incompetence, what a Bolshevist might have done from design.")

The German government planned, apparently, to recover its expenses out of the reparations that the enemy would have to pay once Hindenburg and Ludendorff had captured Paris. Now that the Germans had to confront reality, now that the French were assessing the reparations, Finance Minister Erzberger attacked the problem with characteristic toughness. He instituted the first national system of tax collection, which had traditionally been left to the state governments. He imposed stiff levies on war profits, and on various luxuries. And in defending his program, he denounced the Kaiser's chief economic official, Dr. Karl Helfferich, as "the most frivolous of finance ministers."

Helfferich, now sitting in the Reichstag as a representative of the Nationalist Party, responded with a ferocious series of articles in the conservative newspaper, the *Kreuzzeitung*. Each article carried the same headline: "Erzberger must go!" "This is Herr Erzberger," Helfferich wrote, "who is charged on all sides with intentional deceits, not twice or three times but ten and twenty times; who . . . dishonestly mixed political activities with personal financial interests; who does not answer all these accusations by bringing legal action, but shirks, and like a menaced cuttlefish darkens the water in order to escape. . . . This is Herr Erzberger, whose name appears rightly at the bottom of the miserable armistice agreement . . . ! This is Herr Erzberger who, if not finally stopped, will lead the German nation . . . to total destruction."

After that challenge, Erzberger had no choice but to sue for libel, and so, in January of 1920, the two Finance Ministers of the Empire and the Republic confronted one another in the First District Court of Berlin. The courtroom itself, dominated by a gigantic painting of King Friedrich Wilhelm III, was somewhat less than impartial. A large number of conservatives, particularly wealthy women, packed the chamber to cheer for Helfferich and boo at Erzberger. And then, at the end of the very first week of the trial, a twenty-year-old former naval cadet named Oltwig von Hirschfeld followed Erzberger out of the court, climbed onto the running board of the minister's car, and fired two shots at him. One bullet wounded Erzberger in the right shoulder; the other might have pierced his lung but was deflected by his gold watch chain. Hirschfeld, who subsequently testified that Helfferich's articles had convinced him that Erzberger was responsible for the loss of the war, got a prison sentence of only eighteen months, and the libel trial went on.

The German libel laws permit the defendant to pursue almost any line of counterattack, and Helfferich was a resolute antagonist, with a private army of right-wing supporters. One of them even stole and published Erzberger's personal income tax returns. And in the course of the two-month trial, it turned out that Erzberger had indeed engaged in a number of dubious business alliances. On March 12, the court formally decreed that Helfferich was technically guilty of libel and ordered him to pay a fine of $75, but it also declared that Helfferich had proved many of his accusations against Erzberger, specifically three cases of impropriety, six of perjury, and seven of mixing politics with business. "A man of undoubted ability [and] exemplary industry," the judge said of Erzberger, "but on the other hand of a regrettable lack of judgment."

Erzberger immediately resigned from the cabinet and devoted the rest of his life to clearing his reputation. The time left to him for that task was scarcely more than a year.

On the day of the Erzberger verdict—coincidentally, but not entirely so—the Ehrhardt Brigade was ready to march on Berlin.

Defense Minister Noske had shown surprisingly little concern about the threatening proclamations by General Lüttwitz. He believed that he himself had more military supporters than did Lüttwitz, and his only response to the turbulence in the Döberitz garrison was to order the Ehrhardt Brigade moved back under the jurisdiction of the navy commander, Admiral Adolf von Trotha.

General Lüttwitz immediately demanded a confrontation with President Ebert. He insisted not only that the Ehrhardt Brigade remain in his control but that all orders for the dissolution of the Freikorps be rescinded. Ebert, with Noske at his side, asked sharply whether the general might also have a political program to recommend. Lüttwitz paused for a moment and then recited the program he had heard from the two right-wing politicians who had visited him the week before—new elections for both the presidency and the parliament, formation of a cabinet of "experts," appointment of a "harder" man as army commander. Ebert discussed the general's demands for a few minutes, but Noske was less cordial. "Matters have gone far enough," he said to Lüttwitz. "The time has come when you either obey orders or resign."

Lüttwitz and two subordinate generals marched out in silence. Noske apparently believed that Lüttwitz would promptly send in his resignation, and when he did not receive it the following day, he issued orders relieving the general of the Berlin command. He also ordered the arrest of a half-dozen leaders of a right-wing military group called the National Union, but when police arrived at the Union's headquarters, they found it empty. The Union had been organized with the blessings of Ludendorff, of course, but the general had refused all the conspirators' pleas that he himself should publicly assume command of the movement.

Instead, the insurgents had decided to use as their political figurehead the relatively obscure Wolfgang Kapp. Born in New York, where his liberal-minded father had moved after the unsuccessful revolution of 1848, Kapp had returned to Germany and become, during the war, one of the most fervent nationalists in the Reichstag. As a founder of the right-wing Fatherland Party, he had served as a spokesman in parliament for Ludendorff's aggressive views. After the war, Kapp had faded into the position of director-general of the province of East Prussia—a man without any political following whatever—but Ludendorff apparently still considered him an eminently suitable Chancellor. The insurgent generals, however, treated him with very little regard. When Lüttwitz found himself under pressure from Noske, he didn't even bother to inform Kapp of his plans for retaliation.

By March 12, the day after Noske had dismissed Lüttwitz, the Berlin press was full of rumors that the Ehrhardt Brigade was mobilizing for a coup. Noske complacently sent Admiral von Trotha out to see what was happening at Döberitz, and the admiral telephoned the garrison in advance to make sure that he would see nothing disquieting. At ten o'clock that evening, he returned to Berlin and reported to Noske: "All quiet." An hour later, under a full moon, the Ehrhardt Brigade began its march on Berlin, singing lustily. The rebels flew the black-red-white flag of Imperial Germany, and on their helmets they bore one of the favorite Freikorps emblems, the swastika.

At 1 A.M. on March 13, informed by a newspaper reporter that the Ehrhardt Brigade was on its way to Berlin, Ebert and Noske gathered their military commanders together to find out what resistance was possible. Hindenburg had retired by now, and Gröner had resigned in protest against the Versailles Treaty, but the new army commander, General Walter Reinhardt, loyally believed in the defense of the Republic. "In such a situation, there can be no neutrality for the Reichswehr," he said. "The quicker we act, the quicker the spark will be put out." But Reinhardt's own control over his commanders was uncertain, and the ministers now turned to the chief of staff, General Hans von Seeckt. To their dismay, they found Seeckt determined to keep the army neutral. "The Reichswehr does not fire at the Reichswehr," Seeckt said softly, his monocle glinting under the lights. "Do you perhaps intend, Herr Minister, that a battle be fought before the Brandenburger Tor between troops who have fought side by side against the common enemy?"

Noske was indignant. "I'll mobilize the police," he said. Seeckt only smiled coldly and warned that the police might side with the insurgents. Noske threatened to call a general strike. Seeckt only smiled again and said nothing.

"This night has shown the bankruptcy of all my policy," Noske cried. "My faith in the officer corps is shattered. You have all deserted me. There is nothing left but suicide."

But Seeckt had spoken, and Noske had no choice but to order

all troops to remain in their barracks. There, as Seeckt intended, they would wait to see who won.

Angry and desperate, the ministers finally decided to use their last weapon, a general strike. In words that might have been written by Rosa Luxemburg, the government issued a proclamation: "Workers! Party comrades! The military putsch is here. . . . The work of an entire year will fall into ruins. . . . Therefore quit work! Strike! . . . No hand dare move! No proletarian dare help the military dictatorship! General strike all down the line!" The ministers who signed the proclamation apparently had only limited confidence in its success, however, for they decided to flee from their capital that very night. At 5 A.M., a small procession of automobiles carried the whole cabinet out of Berlin on the road to Dresden, a hundred miles to the south.

By that time, the Ehrhardt Brigade was already in the western outskirts of Berlin. Ehrhardt had agreed to give the government until 7 A.M. to accept Lüttwitz's demands, and so the troops stopped for a while at the Pichelsdorfer Bridge and brewed themselves some coffee. Then they marched up the Bismarckstrasse into the Tiergarten, where they met General Ludendorff—who later claimed that he just happened to be out for an early-morning stroll. The general, accompanied by his protégé, Dr. Kapp, saluted the invaders and wished them success. Precisely at seven, the Ehrhardt Brigade marched on through the Brandenburg Gate and turned right toward the Chancellery. They seized the empty building and then started setting up machine guns at the main street intersections. By noon, they ruled Berlin. Not a shot had been fired.

On the day of the Kapp Putsch, a new movie was playing at the Marmorhaus on the Kurfürstendamm. It was a story of murder and madness, and it was to become immensely popular. It was called *The Cabinet of Dr. Caligari.*

All through the war, there had been a growing interest in the new medium of moving pictures. The number of German theatres showing these novelties grew from 28 in 1913 to 245 in 1919, and the German government saw political possibilities in the phenomenon. It was General Ludendorff himself who suggested in 1917 that the various little film companies be merged into a national film monopoly, and the authorities agreed to establish the powerful

Universum Film A. G. (UFA) for the creation of propaganda films. When the war ended, however, the Socialists decided to get out of the movie business. They sold the government's one-third interest in UFA, abolished all censorship, and turned the movie-makers loose to produce whatever the public wanted.

What the public wanted, as might be expected, was sex. The pioneer in this field was a director named Richard Oswald, who had started in 1917 with a film called *Let There Be Light,* warning the population of the dangers of syphilis. In this, he had the formal support of the Society for Combating Venereal Diseases, and his film was such a success that he turned out two sequels in 1918 and yet another in 1919, along with an equally instructive film entitled *Prostitution.* But once the government had abolished censorship, Oswald's competitors felt free to drop the paraphernalia of education. They began cranking out pictures like *Lost Daughters, From the Edge of the Swamp,* and *Hyenas of Lust.* For those with special tastes, they produced *Different from the Others* and *A Man's Girlhood.* "I observed more than once," said the young Ilya Ehrenburg, "with what rapture pale, skinny adolescents watched the screen when rats gnawed a man to death or a venomous snake bit a lovely girl."

The public wanted spectacles, too, and so Ernst Lubitsch began directing for UFA a series of grandiose historic epics—*Madame Du Barry* (one of the most splendid vehicles for the young Pola Negri) and *Anna Boleyn* and *The Loves of Pharaoh.* Almost every day, in the streets of Berlin, there were crowds of demonstrators marching to and fro for one cause or another, but inside the shelter of theUFA-Palast am Zoo, where a symphony orchestra of seventy musicians provided the accompaniment, Berliners could escape into an imaginary world in which Lubitsch's artificial crowds were storming an artificial Bastille or besieging an artificial Tower of London.

But the new medium also attracted more serious people, who saw in the free-roaming camera a possibility that could be found in no other art form. One of them, a young Czech poet named Hans Janowitz, was haunted by an experience he had had in Hamburg just before the war. He had been wandering through a fair near the Reeperbahn, looking for a girl he had just met, when he thought he recognized her laugh in the darkness of a nearby park. He saw a man, who looked like an ordinary businessman, following the sound of laughter into the darkness. Janowitz himself gave up the search, but the next day he read in the newspapers that a girl named Gertrude had been murdered in the park. Suspecting that Gertrude might be the girl he himself had been following, he went to her funeral, and there he spotted the same businessman he had seen in the park. He had no evidence against the man, however, and so he did nothing. He went off to war, serving as an infantry officer, but the murder was still in his mind six years later when he met in Berlin a young Austrian named Carl Mayer, who had nightmares of his own.

Mayer's father had gone bankrupt trying to prove a "scientific" theory of gambling, and then he had shot himself, leaving his sixteen-year-old son to support three younger brothers by peddling barometers and playing bit parts in local theatres. Mayer apparently broke down under the strain and had to undergo a number of psychiatric examinations, which filled him with hatred for the psychiatrist who had examined him. The two youths talked endlessly about writing a movie that would somehow combine Janowitz's recollections of the Hamburg murder and Mayer's resentment of the psychiatrist, but the basic plot eluded them until one night when they went to a fair on the Kantstrasse. There, among the sideshows, they wandered into an exhibition entitled "Man or Machine." They saw a man perform great feats of strength while apparently in a hypnotic trance. During his act, the strong man also muttered mysterious phrases, which the audience took to be prophecies.

That same night, the two young men started writing their movie. It dealt with a mysterious Dr. Caligari (Janowitz found the name in a book of Stendhal's letters), who travels in a carnival with a somnambulist named Cesare. Two students named Alan and Francis attend the carnival and watch Dr. Caligari lead Cesare from his coffin onto the stage, where, under hypnosis, he answers questions about the future. He also, it later turns out, wanders around like a zombie and murders anyone who has incurred Dr. Caligari's anger. When the students start spying on him, Cesare kills one of them and kidnaps their girlfriend, Jane, whom he carries over the rooftops à la King Kong until he finally drops dead (there is no logic in these things) of exhaustion. The surviving student pursues the fleeing Caligari to an insane asylum, where Caligari proves to be not a patient but the director. The student exposes Caligari's double life, and Caligari ends up raving in a strait jacket.

Plot synopses never do justice to a movie, of course, and the authors of *Caligari* intended it not just as a horror movie but as a kind of revolutionary allegory. Caligari, according to Janowitz's subsequent account of the affair, was supposed to represent the insane evil of "an unlimited [state] authority that idolizes power," and Cesare was supposed to represent "the common man who, under the pressure of compulsory military service, is drilled to kill and to be killed." The triumph of the student at the end, therefore, showed that "reason overpowers unreasonable power." These solemn explications could probably serve just as well for any Frankenstein movie, but they are significant not only in the creation of *Caligari* but in its subsequent history.

Erich Pommer, one of the most successful producers of the day, bought the script from the two young poets and assigned it to a director, Robert Wiene. (He had originally expected to get Fritz Lang.) Pommer's plan was to produce an "artistic" movie, and he went to considerable trouble to achieve his effect. He hired a marvelous cast, including Conrad Veidt, thickly rouged as the cadaverous Cesare, and Werner Krauss as Dr. Caligari, a figure of menacing absurdity in spectacles, long white hair, and a top hat. He hired three Expressionist painters to design sets that are still a marvel of insane distortion— crooked windows, tilting chimneys, eerie mixtures of light and shadow. *Caligari* was the first German "art film," the first made entirely inside a studio, the first to exploit the possibilities of a mobile camera.

But there was one problem: Pommer and Wiene didn't like the allegory. Mild as the implications may seem now, they struck the movie authorities of the day as dangerous, and not what the public wanted. And so, in a classic case of political Bowdlerization, they framed the story with opening and closing scenes which show the student as a patient in Dr. Caligari's asylum. It is he, not Caligari, who is insane, and at the end of the student's story, which has been changed from an attack on authority into a madman's fantasy, the kindly old murderer says, "Finally I understand his madness . . . and now I know the way to his cure."

Despite the protesting cries of the authors, the producers' "cure" helped to turn Caligari into a world-wide success. Yet although the original story was perverted, the film still conveys the authors' message, in a new context. "*Caligari* is a very specific premonition," according to the film critic, Siegfried Kracauer, "in the sense that he uses hypnotic power to force his will upon his tool—a technique foreshadowing, in content and purpose, that manipulation of the soul which Hitler was the first to practice on a gigantic scale."

It is raining in Berlin now, and the Marmorhaus, which still stands, an ugly gray stone building about six stories high, is showing new movies. A huge poster outside the theatre offers a buxom girl waving a trumpet as she eludes the grasp of a half-naked man. The movie is entitled *Frau Wirtin Also Likes to Play the Trumpet*. But further down the Kurfürstendamm, on the second floor of an old office building, the Deutsche Kinemathek is still showing *Das Cabinet des Dr. Caligari*. The film looks old and creaky on a screen about ten feet square. The grinding noise of the projector is very loud, and there is something absurd about the titles that flash before us. . . .

"How long will I live?"

"Until dawn."

The little theatre has about fifty seats, but only a dozen of them are occupied, and about half the occupants are young Americans, loudly translating the titles and giggling at the melodrama. In the Berlin of 1970, the allegory of 1920 has become camp.

When the show is over, the audience filters out into the rain. But the Deutsche Kinemathek is a kind of shrine. Outside the projection room, there is a lobby filled with scale models of the sets that were built for this classic production. Here is the carnival once again, two feet high, and the rooftops over which Cesare carried the screaming Jane, and the tiny tracks on which the camera rolled forward for a close-up. Here, too, are blown-up reproductions of the first reviews. On the very day of the Kapp Putsch, *Die Weltbühne* published the praises of Kurt Tucholsky: "This film . . . is something completely new."

As one wanders among the exhibits in the now-deserted lobby, a dark little man sidles up and says, "Here, this is a book I wrote, and if you're interested, you can have it. You don't have to pay me anything for it." One looks down at the book he has offered. It is called *Caligari and Caligarismus*. But when one looks up to thank him, he has disappeared.

President Ebert and his ministers arrived at Dresden at about noon on the day of their flight, but they found their new refuge almost as unsafe as Berlin. The local commander, that familiar

General Maercker, informed Noske that he had orders from Lüttwitz to put the whole cabinet under arrest. Noske answered that the orders were illegal. Maercker equivocated, saying he would be willing to interpret the orders in such a way as to help the Ebert regime. Ebert and Noske thanked him and decided to continue their flight, this time to Stuttgart, 250 miles to the southwest.

In Berlin, however, the unfortunate Dr. Kapp was having difficulties of his own. The general strike that had been proclaimed by the fleeing government proved more paralyzing than anyone had expected. This was a strike that combined, for once, the energies and emotions of the giant Socialist labor unions, the left-wing militants, the ordinary people, and the government itself. Factories shut down, stores closed, the streetcars and buses stopped. There was no water, electricity, or gas. Schools closed. Civil servants stayed home. "The Kapp Putsch, yes," says one old Berliner, dreamily. "That was the day my aunt couldn't get married. Everything had been arranged for that day, but this was different from the other strikes because *nothing* worked. We all stayed home and sat around by candlelight."

Inside the half-deserted Chancellery, the portly Dr. Kapp scurried about in his morning coat and spats, trying to cope with the baffling problems of governing a nation. That first Saturday, he had called on his daughter to type out his manifesto to the people, but Fräulein Kapp wasted hours trying to find a typewriter, and by the time she had finally found a machine and pecked out the new Chancellor's statement of principles, the Sunday newspapers had already gone to press. Kapp had assigned a lawyer named Dr. Hermann to draw up a new constitution, but this gentleman had not yet finished his draft. And the official civil service was doing very little to help the usurpers. One of the Chancellery's chief executives, Arnold Brecht (later a distinguished professor at the New School for Social Research in New York), contributed his share to the confusion by ordering every telephone operator to take a week off, and then walking out of the Chancellery with all the governmental stamps and seals in his overcoat pockets. And the Ehrhardt Brigade wanted its pay. Dr. Kapp told Ehrhardt to go and break into the Reichsbank, but Ehrhardt, who had just seized control of Berlin, had scruples. "I am not a bank robber," he said. To handle such administrative problems, Kapp had counted on the journalist named Handke, alias Dr. Schnitzler, but now he was nowhere to be found.

"Where is Dr. Schnitzler?" cried Kapp, waddling through the empty corridors of the Chancellery. "I cannot govern without Dr. Schnitzler."

"Everything would still have been all right if we had just shot more people," one Freikorps officer said later. But Kapp and Lüttwitz both quailed at the idea of firing on the masses of strikers. Instead, they began a convoluted series of negotiations, with Ludendorff and Seeckt, with uncertain army commanders in the provinces, with conservative politicians who hoped to mediate between the two regimes, with anyone, in fact, who thought he could end the impasse between the beleaguered putschists and the departed cabinet, between the restless Freikorps troops and the stolid strikers.

"Nobody now understands the Kapp Putsch," says Dr. Hans Staudinger, who was then an official in the Economics Ministry and later fled to the New School for Social Research in New York. "The Kapp Putsch was not just against the government. It was against capitalism. Ludendorff was behind Kapp. He wanted that the military and the workers make a new government, a worker government. That would have been the first uniting of nationalism and socialism—and youth."

Dr. Staudinger is eighty years old now, a short, heavy man with silky white hair, blue eyes, and marvelously pink skin. He hurt his hip recently in a fall while on vacation in Martinique, and so we are riding in a taxi up Park Avenue to the doctor's office. Dr. Staudinger wears a black astrakhan hat, a striped bow tie, and a red handkerchief in his breast pocket.

"Young people are terribly cruel," says Dr. Staudinger, settling himself in the taxi. He had once been a leader in the German Youth Movement, the Wandervögel, that odd collection of pre-hippies who used to roam through the German forests, singing songs, cadging food, and sleeping in fields. The war had killed off many of the best of these idealists, and the rest remained politically divided between left and right. Dr. Staudinger had moved toward the Socialists, and he disapproved of the others' drift toward the Freikorps. "We didn't *kill* people," he says.

When the Kapp Putsch began, Dr. Staudinger was one of the many civil servants who sabotaged the new regime. "I told my subordinates that no documents were official without the approval of the minister, and he wasn't there." How could such sabotage work?

"It was an order that I gave," Dr. Staudinger says with a smile, "and when an order was given, it had to be carried out." And what did he tell the Kapp regime? "I told them that everything was in order," Dr. Staudinger says with another smile. "How could they know what was happening?"

One of Kapp's aides, Alexander Rustow, who had served on Ludendorff's staff during the war, asked Staudinger to help find a way out of the impasse. "He sent me a special passport to get through the barbed wire around the center of Berlin, so I went to this meeting in the Wilhelmstrasse." Several top Prussian state officials were there, and the trade-union leaders, and Rustow made an impassioned plea to the union leaders to support the putsch for the rebirth of Germany. One of the labor leaders was tempted, but the head of the Socialist unions, Karl Legien, flatly refused. "Legien made a great speech," Staudinger says.

How could anyone think Kapp could succeed? "Kapp had an understanding of the needs of the young people," says Dr. Staudinger. "But you should ask Lowe."

Dr. Adolph Lowe, another economist at the New School, also took part in those desperate meetings during the Kapp Putsch.

"On the very day of the Kapp Putsch, I came down with the Spanish flu," says Dr. Lowe. "I don't know how I ever survived, but my sickbed somehow became an interesting place for people to meet. Some of the rebels hoped that the unions would support Kapp, which was an utterly crazy idea. And while I lay in bed, with a temperature of 104, in came a former boss of mine, who was the brother-in-law of Ludendorff. He said, 'I come from Ludendorff. He is very worried about this strike.' I said, 'He is quite right to be worried about this strike. I think this is one time when there will be some truth in the Socialist slogans about the strength of the united workers.' So he went away again to Ludendorff, and maybe I helped to change Ludendorff's mind.

"Of course, it's true that the unions were by no means satisfied with the Social Democratic government," says Dr. Lowe. "I remember once when the government put up a lot of posters that said, 'Socialization is on the march.' The next day, a lot of people had written on the posters: 'Where?' And there was some reason for certain officers to think they could take advantage of this. Even in Bismarck's time, there had been a social consciousness among the

military, and then the workers themselves were somewhat militaris-
tic, accustomed to commands. But the idea of bringing these two
forces together politically—that was just romanticism. The Freikorps
were a little like the Green Berets. And if the Green Berets decided
to stage a putsch, who could they get as their political leader?"

Wolfgang Kapp proved to be a leader of almost absurd incompetence. On the first Saturday of his reign, he ordered the Prussian
State Legislature dissolved; on Monday, in order to keep negotiations
alive, he ordered the dissolution canceled. He had the whole Prussian
state cabinet arrested, and then ordered everyone released. He issued
a decree banning further examinations at Berlin University, and another one confiscating all matzoth flour for the coming Passover. By
Wednesday of Kapp's first week in power, with all the machinery of
government at a standstill, the Berlin Security Police held a meeting
and announced that they had lost confidence in the lonely Chancellor.
At that, Kapp gave up. He issued his last decree, declaring that he
had "completed all my aims" and was therefore resigning in favor of
General Lüttwitz. A taxi rolled up to the Chancellery, and Kapp,
muffled in a scarf and a soft hat, climbed in. His personal possessions
had been bundled into a sheet, with the four corners twisted together,
and someone flung the bundle onto the roof of the cab. Then the
weeping Fräulein Kapp clattered down the steps of the Chancellery
and joined the flight. The taxi sped off to Tempelhof field, where a
plane was waiting to take the five-day Chancellor to refuge in
Sweden.

For a few hours, General Lüttwitz believed he might succeed
where Kapp had failed—and Ludendorff apparently encouraged him
in this hope—but on that same afternoon he received a delegation
from the War Ministry, headed by Colonel Wilhelm Heye, chief of
staff of the Northern Army Command, advising him to resign.
Captain Ehrhardt urged Lüttwitz to arrest his critics, but Colonel
Heye convinced him that a majority of the army opposed his regime,
and so he, too, gave in.

Captain Ehrhardt's last request, which was granted, was to march
his brigade back out of Berlin in military formation. And so, late on
March 17, the heavy-booted Freikorps squads lined up once again to
march out of Berlin on the same route by which they had entered it.
A crowd gathered along Unter den Linden, watching in gloating
silence as the troops marched past in defeat. Suddenly, as the last

detachment of the brigade was marching through the Brandenburg Gate, a small boy in the watching crowd burst into laughter. Two of the troopers immediately broke away from the marching column and attacked the boy with their rifle butts, then kicked at his body with their boots. Nobody in the stunned crowd said a word, but somebody hissed. At that, the troopers leveled their machine guns and fired several bursts into the throng of bystanders. Then they marched on, singing.

"I saw them shoot," says Dr. Staudinger. "I had been at the Reichstag building when I saw them marching through the Brandenburg Gate, and I ran over to watch, and then they started shooting. And the interesting thing is that the officers did not give the command to shoot. It was the young soldiers themselves who decided to open fire. Young people are very cruel. They believe they are in the sign of God."

On the first day of the Kapp Putsch, in the middle of the general strike, a small group of enthusiasts gathered in a building on the Spichernstrasse to hear a lecture. The lecturer was Karl Abraham, a coolly self-contained man of forty-three, with closely cropped hair and a thick mustache, and though he had no explanation for the madness taking place in the streets of Berlin, he did outline a new theory to explain the basic causes for irrational behavior. His talk was entitled "Elements of Psychoanalysis," and Abraham, the first practicing psychoanalyst in Germany, was delivering the first lecture at the newly opened Berlin Psychoanalytic Institute.

For the psychoanalytic movement, this was a major step forward during a rather dark period. Sigmund Freud had by now completed most of his major work, but it had still won little acceptance in the universities and hospitals of Europe. "The decision to become a psychoanalyst placed a physician outside the medical fraternity," as one of the pioneers put it. Several of Freud's most talented early followers—Jung, Adler, and Stekel—had already broken away from his leadership, and Freud himself, at sixty-four, was already suffering from the mouth cancer that was to torture him during his last twenty years. He was, then, little more than a theorist, the author of several interesting books. But Freud's closest disciples were an extraordinarily devoted group. They even formed a Committee of the Seven Rings, to each of whom Freud gave an ancient Greek intaglio to be mounted in a ring. Out of this nucleus grew an organization—and it was organization that differentiated Freud's work from that of his rivals—that spread it around the world.

The organization started in Berlin because three of the seven companions of the ring now lived there—Karl Abraham, Hanns Sachs, and Max Eitingon. And of these, Eitingon had a particular value, for he, almost alone among the early psychoanalysts, had a private income. He was a shy, stammering man with a bald head, steel-rimmed spectacles, and a plaintive mustache, but his income provided him with a large, musty apartment, its parquet floors covered with oriental rugs, and here the members of the ring established the Berlin Psychoanalytic Institute and Polyclinic. Eitingon not only provided the room but paid all the bills.

Everything was very informal. There was no official enrollment. Evening lectures were free to anyone who wanted to attend. Patients paid little or nothing. "Sometimes we even *paid* the patients to come," says one survivor of those early years. "And many of the patients who came free got their carfare from us." What made the Institute unique, however, was a system of standardized training for all analysts. Abraham himself analyzed many of the newcomers—Theodor Reik, Karen Horney, Sandor Rado, Helene Deutsch—and the newcomers passed on their training to others. In very little time, Berlin became "the strongest center of psychoanalysis," according to Franz Alexander, who had been the first student to join the Institute.

It is interesting to speculate why Berlin, rather than Freud's Vienna, exerted such an attraction on young psychoanalysts. "The political atmosphere was better," says Dr. Henry Lowenfeld, a mild-mannered, gray-haired analyst who once studied at the Berlin Institute and now practices in New York. We are sitting in the twilight in Dr. Lowenfeld's book-lined apartment on Central Park West, and he is talking reflectively, in a rather high, soft voice. "The political situation was not good, but it was better than Vienna."

"And they were all oppressed in Vienna by the Giant," says Mrs. Lowenfeld, also a doctor, a strikingly handsome woman with short-cut hair and blue slacks.

"No, it's more complicated," says Dr. Lowenfeld. "Many of them were Marxists, these young men, and they had a feeling of freedom when they came to Berlin."

"Many were Jews, too," says Mrs. Lowenfeld.

"Yes, there was always anti-Semitism in Austria," says Dr. Lowenfeld, "but not in Berlin, not until much later."

While the organization grew in Berlin, however, it continued to look to Vienna for its leadership. "Freud felt that the [Psychoanalytic] Society should be organized not as in a democracy but as a hierarchy," said Franz Alexander, "perhaps as a reflection of the monarchistic attitude natural to a Viennese." "*Mein Reich*," indeed, was not the Emperor's term for his followers; it was Freud's term.

When Adolf Hitler finally came to power, he acted almost immediately to suppress the practice of "Jewish" psychoanalysis, but by then the organization hatched in Max Eitingon's apartment had become international. The first psychoanalytic clinic in America had been founded in New York in 1930, the second in Boston shortly afterward, then the third in Chicago, all organized and operated by émigrés from Berlin.

The failure of the Kapp Putsch gave Ebert and the Socialists perhaps their last great chance to carry out the basic reforms they had long promised, to liberalize the army and the civil service, to base the government's power more on the labor unions and less on the Freikorps. Karl Legien, the head of the labor-union federation, was actually a conservative Socialist, a supporter of the war, an opponent of Liebknecht, but now he took full credit for the strike that broke the putsch, and he wanted his reward. He demanded not only that Noske be dismissed but "that the Trade Union Federation be decisive in the reconstruction of the government [and] have the key role in economic and social-political affairs. All those who had collaborated with the putschists should be strictly punished; all Reich and state police troops should be thoroughly purged of anti-Republican and dubious elements." Until he got his way, Legien said, the strike would continue.

The extent of his success can be measured by the fate of the putschists themselves. General Ludendorff escaped to Munich, under the name of "Herr Lange," and resumed his conspiracies in a luxurious villa placed at his disposal by a sympathetic baron. General von Lüttwitz took refuge at an estate in Hungary, where he remained until a general amnesty permitted him to return to Germany in 1925. A number of his officers underwent a similarly comfortable and temporary exile. Only three of the putschists were actually brought to trial for treason. Of these, two were acquitted. The other, Traugott von Jagow, former police chief in Berlin and Kapp's Interior Minister, received a sentence of five years but served only part of that term (he later sued successfully for retroactive payment of his pension). Only poor Wolfgang Kapp, who returned to Germany and gave himself up in the hope of judicial leniency, died ignominiously in prison while awaiting trial.

The unions did succeed in getting Noske removed from the Defense Ministry, but it was a Pyrrhic victory. General Reinhardt, the only general who had proposed resistance to the Kapp Putsch, resigned in protest, and his post as army commander fell to the general who had refused to fight, Hans von Seeckt. And as for the Ehrhardt Brigade, which had done its best to overthrow the Ebert regime, the government not only granted its troopers an amnesty but actually paid them a sixteen-thousand-mark bonus that had been promised them by Kapp for their efforts in seizing Berlin. "The soldiers were happy and said that everything would still turn out for the best," one of them said later. "The government showed us the best of good will. . . ."

The reason for this astonishing leniency was that the Socialist unions had once again proved unable to control their radical minority. The Communists again seized the opportunity for disruption, and the Socialist leaders again felt they must send the Freikorps into battle. Under cover of the general strike, the Communists in the Ruhr had organized a well-armed militia of some fifty thousand workers who called themselves the Red Ruhr Army. Throughout the week of the Kapp regime, the Red Ruhr Army attacked various military headquarters in the region, seizing the cities of Dortmund, Düsseldorf, and Essen, and, on at least two occasions, massacring the Freikorps units that opposed them. Even after the Kapp Putsch had collapsed in Berlin, and the Socialist leaders were trying to negotiate a compromise with the labor unions, a Communist newspaper in the Ruhr declared: "There can be only one salvation for the German people. The red flag must wave victoriously over the whole of Germany." For two weeks, the Socialist leaders tried to mediate between the Red Ruhr Army and the Freikorps. There were two armistices. Then the Freikorps struck. "The enthusiasm is terrific—unbelievable," one Freikorps youth wrote to his family. "Anyone who falls into our hands first gets the rifle butt and then is finished off with a bullet. . . . We even shot ten Red Cross nurses on sight because they were carrying pistols. We shot those little ladies with pleasure—how they cried and pleaded with us to save their lives. Nothing doing! Anyone with a gun is our enemy."

Once again, as after the Spartakus uprising, Ebert and his ministers wanted to take their case to the German people. Chancellor Bauer, who had come to office mainly to sign the Versailles Treaty, resigned after the Kapp Putsch. His Foreign Minister, Hermann Müller, also a Socialist, succeeded to the Chancellery and promptly called a general election for June 6. Presumably, he thought that the suppression of both right-wing and left-wing extremists would bring the Socialists a resounding vote of confidence. The results were quite different, and quite bewildering. The votes for the so-called "Weimar coalition" dropped from 19 million to 11 million. The Socialists remained the largest single party, but they lost 50 seats and ended up with only 113 in a Reichstag of 466 members. Their smaller allies, the Center and the Democrats, also fared badly. The two main conservative parties doubled their strength, winning more than 9 million votes, and so did the leftists, climbing to 5 million.

For the first time, the sharp divisions within German society had been expressed at the polls, creating a political monster that was to live on, in various forms, throughout the 1920's—a Reichstag without a pro-democratic majority, a Reichstag that nobody could govern. After some tortuous negotiations, the Socialists quit the government. The new Chancellor, an undistinguished Center Party leader named Konstantin Fehrenbach, could not achieve a parliamentary majority and did not even ask for a vote of confidence from the divided Reichstag.

George Grosz did not like the army. He drew endless varieties of pictures of its officers. He drew officers marching, officers lounging, officers sneering, officers strolling (occasionally without their trousers). They were all variations on a basic type. Kurt Tucholsky described it: "A man who, with his chest thrown out, trumpets forth each word, letting two beady, cold eyes set in a low forehead flash forth imperiously . . . a man who . . . perhaps has a badly healed scar on his cheek, who squeezes on a monocle when he wants to read something that he won't understand . . . a man who looks cowardly and brutal at the same time and whose entire bearing is redolent of a barely civilized slaughterhouse hand who is about to start a row on the dance floor."

The army officers didn't like George Grosz either, and in 1920 the Berlin police confiscated a series of Grosz's drawings. He and his publisher were both prosecuted for defaming the reputation of the army. Both men were convicted. Grosz was fined a nominal three hundred marks and the publisher six hundred. Tucholsky estimated the fines to be "about what it costs to murder a pacifist."

"A Welter of Tears and Vodka" 1921

> The author that interested me most was naturally Sirin. . . . He was the loneliest and most arrogant one. . . . Across the dark sky of exile, Sirin passed . . . like a meteor, and disappeared, leaving nothing much else behind him than a vague sense of uneasiness.
>
> VLADIMIR NABOKOV

GENERAL HANS VON SEECKT once declared that the three outstanding traits in his character were vanity, a sense of beauty, and the cavalier's instinct. It was a strange self-assessment for a bemonocled Prussian general to make, but Seeckt was a strange general. A frail man with a long neck and slender hands, he was a connoisseur of art and wine, a wanderer not only through Europe but to Africa and India. An army professional since the age of nineteen, he had shown himself a brilliant staff officer during the war, mastermind of both the Gorlice breakthrough in the East and the Soissons breakthrough in the West. When the war ended in defeat, he wept, for military combat represented to him a kind of mystical self-immolation. "War is the highest summit of human achievement," he wrote. "It is the natural, the final stage in the historical development of humanity." And of war's purpose, he added: "The Reich! There is something supernatural in this word. It embraces far more and connotes something other than the conception of a State."

Seeckt had served as the military member of the German delega-

79

tion to Versailles, and so he knew at first hand how fiercely the French planned to enforce German disarmament. But though Seeckt acquiesced in the signing of the peace treaty, he now saw it as his duty, as the new commander of the German armed forces, to break that treaty in any way he could. He knew that the roving Freikorps eventually had to be broken up ("I must assume of everyone who remains in the army," he said briskly in his first order of the day, "that he loyally respects his oath [to] the constitution"), but he also believed that the Versailles limit of 100,000 troops prevented him from defending the eastern frontier against the fractious Poles, and so he organized a secret eastern army of twenty thousand so-called "Work Commandos," which soon became known as the "Black Reichswehr." And although the Versailles Treaty banned the German General Staff, Seeckt coolly reconstituted it under the modest name of *Truppenamt,* or Troop Office. But these were simply tactical maneuvers. Seeckt's long-range plan was to build a new army that would be able to defeat the French when, inevitably, the next war began. "The whole future of warfare appears to me to be in the employment of mobile armies," Seeckt declared, "relatively small but of high quality, and rendered distinctly more effective by the addition of aircraft." He planned, in short, the force that ultimately waged Hitler's Blitzkrieg of 1939 and 1940.

The Versailles Treaty specifically forbade Germany to own or acquire the tanks and airplanes that were the essential weapons of a Blitzkrieg, but Seeckt figured out a solution to that. Beyond Poland, and equally hostile to the Poles' ambitions, there were other generals who also wanted to build a modern army. Russia was not a participant in the Versailles Treaty anyway, so it was quite legal for Seeckt to plan on sending some of his best officers to train the Russians (and themselves) in the use of modern weapons. There was geopolitical theory in this too. The Germans had long felt themselves threatened from both east and west, and that sense of threat had nurtured the growth of Prussian militarism. No rational German strategist, however, wanted to wage war in both east and west. That had been a major error in World War I (to be duplicated, of course, in World War II), and Seeckt, comparing the dangers on both sides of the Reich, reached the firm conclusion that the greatest threat came from the vengeful French—made all the worse by the French support of Poland. "The existence of Poland is intolerable and incompatible with Germany's vital interests," said Seeckt. "She must disappear and will do so through her own inner weakness and through Russia —with our help. . . . The attainment of this objective must be one of the firmest guiding principles of German policy . . . through Russia or with her help."

It mattered not in the slightest to the conservative Seeckt that Russia was the center of Bolshevism, and it apparently mattered equally little to the Red Army that Seeckt's troops were actively engaged in suppressing German Communism. Seeckt assigned a group of staff officers—including, inevitably, the clever Major Kurt von Schlcicher, whom Seeckt had inherited from General Gröner—to develop contacts with the Soviets. The first open result of these contacts was a German-Russian trade agreement signed on May 6, 1921, but Seeckt followed that with secret negotiations for a military accord. The talks took place in Schleicher's apartment in Berlin, with Seeckt dropping in from time to time. Both the Chancellor—Josef Wirth, another Center leader who had replaced the ineffectual Fehrenbach—and the Foreign Minister, Walther Rathenau, knew of these secret and semi-illegal discussions, but no official treaty was ever made public. The talks resulted, however, in the creation of a government-financed corporation innocuously called Society for the Promotion of Industrial Enterprises. The industrial enterprises it promoted were the building of Junkers airplane factories near Moscow and Kharkov, the production of 300,000 artillery shells at three Russian factories, and the manufacture of poison gas at a remote plant in Samara province. The two armies also agreed to establish a number of schools in Russia for the training of both Russian and German aviators and tank officers.

Neither side realized, apparently, that this was just another temporary phase in the long, perverse relationship between these two great peoples. For centuries, the Germans and the Russians had fought each other, feared each other, and fascinated each other. Now, in 1921, they were bound together by what Winston Churchill called their "comradeship in misfortune." They were both so weak that they genuinely worried about the rambunctious Poles who stood between them. Ultimately, of course, the officers trained in General Seeckt's Russian schools would unite to crush Poland and then fight each other from the Elbe to the Volga in the most massive battles that have ever been waged on earth.

Ilya Ehrenburg, one of the many intellectuals who left revolutionary Russia and one of the few who later went back, came to Berlin in 1921 and found it a city of violence and misery. "The Germans were living as though they were at a railway station," he wrote, "no one knowing what would happen the next day. . . . Shopkeepers changed their price-tickets every day: the mark was falling. Herds of foreigners wandered along the Kurfürstendamm: they were buying up the remnants of former luxury for a song. In the poorer quarters several bakeries were looted. It seemed as though everything was bound to collapse, but factory chimneys went on smoking, bank-clerks neatly wrote out astronomical figures, prostitutes painstakingly made up their faces. . . . At every turn there were small *Diele*, dance-halls where lean couples conscientiously jigged up and down. Jazz blared. I remember two popular songs: 'Yes, we have no bananas' and 'Tomorrow's the end of the world.' However, the end of the world was postponed from one day to the next."

Ehrenburg took a room in a boardinghouse in the Prager Platz, not far from the Kurfürstendamm, and began wandering around. He noted that clothing stores featured pink and blue dickeys as substitutes for shirts. He noted that the cakes in the Josty Café had been made from frostbitten potatoes. He noted that cigars with Havana labels had been made out of cabbage leaves steeped in nicotine. He was accosted by a man who offered to take him to an interesting night spot. "We traveled by underground . . . and finally found ourselves in a respectable flat. On the walls hung portraits of members of the family in officer's uniform and a painting of a sunset. We were given champagne—lemonade laced with spirits. Then the host's two daughters appeared—naked—and began to dance. One of them talked . . . [about] Dostoyevsky's novels. The mother hopefully eyed the foreign guests: perhaps they would be tempted by her daughters and would pay: in dollars of course. . . . 'Is this life?' sighed the respectable mamma."

Most of all, though, Ehrenburg took note of the Russians who had flocked to Berlin, monarchists, anarchists, poets, businessmen, all searching for at least a temporary sanctuary from the upheavals at home. "At every step, you could hear Russian spoken. Dozens of Russian restaurants were opened—with balalaikas, and zurnas, with gypsies, pancakes, shashliks and, naturally, the inevitable heartbreak. There was a little theatre that put on sketches. Three daily newspapers and five weeklies appeared in Russian. In one year seventeen Russian publishing firms were started. . . .

"Russian writers sometimes went to the café Prager Diele. Their conversations were noisy and confused. . . . On one occasion Andrey Bely got into an argument with Shestov; they were talking about the disintegration of personality and used the kind of language that only professional philosophers can understand. Then the curfew hour struck, the lights in the café went out, but the philosophical dispute was still not finished. Never shall I forget the scene that ensued. In two of the segments of the revolving door Andrey Bely and Shestov were shouting. Each, without noticing it, was pushing at his part of the door, and they could not get out into the street. Shestov, with his hat, his beard, his large walking-stick, looked like the Wandering Jew, while Bely fulminated, wildly gesticulating, his fluffy hair on end. An old waiter, who had seen much in his day, said to me: 'That Russian must be a famous man.' "

There were many strange confrontations among these flocks of Russians who suddenly appeared in Berlin. Boris Chaliapin, for example, had spent the revolutionary years giving concerts in exchange for sacks of flour or potatoes, and when enterprising European reporters asked him what he thought of the Bolshevik regime, the singer was outspoken in his criticisms. These criticisms angered Maxim Gorki so much that he refused to speak to his old friend, but Sol Hurok, who had become Chaliapin's manager, was determined to reunite the singer and the writer. "One day, with Chaliapin beside me, I knocked on the door of Gorki's suite in the Adlon Hotel in Berlin," Hurok recalled. "I had called [and] asked Gorki if I might bring Chaliapin to see him. 'Where is that fool?' Gorki roared into my ear. . . . Chaliapin stepped in and enveloped Gorki in his arms like a huge bear. Thus they greeted each other. How they parted I cannot say, for I stayed only six to eight hours and then left them together, in a welter of tears and vodka."

Russians being Russians, there was a free exchange in Berlin among those who had fled Lenin's regime and those who had made their peace with it. Stanislavski brought his Moscow Art Theatre on a visit to Berlin, and Sergei Eisenstein came to study the film techniques being developed at the UFA studios in suburban Babelsberg. Wassily Kandinsky arrived to start a new life on the sale of some paintings he had left at a Berlin gallery before the war; he found that the paintings had been sold, but most of the proceeds had been swallowed by the inflation. And Isadora Duncan, who had been invited to Russia by the Soviets in 1921, reappeared in Berlin with a new husband eleven years her junior, the brilliant but half-demented poet Sergei Essenin, who promptly began a drunken spree through the shops and cafés of the Kurfürstendamm. Mayakovsky came, too, to give readings of his poetry, and the young Vladimir Horowitz, whose first recital went almost unnoticed. "I was very nervous," Horowitz said later. "I didn't play well, but I was fortunate. No critics came."

They met in the Russian restaurants and cabarets that opened everywhere—the Bear, the Eagle, the Coq d'Or, the Russian Tea Room, the Blue Bird, and, particularly, the Allaverdi, a Ukrainian place that offered a wide variety of zakuski, blini, shashlik, borscht, and other national delicacies, along with a whole orchestra of balalaikas. One corner table was reserved for the Soviets, and Lenin's personal envoy, Karl Radek, often appeared there, sometimes exchanging barbed remarks with the former grand dukes who waited on table. Behind the bar of the Allaverdi, there was a circular stairway that led down to an after-hours club in the cellar, where the more prosperous refugees could enjoy champagne and pickled mushrooms and violin music until dawn.

The young playwright, Carl Zuckmayer, was in the cellar club one night when a buzz of excited whispering suddenly went from table to table. "Then there was a sudden silence," he said, "and many of the men stood up to bow in the direction of a small sofa in one corner. There sat an inconspicuously dressed woman with a silk shawl over her head. It was Pavlova. She was obviously in no way annoyed by this classless homage. On the contrary, she suddenly rose and with an expressive gesture removed her shawl and the jacket to her suit, under which she was wearing a sleeveless white blouse. In a moment, all the tables and chairs had been whisked into an adjacent cellar. Everyone crowded against the walls and bottle racks. Pavlova whispered briefly with the violinist, who began the melody of *The Dying Swan*. And for five minutes, she floated about that narrow space like a phantom, then with a deep bow of her whole body sank to the stone floor. The cheers that burst out seemed on the point of shattering the vaulted ceiling, but she silenced them with another gesture of her lovely arms, then returned to the small sofa and her companions. Thereafter, no one looked in her direction."

Among the most talented Russians who fled to Berlin in this period was the nineteen-year-old cellist Gregor Piatigorsky, who swam across the Sbruch River one night, holding his cello over his head while border guards fired their rifles into the water around him. Piatigorsky now is honored as one of the great classical cellists, but he supported himself in adolescence by playing waltzes in restaurants and nightclubs, and so he was able to scrounge his way westward through the cafés of Lwow and Warsaw, always finding help from the extraordinary network of refugee Russian musicians. Berlin was full of Russians, too, but jobs were scarce, and Piatigorsky soon found himself sleeping on a bench in the Tiergarten, storing his cello under the bench and hoping that the police would understand. One night, it rained, and Piatigorsky took refuge in the men's room of the Zoo Station. When the rain finally stopped, he was so depressed by the idea of returning to his bench in the park that he headed instead for the nearby Philharmonic Hall. Carrying his cello like a badge of office, he marched through the stage entrance, and then sneaked into the hall in time to hear the great Busoni conduct Beethoven's Eighth Symphony.

"After the concert," Piatigorsky recalled later, "I took my cello without being questioned by anyone. As I was about to step out of the building, the icy wind stopped me and I turned back. My shirt and socks were damp and I was miserably cold. . . . The last people were leaving. A little later the doors were locked and there was complete darkness. The silence and emptiness of the huge building were ghastly. For a long time I stood still, my heart pounding. I felt trapped and wanted to cry for help. . . . I saw a door leading to a loge. . . . Soon I was undressed and settled for the night. How warm and comfortable it [was] here, and what an improvement over the bench in the Tiergarten. . . . I was ready to fall asleep, but . . . a sudden irresistible urge to play seized me. I got up, grabbed my cello, and, naked as I was, moved toward the stage. I could not find the stairs leading to it, so I climbed onto it from the hall . . . and began to play. The sound of the cello, eerie yet humanly full-throated, came back to me from the dark immensity of the hall. Held fast by this unique experience, I played to the limits of my endurance. Exhausted but elated, I finally returned to the loge. In the morning, I was awakened by the orchestra playing a Schumann symphony. I thought it rather nice to rest on the couch there, unseen, and enjoy fine music in the morning. . . . The orchestra was still rehearsing when I walked out of the building."

"Yes, I knew Nabokov then," says Michael Josselson. "I met him on the tennis court, I think. I can see him quite clearly on the tennis court, on the Lietzenburger Strasse, just off the Kurfürstendamm, right near where we lived. He was a very good tennis player, and he was already known as—well, he wrote extremely well. We all read his short stories and articles, which he wrote under the name of Sirin."

Josselson is a rather thin, dark-haired man, partly bald, wearing a red turtleneck sweater. He came to Berlin from Estonia, studied at the university, and then went into business. He was a buyer for Gimbels and Saks, as a matter of fact, working out of an office on the Ritterstrasse, near the now-empty fields of crabgrass that were once the garment district. Moving to New York in the thirties, he eventually tired of the dry-goods business—"They were only interested in money, nothing else"—and he returned to Berlin with the American Army at the end of the war. He then played a major role —along with Nicholas Nabokov, the composer, a cousin of the writer —in establishing the Congress for Cultural Freedom. The Congress was supposed to represent the "free world" response to official Soviet culture organizations, but it later turned out to have been a beneficiary, through various supposedly unofficial foundations, of subsidies from the CIA. The role of émigré Russians in Berlin has always been ambiguous.

"The Russian colony in Berlin in the twenties was quite large— perhaps fifty thousand, perhaps more," says Josselson. We are drinking coffee now in his new apartment overlooking a small park in Geneva, Switzerland. "And it was not just intellectuals. It was a world in itself. There were doctors, lawyers, businessmen. There were several very good tennis players, as a matter of fact. One of them—Prenn was his name—became a member of the German Davis Cup team. I remember, I saw Prenn play against Tilden. He also played on one of our soccer teams. We had two Russian soccer teams in Berlin. They were not part of the regular league, but they played the other Berlin teams. I myself was a halfback on the junior team.

"But Nabokov. What was Nabokov like in those days? Very handsome. And very nice. As he is now, when he wants to be, when he decides that he likes you. Have you tried to see him? He lives in Montreux, just at the other end of the lake. It's always very complicated, though. First you have to call the concierge at the Montreux Palace Hotel, and then the concierge says, 'Hold the wire,' because he has to check with Vera, Mrs. Nabokov. There are always these two intermediaries. And sometimes, while he's officially in Montreux, he likes to hide out in Bex, a resort, or *Kurort*, as the Germans say, about half an hour from Montreux. But only the concierge can tell."

Montreux turns out to be a town of extraordinary beauty. Acres of tulips bloom red and yellow along the entire waterfront, and just across the lake, the mountains rise steeply toward a crown of snow, which turns pink and orange in the setting sun. The Montreux Palace is an archbishop among hotels. Its thickly carpeted corridors extend for miles, its scores of verandas overlook not only the lake but the hotel's own gardens and swimming pool and tennis courts and golf course. Its bath towels are four feet by six. But the black-uniformed concierge insists that Vladimir Nabokov is not here, nor in Bex either. He is in Sicily, where it is now the best season to hunt for butterflies.

But the phantom novelist can always be found in his books, for he has written—and not written—a good deal about his fourteen years in Berlin. "As I look back on those years of exile," he once said, "I see myself, and thousands of other Russians, leading an odd but by no means unpleasant existence, in material indigence and intellectual luxury, among perfectly unimportant strangers, spectral Germans and Frenchmen in whose more or less illusory cities we, émigrés, happen to dwell. These aborigines were to the mind's eye as flat and transparent as figures cut out of cellophane, and although we used their gadgets, applauded their clowns, picked their roadside plums and apples, no real communication . . . existed between us and them. . . . But occasionally, quite often in fact, the spectral world through which we serenely paraded our sores and our arts would produce a kind of awful convulsion and show us who was the discarnate captive and who the true lord."

There is a recurring image of sudden and absurd death in Nabokov's novels—Lolita's mother struck down by an automobile, for example—but the first "awful convulsion" that Nabokov experienced in Berlin is scarcely mentioned in his autobiography, *Speak, Memory*. In one sentence, in half a sentence, he records that his father was shot to death at a public meeting. Nabokov was twenty-two then, still a student at Cambridge, on a visit to his family in Berlin. Nabokov's father, a former member of the Russian parliament, was editor of the leading Russian daily newspaper in Berlin, *Rul'* (*The Rudder,*) and he took an active part in émigré politics. The Kadet Party, a mildly liberal group, had split into two factions over the issue of whether to remain in exile indefinitely or to return to Russia and make peace with the Bolsheviks. The elder Nabokov was the leader of the faction that argued against any compromise with Lenin; the head of the other faction was an old friend, Pavel Miliukov. To debate the matter, in the best Russian liberal tradition, they hired the Berlin Philharmonic Hall and sent out announcements.

The news of the meeting eventually reached Munich, where two right-wing émigrés named Shabelsky and Taboritsky, who lived together in a shabby boardinghouse, determined to murder Miliukov as a betrayer of the fallen Czar. "Right-wing" is actually too simple a term. Peter Shabelsky, the twenty-nine-year-old son of a rich Caucasian landowner, had suffered from shell shock during the war, and he raged at the Bolsheviks for having killed his fiancée while they were trying to escape from Russia; Taboritsky is a more shadowy figure who had worked for two monarchist newspapers. Both of them later denied belonging to any organization, but they had no explanation for how they had financed their trip from Munich to Berlin.

As soon as the meeting opened at the Berlin Philharmonic, Shabelsky and Taboritsky both rose from their seats in the second row and began marching toward the dais, singing patriotic Russian songs, and brandishing their pistols. Several people in the audience shouted warnings, and women began to scream. As Shabelsky aimed his pistol at Miliukov, Nabokov lunged between them, and Shabelsky's bullet hit him in the side. Taboritsky climbed onto the stage and fired three more bullets at Nabokov—the wrong target—before a bystander tackled him. Nabokov was already dead by the time someone telephoned his home and summoned his son to the Philharmonic to see what had happened.

Young Vladimir Nabokov moved to Germany the following year and began writing, under the name of Sirin, his Berlin novels—notably *Mary; King, Queen, Knave; The Eye; The Defense; Laughter in the Dark; Despair;* and *The Gift.* Nabokov has repeatedly stated that these are not Berlin novels, or rather, that their characters are not Berliners. "I spoke no German, had no German friends, had not read a single German novel either in the original or in translation," he once wrote. "But in art, as in nature, a glaring disadvantage may turn out to be a subtle protective device." It is true that many of the characters in Nabokov's Berlin novels are Russians, for Nabokov spent much of his time within that closed community, occupying himself not only by giving tennis and English lessons but also in translating *Alice in Wonderland* into Russian, and by devising, for his father's newspaper, the first Russian crossword puzzles. But the Russians played an important part in the Berlin of the 1920's, as does any major ethnic group in New York today, and Nabokov has left us a matchless portrait of their peculiar society, their teas and intrigues, and their interminable poetry readings.

Here, for example, is an account of one meeting, in a hall "which belonged to a society of dentists, judging by the portraits of venerable tooth doctors that looked down from the walls." First comes "a gray-haired, clean-shaven old man rather resembling a hoopoe," who reads "a tale of Petersburg life on the eve of the revolution, with an ether-sniffing vamp, chic spies, champagne, Rasputin and apocalyptically apoplectic sunsets over the Neva. After him a certain Kron, writing under the pseudonym of Rostislav Stranyy (Rostislav the Strange), gladdened us with a long story about a romantic adventure in the town of a hundred eyes; for the sake of beauty . . . the word *storozhko,* 'warily,' was repeated about a dozen times ('She warily let fall a smile;' 'The chestnuts broke warily into blossom'). After the interval poets came thick and fast: A tall youth with a buttonlike face . . . an elderly lady wearing a pince-nez. . . ."

And all around him, Nabokov saw a city that he could not resist describing. Here is Fyodor, the hero of *The Gift,* waiting for a bus on the Kurfürstendamm: "In wicker armchairs on the terrace of a neighboring café businessmen sprawled in identical poses with their hands identically gabled in front of them, all very similar to one another as regards snouts and ties but probably varied in the extent of their solvency; and by the curb stood a small car with . . . broken windows and a bloody handkerchief on the running board; a half-dozen people still loafed around, gaping at it. Everything was sun mottled. . . . Across the sidewalk an elderly, rosy-faced beggar woman with legs cut off at the pelvis was set down like a bust at the foot of a wall and was selling paradoxical shoelaces." Or here, Fyodor is wandering among the sunbathers in the Grunewald, observing "old men's gray legs covered with growths and swollen veins; flat feet; the tawny crust of corns; pink porcine paunches; wet, shivering, pale, hoarse-voiced adolescents . . . the pimply shoulder-blades of bandy-legged girls; the sturdy necks and buttocks of muscular hooligans; the hopeless, godless vacancy of satisfied faces."

Nabokov clearly felt no great affection for his surroundings, and when he first began creating German characters, in *King, Queen, Knave,* he argued that "the fairy-tale freedom inherent in an unknown milieu answered my dream of pure invention. I might have staged KQK in Rumania or Holland. Familiarity with the map and weather of Berlin settled my choice." Despite Nabokov's disavowals, however, *King, Queen, Knave* presents a splendidly idiomatic portrait of life in Berlin during the 1920's. Its heroine, Martha, sleek, restless, sensuous, is a paradigm of the city's self-indulgent upper middle class; her husband, Kurt Dreyer, proprietor of the Dandy department store, dreams of quick profits through the invention of a robot mannequin and takes not one but two girls on a skiing trip to Davos. And of all the gawky young bumpkins who came to Berlin to seek their fortunes, none could be more horridly typical than Dreyer's nephew, Franz, with his myopia, his tattered long underwear, his letters to his mother, and his inability to do anything right.

Dreyer regards his nephew as "an amusing simpleton," but the bored Martha goes to his shabby room and seduces him. And then begins one of the most preposterous love affairs in modern literature. All three of them go to the circus, for instance, and watch four Japanese fly to and fro "on rhythmically creaking trapezes" and a seal dive into a pool "where a half-naked girl greeted the happy beast with a kiss on the nose." Martha and the young Franz begin holding hands in the darkness while a lady in a spangled evening dress plays "a luminous violin [with] a star-flashing bow." Dreyer startles the lovers by saying, "Let me know when this obscene abomination is over," and Franz thinks that Dreyer has seen their fumbling in the dark, but Martha only snaps at her husband, "You understand absolutely nothing about art."

Dreyer is as jaded as his wife. He gives a Christmas party, and in the midst of the revelry, paper hats, and drunken dancing, the lights go out. "A masked man suddenly appeared, dressed in an old military coat and carrying a menacing flashlight in his fist [while] the phonograph [went] on dutifully playing in the dark." The masked man is Dreyer himself, trying to create some excitement, but Martha, who recognizes him, screams wildly for help in the vain hope that Franz will defend her by bludgeoning her unwanted husband. For by now, Martha is determined to murder Dreyer so that she and Franz can live on his fortune. They are farcically incompetent conspirators. They start by looking futilely through an encyclopedia for a suitable poison—"They discovered that strychnine caused spasms in frogs and laughing fits in some islanders. Martha was beginning to fume." They devise a complicated plan to shoot Dreyer during a fake burglary, but they don't know how to get a gun. Martha excitedly discovers one in Dreyer's desk but then finds that it is a fake, actually a cigar-lighter.

Cheerfully ignorant of all this, Dreyer wanders, at the request of the inventor whose robot mannequin he is subsidizing, into a police exhibition on crime. "One respectable burgher, who suddenly, for no good reason, had dismembered a neighbor's child, was found to have in his apartment an artificial woman. She could walk, wring her hands, and make water. . . . Impelled by professional anxiety, the Inventor wanted to take a look at her. . . . The poor woman turned out to be rather crudely made. . . . A clockwork device permitted her to close her glass eyes and spread her legs. They could be filled up with hot water. . . . The scornful and happy Inventor left at once but Dreyer, always afraid of missing something entertaining, strolled through all the rooms. He examined the faces of criminals, enlarged photographs of ears, messy fingerprints, kitchen knives, ropes . . . and the puffy faces of their victims who in death came to resemble them; and it was all so shabby, so stupid, that Dreyer could not help smiling. . . . It was lovely outside, a lush wind was blowing. . . . How lovely, blue and fragrant, our Berlin is in the summer. . . . How amusing it would be, he thought, to search the faces of those workmen, of those passers-by, for the facial expressions he had just seen in countless photographs. And to his surprise, in everyone he met

Dreyer recognized a criminal, past, present, or future. . . . Face after face slipped by, eyes avoided his, and even in plump, motherly housewives, he distinguished the skeletons of murder."

Dreyer's observation is a curious forecast of the feelings with which one walked the streets of Berlin in 1945 and 1946—and even, to some extent, today—wondering which of these people was guilty for what happened. But Nabokov was writing in the mid-twenties, and Dreyer's vision was not wholly accurate, for when he finally rejoined his scheming wife and nephew, "he felt a pleasant relief at seeing at last two familiar, two perfectly human faces."

The two lovers have by now acquired the kind of domesticity that Nabokov ascribes to the Germans.

" 'Darling, hurry up,' said Martha from under the blankets.

" 'God, what a corn I've developed,' he grunted, placing his bare foot on the edge of the chair and examining the hard yellow bump on his fifth toe. . . .

" 'Franz, do come, dear. You can inspect it later.' "

Martha has finally devised the perfect scheme for disposing of Dreyer. Like so many Berliners, they will all take a vacation on the Baltic coast, and there the two murderers will lure Dreyer, who can't swim, into a rowboat. They do finally succeed in their plot, but at the last minute Dreyer remarks, "Tomorrow, I'm making a hundred thousand dollars at one stroke." The greedy Martha quickly decides to postpone the plan to push him overboard, and Dreyer returns to the city to sell the patents in the robot mannequin to a gullible American (who is also investigating another Berlin inventor's plan to make hotel water faucets play music—"Wash your hands in a barcarolle, bathe in *Lohengrin* . . ."). It is Martha who catches pneumonia, and, after pleading for someone to bring her emeralds to her bedside, dies. And while she is dying, attended only by the grief-stricken Dreyer, young Franz is still wandering through the little stores at the beach resort, shopping for a pair of plus fours and trying to "decide which he wanted, the brown or the purplish tweed."

The Russian influence on Berlin, the "comradeship in misfortune," was not limited to the military plans of General von Seeckt, or to the cultural gifts of the émigrés. There were also malign political winds from the east.

Among the Communists, it had been assumed from the beginning that the Russian Revolution was only a prelude to the German Revolution, and they promptly set out to make the Soviet Embassy on Unter den Linden the headquarters of the coming battle. As early as the spring of 1918, when Ludendorff was still waging his last great offensives in France, a wealthy young Crimean Jew named Adolf Yoffe (also a neurotic who had been treated in Vienna by Alfred Adler) arrived in Berlin as Lenin's ambassador. He brought along a gigantic staff of more than three hundred assistants, whom he promptly sent all over Germany to foment revolt. By means of the diplomatic pouch, Yoffe also brought and disbursed large quantities of money and revolutionary propaganda, and he made little secret of his intentions. Over the embassy, he hoisted a huge red flag carrying the words: "Workers of all countries, unite!" Yoffe was more radical than even Liebknecht, and when Liebknecht expressed doubts about an immediate revolution, the Russian answered: "Within a week the red flag will be flying over the Berlin palace."

The harassed Social Democrats did not look with great favor on the new ambassador's activities, however, and during the critical days of early November, 1918, Scheidemann suggested that it might be useful to have some of the Russians' incoming shipments be "accidentally" broken open. From the "accident," the police promptly produced a pile of incriminating documents (there is some evidence that the police planted this material), and Yoffe was forthwith expelled. Yoffe tried to return to Berlin the very next month as the head of a five-man Soviet delegation to the National Congress of Workers' and Soldiers' Councils, but he was turned back at gunpoint by German troops guarding the frontier. One of the Soviet delegates, however, was an ambitious Polish radical named Karl Radek, who disguised himself as a wounded German soldier and slipped across the border with a group of repatriated war prisoners.

Radek, like many of the early revolutionaries, was a Jew, a short, solid man with curly black sideburns and thick glasses, and a great ability for both organization and rhetoric. As Lenin's personal envoy to Berlin, he soon achieved a position next to Liebknecht in the leadership of German radicalism, but he was not without enemies. Rosa Luxemburg, in particular, attacked him for the Bolsheviks' use of terrorism. Radek had the standard answer—Lenin applied terror, he said, only against "classes whom history has sentenced to death." Others thought Radek purely an opportunist. One observer, after hearing him make a speech, remarked that behind his "mask of youthful ardor" there lay an expression that resembled partly a wolf and partly "a street urchin after a particularly successful prank. A truly impertinent, amusing, and frightening Mephistophelian face."

Like Rosa Luxemburg, Radek opposed the Spartakist uprisings as premature, and when the vengeful Freikorps troops swept through Berlin, Lenin's emissary fled for his life. He was arrested, finally, and put in solitary confinement, but in prison, oddly enough, he became more influential than ever before. To his cell in Moabit Prison came not just the remaining leaders of the badly wounded Communist Party, seeking guidance and advice, but also a strange congeries of moderate and even right-wing leaders. Walther Rathenau came to Moabit to consult the imprisoned Bolshevik, and so did Ludendorff's adjutant, Colonel Walter Bauer, and so did a number of other businessmen and army officers. To all of them, Radek preached the same doctrine—an alliance, regardless of ideologies, between Russia and Germany. Radek, before his imprisonment, had even proposed a formal alliance to Ebert, but the proposal had been turned down, and the Weimar regime finally decided to send Lenin's envoy back to Russia. His policy lived on, however, because it was also the policy of General von Seeckt.

At the time, it seemed to the good burghers of the Weimar government that the greatest danger from Russia was the influence of dedicated Bolsheviks like Yoffe and Radek, but from a later vantage point, we can see a very different infection spreading westward from Russia. Most of the Russian refugees were either moderately liberal or without any real political convictions at all, but the great emigration also included every variety of monarchist, reactionary and even Fascist, and they, too, played a part in the life of Berlin. Count Kessler noted in his diary one evening when he "went to a reactionary Russian cabaret on the Kurfürstendamm. Extravagantly modern décor and production: a lamentation for Old Russia's downfall sublimated in a cabaret-like presentation and set over against an invincible faith in Russia's future. . . . Into the middle of the performance burst the shocking news of the murder of . . . Nabokov during the course of a lecture. . . . The rumour swept the best part of the audience, almost exclusively Russian, out of the cabaret like a tidal wave. After a few moments we were practically alone in what had been an auditorium full to overflowing. Only three elegant young Russians (there is a grand duke in the chorus) sat on at the table next to us. When I asked one of them how much truth there was in the report, he replied, 'Well, yes . . . Infamous, that fifteen thousand Russian officers should have let themselves be slaughtered by the Revolution without raising a hand in self-defence! Why didn't they act like the Germans, who killed Rosa Luxemburg in such a way that not a smell of her has remained?' "

The cabaret was an appropriate setting for such declarations, since many of the most militant Russian reactionaries in Berlin were purely music-hall characters. There was Prince Bermont-Avalov, for instance, who boasted of the private army with which he had fought the Bolsheviks in the Baltic in 1919, though a number of people said that he was no general and even less a prince. Somewhat more serious was General Vasili Biskupsky, a heavy gambler who had once commanded the Third Army Corps in Odessa (and who also employed the two youths who murdered Nabokov); he took it upon himself to sign a "Russian-German" treaty of alliance with General Ludendorff, to take effect when the two of them had returned to power. Then there was Nikolai Markov, a landowner from Kursk who had railed against Socialism in the Russian parliament. Now, in Berlin, he wrote tracts about ritual slaughters and Masonic plots, in which, among other things, he portrayed Karl Radek as an agent of the Chief Rabbi of Constantinople.

Among these prophets and warriors, a special place should be reserved for Fyodor Vinberg, a former Czarist officer who came to Berlin and founded a small daily newspaper called *Prizyv*. Vinberg was an early advocate of "the final solution." He argued quite explicitly that all Jews should be killed. And in support of his theories, he brought to Germany the first copies of a peculiar Russian work called *The Protocols of the Elders of Zion*. A fraud concocted in 1895, apparently by the Czarist secret police, the *Protocols* were an amalgamation of a forty-year-old novel entitled *Biarritz*, by Hermann Goodsche, plus an equally dated and equally fictitious chronicle entitled *Dialogues aux Enfers entre Machiavel et Montesquieu*, by Maurice Joly, plus some arabesques by the anonymous author.

The whole work purported to be a verbatim record of twenty-four secret meetings of the leaders of a Jewish conspiracy, who announce their determination to overthrow all states and religions, by such tricks as democracy and socialism, and to replace them with a world-wide Jewish empire. And if their conspiracy were discovered, it was said, the Elders of Zion had a plan to undermine all major cities with a network of underground railways, from which they would blow up all gentiles. This implausible document attracted little enough attention in prewar Russia, but when the Russian emigration brought it to Germany, a new edition there soon sold more than 100,000 copies (and not there alone, for an American edition sponsored by Henry Ford also achieved wide distribution).

These activities among the Russian émigrés were not without interest to certain Germans (some of the editors of Vinberg's *Prizyv* were involved in the preparations for the Kapp Putsch, leading to a ban on the paper after Ebert's government returned to Berlin), but the Germans were appalled by the Russians' passion for fighting among themselves. They even had, by now, two émigré pretenders to the nonexistent Russian throne. In June of 1921, therefore, a meeting was convoked in the Bavarian resort of Bad Reichenhall for the purpose of bringing the Russians together. One of the meeting's covert sponsors was General Ludendorff, and one of its main organizers was a rather mysterious Baltic German named Max von Scheubner-Richter (born Max Richter), who had become the chief political adviser to the young Adolf Hitler.

Some 130 Russian delegates from various countries gathered in the Post Restaurant in Bad Reichenhall, and they must have provided a grand spectacle for the Bavarian villagers—Generals Biskupsky and Zakharov, Bishop Antoni of Kiev, Senators Bellegarde and Rimsky-Korsakov. They convened promptly at 10 A.M. every day and discussed the need for economic reconstruction and agricultural reform as soon as the Russian monarchy was restored. They also argued in the corridors about which delegates were German agents and which were in the pay of the French. They could not agree, however, on which royal pretender to support, or on anything else, and so they finally disbanded and returned to their various homes in exile.

But the poison remained. Scheubner-Richter continued his efforts to organize an anti-Communist coalition of German nationalists, and *The Protocols of the Elders of Zion* had a great influence on the Nazi theoretician, Alfred Rosenberg, and both of them, in turn, exercised a considerable influence on the evolving plans of Adolf Hitler. In the beginning, Hitler cared relatively little about Soviet

Communism; even toward the Jews, he felt only the conventional hostility of the ignorant Austrian peasant; it was the French whom he hated with a boundless passion. But from the Russian émigrés who streamed into Berlin at the end of the war, he acquired, slowly, indirectly, the doctrines that would ultimately send General von Seeckt's panzer divisions to their destruction on the Volga.

"A Certain Champagne Sparkle" 1922

Knallt ab den Walther Rathenau,
Die Gottverfluchte Judensau.

(Shoot down Walther Rathenau.
He's a goddamn dirty Jew.)

FREIKORPS MARCHING SONG

IN MAY OF 1922, Chancellor Josef Wirth received a visit from a Catholic priest, who brought a warning that filled him with dread. The nationalist agitation against Foreign Minister Walther Rathenau —grave, stately Walther Rathenau, the millionaire industrialist, the exquisitely polished connoisseur of music and poetry, the lonely bachelor, the black-bearded Jew—was no longer a matter of chants and slogans. A number of young radicals had organized a plot to murder him, the priest said, and the attack might come at any moment.

Chancellor Wirth, appalled, summoned Rathenau to his office and insisted that he accept substantial police protection. "My words impressed Rathenau deeply," Wirth recalled later. "He stood motionless and pale for about two minutes. None of us dared break the silence or speak a single word. Rathenau seemed to be gazing on some distant land. He was visibly struggling with his own feelings. Suddenly his face and his eyes took on an expression of infinite benevolence and gentleness. With a calm such as I had never witnessed in him . . . he stepped up to me, and putting both his hands

98

on my shoulders said: 'Dear friend, it is nothing. Who would do me any harm?' "

In this same season, late one afternoon, three young men were sitting on a bench in the Zoological Garden in the heart of Berlin. One of them was a former lieutenant in the Imperial Navy, Erwin Kern, aged twenty-five, handsome, blond, blue-eyed, and, in his way, insane. With him were two of his followers, a quiet engineer named Hermann Fischer, also twenty-five, and a twenty-year-old ex-cadet, Ernst von Salomon. All of them had taken part in the Freikorps campaigns, and now they were all engaged in guerrilla warfare against the Republic, in gun-running and bomb-throwing and other acts of terrorism. Kern had organized a new plot, but he was reluctant to tell his confederates about his plans. On the park bench, Salomon persisted in his questions. "Kern . . . sat leaning forward, with his arms resting on his knees, watching the people stroll in the soft twilight," Salomon said. "Sounds of distant music reached us faintly. . . . Kern said: 'If this final act is not attempted now, it may be impossible for decades. We want a revolution. We are free from the hindrance of plans, methods and systems. Therefore, it is our duty to take the first step, to storm the breach. We must retire the moment our task is done. For the task is attack, not government.' "

"I intend," Kern said, "to shoot the man who is greater than all those who surround him."

"Rathenau?" Salomon asked.

"Rathenau," Kern said.

The conspirators had chosen their target well, for Walther Rathenau was one of the most distinguished men in Germany. He had been born in 1867 in a working-class district of North Berlin, the son of a passionate technocrat named Emil Rathenau. The elder Rathenau owned a small iron foundry, but he felt constricted by the limitations of his business. He sold the foundry and began looking around for new opportunities. Wandering through the circuit of European industrial exhibitions of the 1870's, he became interested in a new invention by an American named Thomas Edison, and so, in one of those decisions that make commercial history, he bought the European patents for the electric light. With borrowed money, he founded the factory that eventually became the German equivalent of General Electric (AEG).

His son did his best to escape from the father's influence. He studied physics and chemistry and then spent seven years at a factory in Saxony, making himself financially independent. "In 1899," Rathenau wrote, "I decided to retire from industry in order to devote myself to literature. The AEG, however, invited me to join their board of directors and take over the department for constructing power stations. I . . . built a number of stations—e.g. in Manchester, Amsterdam, Buenos Aires and Baku. . . . In 1902 I left the AEG in order to enter finance . . . and belonged at that time to nearly a hundred different concerns." By 1914, Rathenau was a friend of the Kaiser and an influential member of the international capitalist superstructure. "Three hundred men, all acquainted with each other," as Rathenau himself wrote, "control the economic destiny of the Continent. "

This comfortable fraternity split wide open in the fall of 1914, and though ignorant crowds cheered the soldiers marching to the front, visionaries like Rathenau took a less optimistic view of the future. "Rathenau seemed completely overwhelmed," according to his friend and biographer, Count Kessler. "While the people were seized with a delirious excitement . . . Rathenau was wringing his hands in despair. An old friend . . . describes how he came to her and sat in silence, while the tears rolled down his cheeks. . . . The outbreak of war was a crisis from which Rathenau never recovered. It was the crisis of his life."

Rathenau was by no means a pacifist, however. When he received a visit from a Jewish hat manufacturer named Felix Heimann, who wondered whether the cavalry officers on the General Staff had ever thought about accumulating the raw materials necessary for a modern war, Rathenau carried the question to the War Ministry. The Ministry expressed surprise. This campaign, like those of 1866 and 1870, was to last no more than a few months. The strategic plans left by the late General von Schlieffen virtually guaranteed the fall of France. But there was no official objection to the ministerial decree that established a "War Raw Materials Department," consisting of Rathenau, a retired colonel, and five assistants. The little group began by overseeing the production of metals, then chemicals, then wool, rubber, cotton, leather. Eventually, for better or for worse, Rathenau's organization enabled Germany to continue the war at least a year, perhaps two years, longer than would otherwise have been possible.

Rathenau's plans went far beyond the war, however. Indeed, they went beyond anything conceived by the industrialists of his time. "Property, consumption and demand are not private matters," he wrote in a book called *In Days to Come*. "In days to come, people will find it difficult to understand that the will of a dead man could bind the living; that any individual was empowered to enclose for his private gratification mile upon mile of land; that without requiring any authorization from the state he could leave cultivable land untilled, could demolish buildings or erect them, ruin beautiful landscapes, secrete or disfigure works of art; that he conceived himself justified, by appropriate business methods, in bringing whatever portion he could of the communal property under his own private control; justified, provided he could pay his taxes, in using this property as he pleased, in taking any number of men into his own service, and setting them to whatever work seemed good to him, so long as there was no technical violation of the law; justified in engaging in any kind of business, so long as he did not infringe a state monopoly or promote any enterprise legally defined as a swindle; justified in any practice, however absurd or however harmful to the community, provided always he remained able to pay his way."

In short, Rathenau, the millionaire, wondered how society could continue to tolerate the system of private enterprise based on the profit motive. Rathenau argued that the labor devoted to fine textiles was "filched" from the manufacture of adequate clothing for the poor, that even the manpower devoted to yachting could and should be used in commercial shipping. "Whoever squanders labor," Rathenau said, "is robbing the community." His solution was to impose heavy taxes on every form of what he considered "luxurious" consumption: tobacco, liquor, "large private parks . . . horses, carriages . . . costly furniture."

Beyond that, Rathenau advocated sharp restrictions on competition, the merging of firms within the same industry, the participation of both government and labor unions in the management of large corporations, and the redistribution of political power according to economic functions rather than according to regional population. It is scarcely surprising that Rathenau's colleagues considered him a Bolshevik, but his two main books of social theory, *In Days to Come* (1917) and *The New Economy* (1918), both became huge best-sellers. The first sold 65,000 copies in its first year, the second 30,000 in its first month. "Walther Rathenau became," said Kessler, "the most widely read and most passionately discussed of German writers."

Inevitably, Rathenau began thinking, despite his protestations of modesty, of political power for himself. And it may have been this ambition that led him to some of his most ill-considered expressions of nationalism. In the middle of the war, he fell under the influence of General Ludendorff and publicly supported the General Staff's program for the forced deportation of 700,000 Belgians to German factories. Even after Ludendorff had given up and appealed for an armistice, Rathenau demanded that the defeated nation be called to arms in a *levée en masse*. And when the Freikorps were first being mobilized, Rathenau not only supported them but raised $5 million to finance them.

As early as 1911, there had been proposals to have Rathenau run for election to the Reichstag from Frankfurt-on-the-Oder, but local politicians reported that many voters expressed opposition to being represented by a liberal and a Jew, so Rathenau withdrew. In 1919, when the constitutional convention in Weimar received nominations for the presidency, an expatriate German in Stockholm offered the name of Rathenau, and the offer was met, according to the official shorthand report, with "much merriment on the right." Rathenau reacted with considerable anguish. Disavowing the nomination as "misguided," he bitterly and rather pompously denounced the delegates' laughter: "The Parliament of any other civilized state would have shown sufficient respect for a man of recognized intellectual standing to have passed over in silence this act of bad taste. But the First Parliament of the German Republic . . . greeted it with roars and shrieks of laughter. . . . This was their way of greeting a German whose intellectual achievements they either did or did not know."

Rathenau obviously was not destined for a great career in the turmoil of democratic politics. He liked to improvise on the piano, to paint, and to write aphorisms, which he published under a pseudonym, and even his friend, Count Kessler, observed that "he was by no means always easy to get on with; on the contrary, he was easily irritated by contradiction, and when he let himself go he could be extraordinarily unpleasant." The surviving portraits convey a similar effect—a very tall man, in his mid-fifties, and handsome according to the standard of the period. He had a bald head and a short black beard, flecked with gray, and extraordinary dark eyes. His cutaway suits were always coolly impeccable, but a number of observers noticed that he was inordinately given to fingering the long, golden chain that he often wore around his neck.

Another admirer, Stefan Zweig, described him with rather mixed feelings: "His mind was always on the alert, an instrument of such precision and rapidity as I have never seen in anyone else. . . . He spoke French, English, and Italian as well as he did German. His memory never failed him. . . . In speaking with him, one felt stupid, faultily educated, uncertain and confused in the presence of his calm, deliberate and clear-thinking objectivity. But there was something in the blinding brilliance, the crystal clarity of his thinking, just as there was something in the choice furniture and fine pictures in his home, that made one feel uncomfortable. His mind had the effect of an ingeniously contrived apparatus, his home that of a museum. . . . Rarely have I sensed the tragedy of the Jew more strongly than in his personality which, with all of its apparent superiority, was full of a deep unrest and uncertainty."

For such a man, the only road to power lay in his being appointed to office, and Chancellor Wirth, an amiable moderate, duly persuaded Rathenau to become Minister of Reconstruction. Rathenau accepted largely because he believed in the need to end the futile arguments against the Versailles Treaty. "I have entered a cabinet of fulfillment," he said in his first speech before the Reichstag. "We must discover some means of linking ourselves up with the world again."

The diplomatic confrontations with the Western Allies were not easy, however, and they soon proved too much for Wirth's Foreign Minister, Dr. Friedrich Rosen, a veteran diplomat whose chief claim to fame lay in his authority on Persian poetry. When Rosen wearily resigned, Wirth turned to Rathenau as his successor. Rathenau's mother, to whom he was devoted, desperately opposed her son's accepting such a post at a time of nationalist agitation against the principal officials of the Republic. As a result, he did not tell her of his decision to accept the Foreign Ministry, and she learned of it only from the newspapers. "Rathenau lunched as usual with his mother," according to a friend of the family. "They sat opposite one another, toying about with their food, until finally his mother asked him: 'Walther, why have you done this to me?' And he replied, 'I really had to, Mama, because they couldn't find anyone else.' "

"Actually," said one of the conspirators, many years later, "there was only one political common denominator that held the whole 'national movement' together at that time, and . . . it amounted to this: 'We must make an end to . . . the Versailles Treaty and cooperating with the West.'. . . I think it was Kern himself . . . who finally said, during a heated argument, that in that case the only course open was to eliminate every [Versailles] politician. To eliminate in that context is, of course, to kill. . . . 'Lists' were drawn up. And on one of our lists, among many others, was Rathenau's name."

"That list!" said another one of the conspirators. "It was, in fact, a single dirty sheet of paper with names scribbled all over it in pencil, with some crossed out, some written in again. Many of the names meant absolutely nothing to me. . . . It was pure chance that I took part in the murder of Rathenau. . . . In fact Rathenau was the only Jew whom we murdered."

"But we were anti-Semitic," said the first conspirator.

"Indeed we were," said the second.

The second conspirator, Ernst von Salomon, who has felt a compulsive need to write about these events, joined forces with ex-Lieutenant Kern in Hamburg, and they engaged in endless discussions on the overthrow of the government, and the best means to achieve that end. Both of them felt a sense of rage and shame about the outcome of the war. Salomon, the young cadet who had never reached the front, asked Kern how a naval officer could survive the humiliation of defeat and surrender, and Kern answered, "I did not survive it. . . . I am dead. . . . I will not be other than the two million who died. . . . My actions are the sole motive force within me. This force is destructive—hence I destroy." In his search for destruction, Kern deliberately aimed not at the worst but at the best. Rathenau, he said, during an all-night argument in a room filled with cached rifles and hand grenades, "is the finest and ripest fruit of his age. He unites in himself everything in this age that is of value in thought, in honor, and in spirituality." And it was precisely this superiority that inspired the young nihilists to murder him. "I couldn't bear it," Kern said, "if again something great were to rise out of the chaotic, the insane age in which we live. . . . We are not fighting to make the nation happy—we are fighting to make it walk in the path of its destiny."

In the newspapers, the conspirators read of Rathenau's triumphs at the Genoa conference, a meeting ostensibly organized to discuss problems of world trade. From the Germans' point of view, it was the first chance to take part in an international conference as equal partners. The French did their best to upset this equality, and they sponsored a series of private meetings, without the Germans, to determine the extent of German reparations to Russia (which, incidentally, would enable the Soviets to pay off Imperial Russian debts to France). When these private discussions became deadlocked, the Russians proposed a separate treaty of friendship with the Germans, and Rathenau met the Russians at a nearby resort to sign the celebrated Treaty of Rapallo.

None of this had any great practical significance, but the processes of diplomacy are slow and strange. "Looking backwards, one cannot help seeing that Genoa marked the turning of the tide in post-war history," wrote Count Kessler, himself a minor participant at the conference. "Germany . . . had regained her status as a great power. Besides this, she was bringing home, in the teeth of French opposition, her treaty with Russia; and Rathenau had prepared the ground for a further advance on the path of negotiation and understanding by establishing relations of mutual confidence with some at least of the Allied statesmen."

Kern was not the only young fanatic who was planning to murder Rathenau. There was also a seventeen-year-old schoolboy named Hans Stubenrauch, the son of a general, who had decided on the same mission. He had become obsessed by one of Rathenau's rather ambiguous wartime predictions: "That day will never come on which the Kaiser will ride victorious through the Brandenburger Tor. On that day history would have lost all meaning." To Stubenrauch, this Delphic pronouncement was proof that Rathenau had not wanted Germany to win the war, and therefore deserved to die. Stubenrauch confided his plans to another youth named Günther, and Günther put him in touch with Kern, who approved of the idea but not of the young Stubenrauch. Kern was more professional. He and his friend Fischer were both members of Organisation Consul, a terrorist organization headed by that same Captain Ehrhardt who had staged the Kapp Putsch. Kern assigned the schoolboy to minor duties on the fringes of the plot. To carry out the technical details of the conspiracy, Kern joined forces with the Berlin representative of Organisation Consul, Ernst-Werner Techow, twenty-one, the son of a Berlin magistrate, and Techow brought along his younger brother, Gerd, aged sixteen.

On June 18, Kern, Fischer, and Günther went to the home of the Techows' widowed mother, and the five youths worked out a plan to ambush Rathenau's car as he drove from his villa in the wooded suburb of Grunewald to his office at the Foreign Ministry. On June 20, the conspirators met again at the Steglitzer Rathskeller and went over the details. Kern was worried that an ordinary pistol might not be effective in a quick attack. To check the problems, the youths borrowed a six-seater car and drove out to Grunewald the next day to rehearse the assassination. The rehearsal convinced Kern that they needed an automatic pistol, and so he went to a small town in Mecklenburg to get such a weapon, which he had left in the hands of a former naval cadet.

A day or two before the assassination, the conspirators went to the Reichstag to hear Rathenau deliver a speech on the results of the Genoa conference. Wandering home along Unter den Linden, they stopped in front of a photographer's shop, which displayed a portrait of Rathenau in the window. "The strange, dark, eager yet self-possessed eyes looked at us almost searchingly out of the narrow aristocratic face," Salomon recalled. "Fischer, after a long scrutiny, said: 'He looks a decent sort.'" And so they wandered on down the street. With everything ready, the conspirators spent the night of June 23 in a tavern, drinking quantities of beer, wine, and cognac. Techow apparently had misgivings about the assassination, but Kern told him that Rathenau was a Bolshevik, that he wanted to bring all of Germany under the domination of the Jews, and that his policy of cooperation with the Western Allies was a betrayal of the Fatherland.

That same night, Rathenau was a guest at the American Embassy. He was upset, because Karl Helfferich, the Nationalist leader, had just delivered a violent attack against him in the Reichstag. Only two days earlier, Rathenau had invited Helfferich to a quiet dinner at his palatial house in Grunewald, in an effort to settle their differences. The meeting had gone well, Rathenau thought, but now Helfferich had taken the offensive again. "The policy of fulfillment has brought in its train the appalling depreciation of German currency," Helfferich had declared in the Reichstag that afternoon, "it has utterly crushed the middle classes, it has brought poverty and misery on countless families, it has driven countless people to suicide and despair."

At the American Embassy, however, the arguments were more peaceful. There was some discussion of Germany's difficulties in meeting its coal deliveries to the Allies, and Rathenau suggested that the Ruhr coal baron, Hugo Stinnes, be invited to join the party. Stinnes was an old antagonist of Rathenau's, but he agreed to come to the embassy as soon as he had finished dinner. He arrived at ten, and there began what one observer called "a lively political debate, which went on till long past midnight, and which was continued, after they had left the Embassy, at the Esplanade Hotel till almost four o'clock in the morning."

The next day, June 24, at about ten o'clock in the morning, the conspirators' light-gray, six-seater car stood parked on a side street off the Königsallee in Grunewald. All the conspirators had outfitted themselves in leather coats and motoring caps. Fischer kept watch at the corner, looking for some sign of Rathenau's open car. The assassins knew that the Foreign Minister invariably followed the same route, and that his chauffeur drove slowly (the Prussian chief of police had warned Rathenau the previous day, as a matter of fact, that if he insisted on driving to work in a slow, open car, no police could protect him). The assassins' car had unexpectedly developed troubles, however. Techow bent over the hood, poking around in the inside. He told Kern that the oil-feed was broken. The car could only go a short distance. But Kern cheerfully summoned his two confederates and gave the order to start. Salomon, whom Kern had forbidden to take part in the attack, was still worrying about the consequences.

"What motive shall I give if we're caught?" he asked.

"Lord, it doesn't matter what you say," Kern answered. "For all I care, you can say he's one of the Wise Men of Zion, or . . . anything you like. . . . They'll never understand our real motives."

Then Techow started up the car, and it puttered down the little street and turned the corner.

Looking back, past the fires of Auschwitz, it is customary to assume that the Germans have always felt a murderous hostility toward Jews, and even that the disease of anti-Semitism was incubated

somewhere between the Rhine and the Elbe. The assumptions are
not wholly false, but they are far from being the truth.

The tormented relationship between Germany's Jews and gentiles
has endured for nearly two millennia. The first Jewish settlement on
the Rhine was established in the second century A.D., and the German Jews took pride in their local traditions. "If you tell me the name
of any German Jew—Guggenheim, Sulzberger, anyone you like—I
can tell you the name of the city he comes from," says Rabbi
Joachim Prinz, twiddling with a saber-shaped letter-opener on his
desk. "I tell you, there were some Jewish families who lived in the
same *house* for three hundred years."

The earliest known document on the Jews in Berlin dates back to
1295, when the town was little more than a collection of huts, and
this document, prophetically, was a discriminatory decree. It forbade
the weavers of Berlin to buy their yarn from Jews. Although the
number of Jews cannot have been large, they were the scapegoats
for every disaster. In 1348, during the Black Death, they were
blamed for the plague and expelled from the city. From that time
forward, according to one chronicler, "there were repeated expulsions and readmissions, but the details and reasons have been
forgotten." In 1500, seven Jews were accused of the ritual murder
of a boy, a number of others were implicated, and some thirty of
them were burned at the stake in the Neuer Markt, just across
from where the red-brick City Hall now stands. Once again, all Jews
were expelled from Berlin, but a complicated legal proceeding
finally proved, a quarter-century after the burnings, that the executed
"ritual murderers" had been innocent, and so the Elector of Brandenburg readmitted Jews to Berlin. When the Elector suddenly died,
however, there were rumors that the Jews had poisoned him, and a
series of anti-Semitic riots broke out. The Jews were expelled again,
in 1573, "for all eternity."

Nothing can atone for this history of persecutions, of course, but
it may be misleading to imply a historical relationship between the
executions in the Neuer Markt and the massacres in Hitler's death
camps. These were the centuries of the Roman Church triumphant,
and not only were Jews harassed all over Europe but all manner of
Christian heretics were tortured and put to the stake. The reforms
of Martin Luther were scarcely a blessing for the Jews, however,
since Luther advocated that "their assets be sequestered, their homes

razed, their synagogues leveled, that they be driven off the roads . . . assigned to the mines and quarries, compelled to fell trees . . . in misery and captivity as they incessantly lament and complain to God about us." But the religious wars that followed the Reformation took no special toll of Jews, for the ravaging armies that swept to and fro across Germany butchered Catholics and Protestants with equal ferocity.

The modern history of the Jewish community in Berlin begins in 1671, when fifty families received permission to resettle in the neighboring Kurmark. The fifty families soon grew to ninety-six, and more Jews kept slipping in illegally, and being driven out again. Frederick the Great tried to limit the Jewish population by decreeing that only one son in each family could marry and establish his own household. Each of these husbands was required by law to wear a long beard, and none of them could engage in farming or handicrafts. Nor could they trade in leather, wood, furs, and various other goods. Even within these limitations, however, a Jewish subculture began to flourish. Moses Mendelssohn translated the Pentateuch into German in 1783 and became a leading proponent of German-Jewish assimilation (when Mendelssohn himself was proposed for membership in the Prussian Academy of Science, King Frederick personally removed his name from the list of candidates). Among the most brilliant literary salons in Berlin was that of Rahel Levin, who described her own racial destiny as "one long bleeding to death."

It was the French Revolution that finally brought the Jews a theoretical equality. The idea that all men were equal spread from Paris to Kassell, where Napoleon established his brother Jerome as the "King of Westphalia," and from there to the German principalities of the east. But even though a Prussian royal edict of 1812 granted the Jews full citizenship, they did not win their full civil rights until Bismarck promulgated the Constitution of a united Germany in 1871—and even then their rights were disputed. Bismarck, who had financed his wars by means of loans from a Jewish banker named Gerson Bleichroder, once remarked that "the Jews bring to the mixture of different German breeds a certain champagne sparkle which must not be underestimated," and he was consequently attacked by German nationalists as "a lickspittle of the Jews."

As Jews began to emerge in business and the professions, there came outbreaks of anti-Semitic rioting in the 1880's, and the celebrated Professor Heinrich von Treitschke of the University of Berlin wrote that anti-Semitism was "a natural reaction of the German national feeling against a foreign element which had usurped too large a place in our life." Twisting some lines by Heine, Treitschke coined a phrase that Joseph Goebbels later adopted as a slogan: *"Die Juden sind unser Unglück"* ("The Jews are our misfortune"). These slurs did not go unanswered, however. When the Kaiser's court chaplain, Adolf Stöcker, founded his Christian Socialist Party and demanded the enforced conversion of the Jews, more liberal Christians founded a Union to Combat Anti-Semitism. Its leader, Heinrich Rickert, told Stöcker on the floor of the Reichstag: "I am convinced that three-quarters of the German nation are on my side."

When World War I began, the Jews expressed their sense of German nationalism by swarming into the army with an ardor as lemming-like as that of the gentiles. Some 100,000 Jews (one out of every six, including the women and children) entered the German Army. Of these, 80,000 served in front-line trenches, 35,000 were decorated for bravery, and 12,000 were killed. "The Jews were pathologically patriotic," says Rabbi Prinz. "My father served in the war, and my *grandfather* was wounded in 1866, in the war against the Austrians. He was enormously proud of that." And only an American reporter thought it odd that a segregated cemetery should have been created for the Jews who had been killed. "It was a vast place," Ben Hecht said, "acres and acres of earth covered with rows of little marble slabs. . . . [My guide said:] 'They fought bravely for their Fatherland. More Jews were killed in battle than Germans. The Jewish population of Germany was only one half of one percent. The Jewish deaths in the war were three percent.' "

Only after the war, finally, did the Jews attain the full equality that had been promised them in 1812 and 1871. Numerically, they remained a tiny minority, never more than about one percent of the population. Those few, however, tended to congregate in Berlin. The 50 families of 1671 grew to a population of 3,322 in 1800, to 92,000 in 1900, to a peak of 173,000 in 1925 (about six times the 29,000 in Frankfurt, Germany's second-largest Jewish community). Even during this increase, Berlin's Jews never numbered more than 5 percent of the city's population, but they managed to acquire some very visible positions of power and prestige. They were enormously influential in commerce, dominating the giant Deutsche, Dresdener, and Darmstadter banks, and huge department stores like Wertheim, Tietz, and Kaufhaus Israel. The most important newspaper groups, Ullstein and Mosse, were owned by Jews, and, to a very considerable extent, the spectacular culture of Berlin in the 1920's, the culture dominated by men like Max Reinhardt and Bruno Walter and Albert Einstein, was a Jewish culture.

To the Jews, this was naturally a matter of pride, and more than one Jewish chronicler has pointed out that one-quarter of all the Nobel Prizes won by Germans in the first third of this century were won by German Jews. To many gentiles, however, even those who vehemently deny the accusation of anti-Semitism, this flowering of Jewish life represented the triumph of an alien and vaguely threatening force. Whatever the Jewish hopes for assimilation might be—and they were considerable ("Jews are political idiots," says Rabbi Prinz. "They are too optimistic, too hopeful. They do not understand an enemy")—the unusual structure of German religious life tended to keep them permanently separate.

German religious groups are not private organizations, as in America, but officially authorized "congregations," which get their money from special taxes that the government levies on all members of the religious community. Until the present century, this meant that the status of the Jews was the status of a religious minority, and a Jew could escape from discriminatory laws, at the price of his heritage, by converting to Christianity. In our more secular age, however, people no longer accept a purely religious definition of themselves, and so, even as an increasing number of Jews abandoned their religious traditions, an increasing number of gentiles came to agree with the Talmudic decree: Even though a Jew may sin (i.e., become converted), he remains a Jew. By now, the idea of the Jews as a race rather than a religion (or as well as a religion) has become so generally accepted that the terms "Jew" and "German" are used by both groups as though they were mutually exclusive.

To a nation shattered by defeat and revolution, the emergence of Jews in public life seemed a somehow sinister development, quite apart from the old religious antagonisms. Wasn't Trotsky a Jew, after all? And Rosa Luxemburg? And Karl Radek? Even in more ordinary situations, the quantity of Jewish publishers and doctors and lawyers seemed to many anxious gentiles something other than the triumph of the fittest. "The 1920's were governed, in science, medicine, in culture, by the Jews," says one embittered survivor of that period. "The professors at the university were Jews. If a student was a Jew, he would get the best job. If you had a Jewish lawyer, you could win a case, but if you didn't, you would lose. And any job which promised to get money out of it was in the control of the Jews. For us, for the Germans, it was very bad."

To people like this, and they ranged from ordinary Berlin workmen to the deposed Kaiser in Holland, there came wonderful revelations in the works of now-forgotten sages like Houston Stewart Chamberlain. In *Foundations of the Nineteenth Century*, a book that was first published in 1899 and ultimately sold more than a million copies, Chamberlain argued that "The Jewish race is altogether bastardized . . . a crime against the holy laws of life." What Chamberlain argued as theory seemed to acquire proof from those spurious documents called *The Protocols of the Elders of Zion*. They offered "proof" that there was a Jewish conspiracy after all, and the mythical Elders of Zion not only admitted but boasted of their plot to dominate the world.

Of all the men who might personify this dark conspiracy, who fitted the image of ignorant public fears more perfectly than the intellectual millionaire who had once said that "Three hundred men, all acquainted with each other, control the economic destiny of the continent"? And yet the irony of Walther Rathenau's fate is that he was not only one of the most nationalistic of Germany's foreign ministers but one of the most anti-Semitic of its Jews. "Strange sight!" said Rathenau of the despised *Ostjuden*, those bearded Eastern refugees, who never numbered more than eighty thousand in all of Germany but seemed to alarm everyone who saw them. "There in the midst of German life is an alien and isolated race of men. Loud and self-conscious in their dress, hot-blooded and restless in their manner. An Asiatic horde on the sandy plains of Prussia . . . forming among themselves a closed corporation, rigorously shut off from the rest of the world. Thus they live half-willingly in their invisible ghetto, not a living limb of the people, but an alien organism in its body. . . . So what is to be done? An event without historical precedent: the conscious effort of a race to adapt itself to alien conditions . . . The goal of the process should be, not imitation Germans, but Jews bred and educated as Germans."

As for himself, Rathenau declared that he had already gone through that process. "I am a German of Jewish descent," he said. "My people is the German people, my fatherland is Germany, my religion that Germanic faith which is above all religions."

Rathenau was a little late getting up on the morning of June 24, and so it was 10:45 A.M. when his open car reached the place that the assassins had chosen for the ambush. Young Ernst-Werner Techow was waiting for him. He set out in pursuit of the Foreign Minister's car, and then, when Rathenau's driver slowed down to cross some streetcar tracks, Techow passed him.

A bricklayer named Krischbin, working on a new building nearby, saw the passing cars and noticed the young men in their new leather coats. When the assassins' six-seater was about half a length ahead of Rathenau, Krischbin said later, Rathenau "looked over to see if there was going to be a collision, and at that moment one of the gentlemen in the smart leather coats [Kern] leaned forward, pulled out a long pistol, rested the butt in his armpit, and opened fire on the gentleman in the other car. There was no need for him to aim even, it was such close range. I saw him, so to speak, straight in the face. It was a healthy, open face, the sort of face we call an officer's face. I took cover, because the shots might easily have got us too. They rang out in quick succession like a machine gun.

"When he had finished shooting, the other man [Fischer] stood up, swung his weapon—it was a hand grenade—and threw it into the other car. . . . The gentleman had already sunk down into his seat and lay on his side. At this point the chauffeur stopped the car, just by the Erdener Strasse, where there was a dustheap, and shouted out, 'Help, help!' Then the big car sprang forward with the engine full on and tore down the Wallotstrasse. Meanwhile the other car had come to rest by the pavement. At that moment there was a bang and the hand grenade exploded. The impact raised the gentleman in the back some way off his seat, and even gave the car a slight jerk forward."

A middle-aged woman who happened to be passing by jumped into the back seat of Rathenau's car, and the chauffeur, starting the car again, drove toward a nearby police station. The woman, small and pale, was a nurse named Helene Kaiser, and she did her best to help the dying man. "Rathenau, who was bleeding hard, was still alive and was looking up at me," she testified later at the trial of the conspirators. "But he seemed to be already unconscious."

The distraught chauffeur drove to a police station only thirty yards up the Königsallee, and then continued immediately back to Rathenau's house. Servants carried the Foreign Minister into his study and called for a doctor. Rathenau opened his eyes once more, lying there in the study, but by the time the doctor arrived, he was dead. Five of Kern's bullets had hit him, smashing his jaw and his spine.

Throughout that day, and the next, the body remained in an open coffin in the study. "He wore a very peaceful expression," wrote Count Kessler, "and yet there was immeasurable tragedy in the deeply furrowed, dead, wounded face. A handkerchief covered the lower broken part; only the short gray crumpled moustache was visible."

The assassins' car apparently broke down on a side street only a few hundred yards beyond the site of the ambush. Techow jumped out and flung up the hood of the car. Kern threw the automatic pistol over a wall into a nearby garden. All three men tore off their leather coats. The police, racing around the corner, ignored the youths working on the broken-down car and sped past them in pursuit of the killers. Kern and his friends then drifted back into the city, where crowds were already gathering to protest the murder.

It was an extraordinary demonstration. By noon, when the news became generally known, hundreds of thousands of workers streamed out of the factories and began marching through the streets. "These soon merged into one and moved solemnly and irresistibly through the streets of the middle- and upper-class West," Kessler reported. "Four deep they marched in their hundred thousands, beneath their mourning banners, the red of Socialism and the black-red-gold of the Republic, in one endless disciplined procession, passing like a portent silently along the great thoroughfares lined by immense crowds, wave after wave, from the early afternoon till late into the June sunset."

The Reichstag met that afternoon, and Karl Helfferich, who had denounced Rathenau on the previous day, was greeted with shouts of "Murderer! Murderer! Out with the murderers!" Helfferich tried for a while to ride out the storm but then rose and walked out of the chamber. Chancellor Josef Wirth spoke bitterly against not just the assassins but the men who supported such terrorist groups. "Ever since we first began to serve this new state under the flag of the Republic," he said, "millions have been spent in pouring a deadly poison into the body of our people . . . and then people are surprised when mere deluded boys resort to murder."

Kern and his confederates apparently continued drifting through the midst of the angry crowds. At the Alexanderplatz, they stood for a time and listened to people cursing the murderers. Then they returned to the west, to the elongated lake known as the Wannsee, where they took a steamer to the Baltic Sea port of Warnemünde, 150 miles north of Berlin. There, they expected to find another ship that would carry them to safety in Sweden. When they got to Warnemünde, however, they found no sign of the ship, and so they bought bicycles and turned back southward into the forests of Mecklenburg.

Rathenau's body lay in state in the Reichstag during the first two days of that week. Rathenau's mother, pale and numb, sat in the box that had once been reserved for the Kaiser. "I had the orchestra play the funeral music from *Siegfried*," says Dr. Edwin Redslob, the Culture Minister who had sponsored the Weimar eagle. "Rathenau was not really a Siegfried, but all of Germany's real heroes, like Rathenau, get stabbed in the back. We honor the Hagens." President Ebert delivered the funeral oration and said: "This atrocious crime has struck not only at Rathenau the man but at the whole German people." Outside, the labor unions had declared a national day of mourning, and stupendous parades wound through every city in Germany. In Berlin alone, the number of marchers was estimated at one million; in other cities, the number totaled several million more.

Techow, the driver of the assassins' car, fled to a country estate owned by his uncle, on the outskirts of Berlin. He pleaded for safety and protection, but the uncle called in the police. Kern and Fischer, however, proved more elusive. On their bicycles, they rode through mile after mile of forest, stopping for the night in farmers' barns, or, occasionally, at the homes of friends. By this time, they were known and hunted, for a minor participant in the conspiracy had gone to the police and sold his story for cash. The government had put a price of one million marks on the heads of the two fugitives. They were nearly caught when they hired a boatman to ferry them across the Elbe, and a pursuing posse shouted curses at them from the northern bank. The boatman doggedly continued on his course, and the pair continued their flight southward toward Thuringia.

The forests of Germany are vast and dark, and for almost a month, the fugitives found shelter in these woods. Once, after begging food from the cottage of a lonely farmer, they were spotted and reported, and the police threw out a huge dragnet. Hundreds of men formed a circle around the area, beating their way through the thickets, but Kern and Fischer somehow managed to escape back into the forests. Southward, still southward, they wandered, toward a deserted castle near Kösen, some 150 miles south of Berlin, which had once provided a sanctuary for the nationalist cause. After their weeks of flight, they finally arrived at the twin-towered Saaleck Castle, threw their bicycles into the nearby Saale River, and prepared to go into hiding.

Because the castle was supposed to be unoccupied, however, two villagers noticed lights in the east tower and began investigating. They recognized Kern, whose picture was by now posted on billboards all over Germany, and called the police. The police were skeptical, but the two villagers demanded the reward, which had been augmented by voluntary contributions until it reached more than four million marks, and so the authorities in Halle sent two detectives to the castle.

On the dark gray morning of July 17, the two detectives broke into the east tower and started up the narrow stone stairway. At the head of the stairs, a door opened, and Kern appeared with a pistol in his hand. The two detectives ducked for cover and then ran to get reinforcements. Within an hour, the castle was surrounded by a hundred police. The skies had continued to darken, and now a fierce storm burst over the castle. Gusts of wind tore branches from the surrounding trees, and rain poured down on the besieging force. From the valley of the Saale River, a thick mist swirled upward into the woods around the castle. While the police waited for a break in the weather, they saw a crowd gathering. The villagers from nearby towns had come to watch, and soon the hillsides were speckled with onlookers, waiting for the kill.

Kern and Fischer also saw the crowd. They climbed out onto the battlements and began shouting their explanations of the murder. "We live and die for ideals," one of them cried. "Others will follow us." They even tried to throw down written messages, weighted with stones, but the wind carried the papers off into the woods, and so the two assassins retreated back into their lair at the top of the eastern tower. By now, the police had seized the western tower, and through the wind and rain, they opened fire. Kern, crouching by the window, was hit just below the right temple. Fischer tore up sheets from the bed and tried to bandage Kern's wound, but Kern was already dead. Fischer lifted up Kern's body and carried it to the bed. It bothered him, apparently, that Kern's muddy shoes dirtied the sheets, and so he got some brown paper and put it under Kern's feet. Then he folded Kern's arms across his chest and closed his eyes. Slumping down on the other bed, he raised his pistol to his forehead and pulled the trigger. When the police broke into the tower room, they found only two corpses.

For the thirteen surviving conspirators, there was a trial. Techow duly testified: "Kern told me that Rathenau belonged to the 'veiled' Bolshevist movement, that he was one of the three hundred Elders of Zion who was seeking to bring the world under the rule of the Jews." The court sentenced him to fifteen years in prison, a term that was later commuted to seven years. He actually served only four years, then went back to school and became a lawyer. Near the end of World War II, he was captured by the Soviets and died in a prison camp. Von Salomon served five years in prison and eventually became a movie writer, still living in Hamburg. The others got relatively short terms and then went their separate ways.

Some fled to new opportunities abroad, some buried themselves in quiet and orderly private lives, but none of them ever escaped the clawing question of why they had done what they had done. On the eve of the Nazi rise to power, one of the conspirators strode up to Dr. Joseph Goebbels, Gauleiter of Berlin, and hit him on the side of the head and shouted, "It wasn't for swine like you that we shot Rathenau!" But the Nazis knew how to make use of even the most unwilling martyrs. On July 17, 1933, exactly eleven years after the death of the two assassins, there was a great parade to their graves. Heinrich Himmler laid the official wreath, and Ernst Röhm gave the main oration. "Your spirit, Kern and Fischer," said Röhm, "is the spirit of the SS, Hitler's black soldiers."

The murder of Rathenau was not by any means unique. On the contrary, if the Weimar Republic failed through a lack of leadership, it was partly because of the assassins who cut down so many of the men who might have provided that leadership. Karl Liebknecht and Rosa Luxemburg, beaten and shot to death by army officers; Matthias Erzberger, Finance Minister and signer of the armistice, shot to death while walking in the Black Forest; Kurt Eisner, Prime Minister of Bavaria, shot to death on a main street of Munich; Hugo Haase, leader of the Independent Socialist Party, shot to death on the steps of the Reichstag.

Not every attack ended in death, but the unsuccessful attempts also had their effect. Philipp Scheidemann, the first republican Chancellor under Ebert, was scarred by an assailant who tried to blind him with prussic acid. Maximilian Harden, the crusading editor of *Zukunft (Future)*, was beaten nearly to death by a thug wielding a heavy steel rod. Most of these victims were liberals, and many of them were Jews, and the threat of such a fate inevitably intimidated a good many potential victims who were never actually attacked at all.

This intimidation was all the more effective because of the general knowledge that the conservative bureaucrats entrenched in the police and judiciary had relatively little interest in punishing the assassins. According to a classic study called *Four Years of Political Murder*, published in 1922 by Emil J. Gumbel, there were 354 political murders committed by right-wing groups during the four years after the war and 22 such murders committed by left-wing groups. In the 22 left-wing murders, 17 brought heavy sentences, including 10 executions, whereas 326 of the 354 right-wing murders went unpunished. The average prison sentence per murder, according to Gumbel's statistics, was fifteen years for left-wingers and four months for right-wingers.

Still, there was a special horror to the Rathenau murder, and, as with the death of John Kennedy, everyone who was in Berlin on that June day in 1922 still remembers the moment with a vividness that has defied time. "I was attending a course given by Professor Troeltsch, the theologian, and he came late to class that day," says Rabbi Prinz. "He was white, absolutely white, and trembling, and he said to the class, 'Our friend, Walther Rathenau, has just been assassinated.' I remember, I went off in the woods with some friends, just to think. To us, this was the beginning of the end for German Jewry." "I was at the UFA movie theatre near the Zoo," says Fritz

Bamberger, now a college executive in New York, "and I remember that we went out on the roof of the building and watched the workers marching for Rathenau. It was strange. Here was a highly sophisticated product of capitalism—a rather esoteric man—who never could have talked to a worker without embarrassment. But the workers were pouring through the streets, thousands of them, to demonstrate for him. Everyone realized that this was not just an isolated thing. This would lead to something."

On the Königsallee, the spirit of Walther Rathenau is now only a flickering shadow. His villa, from which he set off to work on that morning almost fifty years ago, still stands, a three-story building of yellow stone, encircled by a band of gray rosettes. Four signs on the iron fence disclose that several small publishing firms now occupy the place, but one is told that the whole building will soon be demolished. The owner can't afford to keep it up, and he has been unable to find a buyer. Soon, it will be torn down and replaced by an apartment house.

This was once considered the countryside, but now the Königsallee is a busy highway, and fleets of cars speed past on their way to the Kurfürstendamm. One starts the car again and slips back into the flow of traffic, following the route of Rathenau's last drive. He did not get far. It is only three blocks before the Königsallee swings to the right in that fatal curve where Rathenau's chauffeur slowed down, and the three young assassins overtook him.

There is a dark granite memorial stone here, about six feet high, on a tiny wedge of land carved out of the Mendelssohn estate that extends beyond it. On the stone, a dark metal plaque records that Walther Rathenau "fell on this spot by the hand of a murderer." It adds the observation: "The health of a people comes only from its inner life—from the life of its soul and its spirit." The stone is surrounded by some rather small yews, and two benches stand nearby, and on a recent spring morning, there were daffodils blooming brightly yellow in a light Berlin rain, but the stream of cars never stops here, and the benches are usually empty, and the daffodils, which need no tending, are no different from any others.

"A Kind of Madness"   1923

Nothing expressed the cynical relationship between the grim architecture and the feckless population more than the belief of the Berlin population that one of the stone lions outside the palace at the end of the Unter den Linden roared whenever a virgin walked by.

STEPHEN SPENDER

"WHEN I WAS IN COLLEGE, back in the 1940's, I went through a phase of wearing strange clothes," says a conservatively dressed lawyer who now practices in New York. "It wasn't like nowadays, when strange clothes are sort of a uniform. In those days, strange clothes were considered really strange, but I used to wander around Harvard Square in a Borsalino hat, and Windsor ties, and a Florentine sword-cane, and various cloaks and boots and rags. My mother tried to humor me by giving me her father's Waltham watch, which hadn't run for years but fitted nicely into my waistcoat pocket, and then my father tried to help out by turning over this old German watch chain, which consisted of a string of little iron plaques, with one word on each plaque, saying, 'Gold für Wehr, Eisen für Ehr,' which means, 'Gold for defense, iron for honor.' You see, his parents had turned all their gold over to the German government during the First World War, including my grandfather's gold watch chain, and this was what they got in exchange. And this exchange—some scrap metal and a few words in exchange for their gold—is the story of a whole generation of the German middle class."

The middle class had worked and saved, and it had put its savings into gold. Gold, thought the middle class, would survive all the typhoons of war and revolution. When the typhoons came, the

Kaiser's wartime ministers were too timorous—or perhaps too middle-class—to simply seize the gold they needed. Or perhaps they also believed in the mythology of hoarded gold, inviolable, a Nibelungen treasure. Since they did need this treasure, however, they "borrowed" it, giving in return paper notes (and iron watch chains). "By a continuing process of inflation," as Keynes said, "governments can confiscate, secretly and unobserved, an important part of the wealth of their citizens. . . . The process engages all the hidden forces of economic law on the side of destruction, and it does it in a manner which not one man in a million is able to diagnose."

The ultimate repayment, the Germans assumed, would have to come from the defeated French and English. Bismarck, after all, had imposed an indemnity of five billion francs on the defeated French in 1871, which not only paid for the war but financed the rapid postwar growth of Berlin. To meet the vastly greater costs of the World War, Imperial Finance Minister Karl Helfferich was believed ready to demand 150 billion marks as soon as the fighting ended. Unfortunately, it was Clemenceau who announced at Versailles, "The hour has struck for the weighty settlement of our accounts." Clemenceau demanded total payment for all of France's war damages, its 5 million dead and wounded, its 4,000 ruined towns and 20,000 destroyed businesses. He declared that the Germans must pay for up to a hundred years, if necessary—with interest—and the British were not far behind. London's claims were limited only by a slightly more realistic idea of the German capacity to pay, but one commission of British experts fixed that capacity at 800 billion marks, considerably more than the total of German national wealth. The Germans offered to pay 100 billion, without interest, but the Allies rejected this offer with disdain. Instead, they fixed the initial payment at $5 billion in gold, along with considerable quantities of coal, chemicals, and shipping, to be delivered by May of 1921. The ultimate amount of reparations was left to future negotiation. And because the negotiators failed to agree on this basic economic problem, the reparations issue, which Winston Churchill called "a sad story of complicated idiocy," became not only a cause of endless wrangling between Germany and the Allies but also a partial cause for the ruinous fall of the German mark.

The descent was not disastrous during the first year or two. Between 1918 and the summer of 1921, the mark slid from its traditional rate of 4.20 per dollar to 75—bad, but not beyond comparison with what we have experienced in other times in other countries. And besides, people were still preoccupied with more basic problems. "*Hunger* is what I remember most from those years, 1919, 1920," says Salka Viertel, a darkly attractive actress in those days and now a white-haired lady living in the Swiss mountain village of Klosters. "I was always hungry, and cold. And sometimes slightly drunk, because that was one thing you could always get if you had any money at all."

Even those who had money, though, found that what they had was evaporating. "My father had left a fortune of 800,000 marks," says a Harvard professor, recalling those days, "but by the summer of 1922, the value of the mark had dropped to 400 per dollar. Every month, it got worse. My mother finally used her last 65,000 marks to buy a typewriter, and she began typing students' theses to support the youngest children. I went to Holland that spring, looking for anything that would earn hard currency, and I found a job at the Queen Anna coal mines in the province of Limburg. We worked far down, at the bottom of the mine, hacking away with pickaxes. It was tremendously hot, usually one hundred degrees or so, and full of dust, but by the end of the spring vacation I'd saved fifty guilders, which was about twenty-five dollars. Then I figured out how to beat the inflation. I used the guilders as security for a short-term bank loan, and then I'd repay the bank loan with the deflated marks and take out another loan. I paid for a whole semester at Heidelberg that way, and at the end I still had the same fifty guilders."

The assassination of Walther Rathenau shook what little faith there was in the prospects for German recovery. From a rate of 400 per dollar in the summer of 1922, the mark sank to 7,000 by the first of January, 1923, and every week it sank further. Peter Wallenberg, then a student, now a retired UN correspondent, recalls the period as a golden era for confidence games. "I sold gold," he says with a wink. "I told the other students in my school that my parents had gold in the closet. I don't know why anyone believed me, but I had imagination. I took their money and hid it in a suitcase under my bed, and when my mother found it, she asked, 'What's all this?' The whole suitcase was full of ten-mark notes, twenty-mark notes, but of course by then they were all worthless."

That cold January of 1923, the crisis became a disaster. The government of Chancellor Wirth had collapsed at the end of 1922, when the Socialists withdrew their support. President Ebert then tried to form a more conservative coalition, one that could win the support of big business and deal with the economic problem. The new Chancellor he selected was Superior Privy Councilor Wilhelm Cuno, director of the Hamburg-America shipping line, a man whose elegant manners and appearance disguised, for a time, his total inability to rule a disintegrating nation. ("Cuno is a fat cigar," Rathenau had once said, "which will have to be smoked someday because of its lovely band.")

And the arguments over reparations went on. The Germans asked for a moratorium and dawdled in their deliveries of raw materials while they tried to negotiate for better terms. France's vengeful Premier Raymond Poincaré refused to tolerate such tactics. He was eager, in fact, for any pretext that would permit the French to claim a violation of the Versailles Treaty and to justify a new invasion of Germany. "Whatever happens," he had warned British Prime Minister Bonar Law, "I shall advance into the Ruhr on January 15." When the Germans continued stalling, the French made a formal complaint that the Germans had failed to deliver half of the 200,000 telephone poles due for shipment to France during 1922. The Germans blamed the delay on their state governments, which owned the forests that contained the trees that had to be cut down for telephone poles. The British hardly took the French charge seriously—history had recorded no such political use of wood, said British Envoy Sir John Bradbury, since the Greeks had built a horse outside Troy—but the French now added a new complaint about shortages of coal deliveries from the Ruhr. Overriding British protests, they sent a Franco-Belgian "technical commission" to the Ruhr, on January 11, 1923, to find out what was going on.

The first thing they found was that the German Coal Syndicate had just moved out of the Ruhr and pitched camp in Hamburg. The French, who had sent only a few troops to "protect" their commissioners, following up with additional troops. The German government then suspended all reparations deliveries and called on everyone in the Ruhr to meet the French invasion with passive resistance. The French responded by dismissing any Ruhr official who disobeyed their orders and arresting anyone who attempted to use force. On March 31, there was a clash at the Krupp works in Essen, and French troops opened fire on a crowd of workers, killing thirteen of them. By now the French had put the entire Ruhr under their military rule, and Germany had lost its industrial center, the source of 80 percent of its coal, iron, and steel, the machinery of its own recovery.

The German mark sank more rapidly than ever. From a rate of 7,000 to the dollar in January, when the French invaded the Ruhr, it fell to 160,000 by July. One month later, the rate was 1 million. And the German government, which now felt an obligation to subsidize the idled workers of the Ruhr, kept printing more banknotes. At the Ullstein newspaper headquarters on the Kochstrasse, officials requisitioned presses to turn out the increasingly worthless paper. "All doors were locked and officials of the Reichsbank were placed on guard," said one of the owners, Hermann Ullstein. "Round the machines sat elderly women, staring fascinated at those parts of the machines from which the finished products came pouring out. It was the duty of these women to see that these billion-mark notes were placed in the right baskets and handed to the officials. They had to keep an eye on every single billion. Officials are so funny sometimes."

By the middle of 1923, the whole of Germany had become delirious. Whoever had a job got paid every day, usually at noon, and then ran to the nearest store, with a sack full of banknotes, to buy anything he could get, at any price. In their frenzy, people paid millions and even billions of marks for cuckoo clocks, shoes that didn't fit, anything that could be traded for something else. The celebrated conductor, Bruno Walter, had to break up his rehearsals in mid-symphony for the regular midday rush, and after a typical scramble, he recalled, one of his musicians triumphantly displayed his reward for a day's work, a bag of salt. The battle for survival paid people in other strange currencies. "I taught anatomy to three Chinese," says Mrs. Henry Lowenfeld, the psychoanalyst's wife. "I spoke not a word of Chinese, and they spoke not a word of German, so I had to teach them with diagrams and sign language, and after each lesson I got paid with tea—wonderful tea—and little cakes." Artur Schnabel gave a concert and received his fee in a suitcase full of bills. "I had to ask a man to help me carry my fee home," he said later. "On my way home, I passed a delicatessen and to relieve my helper I spent half my fee on a couple of sausages. The next morning I saw in the paper that I could not even get one sausage for the other half of my fee."

Food, indeed, became both a currency and an obsession. It was, according to George Grosz, "the only popular subject of the day. . . . Mornings, at a breakfast of turnip coffee, mildewed bread and synthetic honey, one discussed lunch. At lunch of turnip cutlets, muscle pudding and turnip coffee, one discussed a dinner of muscle wurst." And if food was a currency, a new kind of banker inevitably appeared—the hoarder. One of these dealers took Grosz to his head-quarters, an apartment crammed with tubs of butter, sacks of flour, and various other riches. "Cans of Russian caviar were piled up to the ceiling," Grosz observed, "that is, as much as one could see of the ceiling, because from it dangled all kinds of wurst . . . spiced Italian salamis, tongue bolognas . . . countless slabs of bacon, both lean and fat." The black marketeer, a restaurant cook, gave Grosz a ham sandwich and a glass of gin and said, "*Prosit*, my dear. Long live this fool's paradise."

For foreigners, too, the Berlin of 1923 seemed like some Brueghel fantasy of daydreams fulfilled. Malcolm Cowley, the critic, went to Berlin to visit his friends Matthew Josephson and Harold Loeb, who had moved there because it was so much cheaper to publish their little magazine, *Broom*. Cowley found that "for a salary of a hundred dollars a month in American currency, Josephson lived in a duplex apartment with two maids, riding lessons for his wife, dinners only in the most expensive restaurants, tips to the orchestra, pictures col-lected, charities to struggling German writers—it was an insane life for foreigners in Berlin and nobody could be happy there. We hurried back to France on an international express full of smug-glers."

By one means or another, by bartering and maneuvering, the Berliners managed to survive, and, in some cases, even to flourish. Berthold Viertel, for example, was an ambitious young director who had always wanted his own theatre, and the inflation brought him a sponsor, a currency speculator who yearned for cultural prestige. Viertel (the model for the temperamental director in Christopher Isherwood's *Prater Violet*) promptly organized a repertory company called *Die Truppe* (The Troupe) and commissioned two Bauhaus students to design a modern setting for *The Merchant of Venice*, with Fritz Kortner as Shylock. The actors got a minimum of nine million marks a year, plus a sliding scale of raises, but the mark kept sliding faster. "Night after night we were sold out," according to Viertel's wife, Salka, "only to see in the morning paper that we were just as broke as ever."

The survivors smile now at the madness of 1923, but the destruction of an economy brings considerable suffering to the poor and the helpless, and even though the inflation made everyone poor, it made some people poorer than others. Louis Lochner, who arrived in Berlin during this period and eventually became bureau chief for the Associated Press, got the usual first impression of "cafés crowded with stylishly garbed ladies" but soon found a different story on the side streets off the fashionable boulevards. "I visited a typical Youth Welfare Station," he said later. "Children who looked as though they were eight or nine years old proved to be thirteen. I learned that there were then 15,000 tubercular children in Berlin; that 23 percent of the children examined by the city health authorities were badly undernourished." The old were equally helpless. One elderly writer named Maximilian Bern withdrew all his savings, more than 100,-000 marks, and spent them on one subway ticket. He took a ride around Berlin and then locked himself in his apartment and starved to death. "Barbarism prevailed," said George Grosz. "The streets became dangerous. . . . We kept ducking in and out of doorways because restless people, unable to remain in their houses, would go up on the rooftops and shoot indiscriminately at anything they saw. Once, when one of these snipers was caught and faced with the man he had shot in the arm, his only explanation was, 'But I thought it was a big pigeon.'"

The fundamental quality of the disaster was a complete loss of faith in the functioning of society. Money is important not just as a medium of economic exchange, after all, but as a standard by which society judges our work, and thus our selves. If all money becomes worthless, then so does all government, and all society, and all standards. In the madness of 1923, a workman's work was worthless, a widow's savings were worthless, everything was worthless. "The collapse of the currency not only meant the end of trade, bankrupt businesses, food shortages in the big cities and unemployment," according to one historian, Alan Bullock. "It had the effect, which is the unique quality of economic catastrophe, of reaching down to and touching every single member of the community in a way which no political event can. The savings of the middle classes and the working classes were wiped out at a single blow with a ruthlessness which no revolution could ever equal. . . . The result of the inflation was to undermine the foundations of German society in a way which neither the war, nor the revolution of November, 1918, nor the Treaty of Versailles had ever done. The real revolution in Germany was the inflation."

"Yes, the inflation was by far the most important event of this period," says a seventy-five-year-old journalist, a woman who still lives in Berlin. She is white-haired and rather large, and she nibbles cookies as she talks, forgetting that it is already two in the morning. "The inflation wiped out the savings of the entire middle class, but those are just words. You have to realize what that *meant*. There was not a single girl in the entire German middle class who could get *married* without her father paying a dowry. Even the maids—they never spent a penny of their wages. They saved and saved so that they could get married. When the money became worthless, it destroyed the whole system for getting married, and so it destroyed the whole idea of remaining chaste until marriage.

"The rich had never lived up to their own standards, of course, and the poor had different standards anyway, but the middle class, by and large, obeyed the rules. Not every girl was a virgin when she was married, but it was generally accepted that one *should* be. But what happened from the inflation was that the girls learned that virginity didn't matter any more. The women were liberated."

Professor Fritz Bamberger is drawing a map. The horizontal lines show Unter den Linden, and the vertical lines show its main cross street, the Friedrichstrasse. Professor Bamberger sits in a study on the East Side of Manhattan, filled with leather-bound volumes of Spinoza, and he writes carefully with a silver pencil on a small pad of paper. Though he is in his sixties now, rather courtly, with a gray mustache and a cigar, he remembers the scene vividly. "To the north here," he says, drawing neatly, "there was a little bridge, the Weidendammbrücke, and then it turned into the Chausseestrasse, and that whole street was filled with little girls. And older ones, who made themselves up to look like young girls. They all wore special clothes—mini-minidresses—and they would swing their handbags. There were cheap hotels all around, and dance halls. . . ."

(It is different in East Berlin now, and yet not different. As you walk north from the dark old railroad station, you see that the bars and dance halls along the Friedrichstrasse have been replaced by the House of Czech Culture and the House of Polish Culture, both filled with exhibitions of local handicrafts, and as you walk across the Weidendammbrücke, where the dark, iron eagles still perch on top of the lampposts, the girls look quite ordinary, scurrying along in their drab brown raincoats and clutching their shopping bags as they try to escape from the thunderstorm that lowers overhead. But perhaps it is just too early in the afternoon. "Come back any evening at around seven," says a woman who lives further up the Friedrichstrasse, "and you'll see the subways arriving from the West with swarms of Italian workers, and Arabs, and all kinds of people, all looking for girls. Girls are still cheaper here than in the West.")

"Well, sure, prostitution was one of the great joys of the city," says another old Berliner. "All the girls registered with the police, and they had to have medical checkups, and if you caught anything from one of them, you could even sue her and make some money for having been 'a victim of bodily injury.' It was a great thing."

They wandered up and down the Friedrichstrasse and the Kurfürstendamm, and they stood in clusters along the Tauentzienstrasse, just beyond the Kaiser Wilhelm Memorial Church, and everyone remembers their peculiar costumes. Klaus Mann, the son of the novelist, described them as looking "like fierce amazons, strutting in high boots made of green, glossy leather. One of them brandished a supple cane and leered at me as I passed by. . . . She whispered into my ear: 'Want to be my slave? Costs only six billions and a cigarette. A bargain. Come along, honey!'" Josef Sternberg, the movie director, noted a different type, which, "flaunting pigtails and schoolbooks, paraded to appeal to those who hurried to meet them with set jaw and clenched fists." And Anita Loos, on a visit from Hollywood, remarked that "any Berlin lady of the evening might turn out to be a man; the prettiest girl on the street was Conrad Veidt, who later became an international film star."

"All values were changed, and . . . Berlin was transformed into the Babylon of the world," said Stefan Zweig. "Bars, amusement parks, honky-tonks sprang up like mushrooms. . . . Along the entire Kurfürstendamm powdered and rouged young men sauntered and they were not all professionals; every high school boy wanted to earn some money and in the dimly lit bars one might see government officials and men of the world of finance tenderly courting drunken sailors without any shame. Even the Rome of Suetonius had never known such orgies as the pervert balls of Berlin, where hundreds of men costumed as women and hundreds of women as men danced under the benevolent eyes of the police. In the collapse of all values a kind of madness gained hold particularly in the bourgeois circles which until then had been unshakeable in their probity. . . . But the most revolting thing about this pathetic eroticism was its spuriousness. At bottom the orgiastic period which broke out in Germany simultaneously with the inflation was nothing more than a feverish imitation. . . . The whole nation, tired of war, actually longed only for order."

It was customary for moralizing observers like Zweig to ogle the girls on the streets and then to bemoan the consequences of economic hardship and spiritual confusion, and yet the Kurfürstendamm, in these times of prosperity, is still full of girls. They are young and pretty, too, unlike the furtive creatures of the side streets, and they are as bold in their invitations as they ever were. Their boots are in high fashion, and they still carry umbrellas, not, one suspects, because of any peculiar fetishism, but because, on an average day in Berlin, a sudden shower drenches the city for fifteen or twenty minutes, and then a rainbow arches overhead. The nights are cool. The wind is brisk. "Na?" she asks, on the glittering, wet street, striped red and blue from the neon lights. "Spazierengehen? Like to take a walk?"

A harmless encounter. Organized vice requires organization.

"What ever happened to those famous old nightclubs?" one asks Christopher Isherwood. "It there anything left of them?"

At sixty-six, the novelist is a slim, tanned, and still rather boyish figure. His eyes are bright blue, and he wears a frayed blue shirt, a blue silk scarf, a blue tweed jacket, and blue slacks, all different shades of blue, and he is pacing up and down a white-walled living room off Cadogan Square, waiting for news that his latest play will get a London production.

"Well, the Cozy Corner is now a dentist's office," he says with a wry smile, "but I've heard that the Kleist Casino is still the Kleist Casino."

The Kleist Casino is on the Kleiststrasse, but there is no sign outside except for the letters "KC" in white script on the hostile door. There are no windows in the blank wall, and the inside is dark and gloomy. In a small foyer, two nondescript young men lounge behind a counter. One of them demands that coats be checked, for fifty pfennigs, while the other one, in boots, continues idly leafing through a magazine called *Him*. Inside, at the end of a corridor, the Kleist Casino turns out to be a glum parody of elegance. Striped blue and white awnings sag from the ceiling, bunches of faded flowers hang from the maroon wallpaper, and the bar is illuminated by two lamps supported by half-size torsos, without figleaves. About fifty young men sit around in morose silence, about a quarter of them affecting leather jackets, the rest in timid business suits. The two bartenders absent-mindedly twitch to the beat of a rather mild rock-'n'-roll, and at the far end of the room, there are two couples engaged in a halfhearted twist. One of the dancers appears to be a girl, with long black hair, but if so, she would be the only girl here, and in the darkness it is hard to tell. It is odd to remember, suddenly, that Kleist himself was a great poet, who committed suicide in Berlin at the age of thirty-four. He lies buried by the shores of the Kleine Wannsee, and the inscription on his grave says: "Now, immortality—you are entirely mine."

Is this all there is, or ever was, to the famous night life of Berlin? In describing it as "by far the most immoral city of Europe," Walter Slezak, the actor, had singled out another place: "The Eldorado nightclub, where female impersonators and transvestites performed, was patronized by homosexuals and curious tourists and operated openly." A half-century later, it is still there, still operating openly, and still an attraction for "curious tourists." One of the standard guidebooks, Arthur Frommer's *Europe on $5 a Day*, describes how even the budget-minded traveler can see freak shows at modest cost: "Now for the action. . . . The connoisseurs among you . . . will want to sample some of the more erotic nightspots in Berlin. One of the typically weird (though not inexpensive) ones is the Eldorado, 28 Martin Lutherstrasse, where every one of the 'waitresses,' 'hat-check girls' and 'bar maids' is a female impersonator. You'll want to see this, but you won't want to spend more than an hour at it. Therefore, sit at the bar, where a couple can have a cognac and beer, as Hope and I did, and not be pressed to have a single thing more. There's a 2-mark (50¢) admission charge; then 8 marks for your first drink, 2.50 marks thereafter."

It seems a rather high price to pay for the unedifying spectacle of men parading around in women's clothes, and one senses that the whole mythology of vice in the 1920's has been overtaken by events. Right across from the bombed hulk of the Kaiser Wilhelm Memorial Church, for instance, there flourishes a kind of sexual supermarket called Beate Uhse. Miss Uhse was a pilot during World War II, and then, looking around for some way to take part in the postwar "economic miracle," she decided to open a store for people in need of erotic materials. It was such a success that it has become a chain of stores throughout Germany. The windows of the Berlin headquarters emphasize mainly books with titles like *Die Sexspiele des Alfred Kindermacher* (*The Sex Plays of Alfred Childrenmaker*), but the doorway offers an inviting blast of rock-'n'-roll, and throngs of people crowd in to inspect racks of color pictures, "adult" records (*"Gruppensex Tralala"*), and long counters containing every variety of pills and creams, aphrodisiacs and contraceptives—*Erekta Prompt, End-spurt, Topcraft, Energie,* and *Happy End*—and an artificial implement advertised as a "cordless electric vibrator."

This is nothing very special, of course. We can find the same kind of equipment in Times Square in New York. And from the miasmal swamps of the current "sexual revolution," we can look back on the "sexual revolution" of the 1920's and see that Scott Fitzgerald considered revolution a matter of necking in the rumble seat. Berlin was, as always, ahead of its time, but now that this time has come, even the most flamboyant hedonism of the 1920's acquires, in retrospect, a quality of guileless innocence.

On the vertiginously spiraling ramps of New York's Guggenheim Museum, there was an exhibition not long ago of the paintings of Laszlo Moholy-Nagy, one of the major figures of the Bauhaus. Most of the paintings were a rather repetitious series of squares, planes, lines, crosses, and three-dimensional variations that Moholy-Nagy called "space modulators." One picture stood out alone, however. It was a collage, entitled "25 *Pleitegeier*" ("bankruptcy vultures"), showing a large bird hovering ominously over two silhouetted men.

The most striking aspect of the collage was that it had been made entirely out of banknotes. "In the dismal winter of 1922–23," Moholy-Nagy said in an explanatory note, "I roomed with Kurt Schwitters in an almost unheatable attic studio in Spichernstrasse, Berlin. The German mark had reached an inflationary value of 25 million. We had no money to buy paint and canvas. So Kurt inspired me to follow his example and use the 'currency' of the day to make collages."

There were, then—and everyone felt it—bankruptcy vultures, people who were causing the disaster, or, at the very least, taking advantage of it. Economic systems do not collapse by themselves —or so we like to think—so somebody must be responsible. At the lowest and most innocent level, in a time when the use of currency had given way to the bartering of goods and services, even the children found that there were new ways to get rich. "Messenger boys established foreign exchange businesses and speculated in the currencies of all lands," said Stefan Zweig. "Some adolescent boys who had found a case of soap forgotten in the harbor disported themselves for months in cars and lived like kings, selling a cake every day, while their parents, formerly well-to-do, slunk around like beggars."

Then there were the foreigners—or so the Germans, not without xenophobia, thought. "Thousands of homes had to be abandoned," says one Berlin businessman, who bitterly remembers how the inflation bankrupted and nearly maddened his own father-in-law. "And who got them? People from Poland or Holland, anybody with foreign money. You could buy a house, which was worth fifty thousand marks, for five hundred dollars. I know whole streets which belonged completely to Czechs, French, Swiss. They bought up all of Berlin, and not just Berlin."

The acquisition of foreign currency was not beyond the capacities of Germany's entrepreneurs, however. Publishers who could sell even a small fraction of their newspapers in Switzerland, for example, could support their whole corporations with the profits; a movie producer who could sell a film to Hollywood became a Croesus. And even apart from foreign earnings, any businessman with good credit could buy supplies with borrowed money, pay his workers minimal wages, and then settle both his debts and his taxes with depreciated currency.

The greatest master of all those who saw opportunity in the national ruin was a dark and stormy man named Hugo Stinnes. Though born of well-to-do parents, Stinnes started out as a clerk, then worked as a coal miner, and finally opened a small coal business in 1893. He had a swarthy skin and a black beard, and even after he became a millionaire, he affected workman's clothes and heavy boots, prompting Count Kessler to describe him as "a cross between a patriarch, a commercial traveller, and the Flying Dutchman."

"He kept everything in his pockets," recalls Hans Staudinger, the economist, demonstrating, filching around in his pockets and bringing out bits and pieces of paper. "Everything, his accounts, names of companies he wanted to buy. And then he telephoned day and night, running all his businesses. He spoke in a high voice, and always very slowly. I asked him once why he always spoke so slowly. He said, 'Because then people listen.' The trouble was that he believed in the eternity of inflation. He believed it would never end. And so he lived on credit. He had a bank of his own in Holland, and German businessmen would put their money there for safety, and Stinnes would take it out and buy their own companies from them. He told me so himself."

But it was the mines that formed the basis of Stinnes' wealth. The mines produced coal, and coal produced foreign currency, and with foreign currency, one needed only daring and ruthlessness to build an empire. On credit, Stinnes bought everything he could find for sale—shipping lines, factories, country mansions—until he had created the biggest industrial trust in Europe. He owned, in all, some two thousand companies. "He had become a legendary figure," according to Kessler's account, "a wizard, a Klingsor who alone possessed the secret of conjuring forth magic gardens from the stony ruins of German industry."

The question remains: What caused the inflation in the first place? Germans of a nationalist persuasion have always placed most of the blame on the Allied demands for reparations, and it is undoubtedly true that any currency must suffer when the national wealth and the national production are drained to pay international commitments. More hostile observers, on the other hand, accuse the German government itself of trying to perpetrate a gigantic fraud. "Goaded by the big industrialists and landlords," as William Shirer put it in *The Rise and Fall of the Third Reich*, "the government deliberately let the mark tumble in order to free the state of its public debts, to escape from paying reparations. . . . Moreover the destruction of the currency enabled German heavy industry to wipe out its indebtedness by refunding its obligations in worthless marks."

This, too, is partly true, but conspiracy theories of history are generally to be mistrusted, particularly when it is possible to find more fundamental causes in sheer ignorance. There are few subjects about which we are so ignorant, even today, as the control of economic cycles, and, more specifically, currency values. In the United States, too, after all, the Republican administrations of the 1920's, not to mention more recent ones, proved somewhat less than successful in maintaining economic stability. So perhaps it was simply Prussian doggedness, rather than Prussian scheming, that led Reichsbank President Rudolf Havenstein to keep printing more and more banknotes.

"Today it requires handcuffs to stay the hand which turns the crank of the printing press," the British Ambassador, Viscount D'Abernon, observed angrily. "Last week, when, by the blessing of Providence, the printers struck and the printing of notes was perforce interrupted, Havenstein brought in strike-breakers in order to get the presses going again." That was in the summer of 1922; a year later, Havenstein went before the Reichsrat (Senate) to boast that his round-the-clock operation of the printing presses now enabled him to produce 46 billion marks in new currency every day. Not a single member of the Reichsrat objected, and it was only Lord D'Abernon who remarked that any bank president who understood so little about money should have been hanged.

"There was a considerable element of stupidity about economic theory," says Adolph Lowe, a birdlike figure of seventy-seven, with a tanned face, wispy white hair, and an academic gray sweater underneath his brown tweed jacket. We are sitting on the third floor of the New School for Social Research, in the heart of Greenwich Village. In the lobby downstairs, Maoist students are passing out Maoist pamphlets, but it is very peaceful in Dr. Lowe's little office, with rain beating on the windows, and Dr. Lowe, who was an official in the Economics Ministry in Berlin, wants to explain the quantity theory of money. "You know the quantity theory of money? That the level of prices depends somehow on the quantity of money in circulation. Of course, everyone is a Keynesian nowadays, but the general theory in Germany then was that prices rose or fell by themselves, and the government had to *adjust* the amount of money to provide what was needed to satisfy the demand for money."

"Is it possible," a visitor asks, "for a country's whole supply of economists to be uniformly wrong?"

Dr. Lowe smiles cheerfully, but the recollection of old arguments still sharpens his voice.

"You must understand that the German universities had cut themselves off from classical economic thinking fifty years earlier," he says. "They developed instead what was called the 'historic school' of economics, and this dominated the universities where all the economists were trained. I tell you, in all of Germany, there were only three teachers who really understood economics, and two of them were not even full members of their faculties."

"But surely somebody must have seen that the prevailing economic theories weren't working."

"Yes, of course," says Dr. Lowe, "but the wrong theory was very handy for two important groups. First, those who didn't want to pay reparations, who thought it was a patriotic duty to destroy Germany's capacity to pay. And second, the large-scale businessmen, people like Stinnes, though he was not the only one, who financed their business with large-scale borrowing."

Even if this is true, it remains mysterious why everyone seemed to accept the disaster as an inevitable manifestation of destiny. At first, of course, the inflation probably appeared relatively harmless, certainly less painful than the large tax increase that would have been needed to stop it. The shopkeeper's sales went up, and so did the workman's wages, and the constant upward movement came to be considered normal. This is now known as "the inflation psychology."

Among government officials, then, it seemed natural to call on bankers and businessmen for advice, and the most prominent among these counselors gave, whether from dogma or from greed, the wrong advice. And yet the government had to meet its payrolls—it paid not just the bureaucrats but the professors and the clergy and the railroad conductors and now the idled workers of the Ruhr—as well as the compulsory reparations demanded by the Allies. So Chancellor after Chancellor did as he was told—and kept the presses running.

There was a time, though, late in 1922, when Chancellor Josef

Wirth attempted to get an expert opinion from the outside world. At his request, John Maynard Keynes and three other economists came to Berlin, surveyed the problem, and offered a solution. They recommended, among other things, a two-year moratorium on reparations, stabilization of the mark at three thousand to the dollar, a curb on the printing of banknotes, and a balanced budget. The only trouble with this cure was that the patient still seemed to prefer his sickness, and so the Keynes report was ignored by Germans and Allies alike. "Currency experts—or, to speak more correctly, people who assume to be oracles on currency—have a sad fate," Lord D'Abernon remarked. "During life they empty every room in which they hold forth, and death finds them in madhouses."

The hapless Dr. Cuno gave up in August of 1923 and resigned his brief chancellorship. President Ebert then turned, finally, to one of the most extraordinary figures of the Weimar Republic. A stocky, bald, thick-necked man, son of a beer merchant, Gustav Stresemann had been a successful businessman before the war, then, in the Reichstag, a vehement supporter of Ludendorff's pan-German ambitions, and a devout monarchist even after the ignominious flight of Kaiser Wilhelm. Yet he was to become the Weimar Republic's quasi-permanent Foreign Minister, architect of rapprochement with France, and, at his death in 1929, one of its most deeply mourned statesmen. Now, in the anarchy of mid-1923, he undertook to form a "grand coalition" including all parties from the Socialists on the left to his own German People's Party on the right.

By this time, the Republic faced not only economic collapse but actual geographical disintegration. The united nation of Germany was still scarcely half a century old, after all, and although Prussia was the dominant state, including more than half the territory and population of the Reich, the smaller states retained a good deal of autonomy. Bavaria and Württemberg, for example, had entered World War I as autonomous monarchies, and even the most docile states retained control of their own police, courts, and educational systems. Prussia, the birthplace of German militarism, was now in the hands of the Social Democrats—Otto Braun, an ex-printer, a tall, heavy man with a beaked nose and bushy eyebrows, had become the state Premier after the Kapp Putsch and remained in power for most of the next twelve years. But if Prussian leadership had seemed attractive in 1871, it seemed much less so now, and a number of provincial leaders were considering the advantages of seceding from the tottering Republic.

Chancellor Stresemann's first major act, on September 26, was to announce the end of passive resistance in the Ruhr and the resumption of reparations shipments to France. The same day, he had President Ebert decree a state of emergency, giving broad powers to the federal government, and specifically to the army commander, General Hans von Seeckt. The southern province of Bavaria had already declared its own state of emergency, however, and given equally broad powers to a new right-wing governor, Gustav von Kahr. It was a large step toward secession, and President Ebert wanted to know where the army stood. General Seeckt's answer was ambiguous. "The army, Herr President, stands behind me," he said.

In the province of Saxony, located roughly between Bavaria and Berlin, a diametrically opposite movement was under way. On October 10, Saxon Premier Erich Zeigner formed a "popular front" by taking two Communists into his cabinet "to preclude the danger of a plutocratic military dictatorship." A few days later, the state government of Thuringia made a similar move. In Hamburg, too, there was a Communist uprising, which led to the death of sixty-five people. And on October 21, the French intrigues to gain control of the Rhineland culminated in the mobilization of local separatists, who proclaimed themselves the government of an independent Rhenish Republic.

General Seeckt, who distrusted Stresemann as "pro-French," believed that he could best hold the Reich together by establishing himself as the head of a right-wing government. He even proposed the change to President Ebert, and when Ebert dared him to make his proposal directly to Stresemann, Seeckt did not shirk the challenge.

"Herr Chancellor," said Seeckt, "it is impossible to carry on the struggle under you. You do not have the confidence of the troops."

"Are you withdrawing the army's support from me?" Stresemann demanded.

Seeckt was about to reply, but he was interrupted by Defense Minister Otto Gessler, who had insisted on being present at the confrontation, and who now insisted on the principle of civilian control over the military.

"Herr Chancellor, only I can do that," said Gessler. When

Seeckt remained silent, Stresemann still retained his tenuous hold on power. He immediately placated the army, however, by ordering the troops to suppress the left-wing governments in Saxony and Thuringia, an operation that was carried out within a few days. The Rhenish Republic never really acquired more than a phantom sovereignty. That left only the problem of Bavaria, and Adolf Hitler.

About five years had passed since the little Austrian, lying blinded and enraged in a hospital outside Berlin, had "decided to go into politics." He had drifted southward to the Bavarian capital of Munich, where he found political conditions in a promising state of turbulence. Bavaria had also had a short-lived revolution, and Hitler applied to army headquarters as an informer. His disclosures, of dubious accuracy, helped to keep the Freikorps firing squads busy. He then got a job in the Press and News Bureau of the Army's VII District Command. He attracted the attention of the command's intelligence chief, a crude but able officer named Captain Ernst Röhm. In the confusion of Munich politics—Ludendorff had taken refuge here, and Captain Ehrhardt, and numerous others—Röhm liked to send out spies to keep him informed on the myriad local "patriotic" movements. He sent his protégé, Adolf Hitler, to investigate and infiltrate one of the least significant of these little groups.

"One day," Hitler wrote later, "I received an order from my headquarters to find out what was behind an apparently political organization which was planning to hold a meeting within the next few days under the name of 'German Workers' Party.' . . . Wednesday came. The tavern in which the said meeting was to take place was the 'Altes Rosenbad' in the Herrenstrasse, a very run-down place. . . . I went through the ill-lit dining room in which not a soul was sitting, opened the door to the back room, and the 'session' was before me. In the dim light of a broken-down gas lamp four young people sat at a table. . . . The minutes of the last meeting were read and the secretary was given a vote of confidence. Next came the treasury report—all in all the association possessed seven marks and fifty pfennigs. . . . Terrible, terrible! This was club life of the worst manner and sort. Was I to join this organization?"

He did. He became the party's seventh member. The following month, he even gave his first speech, before an audience of 111 people. The party's chairman, Karl Harrer, considered him a failure, but Hitler worked on. By the start of 1920, he had become the little party's propaganda chief. He organized more meetings. People began to listen. In Munich, any tirade against Marxism and foreigners could attract an audience. And the authorities didn't mind. The Munich police commissioner was a reactionary named Ernst Pöhner, who, when asked whether he knew that the city was full of political assassins, answered, "Yes, but not enough of them." His assistant was a chilly bureaucrat, Wilhelm Frick, who eventually became the first Interior Minister of Nazi Germany and died on the scaffold at Nürnberg.

The army, too, was sympathetic. The local commander was Major General Franz Ritter von Epp, a former Freikorps commander, who, at Röhm's urging, helped raise sixty thousand marks to buy Hitler's party a weekly newspaper, the *Völkischer Beobachter* (*People's Observer*). Röhm himself steered a number of wandering Freikorps troopers into Hitler's growing force. General Ludendorff, too, became interested, and Ludendorff had access to wealthy people. In 1920, Hitler persuaded his group to take a more ideological name: The National Socialist German Workers' Party. He provided it with a new party emblem: the swastika. In 1921, he officially took control as chairman, and he organized a number of Freikorps veterans into a fighting unit called the *Sturmabteilung* (SA), the Storm Troopers. Captain Röhm controlled a number of military weapons caches; he would supply arms.

None of this attracted great attention in Berlin, of course (though General von Seeckt took the precaution of replacing General von Epp), but the discontented citizens of Munich seemed to enjoy their local orator. Every time he spoke, the crowds grew. "The first thing we must do," the young Hitler declared in April of 1923, "is to rescue [Germany] from the Jew who is ruining our country. . . . We want to stir up a storm. . . . We want to prevent Germany from suffering, as Another did, the death upon the cross." In Berlin, General Seeckt heard and disapproved. The following week, when Hitler mobilized fifteen thousand Storm Troopers to break up the Socialists' traditional May Day parade, the army announced that its troops would fire on anyone who disturbed the peace. Captain Röhm had secretly provided the Nazis with a large supply of arms, but Seeckt's orders prevailed. Hitler surrendered his weapons and sent his Storm Troopers home in defeat.

Hitler spent most of the summer sulking in Berchtesgaden. By autumn, however, the national disintegration was proceeding so rapidly that he decided to try to mobilize his forces once again. He called a series of mass meetings; the Bavarian government banned them. But in the hostility between Berlin and Bavaria's separatist Governor Kahr, Hitler saw a new opportunity. He learned that Kahr was to speak at the Bürgerbräukeller on the night of November 8, so he ordered Hermann Goering, head of the SA, to collect six hundred Storm Troopers and surround the building. He also sent one of his aides to bring General Ludendorff to act as a figurehead for the putsch. Twenty minutes after Kahr began his speech to about three thousand beer-drinking citizens, Goering burst in with an escort of twenty-five armed Brown Shirts.

Hitler, who until then had been standing unnoticed in a trench coat next to a pillar, suddenly leaped on a chair and fired a pistol shot at the ceiling. "The national revolution has begun," he cried. "This hall is occupied by six hundred heavily armed men. . . . The Bavarian and Reich governments have been removed and a provisional national government formed. The army and police barracks have been occupied." Most of these statements were pure lies, but there was no way for Kahr to know that. He and his chief aides docilely accompanied Hitler to an adjoining room, where their wild-eyed captor put his gun to his head and announced, "If I am not victorious by tomorrow afternoon, I shall be a dead man!"

Under such circumstances, Kahr agreed to Hitler's proposals for a new regime that would give Hitler "the direction of policy in the National Government." Even Ludendorff, who arrived in the middle of the scene, agreed to join in the putsch—and in what Hitler called "the march on that sinful Babel, Berlin." By this time, Hitler had taken off his trench coat and proved to be wearing a cheap black tailcoat, which, according to one witness, made him look like a provincial bridegroom. But the beer-hall crowd cheered loudly when he declared: "I am going to fulfill a vow I made to myself five years ago when I was a blind cripple in a military hospital: to know neither rest nor peace until . . . there shall have arisen once more a Germany of power and greatness." Then they all sang "Deutschland Über Alles."

Governor Kahr soon took the opportunity to slip out a side door, and so there was no official support for the Nazi forces which organized that night for the conquest of Munich. By dawn, Hitler was in a panic and wanted to disband, but Ludendorff convinced the ex-corporal that the very presence of the former commander was enough to guarantee success. "We march!" said Ludendorff. And so, just after eleven o'clock in the morning, an uncertain regiment of somewhat more than two thousand men set off from the Bürgerbräukeller. Hitler carried a pistol, and someone else waved the swastika flag. At the Marienplatz, where the giant Frauenkirche and the Gothic City Hall still loom over the medieval marketplace, the Nazi columns turned into the Residenzstrasse, a narrow, arcaded street that leads to a broad square called the Odeonsplatz. If the marching Nazis were to be stopped, the outnumbered police would have to stop them before they reached that large square, and so they had established a cordon at the end of the Residenzstrasse.

The police, armed with carbines, ordered a halt. "Surrender!" Hitler shouted. A police officer opened fire, and then both sides began shooting. Hitler was marching arm in arm with his political adviser, Max von Scheubner-Richter, and the first volley killed Scheubner-Richter instantly. Hitler fell heavily, dislocating a shoulder, then rose and staggered toward the rear. Goering fell with a severe wound to the hip and groin. Another leader of the march burst into tears, and the rest began to retreat in confusion. Only General Ludendorff, quite confident that no German would ever fire at him, marched serenely forward. Accompanied by an adjutant named Major Streck, he strode straight through the police lines and entered the Odeonsplatz, all alone.

Hitler fled in a yellow car to a friend's house in the suburb of Uffing, where the police found him, two days later, hiding in the wardrobe cupboard of his hostess. In due time, he was tried, convicted, and confined to prison for just over one year. As for Ludendorff, he was acquitted.

Still the mark kept sinking. The French occupation of the Ruhr had been a devastating blow, and neither passive resistance nor the suspension of reparations could compensate for the loss of Germany's basic industry. From a rate of 1 million per dollar on August 1, the mark plummeted every day until it reached 130 billion by the first of November. Two weeks later, the rate was 1.3 trillion.

The bureaucrats kept numbly at their work, and every stamp

collector still has specimens of postage stamps costing tens and hundreds of billions. But Germany was now, in effect, without any currency at all. Everything had collapsed. The main question, inevitably, was how to devise some new medium of exchange, and what to use to support it.

Traditionally, of course, a currency was supposed to be backed by gold, but the Weimar government simply didn't have enough gold, and so there were plans to base the mark on coal, or even potash. One survivor of that period recalls trying to work out a system to peg currency to an index of consumer prices. "This was a theory of James Harvey Rogers, who was at Yale," he says, "and Rogers himself was willing to pay for research—which cost very little in dollars—so we opened an office in Berlin and hired about a dozen people to go around to stores and make charts of the prices of consumer goods."

It was Karl Helfferich, the Imperial Treasury Minister who had failed so egregiously to finance the war effort, who finally came up with the basic idea for a solution. He proposed the creation of a National Mortgage Bank (Rentenbank), which would claim a mortgage on all of Germany's agricultural land and issue banknotes pegged to the price of rye. The Socialist Finance Minister, Rudolf Hilferding, found this an interesting plan but argued that the so-called *Roggenmark* (rye-mark) would be inordinately beneficial to the rye-growing peasants. Since Hilferding could not provide an alternative solution, however, Chancellor Stresemann replaced him with a less intellectual but more organized Finance Minister, Hans Luther.

Under Luther's guidance, a program for currency reform was finally worked out: The Rentenbank was to be instituted, as of November 15, and to begin issuing Rentenmarks, backed by a "mortgage" on the nation's gold supplies, which was to be backed, in turn, by a "mortgage" on all of Germany's land and assets. This so-called "mortgage" actually "meant nothing," says Adolph Lowe in his little office at the New School for Social Research. "It was just a cover for the new money, but the silent majority believed in it. They reduced their spending, and that made it work." Another former Weimar official puts it slightly differently: "It was still printed paper, but nicely printed paper. It had confidence."

At the very moment of change, however, this was still a matter of theory. "I'm not here to boast about my own doings," Adolph Lowe continues, "but the night before the stabilization, I was at a meeting with the top officials of the ministry, and the mark was then 3.8 trillion to the dollar, and I said, 'Let's decrease it still a little more, to 4.2 trillion, and then tomorrow we can wipe out twelve zeros on every bill and re-establish the mark at the prewar level.'"

To translate this theory into reality, Luther called on a prickly young financier named Hjalmar Horace Greeley Schacht, then head of the Darmstadt National Bank, and made him Commissioner for National Currency. Schacht promptly moved into a little office in the Finance Ministry, which had previously been a storeroom for cleaning supplies, and set to work. His first task was to suppress the myriad local currencies which various towns and corporations had been issuing on their own authority during the inflation; he simply announced that these currencies would no longer be honored. Then, to stop the speculators who continued to drive the old mark up to a theoretical rate of twelve trillion, he shut off all their credit. Within a month, he had succeeded in holding the new mark to its pegged rate of 4.2 to the dollar.

"What did he do?" Schacht's secretary and only assistant later explained to a reporter. "He sat on his chair and smoked in his little dark room at the Ministry of Finance, which still smelled of old floorcloths. Did he read letters? No, he read no letters. Did he write letters? No, he wrote no letters. He telephoned a great deal—he telephoned in every direction and to every German and international place that had anything to do with money. . . . And he smoked. We did not eat much during that time. We usually went home late. . . . Apart from that, he did nothing."

And so the national madness ended. But not before Chancellor Stresemann himself had fallen. The Socialists, still angry at his suppression of the popular-front governments in Saxony and Thuringia, voted "no-confidence" in his regime. He was replaced by the leader of the Catholic Center Party, Wilhelm Marx, and, with the Socialists in opposition for the next five years, a period of retrenchment and reconstruction began. At first, money was very tight, unemployment increased sharply, bankruptcies were common—"Bankruptcies were *normal*," says one Berlin businessman. "I had to work out balance sheets for lots of my friends. Bankruptcy was not even declared. One paid 10 percent or 20 percent to the creditors, and then one started again on this lower basis." Berthold Viertel's theatrical angel went broke, to cite one typical example, and so Viertel's repertory company had to close down. Even the mighty Hugo Stinnes suddenly dropped dead, and his whole empire, built on credit and inflation, fell in ruins. It was an attractive situation for foreign investors, and British and American loans came pouring in with the capital to launch a new boom. Now began the period in which the big industrialists tightened their control on the economy. Six large chemical companies merged in 1925 to form I. G. Farben. The following year, four steel companies joined to form the gigantic United Steel Works. The cartel—there were eventually two thousand of them—became the standard system for organizing business. By 1925, about 2 percent of all enterprises employed 55 percent of all workers.

Smaller profiteers had a harder time, however, and many of the nightclubs on the side streets of Berlin went out of business. Among the streetwalkers on Unter den Linden, only the professionals remained. "Ten years after the Revolution," one survivor says with a chuckle, "an American journalist asked Ossietzky [the editor of *Die Weltbühne*] what had really changed. He said that the businessmen were still doing business, and the generals were still generals, and the only thing that was different was that the women of Germany had finally been liberated."

"We Feel Young, Free, and Pure" 1924

The Spirit . . . is the Positive, the Creative. It is the Good. *The inspiring White Beam.* This White Beam leads to evolution, to elevation. . . . People are blind. A Black Hand covers their eyes, and this Black Hand belongs to the Hater!

WASSILY KANDINSKY

IT IS A COLD NOVEMBER NIGHT in New York. On the second floor of the Goethe House, in a paneled auditorium decorated with giant vases of red and yellow chrysanthemums, a stout old gentleman named Richard Huelsenbeck is delivering a lecture entitled "*Dada oder der Sinn im Chaos*" ("Dada, or Meaning in Chaos").

The subject—not to mention the language and the weather—might seem somewhat forbidding in the New York of 1970, but the auditorium is overflowing, and the authorities at the Goethe House have even set up folding chairs in an anteroom so that late-comers can sit in darkness and listen to the lecture over an amplifier. The room has its standard quota of elderly Germans, flocking to hear tales of the olden days, but there are also a lot of young people in beards and beads, for this is the age of Pop Art and Happenings and the Music of Chance, and Dada seems to be having a kind of Renaissance.

Richard Huelsenbeck has thick white hair and wears a gray pin-stripe suit and looks rather like a retired doctor, which he is, but he still tells the old stories with gusto. He tells how he was studying medicine in Berlin in 1915, and writing poetry, and painting, and

145

how he met another free spirit named Hugo Ball, and how they staged an art show and poetry reading that produced, he says, "the first signs of Dada." Huelsenbeck, who liked to affect a monocle in those days, beat loudly on a drum while he recited a supposedly African chant, with a chorus that went "Umba-umba-umba."

He was soon called up for military service, but he got another doctor to declare that he was "crazy," and then he went to Zurich, where he found the tall, gaunt figure of Hugo Ball sitting on a bench by the lake. Ball had been supporting himself by playing the piano in a nightclub, and his new wife, Emmy Hennings, sang songs. But now he had just opened a satiric cabaret, which he called the Café Voltaire. It was at No. 1 Spiegelgasse, across the street from the lodgings of an obscure Russian who called himself Lenin. Ball had gathered around him a number of young artists all dedicated to ridiculing conventional society and conventional art, and above all, the war. Tristan Tzara, for one, loudly read his poems in the original Romanian, then produced "accidental poems" out of random words from newspapers, and then began creating "simultaneous poems," to be recited by several people in several languages. The sculptor Hans Arp displayed a work he had made by tearing up scraps of paper, letting them fall onto a board, and gluing them down wherever they fell. And after some folk songs by a balalaika orchestra, Ball himself would appear in a cardboard costume, complete with wings, and recite one of his baffling "sound poems" ("Gadji beri bimba glandridi laula lonni cadori/gadjama gramma berida bimbala . . .").

All they needed, then, was a name for their movement, and so there occurred the famous scene with the dictionary. According to Huelsenbeck, he and Ball were thumbing through a German-French dictionary in an effort to find a stage name for a new singer at the cabaret. "I was standing behind Ball . . . [while his] finger pointed to the first letter of each word descending the page. Suddenly I cried halt. I was struck by a word I had never heard before, the word 'dada.' 'Dada,' Ball read, and added: 'It is a children's word meaning hobbyhorse.' At that moment I understood what advantages the word held for us. 'Let's take the word "dada,"' I said. 'It's just made for our purpose. The child's first sound expresses the primitiveness, the beginning at zero, the new in our art.'"

(It seems odd that one simple scene involving two people should cause so much confusion, but legends grow by a logic of their own.

"Germany's Children Are Starving!" by Käthe Kollwitz

Reichswehr troops battle Spartakists

Freikorps soldier firing
on Spartakus rebels

Spartakist leader Karl Liebknecht

Chancellor Philipp Scheidemann

Foreign Minister Walther Rathenau

President Friedrich Ebert

Edvard Munch's portrait of Count
Harry Kessler

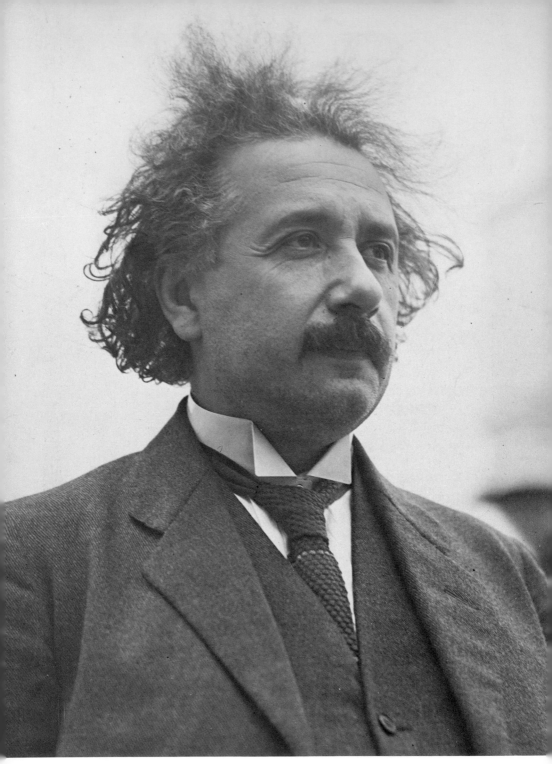

Albert Einstein

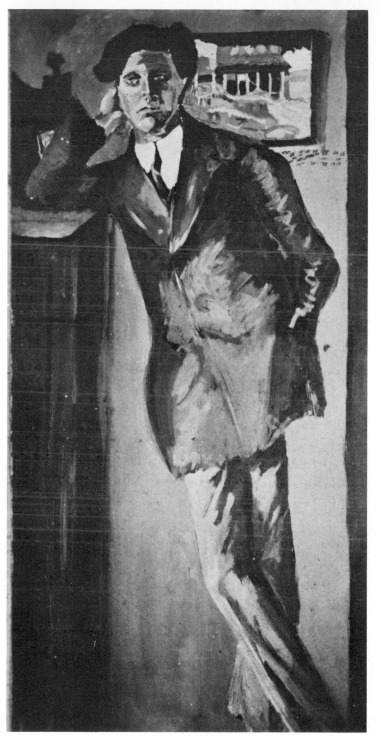

Arnold Schoenberg's portrait of Alban Berg

Pianist Artur Schnabel

Arnold Schoenberg's self-portrait

"The Bankruptcy Vultures," collage by Laszlo Moholy-Nagy

Adolf Hitler's sketch
for a triumphal arch

Ludwig Mies van der Rohe's
first design for a glass
and steel skyscraper

Erich Mendelsohn's
Einstein Tower

Architect Walter Gropius

"The Friedrichstrasse" by George (

"The Brandenburg Gate" by Ernst Ludwig Kirchner

Joseph Goebbels addresses his followers

"Prostitutes" by Otto Dix

Marlene Dietrich in *The Blue Angel*

A revue at the Apollo Theatre

Josephine Baker

Lotte Lenya in *The Threepenny Opera*

The original
The Threepenny Opera

Bertolt Brecht as a young man

Lotte Lenya before a poster of Bertolt Brecht

Director Max Reinhardt

Kurt Weill and Lotte Lenya

Peter Lorre in *M*

Hindenburg and Hitler in 1932
election campaign poster

Clash between Nazis
and Communists in 1933

The Berlin Cathedral in flames during World War II bombing

According to the memoirs of another Dadaist, Tristan Tzara was also present at the moment of discovery, and Ball said, "Here, gentlemen, you have the ism of all isms—Dadaism!" Ball himself never laid claim to the discovery, but Tzara, on the other hand, always took full credit himself: "I found the word Dada by accident in the Larousse dictionary." Then, in the subsequent wars within the movement, Tzara's enemies in Paris spread stories that the word had been discovered not by him but by Hans Arp, who first denied it, then confirmed it, then said he had only been joking.)

Toward the end of the war, the Dadaists began returning to their various capitals, bringing with them this anarchistic movement and finding that it evoked an emotional response all over Europe. In Paris, in particular, where Tzara joined forces with André Breton, the Dadaists staged a series of riotous "manifestations" on behalf of—well, of nonsense. At one public meeting, Tzara read aloud from a newspaper article while an electric bell rang so loudly that it drowned out everything he said. Francis Picabia drew pictures on a wall while André Breton followed behind him and erased everything he drew. Spectators threw eggs and tomatoes and even veal cutlets at the speakers. Others showered the theatre with copies of an anti-Dada leaflet called *Non*.

What did it all mean? "Dada has no meaning," said Tzara in one of the Dada manifestoes, adding: "I am in principle against manifestoes, as I am also against principles." But the manifestoes kept pouring forth: "Order = disorder; ego = non-ego; affirmation = negation. . . . Art is a private matter. . . . Any work of art that can be understood is the product of a journalist." In Berlin, however, where Huelsenbeck brought the new creed back from Zurich (Hugo Ball having retired from the artistic life to work among the poor), the Dadaists had a slightly more coherent program. They were for the newest forms of abstract art (they staged exhibitions of Paul Klee and Wassily Kandinsky), and for the art of chance, of improvisation and the unconscious. And against everything connected with the Establishment. When Friedrich Ebert gathered his delegates in Weimar to found the new Republic, the Chief Dada of Berlin, a bearded architect named Johannes Baader, who had been officially certified by the police as a madman and therefore not liable for his actions, rose up at the opening session of the Constituent Assembly and delivered a speech. While the delegates on both left and right shouted in protest, Baader loudly declared that the very act of creating the Weimar Republic was itself "a Dadaist demonstration." He therefore nominated himself as President of the Republic.

But the Dada demonstrations had a purpose, says Richard Huelsenbeck, clearing his throat and surveying his audience at the Goethe House in New York. "We were against the war," he says. "And so we were against all ideology, because the ideology based on Kant and Fichte and Hegel had become compatible with war. We were against culture because the culture of Goethe and Schiller had become compatible with war. But we were not politicians, we were artists, painters and poets, and so we expressed ourselves in art, even though we were against art. That is the basic paradox of Dadaism, which has not been resolved to this day."

The intellectual and artistic centers of Berlin, as in all big cities in Europe, were its cafés. Here, in the Café des Westens, the Josty, the Schiller, the Monopol, one read the newspapers, met one's friends, exchanged gossip, made deals, wrote poems. Of all these institutions, the legendary one was the Romanische Café, a great barn of a place, seating one thousand customers, just across from the Memorial Church. To the right of the revolving door, the bearded old Expressionist painters held forth at Max Slevogt's *Stammtisch* (a table permanently reserved for a regular customer), and in the balcony, where the chess players sat at rows of little tables, one might encounter the man who had been world champion for twenty-seven years, Emmanuel Lasker.

The young artists flowed in, to challenge and shock their elders. There was, according to one chronicler, "a most curious international mob of people, with long hair, short hair, or shaven skulls, in rags or in furs. . . . George Grosz, who was then both a Dadaist and a Marxist, often appeared there dressed as an American cowboy, booted and spurred." Grosz was, indeed, a paradigm of the young artist home from the war, full of energy and anger. According to another historian of the period, Grosz "paraded through the Berlin streets wearing a death's head and carrying a placard emblazoned 'Dada Über Alles.'" "Those were wild years," Grosz himself said later. "I took an active part in life. Yes, I was part of it all."

Grosz had been born in Berlin, in 1893, but he grew up in the small town of Stolp, in Pomerania, where his father was the manager of a Freemason lodge. The father died when Grosz was seven, and the mother moved back to Berlin for a time, to one of its bleak slums, but then she gave up the struggle of the city and returned to Pomerania, where she managed a club for officers in the Hussars. In later years, when Grosz was renowned as the most savage caricaturist of the German bourgeoisie and its military caste, he ascribed his views to the philosophy of Marxism, but is it not possible that the hatred infusing so much of his work derives from those boyhood years when he first experienced Berlin as an orphan in the slums, and when he saw the monocled officers of the Hussars order his mother around like a servant?

Grosz himself attached great importance to a more pleasant experience of his childhood. One night, he climbed onto a barrel and peeped into the bedroom of a woman who was preparing for sleep. Layer by layer, she peeled off all those chemises and camisoles and corsets that concealed the turn-of-the-century matron, until she finally stood naked before her mirror, still marked on the legs by garter bands, now letting down her long hair and brushing it, completely unaware of the boy perched on a barrel outside her window. The sight "affected me deeply," Grosz wrote many years later. "It was stupendous. . . ! I have never succeeded in erasing that first impression from my mind. Nor have I ever really wanted to do so."

Like much of his generation, Grosz had volunteered for the war, but after suffering an emotional breakdown, he finally returned as a shattered man to a shattered Berlin, a city that appeared, as Johannes Baader had said of the whole country, one great manifestation of Dada. "The city seemed to me like a stone-gray corpse," Grosz recalled later. "The streets seethed with unemployed. To pacify them, they were given chess games instead of work. . . . Many of the younger elements who had never been regularly employed . . . formed small bands that played some kind of imitation jazz for the few pennies dropped into their hats. . . . Real and fake cripples sat around on corners and turned their heads to one side when anyone passed by, quivering, quaking, pretending war injuries. They were called 'shakers.' The people, however, had long since become inured to the strange, unusual, and repulsive. . . . [I] was among those who wanted to extricate themselves from absolute nothingness. We wanted something more, but what the 'more' was we could not exactly say."

Grosz met Huelsenbeck, and the doctor-poet welcomed the painter as a co-founder of the local Dada. They opened a Dada Club and began publishing Dada magazines—*Every Man His Own Football*, *The Bordello*, *Rose-Colored Glasses*, and *Bankrupt*—many of which were banned almost as soon as they appeared. On one occasion, the Dadaists decided to sell their magazines by parading through the streets with a hearse and a band, complete with top hats and frock coats, while the editors trailed behind, hawking copies of their latest issue to bystanders. They were arrested, finally, for serenading the governmental offices on the Wilhelmstrasse and plastering the walls with stickers that said, "Hurrah Dada." At other times, the Dadaists would announce lectures on worthy subjects, and then, when the audience had gathered in search of enlightenment, Grosz would appear on stage and denounce everyone with a barrage of obscenities.

As in Paris, though, people seemed to be fascinated by the young artists who insulted them, and Dada soon acquired a sort of radical chic. "If Dada made no sense to the masses," Grosz observed, "it at least served as an outlet for the rich playboys who financed our movement. One such wealthy admirer had a wine cellar deep under the basement of his villa in Grunewald. He had streets and avenues and thousands of bottles of choice wines and liquors. These streets he named after some of his Dada friends. The George Grosz Alley was piled high with kegs of sherry. He even had a map of his wine empire, a region as fantastic as the catacombs under the streets of Paris. He had a motor scooter with a tremendous headlight attached, to help him get around. . . . Every month we would have a party down there."

The Dada exhibitions in Berlin attracted some of Germany's most interesting young artists, notably Max Ernst, who was already painting the dreamlike absurdities that were to become basic statements of the Surrealist movement, and Kurt Schwitters, who liked to spend his time pasting together collages of old bus tickets, cloakroom stubs, buttons, inner tubes, and pieces of string. (He became so fascinated with junk, in fact, that he first covered all the walls of his house with collages, than began to fill the rooms with various "freestanding objects." From one of his early collages, which he called a "*Merz* picture," because it featured the last half of the word "*Commerz*" ("commerce"), clipped from a newspaper headline, Schwitters became obsessed with producing *Merz* art and *Merz* plays. He took to calling himself *Merz*, and his home the *Merz* Building, which, by the mid-1920's, became so full of trash that he divided it up into various grottoes, with names like Nibelungen Treasure and Sex-Murder Cave. The accumulated rubbish extended from the cistern up to the second floor and then out around the chimney.)

Despite the pranks and games, however, the Dada movement in Berlin, unlike that in other cities, committed itself to left-wing politics. "Dada is German Bolshevism," said Huelsenbeck. In Paris, Tzara had declared that "Dada has no meaning," but at the first International Dada Exhibition in Berlin, the walls were placarded with slogans like "Dada is political" and "Take Dada seriously." The most startling entry in the exhibition was a dummy in the uniform of an army officer. It had the head of a pig, and it hung, floating face down, from the ceiling of the main gallery.

The Berlin Dadaists were a diverse and argumentative group—Huelsenbeck, the bemonocled poet who was soon to wander off as a ship's doctor; Baader, the demented architect who seems to have thought seriously that he was Jesus Christ; Hannah Höch, a sprightly girl who specialized in nightmarish photo-collages. The most important of them, of course, was George Grosz, who was a Dadaist primarily in the sense that he rejected every relic of the old society, and all the formal academic art in which he had been trained before the war. He was also a Cubist, in the sense that he delighted in picturing his subjects from several viewpoints at once; and a Futurist, in the sense that he filled his cityscapes with a furious quality of simultaneous motion. But these various movements actually had relatively little effect on him, for his work is quite unlike anything that anyone else has ever done.

Despite the ferocity of his pictures, he was a rather mild-looking man, prey to doubts and misgivings about himself. A self-portrait he drew in those days shows him looking rather pudgy, slumped despondently in a chair. A photograph is more charitable. It shows a handsome but somewhat conventional face—receding hair, a wide mouth, strong nose and chin. He resembles a banker, or a junior diplomat, or, of all things, an army officer. The only oddity is that he is smoking a corncob pipe. And, of course, that he is sitting with brush and palette before one of his bitter panoramas of the Berlin scene.

He was enormously productive, creating hundreds of vivid portraits of Berlin and its citizens—all, without exception, portraits of decay, corruption, lewdness, death. They do not, of course, give a really comprehensive picture of the city. There seem to be no workmen in Grosz's Berlin, no schoolchildren, no parks or trees. There are no pretty girls, just apathetic whores, or matrons with sagging breasts, who stand and wait for paunchy husbands in suspenders and underwear to finish brushing their teeth. There is nobody, as a matter of fact, who looks as young and eager and clean-cut as Grosz himself, only middle-aged businessmen with bristling mustaches and bald heads and thick cigars; and officers with monocles and ruthless jaws, and, often, no trousers; and, over and over again, sex murderers, real or potential, brandishing knives and hatchets. Even the buildings of Berlin become sinister in Grosz's drawings, hard towers of stone, usually tilted at threatening angles. And there is rarely any sunshine, just the pale light of a crescent moon glowing thinly outside the apartment house where some horror is occurring. And yet, despite their savagery, despite their obsessive repetition of the themes of lust and corruption, Grosz's portraits are fearfully accurate. They may not represent all Berliners, but those figures of hatred did walk up and down the streets of Berlin in the 1920's, and in the days of Hitler. One can tell because one can see them on the streets of Berlin today.

In 1923, Grosz put together a collection of his pictures and published them under the title *Ecce Homo*. It is still the centerpiece of his life work. Here, in sixteen paintings and eighty-four drawings, he produced an unforgettable indictment of the German ruling class, its merchants, its professors, its officers, and its women. And the ruling class, which might put up with the lighthearted absurdities of Dada, would not put up with this. Earlier, Grosz had been prosecuted for "defaming the reputation of the army." Now, under a law that had not been invoked in decades, the authorities charged Grosz with "defaming public morals, corrupting the inborn sense of shame and virtue innate in the German people." He was convicted and fined, and twenty-four of the one hundred plates in *Ecce Homo* were confiscated.

By then, however, Grosz had already broken away from the Dadaists. Despite their theoretical explanations, their pranks seemed an inadequate response to the problems of a country stumbling toward disaster. And, indeed, the whole Dada movement was dying.

For those who still believed in this form of "manifestations," the end came with André Breton's manifesto of 1924, which killed Dada and announced the new movement of Surrealism. But Grosz had already joined forces with the Communists. "Today," he said, "art is an absolutely secondary affair."

The death of Dada in 1924 coincided with the death of another movement, which, although radically different in both techniques and objectives, shared with Dada an innocent optimism about the future of the world, and about the possibility of improving it. The movement had begun in 1905, in Dresden, where Ernst Ludwig Kirchner joined forces with other young painters like Emil Nolde and Max Pechstein in a group called "The Bridge." Five years later, the movement spread to Berlin, under the name of "The New Secession," and began exhibiting under the auspices of Herwarth Walden, an energetic entrepreneur who had started an art gallery and a magazine both named *The Storm*. It was not until the following year, 1911, that an article in Walden's magazine first gave the new movement its name: Expressionism.

The Expressionists considered themselves the German counterparts of Matisse and the Fauves, but they wanted to go much further in transforming art into a representation of inner emotion. They wanted to manifest, according to one account, "the spirit of revolution and reform, the longing for eternity and the sense of God's presence." Or, to use one of the Expressionists' own terms: *"Der Geballter Schrei"* ("the clenched outcry"). This meant, above all, color—passionate color—a red sun, an orange sky, splashes and blotches of whatever might express the painter's feverish emotions.

There is some mysterious contradiction, however, between the Germans and an art based on passion and color. Perhaps it is the climate, those gray skies and arctic winds. Perhaps simply the environment, not the hostility of Grosz's cigar-puffing burghers but the whole cultural tradition of the nation. In countries that border on the Mediterranean, color and passion seem to be in the air, but in the land of Gothic cathedrals and *The Well-Tempered Clavier*, a land of lines and masses and counterpoint, the sensuous blues and yellows of a Matisse or a Bonnard seem somehow artificial, a product of theory rather than experience.

Expressionism remained fairly bucolic in its early years—every respectable German museum is full of garish "modern" landscapes with cows—but the end of the war brought out the Expressionists' still-unfulfilled passion to change the world. They staged exhibitions of their paintings in Berlin railroad stations, so that the workers might benefit from a glance at art on their way to their jobs. They organized, in 1918, a new movement called "The November Group," and issued a manifesto that stated their views in the most idealistic terms: "We believe that our first duty is to dedicate all our energies to the moral regeneration of a young and free Germany. We plead for excellence in all things. . . . We insist upon unlimited freedom of expression. . . . We respect every achievement in every sphere. . . . Our goal—each at his place in hard, tireless, collective creative work. We feel young, free, and pure. Our spotless love belongs to a young, free Germany and we shall fight against all backwardness and reaction, bravely, without reserve, and with all the powers at our command." Along with this effusion, the Expressionists of the November Group sent out a questionnaire on artistic matters "which need clarification." There were questions like "How can one interest the *Volk* once more in a total work of art . . . to take the place of salon art exhibitions?" And again: "Harmony with the *Volk*. How can the efforts of modern artists reach the *Volk* and harmonize with it?"

The answers that came back were ingenuously radical, or radically ingenuous. Walter Gropius, for example, responded to a question about state support of art by saying, "Art and state are irreconcilable concepts." And to a question about art exhibitions, he said, "Since art is dead in the actual life of civilized nations it has been relegated to these grotesque morgues and there prostituted." Instead of such practices, he wanted, among other things, "travelling art shows in brightly painted huts." Another young architect in Berlin, Bruno Taut, proposed that the state begin "a monumental architectural project: something so mighty that it will occupy the spare time of *everyone* perpetually; a vast decoration of earth. . . . To concentrate only upon practical matters is boring. Children who are bored, fight—and nations make war."

The November Group gathered all of these responses into a book entitled *Yes!—Voices of the Workers Council for Art*, published in Berlin in 1919. But once the artists had said their say, what could possibly follow? Expressionist painters went on painting Expressionist pictures, or, as in the case of *Dr. Caligari*, designing sets for Expressionist movies. The theatre, indeed, provided a major medium for Expressionist enthusiasm, and there was a sudden outpouring of plays in which nameless characters, identified only by designations like The Father or The Son, worked out their violent and rather unreal destinies. But as the years passed, the years of the Kapp Putsch and the Rathenau murder, and the first stirrings of Adolf Hitler and his Storm Troopers in Munich, how important was it, really, what the Expressionists thought of their own souls, either in words or in colors?

As early as 1923, an art-gallery director named Dr. Gustav Hartlaub began collecting evidence that the Expressionist movement, still so noisy, still so full of confidence in its own manifestoes and its own self-exhibitions, was dead. By the following year, he was ready to stage a showing of his evidence, illustrating a number of tendencies that he called "The New Objectivity." He did not mean simple realism—among his prize exhibits were works by Grosz, Otto Dix, and Max Beckmann—but he did emphasize the inclination of many artists toward a more literal representation of their physical surroundings. As an explanation for this change, he suggested a fundamental change in the national mood: "The expression [New Objectivity] ought really to apply as a label to the new realism bearing a socialistic flavor. It is related to the general contemporary feeling in Germany of resignation and cynicism after a period of exuberant hopes (which found an outlet in Expressionism). Cynicism and resignation are the negative side of the New Objectivity; the positive side expresses itself in the enthusiasm for the immediate reality . . . the desire to take things entirely objectively . . . without immediately investing them with ideal implications. This healthy disillusionment finds its clearest expression in Germany in architecture."

There were economic reasons, too, for the new mood. The wild tumult of the postwar years, the madness of the inflation, had abruptly ended with the stabilization of the mark, leaving a convalescent Germany with the convalescent's yearning for peace and order and a cautious reconstruction of the essentials of life. The so-called Dawes Plan of 1924, devised by the American banker Charles Dawes, fixed German reparations payments at 2.5 billion marks a year and provided for the evacuation of the Ruhr. It thereby opened the way for American investments in the recovering German economy. Factory owners began installing assembly lines, and the increases in production brought a large increase in jobs. Money was very tight for several years, however, and tight money tends to make people cautious, in the arts just as much as in business.

The term "New Objectivity" thus became not just a label for an art exhibit but a justification and explanation for a whole period of conservatism and retrenchment. In the theatre, the Expressionist heroes who had cried out for revenge against their cruel fathers suddenly seemed, as they perhaps had been from the start, absurd. And in the movies there was an equally marked shift from the painted sets of the UFA studio out into the street. The change was not without its critics, of course. "The main feature of the new realism is its reluctance to ask questions," said one of them. "Reality is portrayed not so as to make the facts yield their implications, but to drown all implications in an ocean of facts." Still, the new emphasis on realism struck some artists as a kind of liberation. Carl Mayer, one of the two poets who had written *Doctor Caligari*, now conceived a plan for a documentary movie called *Berlin, Symphony of a Great City*, and a talented photographer named Karl Freund set to work to, as he put it, "show everything. Men getting up to work, eating breakfast, boarding trams or walking . . . Shooting life. Realism. Ah, that is photography in its purest form."

Theories of art generally appear long after the art they try to explain. Long before there was a "New Objectivity," there was Walter Gropius, who had a revolutionary idea—or rather, a counter-revolutionary idea—about objectivity and objects. The idea was supremely simple: that mankind had failed to control the arrival of the machine, and that this control could, with a certain amount of ingenuity and energy, be recaptured.

The economic consequences of the machine age were already a matter of history. In every situation in which a machine could produce goods more cheaply than human labor, the machine had soon come to dominate a new area of industry. The craftsman, whether a weaver or a buggy-maker, had to either join the factory or go hungry. The consequence was not just a social upheaval but also a deep division between people and objects. When the man who made an object had to give way to the machine, the making of ob-

jects lost value, and the objects themselves became abstractions.
And while the engineers ruled the machines, the artists and designers turned away from the materials of everyday life and produced only ornaments for the salons of the rich. Art, which had
once involved every kind of building and creating, became synonymous with painting, particularly the painting of portraits and landscapes, all confined within ornate golden frames.

The reaction began in the late nineteenth century, led by figures
like John Ruskin and William Morris, who demanded a return to
the old crafts, to hand-made furniture and hand-woven rugs. But
the rejection of the machine was, in the age of the machine, simply
a form of antiquarianism. What Walter Gropius saw was that the
machine could do good work just as well (and just as cheaply) as
bad work. Thus, it could make beautiful things just as easily as ugly
things, and if the engineers who ran the machines didn't know the
difference, then he, Gropius, would find a way to teach them. In
short, the artist, instead of rejecting the machine, or fighting it, or
ignoring it, should try to take control of it.

The idea came naturally to Gropius for he was not an artist in
the landscape-painter sense but an architect, and architecture has
always been the most public and most practical of the arts, the art
that requires of the artist the greatest amount of both technological
and commercial skill, a knowledge of steel and stone, of how much
weight a specific girder can support, and also of tax laws and public
relations, and even the amount of bribery required for corrupt con-
tractors.

Architecture, too, had become estranged from everyday life
during the nineteenth century—the architects designed public
buildings in a neo-classical style, while the new steel factories were
designed by engineers, and most of the housing in the rapidly growing cities was hardly designed at all—but Gropius found his way to
the Berlin studio of one of the pioneers of twentieth-century industrial architecture. His name was Peter Behrens (among his other
young assistants were Ludwig Mies van der Rohe and Le Corbusier),
and, as artistic consultant to Germany's General Electric Company
(AEG), he built a number of installations that attempted to combine functionalism with aesthetic principles.

To the head of AEG, old Emil Rathenau, father of the future
Foreign Minister, Gropius wrote his first major statement of how the

artist might join forces with the technician. He wanted to start a company to produce prefabricated housing. "Due to extensive building speculation and poor management throughout the past decades," he said, "the state of building has deteriorated both in taste and in durability. . . . Our organization now wants to . . . improve on present conditions . . . particularly with respect to the quality of design. . . . Thus art and technology would be happily united." Specifically, Gropius proposed to design houses that could be built of identical ingredients, and thus mass-produced. "Only through mass-production can really good products be provided," he said. "Industrial production methods can be applied to nearly all parts of a house. . . . Entire houses including walls, ceilings, stairs, plumbing, etc. [can be] poured in concrete, using variable forms. . . . [But] each house maintains an individual personality through variations in form, material, and color. . . . The governing principle of the enterprise will be to make these houses comfortable, not in terms of overdone gilded pomp but rather in clear and open spatial arrangements."

This document of 1910, which implies and foretells more than half a century of building design, apparently did not inspire old Emil Rathenau to action, but Gropius was already beginning to carry out his ideas by himself. That same year, he left Behrens' office and opened his own architectural studio in Berlin. From it came some of the earliest examples of what we still call "modern architecture," starkly rectangular creations of steel and glass, completely functional but also bold and new.

Gropius considered architecture "the dominating mother of all arts," and yet his basic idea was not an architectural idea but rather a conviction that there should be a "common citizenship of all forms of creative work," and that good design is "an integral part of the stuff of life, necessary for everyone in a civilized society." By coincidence, Gropius' opportunity to start redesigning Germany came in the same little town where Friedrich Ebert and his supporters had tried to redesign Germany's political structure. For Weimar, 140 miles southwest of Berlin, was the home of both a Grand Ducal Academy of Art and a school of arts and crafts that had been founded at the turn of the century by the Belgian designer Henri van de Velde. As soon as the war ended, the republican authorities merged the two schools and summoned Gropius from Berlin to take charge. He started by giving the institution a new name: the Bauhaus.

Gropius, who had narrowly escaped death during the war, was now thirty-five—getting a little stout, his dark hair beginning to recede over the forehead—and troubled by the disintegration of his marriage to the widow of Gustav Mahler. He was also a man of boundless energy and gusto, gifted not only with the talents of a first-class architect but also with those of a first-class executive. The most important of these talents, as always, was the ability to attract colleagues, to bring to the staid and sleepy town of Weimar the most dynamic artists in Germany, and beyond. "Architects, sculptors, painters, we must all return to the crafts!" said Gropius. The first man he appointed to the position of "master" was an American, Lyonel Feininger. Then came Paul Klee, and Wassily Kandinsky, and Laszlo Moholy-Nagy, and later, when the Bauhaus began training its own masters, Marcel Breuer and Josef Albers. And finally Mies van der Rohe.

The students started with a six-month course on the fundamentals of color and line, then joined one of the Bauhaus workshops to start carrying out the basic Bauhaus idea, the application of modern design to every aspect of modern life. There were workshops in weaving and furniture-making, in metalwork and printing and ceramics and wallpaper and stained glass. (The only building category in which the early Bauhaus did not have a workshop was, curiously enough, architecture. Gropius maintained his own architectural studio in Berlin.) In all these workshops, the students were expected not just to create pretty things but to work out designs that could be leased out for commercial manufacturing (Herbert Bayer even designed new million-mark banknotes for the inflation-ridden state government). And Gropius, constantly in search of funds for his ill-equipped workshops, had no illusions about the need for profit, even during the anarchic period of the inflation. "Gropi can be difficult at times," Feininger wrote to his wife after one staff meeting. "'Whoever cannot now show what he is worth, can go to the Devil with his art,' he said, during the session; so I as a young chap, would have been sent to the Devil long ago. But Gropi has a clear grasp of realities, and that is something we others haven't."

Today, when we look back at the creations of the Bauhaus, we can recognize not only the brilliance of Gropius' idea for reuniting art and technology but also the skill with which he carried out his plans. The tubular chair that stands in every American kitchen, the silverware now known as "Scandinavian," the abstract patterns in our floors and wallpapers, the shapes of fluorescent lights overhead —all these and much more originated just outside Berlin a half-century ago. "We are all graduates of the Bauhaus," as one New York art critic said not long ago. "Indeed, there are no other major modern styles."

In the early days of the Bauhaus, however, Gropius had to confront a ceaseless flow of criticism and complaint. It started with attacks from the traditional protectors of traditional Art. Wilhelm von Bode, the distinguished old collector who had amassed such treasures as Nefertiti and the Pergamon Altar for the Imperial Museum in Berlin, wrote to the Weimar authorities that he was "absolutely appalled" by the fact that Gropius had begun his regime with the appointment of "the cubist Feininger." In Weimar itself, a group of professors in the old Grand Ducal Academy of Art refused to accept the creation of the Bauhaus, challenged the legality of Gropius' rule, and operated their "secessionist" academy in one wing of Gropius' own headquarters.

Even inside the Bauhaus, there was serious opposition to Gropius' idea. Feininger, for one, wrote to his wife that he "rejected" the union of art and technology as "a misinterpretation of art" and "absurd." The main figure of opposition, though, was Johannes Itten, a gifted painter and an even more gifted teacher, who directed the Bauhaus' basic course in design. He had been educated in science and mathematics, but, like Feininger, he had little faith in the union of art and technology. He was preoccupied with form, and patterns of color, and, ultimately, Oriental mysticism. And when he argued with Gropius over the future of the Bauhaus, he argued vehemently, unrelentingly. Gropius, always the executive, accepted Itten's emotional resignation, replaced him with Moholy-Nagy, and pressed ahead on his own course.

The most serious opposition, however, came from the conservative political forces in Weimar and the surrounding state of Thuringia. The townspeople of Weimar knew little about the internal politics of the Bauhaus, but they knew that they disapproved of the sudden influx of students from wicked cities like Hamburg and Berlin, rambunctious young people in sandals and long hair, who liked to sunbathe on the roof of the Gothic Tempelherrenhaus, and who, it was said, lived promiscuously in their dormitories. The students responded with an endless series of parties—kite-flying competitions, or kinetic light shows, or various kinds of "happenings" (there are still photographs of students parading with placards marked "passion," "suspense," "entrance," "orgasm," and, mysteriously, "catastrophe"), or simply dances to jazz provided by the Bauhaus band, which liked to punctuate its improvisations with occasional pistol shots.

There was an element of Dada in all this, along with the usual high spirits of the young, but there was also an element of Gropius' instinct for executive planning. "The Bauhaus was a very revolutionary place internally," according to Mrs. Ilse Gropius. "And if something went wrong and the conflict came to a head, my husband said, 'Let's have a party.' The party was symbolic. It threw a positive light on the benefits of collaboration." (The occasion of her comment was a "Grope Fest," in the spring of 1970, in Cambridge, Massachusetts, where Gropius had died, leaving a will that asked for no mourning but rather "a fiesta—à la Bauhaus—drinking, laughing, loving." And so, according to the *New York Times*, "Two nearly naked women and a man painted in silver from head to toe slithered across the room as eerie electronic music and flashing strobe lights reverberated against walls and ceilings covered with silver paper. Below them, statuesque women in floor-length metallic gowns and men in silver ties whizzed down a chute, bounced off rubber mats in the basement and ran into an inflated plastic bag, where they gleefully threw fistfuls of tiny white pellets at each other.")

For most of its existence, though, the Bauhaus was a public institution, dependent on the approval of public officials and the flow of public money. From the beginning, there had been a certain amount of hostility from conservative politicians—accusations of frivolity and waste—but Gropius, the executive, proved a tireless propagandist for his cause, and the Thuringian state government generally supported him. During the nationwide crisis of 1923, however, when the Socialist leaders of both Thuringia and Saxony tried to counter rightist threats by joining the Communists in popular-front coalitions, Chancellor Stresemann responded by calling out the army to overthrow both regimes and place both states under martial law.

Gropius had always insisted that the Bauhaus remain totally nonpolitical, but the army soon heard reports that the controversial school was a nest of subversives. "Yesterday at 10:30 A.M. I was summoned from my office to my home by a Reichswehr soldier," Gropius protested to the local commander, "for a warrant to search the house had been issued. . . . I am ashamed of my country, Your Excellency, that despite the accomplishments I can claim, I am apparently without protection in my own country, and only because today irresponsible elements are beginning to exploit our army." The commander, General Hasse, retorted with a threat to prosecute Gropius for an "affront to the Reichswehr and insulting me personally."

The conflict became even worse the following spring, when new state elections brought a majority for the rightists. They promptly began harassing the state government with parliamentary questions: "Is it true that the government has not taken any steps so far to phase out such an unprofitable institution as the Bauhaus . . . ? Is it true that doubts have been raised about the moral qualities of the Director of the Bauhaus, Gropius . . . ?" Gropius answered angrily: "The Bauhaus has been hampered in its important work by ignorance and malicious slander. . . . The Bauhaus must protest very strongly against such derogation." But the harassment continued. There was an official investigation of the Bauhaus' somewhat muddled finances (the school had had five different business managers in six years), and finally an official notification that all of the teachers' employment contracts would end as of September, 1924.

The authorities did not want to shut down the Bauhaus, just to eviscerate it. Their plan was to get rid of Gropius and his principal followers, to reduce the budget by more than half, and then to turn over the remnants to private business. Gropius answered this plan by announcing that he and his associates "make known to the public their decision to dissolve the Bauhaus, which they had built out of their initiative and conviction."

In the very moment of its dissolution, however, the Bauhaus suddenly found its salvation. Dr. Fritz Hesse, the Social Democratic Mayor of Dessau, a small industrial city halfway between Weimar and Berlin, invited Gropius and his whole institution to move north. And he did far more besides. He asked Gropius to design his own building for the new Bauhaus, and new housing for all the Bauhaus masters; he also promised the money and political support that had been so lacking in Weimar. Gropius happily accepted, and in less than a year, the Bauhaus reopened in its new home. And there, the plans that had obsessed him for many years, the plans that had barely begun in Weimar, were destined to flourish.

The problem confronting Dr. Einstein was an embarrassing one. He was making a tour of the newly completed "Einstein Tower" in the company of Eric Mendelsohn, the architect who had built it. The tower clearly fulfilled its function—the cupola at the top served as an observatory, from which the rays of cosmic light could be reflected down into a subterranean astrophysical laboratory. But the building itself, in the suburb of Potsdam, looked rather like an ungainly spaceship. Its squat, concrete tower, with four tiers of deeply recessed windows, rose heavily from an elongated base. Einstein and Mendelsohn wandered through the building for some time, and while the young architect waited anxiously for a sign of approval, Einstein said nothing. Only some hours later, during a meeting with the building committee, did Einstein get up and whisper in Mendelsohn's ear the enigmatic one-word judgment: "Organic."

At about this same time, Ludwig Mies van der Rohe sat at his desk and drew a vision of two skyscrapers. One was rectangular, the other cylindrical (neither was ever built, though the latter undoubtedly inspired Chicago's Marina City). Both of them were to be sheathed from the ground to a height of more than twenty stories in nothing but glass. Mies did not want this glass simply to form windows, framed by pillars of steel; the walls themselves were to be glass, the entire buildings were to be giant crystals. "With a single stroke of his pen," according to one architectural expert, "Mies laid the foundation for all the great glass-and-metal skyscrapers we see about us today."

Mies and Mendelsohn stand at opposite extremes of modern architecture, but in their radical use of new materials they both represent the turbulent novelty of postwar Berlin. And they both shared one of the peculiar problems of architecture—the fact that architects need a wasteland to work in. The masterpieces of Christopher Wren, for example, could emerge only from the ashes of the London fire. But the center of Berlin had already been built, and in a style designed to last until Judgment Day. The great builders of the eighteenth and early nineteenth centuries—Andreas Schlüter, George Knobelsdorff, and Karl Friedrich Schinkel—had already created the Royal Palace, the Opera, the university, turning Unter den Linden into one of the world's most grandiose displays of public architecture. Kaisers might come and go, but most of these monuments of neo-classical design still stand to this day.

The need for new building in the 1920's, then, was a need for new houses. The rich were buying up plots of land near the woods of Grunewald and along the shores of the Havel, and they considered it fashionable to commission one of the new architects to build their houses. Mies van der Rohe turned from hypothetical skyscrapers to the designing of suburban villas, one of which was notable for a series of brick walls that reached out into the gardens in all directions. Gropius built an extraordinary house in Dahlem entirely paneled with teak, for which he commissioned the Bauhaus workshops to produce abstract patterns. Like most intellectuals of the period, however, the architects were political liberals, and they felt a sense of obligation to the ideal of mass housing. Gropius, for one, helped to build a huge project for the workers at the Siemens electrical plant in northern Berlin. And bit by bit, the building boom of the 1920's began to change the whole look of the city. Everywhere that the young architects found an opportunity, they started erecting those bleakly rectangular houses and apartment buildings, with white walls and horizontal windows, that still connect the Prussian capital to the suburbs of Los Angeles.

Eric Mendelsohn, too, built rectangular villas for the rich men of Berlin, but his ambitions lay in a different direction. A plump and rather single-minded man, quite stoical about the loss of an eye to cancer, he had decided to become an architect at the age of five, and even while he served in the trenches on the western front, he kept sketching the massive buildings that he wanted to create. Some of those wartime sketches were tiny, no more than an inch high, but they all convey a sense of vast size. And the patterns of machinery keep recurring—rows of cylindrical shapes vaguely evocative of a piston engine, giant horizontal slabs with titles like "warehouse" and "goods station," and that figure of the spaceship, looking a bit like a very broad-beamed submarine, which appears first as "optical factory," then as "skyscraper," and finally as the Einstein Tower. Mendelsohn was passionately interested, like the other young architects of Berlin, in expressing the machine age in his buildings, but unlike them, he conceived the machine age not in terms of abstract rectangles but in terms of power and mass. He became, thus, the architect most ideally suited to translate the new techniques into huge temples of commerce.

The department stores of Berlin were somewhat different from those of other countries, for housewives considered it faintly embarrassing, at least in the early years, to shop for cut-rate prices. The entrepreneurs, therefore, lured them in by creating lavish surroundings. Wertheim's, the gigantic stone palace that had opened on the Leipzigerplatz at the turn of the century, boasted not only three new escalators, eighty-three elevators, and three miles of pneumatic tubes but also marble walls, crystal chandeliers, and fountains ornamented with tiles from the Kaiser's own ceramic works.

A bit further down the Leipziger Strasse, Eric Mendelsohn built the first of his major stores, a showcase for the prosperous fur dealers named Herpich. The new architecture, indeed, was admirably suited to the need for commercial display. While Wertheim's took pride in the 100,000 lightbulbs that illuminated its mausoleum, Mendelsohn produced for Herpich a façade consisting almost entirely of glass. And at night, by a technique that had never been tried before, a band of concealed light served to advertise the fur dealer's wares. When Mendelsohn first designed the store, in 1924, Berlin's Mayor Gustav Böss officially tried to block the construction as "shaming the street"; only eight years later, the city authorities decreed it a landmark and a "masterwork."

Mendelsohn's success in Berlin brought him a number of similar commissions. He built large department stores in Nürnberg, Stuttgart, Breslau, and Chemnitz. In fact, he was, with forty assistants working in his studio, one of the busiest architects in Europe. To the objective eye, his buildings are not impressive as works of art, scarcely comparable to the austere purity of Mies's best work. Despite his insistence on personal expression in the design of every building, his own expression tended to be somewhat ponderous, and he kept repeating his basic ideas, often a horizontal mass ending in a vertical cylinder. Still, he had many admirers, one of whom, for example, wrote that Mendelsohn "succeeds in drawing out his horizontal lines to their fullest extent, almost, at times, to the breaking point, and then, while the eye of the spectator is in full pursuit of these vigorous flowing lines, Mendelsohn arrests them, makes them as it were recoil upon themselves, and always at just the right point. Mendelsohn knows how to play upon form as a violinist plays upon a string."

Whatever his talent, Mendelsohn was very much a representative of the new architecture in Berlin, and during a busy decade, he left his trademark all over the city. On the Kurfürstendamm, he built a complex that included the Universum Cinema, a cabaret theatre, a bachelor hotel, a block of apartments, and a whole side street of little shops. On a triangular site near the Belle-Alliance Platz, he designed a monolithic headquarters for the German Metal Workers Union, and on the Potsdamer Platz, he produced a towering office building called the Columbus House. In between major assignments, he created a yacht club in the suburb of Wannsee and a house for himself on the shores of the Havel.

No one architect, however, not even a school of architecture, can decisively affect a city that is already established. And the ironic fate of the young builders of Berlin was that they had to flee into exile upon the arrival of Hitler, who had architectural ideas of his own, and they could return only after Hitler's dreams had left the center of Berlin a wasteland—the very space they needed for their work. Berlin today represents a kind of Pyrrhic victory for the architects of the 1920's. From the ruins of the Hansa Quarter rises one of Gropius' most cheerful apartment houses; the new Museum of Modern Art is by Mies; all through West Berlin, in fact, the radical ideas of the exiled masters are now a commonplace. Eric Mendelsohn was not one of those who went back to rebuild; he spent his last years in America and Israel. But he had anticipated the event from the beginning of his exile, when he observed the dilapidated streets of Marseille and cried out to his wife the basic creed of the architect: "God! What there is to do still; for the face of the world cannot remain like this."

CHAPTER IX

"The Supremacy of German Music" 1925

You must change that, Schoenberg. Have your pupils read Dostoyevsky, that is more important than counterpoint!

GUSTAV MAHLER

If you are in a position to observe the way Mahler ties his tie, you can learn more counterpoint from this than you can in three years at the conservatory.

ARNOLD SCHOENBERG

THEY NEVER FORGAVE Friedrich Ebert, apparently, for what he had and had not done during the days of the Revolution. As a matter of fact, nobody ever seems to have forgiven him for his working-class origins. George Grosz, for one, wrote contemptuously: "Ebert, the former saddle-maker now president of the Republic, was occupied with having his moustache cut just so, so that he could look like the executive of a large corporation." Kurt Tucholsky derided Ebert's fear of a Communist putsch as "groundless," denounced his efforts to suppress rebellion as "insane," and declared that his whole regime represented nothing but "his lack of courage, his betrayal of comrades." And when, on one occasion, the President went to Wilhelmshaven to launch a ship, the shipyard workers greeted him with total silence. This may have been a show of left-wing hostility, but it may have had other causes. "The truth is, the Germans cannot stand a President in a high hat," Gustav Stresemann observed. "They

167

must have a military uniform with plenty of medals. If it is a mere question of wearing a high hat and looking common in it, each member of the public thinks he can do that for himself."

If the hostility on the left was strong, the hostility on the right was venomous. "I remember one day when Ebert came to visit our town," a history professor in New York says of that period, "and all along the streets that his car was to travel, the shopkeepers hung out underwear from their windows. There were a few flags that the authorities had put up, of course, but all along the President's path, he had to see the shopkeepers' underwear." And if the leftists accused Ebert of betraying the Revolution, the rightists accused him of fomenting it in the first place.

During a presidential visit to Munich in 1922, an extreme nationalist called Emil Gansser broke through police lines and screamed at Ebert that he was a "traitor." When Ebert made the mistake of filing a slander charge against Gansser, the defense lawyer, a Nazi, got the Munich court to subpoena the President for cross-examination. Ebert tried to escape from the entanglement by dropping charges—a mistake even worse than his original decision to prosecute. Gansser was emboldened now to publish an open letter claiming that Ebert had admitted treason and should resign.

A new prosecution forced Gansser to leave the country, but his charge was taken up by another right-wing extremist named Rothardt, who edited a small paper outside Magdeburg. Rothardt reprinted Gansser's open letter and added his own taunts: "Come on, now, Herr Ebert, prove that you really are not a traitor." Once again, Ebert succumbed to the temptation to sue, and once again he had to submit his case to a provincial court. After a two-week trial, the Magdeburg judge sentenced Rothardt to three months in prison but also observed that Ebert, though he might claim extenuating political circumstances, was technically guilty of treason for having joined the general strike on the day of the Kaiser's downfall.

It was absurd, of course, for a provincial judge to claim that the President of the Republic was guilty of "treason," but while Ebert appealed the ruling to a higher court, every Nationalist demagogue could claim judicial "proof" for the accusation that Germany was ruled by the "November criminals" who had betrayed her. Trapped by his policy of suing accusers, Ebert became enmeshed, by the end of 1924, in almost 150 legal actions against various right-wing critics. Nor were these critics limited to the provincial press. On the contrary, they had just won an important role in the national government.

The two general elections in 1924 had brought strong gains for the Nationalists, a right-wing and essentially anti-republican group, who now held 103 seats in the Reichstag, second only to the Social Democrats' 131. Chancellor Wilhelm Marx, of the Catholic Center, tried in vain to patch together a new coalition of moderates, and then Ebert assigned the chancellorship to Hans Luther, the nonpartisan administrator who had organized the currency reform of 1923. Luther recognized the inevitable by including right-wingers in his coalition, and so the Nationalists were in a strong position to exploit one of the biggest corruption scandals of the 1920's, the Barmat case.

The Barmat brothers—Julius, Herschel, Solomon, and Isaak—had come from Poland to the Netherlands, where, in 1907, they set up a small export-import business. After the war, they undertook to ship large quantities of food, particularly lard, to the hungry Germans. In the course of these transactions, they came to know many leading Social Democratic officials. From the office of Friedrich Ebert himself, in fact, Julius Barmat got a permanent visa that enabled him to travel in and out of Germany whenever he liked.

In the course of the next few years, the Barmat brothers established themselves in Berlin and prospered mightily. During the inflation, when business success depended on the acquisition of "real" wealth—food, or fuel, or foreign currency—the Barmats' importing business naturally flourished. After the inflation, when money was tight, the Barmats got even richer by loaning money to smaller companies—and when those companies got into trouble, the Barmats took them over. By the end of 1924, Barmat Enterprises consisted of forty-six different companies, including banks, metalworks, and textile mills. But the Barmats themselves had become overextended, and the brothers now found themselves unable to make the repayments that were due to their creditors. At this point, the creditors turned to the police.

Early in the morning of New Year's Eve, the police set out to capture Julius Barmat in his elegant villa on Schwanenwerder, a thickly wooded island in the Havel River on the western outskirts of Berlin. They worried that the Barmats might try to flee in two speedboats that were kept on the island, so fifteen policemen surrounded the villa at dawn, and several police boats cruised offshore. The Barmats surrendered without any resistance, and then the investigations began. It turned out that their bankruptcy involved a default of somewhere between two and ten million dollars, most of it borrowed from the Prussian State Bank and the National Post Office. It also turned out that the Barmats—all loyal members, whether for business or ideological reasons, of the Social Democratic Party—had provided favors to a wide range of Socialist political leaders.

Gustav Bauer, the former Chancellor who had signed the Versailles Treaty and survived the Kapp Putsch, was now revealed to be a member of the Barmats' board of directors. The President's son, Friedrich Ebert, Jr., had received contributions for the Socialist cause. The Barmats had even loaned $1,000 to Berlin's Police Commissioner Richter to help him build a small house, and Richter had given Julius Barmat a silver cigarette case "in gratitude." The loans and favors extended through all layers of government and business. The Barmats had given, for example, more than $4,000 to the Social Democratic press. And one of their business allies, another East European émigré by the name of Ivan Kutisker, had even bought carloads of geese and distributed them at Christmastime to everyone in the Prussian State Bank, from the directors down to the doormen.

The Reichstag investigated the scandal, the Prussian legislature formed a Barmat Committee to investigate further, a Berlin court weighed charges of fraud and bribery, and the Nationalists took advantage of every new disclosure. Why, they demanded, had Ebert let the Barmats into the country in the first place? Why had he not kept a closer watch on his own secretary, F. Krüger, who died shortly after the disclosure of his involvement in the scandal? Why, the Nationalists demanded, had the whole Weimar Republic turned into what they now took to calling the *"Barmat-Republik"*? The prosecution of Julius Barmat and his associates lasted for more than two years, and at the end, on March 30, 1927, the judge handed down a 545-page verdict, which, after analyzing the incredibly complex affair, convicted Barmat on two counts of bribery and sentenced him to eleven months in prison. Ex-Chancellor Bauer had already been forced to resign from the Reichstag, and Police Commissioner Richter had been dismissed.

But for President Ebert, who was not really implicated in any wrongdoing whatever, the verdict came much too late. Throughout the early months of 1925, when new Nationalist accusations appeared every week, Ebert became obsessed with defending his honor. He suffered from terrible abdominal pains, but he refused to listen to his doctors' recommendations for surgery. "I cannot go away [from my office]," he said to his old comrade, Noske. "My honor is at stake. Or rather the honor of the head of state. Do you know what is happening today? In that Barmat Committee they want to establish today whether I have had sexual relations with one of my office secretaries. . . . The filth which surrounds me! Disgusting!" Five days later, Ebert was dead, at the age of fifty-four. By the time the doctors had persuaded him to undergo surgery for appendicitis and peritonitis, it was too late to save him.

Rudolf Serkin has an invisible keyboard that is always before him. Sitting in a restaurant, or even walking along Rittenhouse Square in Philadelphia, he is apt to illustrate a point by holding forth his arms and letting the fingers flicker over the imaginary keyboard. The piano is not just his profession but his life.

He is a tall man, full of nervous energy, with a crown of closely cut gray hair, and a sudden smile. Now we are eating cold cuts at the Artistic Alliance, a staid little club just around the corner from the Curtis Institute of Music, where Serkin is the director, and he is telling how he first came to Berlin just after the Revolution.

"Yes, we had our own revolution in Vienna, a small one. We took over the palace and used it for the children of the workers. They lived there. I gave them piano lessons. I myself was sixteen. I had tuberculosis then, and they said I should go to Paris for treatment. There was a special train that took children from Vienna to Paris, a tuberculosis train. I was also going to study with Isidore Philipp at the Conservatoire. Some people arranged for me to have a job at the Hôtel de l'Opéra—is there a Hôtel de l'Opéra? Yes? That was it—where I could also practice."

"What kind of a job was that?"

"I don't know—I never went there. I met Adolf Busch in Vienna, where he was giving a series of violin concerts, and he said, 'Why don't you come to Berlin and study with Busoni?' I said I didn't know how to make the arrangements. And Busch said, 'My house is empty. You can live there.' So I went to Berlin.

"The first letter I wrote to Busoni, he never answered. Then his pupil, Egon Petri, arranged a meeting. Busoni was nearly dead then

—his heart." Serkin clutches at his chest. "He said I shouldn't have any lessons. I was seventeen, and he said that was old enough for me to have a style of my own. He said I should go to lots of concerts, and if I liked one, I would learn something. And if I didn't like one, maybe I would also learn something."

"So what did you do? Try somebody else?"

"I took his advice. There was nobody else to study with. I practiced every day, for hours. I gave a concert myself, at the Singakademie. There were only twenty people in the audience, but among them were Busoni, Schnabel, and Einstein."

"What did you play?"

" 'The Goldberg Variations,' " Serkin says promptly. Even after fifty years, the program at a Berlin debut is not forgotten.

"Did you ever play with Einstein?"

"Oh, yes. He was very kind to me."

"I've heard he was a terrible violinist."

"Yes, he always played without any vibrato, so it always went skreek-skreek-skreek. But he loved it so much." Serkin smiles.

"When Busch came back to Berlin," Serkin continues, "Busch and I went to Busoni's house and played his violin sonata for him— a beautiful piece, I love it. When we finished, we asked him, 'Is that the way you imagined it to sound?' He said, 'No.' We said, 'Why? How should it be played?' He said, 'I won't tell you, because that would spoil your spontaneousness.' Only later, when Busoni made an arrangement for two pianos, and he played it with Petri, then we saw what it was. He played the last movement about three times as fast as we had. We had played it very German, full of soul, but he wanted it Italian, like this."

The hands stretch out over the cold cuts and begin playing very rapidly on the invisible keyboard that is always there.

Ferruccio Busoni was a legendary figure. An Italian by birth, rather gaunt and somewhat stooped, with long hair flowing back from a handsome, granitic face, he had come to Berlin in 1894 and soon became a famous personality in the music-loving city. As a pianist, he had narrow hands, which forced him to practice constantly, but his performances were titanic. In one typical recital, he played Beethoven's Hammerklavier Sonata, plus all four Chopin Ballades and the A-flat Polonaise, ending with Liszt's incredibly difficult *"Réminiscences de Robert le Diable."* He created massive sonorities, using the shoulders rather than the wrists for muscular power, and in his rejection of the sentimental traditions of nineteenth-century music, he became known as the founder of modern pianism. As a composer, he dedicated himself with equal energy to an unfashionable but highly individualistic kind of neo-classicism. He produced a gigantic concerto for piano and male chorus, a *"Fantasia Contrappuntistica"* for two pianos, and the operas *Arlecchino* and *Doktor Faust*. As a teacher and editor, finally, he revised much of the piano literature of Bach and created transcriptions of Bach's organ music that are still popular in recital halls.

Throughout his life, Busoni was searching, Faust-like, for a kind of perfection. "I began," he once said, "by getting beyond Schumann and Mendelssohn. I used to misunderstand Liszt, then I worshiped him. Later, I was amazed at him, and then, as a Latin, turned away from him. . . . One of the most difficult things was learning to distinguish between good Beethoven and bad. . . . And through all these twenty years, there stood unchanged, like a lighthouse in a stormy sea, the score of *Figaro*. But as I looked at it again a week ago, I found signs of weaknesses in it for the first time." Nonetheless, when Busoni decided to give a series of farewell concerts in 1922, the great virtuoso played nothing but Mozart—twelve piano concerti in a row.

He was also, in the tradition of Paganini, something of an eccentric. "Busoni was the greatest figure—there is nobody like him," said Artur Schnabel. "Unfortunately I could not see him as often as I wished because he was nearly always surrounded by a group of people who were a bit too expensive—I would say—for me to take into the bargain. He had a great affection for freakish people; he felt a kind of symaphty for them. Every day after lunch he had this group for two or three hours—a strange collection, not very gifted either. He was very good to them. Yet, with a kind of devilish glee he would tell them the most absurd things about music, which he simply invented. They accepted blindly all these fantasies and would afterwards spread them as the last word on music. . . . I shall never forget the last time I saw him. It was . . . shortly before he died, and when he was very ill. I saw him alone. When I entered the room, he said: 'Schnabel, you are acquiring a face.' It impressed me deeply—a great compliment. It meant that I had none until then, of course. I was then forty."

Among the younger pianists in Berlin—Claudio Arrau lived there

then, and Wilhelm Backhaus, and Vladimir Horowitz—it was
Schnabel himself who served as a kind of standard. "He was the
greatest influence on us all," says Rudolf Serkin. "In every way. By
the way he played, by playing all the modern music, by keeping an
open house, by knowing everyone." A square, stocky man with a
thick gray mustache, Schnabel was not a virtuoso—"How is your
friend, the great *adagio* player?" Rachmaninoff once sneered to a
member of the Schnabel circle—but his poetic touch and scrupulous
taste made him the foremost interpreter of Beethoven and Schubert.

Schnabel, too, had his court, and his rather regal way of life. To
his apartment, on one occasion, he summoned some of the best in-
strumentalists in Berlin to begin twenty rehearsals of the first postwar
performance of Arnold Schoenberg's song cycle, *Pierrot Lunaire*. The
violist was Boris Kroyt (later a member of the Budapest Quartet),
and Kroyt recommended a starving young refugee, Gregor Piatigorsky. After the group had rehearsed for an hour or so, Schnabel announced a break for tea. "No one except me was in a hurry to have
tea," Piatigorsky recalled later. "I waited, listening with the others
to Schnabel discoursing on *Pierrot Lunaire,* Communism, and other
interesting topics. However, sensing a rather prolonged dissertation,
I slowly moved into the other room. There I saw sandwiches and a
variety of cakes displayed on a table. I was alone. It was like leaving
baby lambs with a wolf. I devoured the sandwiches one by one. I
worked fast. When there were no sandwiches left, I began the devastation of the sweeter and less satisfying material. These also disappeared with fabulous speed, and only when nothing edible
whatever remained on the table did I rejoin the group, who still
listened to Schnabel."

When Artur Schnabel came from Vienna to Berlin in 1898, "there
was only one opera house, perhaps three playhouses, three concert
halls, one variety show and one house where light opera was given.
. . . All presentations seemed addressed to one and the same group
of persons, numbering ten thousand, I estimate." But as the population soared from 1.8 million in 1900 to more than 4 million in the
1920's, the demand for music became almost insatiable. In 1912, the
Deutsches Opernhaus was opened to accommodate the people who
couldn't get into the State Opera on Unter den Linden. After the
war, the Kroll Theater on the edge of the Tiergarten turned into
Berlin's third opera house. Erich Kleiber, then in his early thirties,

directed the State Opera, Bruno Walter the municipal opera, and Otto Klemperer the Kroll. And when Artur Nikisch died in 1922, Wilhelm Furtwängler took over the Berlin Philharmonic, with Bruno Walter conducting a special series of concerts there as well. The competition among these enormously talented musicians was intense, and it resulted in an outpouring of concerts more rich and varied than anything that could be heard in the rest of Europe. Old Berliners still talk with veneration of Furtwängler's incandescent Beethoven, of Walter's sensuous Mozart, and of such novelties as Klemperer's modern-dress version of Wagner's *Flying Dutchman* (which prompted Wagner's son Siegfried to cry: "*Kulturbolschewismus*," or "Cultural Bolshevism").

"In music, Berlin was still a bastion of the traditional world," Yehudi Menuhin recalls. "Beethoven and Brahms were gods. Furtwängler and Walter were their vicars on earth. And Mrs. Louise Wolff, the producer, was the high priestess. How I remember the great dinner that Mrs. Wolff gave after the dress rehearsal on the morning of my debut. The rehearsal was almost more important than the concert itself, because that was when all the musicians came to listen. At the dinner, there were at least forty people. They all bowed and shook hands. '*MAHLzeit* . . .'"

More than forty years after the event, Menuhin begins, amid the clutter of his New York hotel room, to act out the scene. He shakes the hands of the imaginary diners and repeats that somewhat old-fashioned invitation to eat, roughly the equivalent of the French phrase, "*Bon appétit.*" "And then they *ate*, until the groaning table turned into the groaning guests. Then they got up and bowed again, as deeply as they *could*, which was not as deeply as before. '*MAHLzeit*' again. Well, that world—with the eternal carpet on every table, and the lace on top of the carpet—that world wasn't going to change, not if they could help it.

"I speak of the musical life specifically because that was very important in Berlin in those days," Menuhin goes on. "The musical life represented what colonies, or a Foreign Office, do in a great capital of a great power. The ambition that people might otherwise dedicate to military power was all played out on an opera stage."

Adolf Hitler never liked Berlin. He disliked its wit and its cynicism and its cosmopolitan atmosphere. Someday, he decided, he would tear down and rebuild the whole center of the city. He would rip out the Anhalter and Potsdamer railroad stations and move them back to the south of Tempelhof airfield. That would give him enough room to build a three-mile-long avenue from Tempelhof in the south to the Reichstag in the north.

The plan for the avenue was inspired by the Champs Élysées in Paris, but it was to be two and a half times as long, and, as a matter of principle, seventy feet wider. For the northern end, Hitler himself designed an incredible domed assembly hall, sixteen times the size of St. Peter's in Rome. The dome was to be 825 feet in diameter, and the assembly hall was to seat more than 150,000 people. For the southern end of the avenue, Hitler designed a ponderous triumphal arch, even more ugly than the domed assembly hall. This was to be more than twice as high as the Arch of Triumph in Paris. And into its granite sides, the workmen were to chisel the names of every one of Germany's 1.8 million war dead. When all the rebuilding was finished, Hitler planned to give Berlin a new name: Germania.

The most extraordinary thing about Hitler's plan is that he sketched the designs for his two monster buildings on two small cards in the year 1925—a time when he had just emerged from prison to find his party disintegrating and his political future nil. "I made these drawings ten years ago," said the Führer when he finally turned them over to his pet architect, Albert Speer. "I've always saved them because I never doubted that someday I would build these two edifices. . . . Berlin is a big city but not a real metropolis. . . . We must surpass Paris and Vienna."

Bach and Beethoven are magnificent, of course, but the importance of a musical capital depends on its capacity for encouraging and welcoming new work. "Berlin opened its arms wide," according to Hans Heinsheimer, a music publisher now at the headquarters of G. Schirmer in New York, "to everything that was new, young, daring, different." It was a policy of the Philharmonic to have composers perform their own works, and so Berliners heard the definitive interpretations of the latest creations by Stravinsky, Ravel, Bartok, and Prokofiev.

Of all these visitors, the most interesting was Arnold Schoenberg, who, on the death of Busoni, received an invitation to take over his master class in composition at the official Academy of Art. In September of 1925, Schoenberg moved from Vienna to Berlin, and so the capital of modern music moved with him. He set up his headquarters in an apartment on the Nürnberger Strasse, where his music room contained a piano, a harmonium, and a guitar. Another room was devoted entirely to the composer's passion for Ping-Pong. Since Schoenberg didn't feel like going to work at the Academy on the Pariser Platz, his students, who included the Americans Marc Blitzstein and Henry Cowell, came to his apartment for classes in the analysis of music—not modern music but Bach and Mozart.

Schoenberg was then a rather dour, irritable man of fifty-one, thin, bald-headed, asthmatic, and embittered by years of hardship and opposition. Orphaned at fifteen, he had supported himself as a young man by orchestrating the scores of popular operettas, and this kind of hack work constantly interfered with his own creations. His early masterpiece, the *Gurrelieder*, an operatic oratorio for a gigantic assemblage of five soloists, four different choruses, and an orchestra of almost two hundred instruments (including three different kinds of clarinets, four kinds of trombones, gongs, harps, celesta, and some large iron chains), was largely composed in 1900, but the orchestration took until 1911, and it required two years more for the work to get its first public performance.

Schoenberg sustained himself in the absolute conviction that he was creating a wholly new language for modern music. This language derived logically from Wagner, whose *Tristan* and *Parsifal* had more or less abandoned the traditional system of tonality that had reigned ever since the Renaissance. But while Wagner's fluctuating chromatic harmonies washed up to the frontiers of tonality, Schoenberg determined to move on toward the total abolition of the standard eight-tone system. To replace it, he began experimenting with a technique in which all twelve tones of the chromatic scale would be equal in value. The only difference between consonance and dissonance, he wrote in his *Manual of Harmony* (1911), was that consonance provides a simple relationship to the ground note, whereas dissonance involves a more complex relationship. Ideally, he believed, there should be "no absolute up or down, no right or left, no forward or backward. Every musical configuration, every movement of tones, has to be comprehended as a mutual relation of sound."

In *Pierrot Lunaire*, Schoenberg developed the technique of

Sprechgesang, in which the singer does not sing but rather speaks at a prescribed pitch. But this was only a transitional work. In the "Five Piano Pieces," Opus 23, and the "Serenade," Opus 24, Schoenberg was working out a completely new system of musical composition. During the summer of 1922, while out on a walk with one of his pupils, he finally made the astonishing announcement: "I have discovered something which will guarantee the supremacy of German music for the next hundred years."

This was, of course, the famous "tone row" or "series." The idea, basically, was that a composition would begin with a statement of all twelve tones of the chromatic scale, in any sequence the composer chose, and no note could be repeated until the other eleven had been stated. This tone row then became the basic theme of the piece, to be varied rhythmically, or inverted, or reversed, or transposed to different levels, but not to be fundamentally altered. Other composers had experimented with similar ideas, to be sure. Even in the seventeenth century, Heinrich Schütz had written chord sequences that contained all twelve tones without a repetition, and one of the main themes of Liszt's Faust Symphony was built on four triads that produce a tone row. But it was Schoenberg who insisted on this system as the foundation of all atonal music.

To Schoenberg, and to his growing school of followers, the tone row represented a liberation from the conventional language of music. Finally, all at once, Schoenberg had invented a new medium, providing every other composer with a whole new universe to be explored. And if concert audiences didn't like the sounds that resulted, Schoenberg was contemptuously indifferent. "Beauty appears only from the moment when the unproductive begin to miss it," he declared in the *Manual of Harmony*. "Before that point it does not exist, for the artist has found no conscious need of it. He is satisfied with truthfulness, with having expressed himself, and having said that which had to be said according to the laws of his nature. The laws of nature manifested in a man of genius are but the laws of the men of the future."

It seemed to many people—and, indeed, it still does—that the rigid imposition of the twelve-tone row is an arid and cerebral way of composing music, and Thomas Mann even went so far as to ascribe it, quite literally, to the Devil. In one of his last major novels, *Doctor Faustus*, Mann told the story of a composer named Adrian Leverkühn, who duly announces his invention of the twelve-tone theory (I am following here the stiffly official translation by Mrs. H. T. Lowe-Porter): "One would have to go on from here and make larger words out of the twelve letters, as it were, of the tempered semitone alphabet. Words of twelve letters, certain combinations and interrelations of the twelve semitones, series of notes from which a piece and all the movements of a work must strictly derive."

To carry out his plan, Leverkühn makes the traditional pact with the Devil, who promises him the traditional twenty-four years of success: "Know, then, we pledge you the success of that which with our help you will accomplish. You will lead the way, you will strike up the march of the future." But the Devil also warns him: "Love is forbidden you, in so far as it warms. Thy life shall be cold, therefore shalt thou love no human being." Leverkühn goes on to write a series of masterpieces, but his efforts to find love all end in the deaths of his vicitims. And so, when the allotted time runs out, he summons all his friends to hear a performance of his last work, *The Lamentations of Dr. Faustus*, then confesses his secret to the horrified audience—"I am wedded to Satan . . . I made with him a bond and vow, so that all . . . I brought forth [is] infused by the angel of death." At that point, he cries out in pain and falls to the floor from a stroke that leaves him mad for the rest of his life. Mann acknowledged at the end of the novel that Leverkühn's theory "is in truth the intellectual property of . . . Arnold Schoenberg," and he originally wanted to dedicate his work to the composer. Schoenberg, perhaps understandably, was furious. Now living his last years near Hollywood, still poor, still relatively unappreciated, still determined to go his own way, he angrily denounced his fellow refugee and refused ever to speak to him again.

Still, those who knew Schoenberg well were not dismayed by his apparent coldness and aloofness. Salka Viertel, the actress, met Schoenberg often because her brother, Edward Steuermann, was a pianist who championed modern music, and, indeed, played the premiere of Schoenberg's piano concerto. "Brilliant is a stupid word to use about people," Mrs. Viertel remarks, "but I have known only two men who struck me as completely superior people, men of genius. One was Brecht, and the other was Schoenberg. I don't count my husband, or my brother. Schoenberg had the most incredible mind. On any subject. If you couldn't get a can of tomatoes open, say, he would immediately start to work out a theory on how to make a better kind of can-opener." (Schoenberg did, in fact, invent a more complicated version of chess, with ten squares on each side, which he called "hundred chess.")

"Schoenberg was a fantastic man," says Rudolf Serkin. "I loved him. But I could not love his music. I told him so, and he never forgave me. He said, 'It's up to you to decide, whether you want to be on this side of the barricades or that one.'

"I studied composition with Schoenberg for quite a time," Serkin goes on. "It was very informal, just six or seven of us in a class. But it was also quite technical. He taught counterpoint. He had us write variations on a theme. Once, I wrote a rondo for piano and I brought it to him. He looked at it, and then he said, 'Serkin, I'm going to cut out all the parts that you like best.'" Serkin makes a gesture of a man wielding large shears. "And he did. All the extra things. The ornamental things. He wanted only the essentials. Schoenberg thought that composing was a craft, and that every composition should be well made. He used to use the Mendelssohn Trio in D Minor as an example of a badly written piece."

"But it's so beautiful," one protests. "Wasn't he really against it because it's rather sentimental?"

"No, it was a matter of construction. He thought the second theme was wrong, and the development section was out of proportion. Schoenberg was not against emotion. He always wanted emotion in all his works. And I think he changed his mind later about the Mendelssohn—not so bad after all."

Of all Schoenberg's pupils, the most important and the most dedicated was Alban Berg, also orphaned at fifteen, also a victim of asthma. "He was unusually tall but always slightly stooped," according to Hans Heinsheimer, the music publisher, "as if bowing in grace and elegant humility to the world. His hands were very large, white, and sensitive, covered by a fascinating web of blue veins. He had a beautiful face, a smiling, almost mocking mouth, great warming eyes that always looked straight at you." Berg started his career as a government accountant, dealing with taxes on alcohol and statistics on pig farming, but his brother sent some of his early musical sketches to Schoenberg, who immediately accepted the young bureaucrat as a nonpaying pupil. "He was industrious, eager, and did everything in the best possible way," Schoenberg said later.

Berg, in turn, served Schoenberg as a worshiping disciple. He wrote articles analyzing the older man's compositions, and fought to get them performed.

His own early works were on a relatively small scale—songs, a piano sonata, a string quartet. In the spring of 1914, however, Berg was deeply moved by a Vienna production of Georg Büchner's unfinished play, *Woyzeck*. He saw it several times and then decided to turn it into an opera. Having been a civil servant, and a semi-invalid, Berg must have seen something he recognized in Büchner's gloomy story of the half-mad soldier, browbeaten by his officers, treated as a guinea pig by his doctor, betrayed by his mistress.

There actually was once a Johann Christian Woyzeck, a barber and mercenary soldier, who, at the command of a mysterious voice, stabbed his faithless mistress to death. Some said at the time that Woyzeck was mad, but the official verdict was that the murderer's "erroneous, capricious and superstitious illusions" were the result of "turbulent circulation of the blood," and so he was publicly executed in Leipzig in 1824.

The case fascinated the young Georg Büchner, who was both a revolutionary and a medical student, specializing in nervous disorders. When he began to recreate the character of the executed Woyzeck, he attributed the crime not only to the soldier's mysterious sense of terror but to the taunting voices of the captain and the doctor, both hinting at the faithlessness of his mistress. But Büchner was also a gifted poet, and only a poet could have created the chilling final scene, in which the murdered woman's son rides off on his hobby horse to join the other children in going to look at the corpse. When Büchner died at twenty-three, he left the play as an unfinished series of twenty-seven scenes. It was not published until almost a half-century later, in 1879, but it eventually became recognized as one of the major forerunners of the Expressionist theatre.

If Berg saw something he recognized in this melodrama of murder and madness, the war could only have strengthened that sense of recognition. Although he was too fragile for front-line duty, he found himself consigned to endless drills and guard duties in a provincial barracks. "Report for duty at 6:45 A.M. and command an hour's physical training," Berg wrote to a friend in an accounting of his military life, "then march off to an exercise field. . . . Activity in the guardhouse equals nothing. Sitting around for twenty-four hours in a little room saturated with tobacco smoke, with ten or twelve recruits. Every two hours I have to take one of them out—that is, collect the guard who is on duty and put someone in his place. So this goes on from 12:30 P.M. to 12:30 P.M. on the following day. In the night I can sleep for four hours." And again: "Have you ever heard a lot of people all snoring at the same time? The polyphonic breathing, gasping and groaning make the strangest chorus I have ever heard. It is like a music of the primeval sounds that rises from the abysses of these people's souls." When he finally got a medical discharge, after a complete physical collapse, Berg wrote an oddly beautiful chorus of snoring soldiers at the end of the second act of *Wozzeck*.

In 1917, Berg worked out his own libretto for the opera, following Büchner's work closely but compressing the two dozen scenes into fifteen, and occasionally amplifying or clarifying some of the poet's murkier passages. Schoenberg was not particularly sympathetic to his pupil's project, arguing that the original play was "of such extraordinary tragic power that it seemed forbidding to music," and that it "contained scenes of every-day life, at variance with the concept of opera." Or, as he once put it somewhat more bluntly, music should be concerned with angels rather than servants. Berg was not to be dissuaded. In the course of actually composing the opera, from 1918 to 1920, he devised an extraordinarily complex system to hold the various scenes together by means of the musical structure. The first act was to establish the various characters by a series of set pieces—a suite, rhapsody, march, passacaglia, and rondo. The second act was to develop the plot in the form of a five-movement symphony, and the third was to dramatize the catastrophe in a series of "inventions"—on a theme, on a note, on a rhythm, and so on. The entire work was to be sung in a narrative style that Berg called "rhythmic declamation," with each scene followed by an orchestral transition. This orchestration, which required 113 instruments, including xylophone, celesta, contrabass tuba, and two tam-tams, took Berg most of another year to finish. And when he had finished, he was proudly confident that he had created a masterpiece.

The trouble was that nobody would either produce or publish it. With the financial backing of Alma Mahler, the composer's widow, who was then married to Walter Gropius, Berg finally published the opera himself, thus creating a mountain of unsalable paper. "Do you know of anyone who would buy the score?" Berg wrote plaintively to a friend. "Perhaps on your recommendation . . . I'll never be able to persuade a publisher to pay for it, so I would like to sell a number of them for my own account." Berg also sent free copies to all the main German opera companies and music magazines, but the most notable response was a number of denunciations published by the more conservative critics. It was not until 1924, when the young Erich Kleiber was on a visit to Vienna, that Edward Steuermann played him a piano version of the opera, and Kleiber promptly declared: "It's settled. I am going to do the opera in Berlin, even if it costs me my job."

Kleiber kept his promise, but not without difficulty. Though Berlin might welcome new work, there were limits to what was acceptable at the State Opera. Singers protested at the difficulties of Berg's music, and various critics wrote attacks on the idea of staging such an "ultra-modern" opera. Kleiber demanded an extraordinary number of rehearsals—thirty-four for the orchestra and fourteen more for the full ensemble—and at the opening night on December 14, 1925, the audience reacted violently. "There were fist fights," said Hans Heinsheimer, who was there, "angry challenges shouted across the orchestra seats and from the boxes, deriding laughter, boos, and hostile whistles that threatened for some time to overpower the small but, at last, vigorous group of believers. As the tall, noble figure of the composer appeared before the curtain, the riots increased, the bravos and boos, the waves of enthusiastic excitement and outraged hostility. Berg seemed a little taken aback by it, perhaps a shade paler than usual, but quite unaffected, calm, very sure of his work."

"When I left the State Opera last night," said one of the hostile critics, Paul Zschorlich of the *Deutsche Zeitung*, "I felt that I was not leaving a public place, dedicated to the arts, but a public insane asylum. On the stage, in the orchestra, in the audience—only lunatics. The work of a Chinaman from Vienna . . . a deliberate swindle. Fragments, rags, sobs, belches. Tormenting, ugly-sounding cackle. A fountain-poisoner of German music . . . He is a musical mountebank, a composer dangerous to the public welfare." On the other hand, another critic named H. H. Stückenschmidt declared the exact opposite. "It is difficult," he said, "to do justice to the strange perfection and uniqueness of this work. . . . Berg [shows] evidence of genius."

"We didn't know, of course, what fate had in store for the opera and for us," Heinsheimer observed, ". . . but we knew, then and there, that we had been present at a historic event."

The funeral for Friedrich Ebert was very impressive. Bands played, politicians gave orations, thousands of workmen marched with black arm bands, and millions more suddenly realized that Germany was, to its bewilderment, leaderless.

The creators of the Weimar Constitution had thought, vaguely, that the President would be some national figure, above and beyond politics, but now there was no such figure to replace poor Fritz Ebert. Among the middle-of-the-road politicians of the so-called "Weimar Coalition," the best candidate appeared to be Ebert's old friend, Otto Gessler, the leader of the Democratic Party. He was a liberal, basically, but as a Defense Minister who had steadfastly defended the prerogatives of the army, he was thought to be accept-able to the right. The Nationalists, however, had more ambitious plans. They sabotaged Gessler by spreading rumors that he was having an affair with a Berlin lady of high position, and then, when Gessler's candidacy collapsed, every faction produced a candidate of its own.

The right put forward Karl Jarres, a former Interior Minister and Mayor of the Ruhr city of Duisburg; the moderates united behind Ex-Chancellor Wilhelm Marx; the Socialists nominated the head of the Prussian state government, Otto Braun; the Communists sup-ported their own leader, Ernst Thälmann; and the newly reviving Nazis offered General Ludendorff. The right-wing candidate, Karl Jarres, proved surprisingly strong, winning 10.4 million votes as against 7.8 million for the Socialists' Braun (Ludendorff collected only a pitiful 280,000), but the seven-man race ended in the predict-able stalemate. For the runoff, in which only a plurality was needed, the moderates and Socialists united behind Wilhelm Marx, and their combined votes looked strong enough to win. The conservatives, however, were not interested in going down to defeat with Dr. Jarres. Instead, they began hunting around for a stronger candidate, and they soon decided on an almost invincible name: Marshal Paul von Hindenburg.

The aged marshal was living in retirement in Hannover—his house a mausoleum of war relics, battle flags, a silver ax, bronze elks, and a large collection of pictures of the Madonna. Only occasionally did he venture out to go hunting for chamois in Bavaria, bringing home skulls and horns to be mounted on the walls of the mausoleum. But he was still the nation's greatest hero. Millions of Germans remembered not the defeats on the western front but the great victories of Tannenberg and the Masurian Lakes (which most experts credit to Ludendorff). Millions more remembered the gigantic wooden statue of Hindenburg that had stood, throughout the war, in the Königsplatz outside the Reichstag building; everyone who donated one mark to the Red Cross won the right to pound another nail into the monolithic figure.

He was an immense man, six feet five inches tall and well over two hundred pounds, and he overwhelmed everyone with his glittering blue eyes, his giant, curving mustache. But what the admiring masses failed to recognize was the craftiness of the man. They accepted his pose as a simple soldier—and he was, in many ways, simple—but soldiers do not become field marshals without a certain skill in claiming credit for other men's successes, and avoiding the blame for other men's defeats. Ludendorff's victories in the East became Hindenburg's victories, but Ludendorff's failures in the West remained his own. It was left to General Gröner to convince the Kaiser to abdicate; and to Matthias Erzberger to sign the armistice. In each case when somebody else had to accept a heavy responsibility, Hindenburg clutched the victim by the shoulder, and, with tears glistening in his eyes, offered his deepest sympathies.

The field marshal himself remained the father of his people. When, in 1919, the government held an official inquiry into the reasons for the loss of the war, Hindenburg came out of retirement, voyaged in a special train from Hannover to Berlin, waved paternally to the cheering crowds, and told the Commission of Inquiry that the army had been defeated only by the fact that revolutionaries at home had inflicted a "stab-in-the-back." It was the first public statement of this fraudulent judgment, which had actually been concocted by Ludendorff, but the commissioners never challenged it. "I doubt," the field marshal rumbled on, "whether you gentlemen have ever felt such a responsibility for the Fatherland as we were bound to bear, deep down in our hearts, for years."

It is easy to condemn Hindenburg as a pious hypocrite, but in every judgment of him, one must remember his awesome age. He was born in 1847, a full generation before a united Germany even existed. As a nineteen-year-old lieutenant, he had stormed an Austrian battery during the Battle of Königgrätz, then fought against the French at the Battle of St. Privat. He had grown old in the Kaiser's peacetime army of the nineteenth century, and he had retired before the World War even began. Old men inevitably acquire a certain craftiness, but, more important, they acquire a sense of indifference to the squabblings of this world. Peace and survival, those are the important things. And now, when a delegation of Nationalist politicians came to ask him to run for the presidency, Paul von Hindenburg was already seventy-seven years old, and suffering from a chest cough, and he answered them by saying that he wanted his rest: "*Ich will meine Ruhe haben.*"

The Nationalists refused to be denied. They had considered every other possibility—other generals, like Von Seeckt; various industrialists, like Fritz von Thyssen, regional politicians like the unfortunate Dr. Jarres—and they were convinced that Hindenburg was their man. Not only were they convinced that he would be invincible, but if he was also old and tired and sleepy—so much the better for them. They decided to send as their special emissary another venerable military hero, Grand Admiral Alfred von Tirpitz, the bearded mastermind of the wartime submarine campaign, who had advocated back in 1916 that the Kaiser give way to Hindenburg as military dictator. Now Tirpitz journeyed to Hannover, and, as one old soldier to another, insisted that Hindenburg accept the call of duty. It may be that there were elements of hypocrisy in both the offer and the acceptance, but perhaps we have become too cynical. The call of duty, as he understood it, was something that Hindenburg had tried to serve all his life, and once Tirpitz had convinced him that this meant the presidency, the Nationalists had captured their candidate.

The results were not totally inevitable, but nearly so. The moderates still hoped that their united support might carry Ex-Chancellor Marx to victory. The Nazis had abandoned the discredited General Ludendorff (to his indignation) and rushed to support Hindenburg. The Communists insisted on staying behind their own leader, Ernst Thälmann. The election day was cold and rainy, and as Count Kessler went to the polls in Berlin, he noted very few voters. "The drizzle kept the streets empty. On the Potsdamer Platz just a few swastika-carrying youths, with heavy cudgels, blonde and stupid as young bulls. . . . It poured incessantly. The people in the streets seemed indifferent. The lorries with [various] supporters drove noisily between the crowds taking their Sunday walk under umbrellas. Nobody, looking at the streets, would guess that a decision vital to Germany and Europe was in the course of being made. I have at any rate done my duty."

The result was that Hindenburg got 14.6 million votes, Marx 13.7, and Thälmann 1.9. It has been noted, with some indignation, that if even half the Communists had joined the other left-center parties in voting for Marx, Germany would never have seen the day on which Hindenburg appointed Adolf Hitler to the chancellorship, but the fact remains that, given a choice between a democratic political leader and a conservative military leader, the largest number of German voters supported Paul von Hindenburg.

And at first, the result seemed to bring certain benefits. "Today attended Hindenburg's swearing-in at the Reichstag," said Count Kessler, who had originally considered the electoral verdict "one of the darkest chapters in German history." Now he saw different results. "By eleven o'clock the galleries inside the Reichstag were full to overflowing. . . . The hall was pretty skimpily decorated. Just the black-red-gold presidential standard affixed to a wall-covering behind the Reichstag President's chair and a black-red-gold banner, flanked by blue hydrangeas, draped over the presidential table. . . .

"Hindenburg, standing on the spot where Rathenau's coffin had stood, swore the oath of office . . . and read a declaration from a piece of paper inscribed with such huge letters that it would have been possible, with the aid of an opera-glass, to read them from the gallery. The old gentleman nevertheless had some trouble in deciphering them. . . . The impression was of a somewhat self-conscious old general enunciating unaccustomed and incomprehensible material. The emphasis laid in the declaration on the constitution's *republican* and *democratic* character . . . was however stronger than expected. . . .

"A young diplomat with the Legation at Riga said to me, as we were leaving, 'We have witnessed the *birth* of the German Republic.' With Hindenburg it becomes respectable and so do its black-red-gold colors, which will now appear everywhere with him as his personal banner. Something of the veneration in which he is held will rub off on them and make it more difficult for the swastika-wavers to drag them down in the mud again. Today already they are much more prominent as part of the street decorations in the centre of the city than has been the case so far. . . . If the republicans do not abandon their vigilance and unity, Hindenburg's election may yet turn out even quite useful for the Republic and for peace."

"The Attack Begins on July 4" 1926

The receptivity of the masses is very limited, their intelligence is small, but their power of forgetting is enormous. In consequence of these facts, all effective propaganda must be limited to a few essential points. . . . These slogans must be repeated until every last member of the public understands what you want him to understand.

ADOLF HITLER

"THE NOVEMBER EVENING already hangs heavy and gray over Berlin as my train pulls into the Potsdamer station," Joseph Goebbels wrote. "Scarcely two hours pass, and then there I stand for the first time on the podium. . . . I address the Berlin party. . . ."

It was a lie—he did not address a party meeting until some time after his arrival, nor was this his first trip to Berlin—but he was a chronic liar. Or rather, he had such a passionate vision of himself as a heroic figure, and such an extraordinary ability to believe whatever he wanted to believe, that the distinction between truth and false-hood simply didn't occur to him. What he saw, when he wrote his memoir called *Battle for Berlin*, was the image of himself arriving, lonely and frightened, in the hostile city on a cold winter evening.

He was only twenty-nine years old, a tiny, hunched figure in a shiny suit and a felt hat, scarcely five feet tall and only one hundred pounds. And he limped badly from a childhood attack of infantile paralysis, which had made his left leg four inches shorter than his right. He carried one shabby suitcase, which contained a few clothes and an autographed copy of the first volume of Hitler's *Mein Kampf*. He had just been appointed by Hitler as the Gauleiter of Berlin.

189

Goebbels feared and disliked this new battlefield. "I hate Berlin," he had written in his diary at the start of that year. At another point, he described the capital as "a monster city of stone and asphalt." He considered it "a dark and mysterious enigma." He respected the Berliners for being "hard-working and vital," but he found that they had "more wit than humor," and that they tended—an odd judgment from such a judge—to "fanaticism" and "ruthlessness." Much of this he blamed on "those rootless international Jews," and particularly on the big newspapers of Ullstein and Mosse, which "spew . . . Jewish poison throughout the capital."

As Gauleiter (i.e., leader of the *Gau*, or district), Goebbels was supposed, somehow, to take command of this awesome metropolis, but the forces at his disposal soon proved to be a pitiful little band of malcontents. There were about a thousand of them, leaderless and in debt. "What people in Berlin called a party did not deserve that title in any way," Goebbels said. "It was a wildly confused crowd of several hundred people with national socialist views, each of whom had formed his own private idea of national socialism." And when Goebbels made his first inspection of party headquarters, he found it to be "a sort of dirty cellar in the back of a building on the Potsdamer Strasse. There lived a so-called business manager with a notebook, in which he daily wrote down the income and expenses as well as he knew. Piles of paper and old newspapers lay in the corners. In the anteroom, groups of unemployed party members sat around, smoking and telling dirty jokes. We called this headquarters the 'Opium Den.'"

Goebbels' first directive to his troops was brisk. "On this day," he began, "I am taking over the leadership of the Gau Berlin-Brandenburg. . . . It will be our first task to obtain a new Gau office. The new office will cost money. Punctual payment of dues is accordingly necessary. The Gau office is a place of work. . . . It must not be confused with a place to get warm or a waiting-room. Party comrades are admitted to the office only on party business. The Gau leader is available by appointment during office hours. Appointments to spread gossip or for similar reasons are useless."

The Nazis of Berlin, such as they were, had split into a number of factions. Some supported the regional party chief, Gregor Strasser, and some the leader of the SA (Storm Troopers), Kurt Daluege, and some the departing Gauleiter, a minor bureaucrat named Ernst von

Schlange. Goebbels called everyone together for a meeting in the western suburb of Spandau—"a sad picture," he said later, "with the conference hall half empty"—and told them that the past was finished, that a new day was beginning, and that anyone who didn't want to follow his leadership should leave now. About a third of the members soon drifted away, leaving Goebbels with barely six hundred stalwarts. And from these remnants, the twenty-nine-year-old Gauleiter demanded complete dedication. Since the Nazis were a revolutionary party determined to overthrow "international capitalism," he said, the members would have to finance it themselves, at the rate of three marks (about seventy-five cents) a month.

Was it Yeats who said somewhere, "If they knew we existed, they wouldn't allow it"? Goebbels, in retrospect, had somewhat the same feelings about the ignominious beginnings of his leadership in Berlin. "It was a favorable circumstance for us," he noted, "that we didn't have to anticipate, for the time being, any resistance from outside. We weren't known at all, and to the extent that people knew of our existence, they didn't take us seriously. . . . And that was good. For thus we won the time and the opportunity to put the movement on a healthy basis."

The young Gauleiter's road to Berlin had been tortuous. He was born into a fervently Catholic lower-class family in the town of Rheydt, in the Rhineland. His two grandfathers were a blacksmith and a carpenter, his father a foreman in a factory. His mother yearned to have him become a priest. Even apart from his deformity, which seems to have been caused by a surgical operation that attempted to remedy the paralysis of polio when he was four, Goebbels was a sickly child, thin-chested, with an abnormally large head on his spindly shoulders. Lonely, unpopular, he concentrated on his studies, graduated near the top of his high school class and won an interest-free loan for university studies from a Catholic organization called the Albertus Magnus Society (which had to go to court, years later, to get the famous Dr. Goebbels to repay the loan).

Like many students of those years, Goebbels wandered from one university to another—eight, in his case—ending at Heidelberg, where he studied literature under the celebrated Friedrich Gundolf, a Jew. Goebbels tried, through Gundolf, to gain access to the circle of students who gathered around the poet Stefan George, but Gundolf didn't like Goebbels, and the attempt failed. "I was a pariah," Goebbels complained later, "ostracised . . . not because I was less efficient or less clever than the others but only because I lacked the money which the others enjoyed so abundantly." He was also rejected by the army as physically unfit. The rejection humiliated him at the time and later made him feel deeply self-conscious among the burly ex-soldiers and Freikorps veterans of the Nazi movement. As usual, he tried to lie. Limping along between ranks of Storm Troopers during a parade through Berlin, he shouted: "We who were shot up during the war . . ."

He graduated from Heidelberg in 1921, determined to become a writer. He sent articles to the *Berliner Tageblatt*, but they were all rejected by the editor, Theodor Wolff, who, like Professor Gundolf, was a Jew. He also tried to get a job with the *Tageblatt* and was rejected again. One begins to see the paranoia forming. As early as 1920, after a quarrel with his first girl, Goebbels considered suicide and wrote a "last will and testament," which appointed his older brother as "literary executor" for his sheaves of unpublished poems and half-finished plays. A new girlfriend—Goebbels was, for obvious reasons, a lifelong philanderer—finally got him a job as a clerk in a bank in Cologne, which he hated. Then another friend found him a job on the Cologne stock exchange, calling out the prices of stocks and bonds. Here, too, one sees the origins of the paranoia. If there was one group that Goebbels hated as much as Jewish intellectuals, it was "the international capitalists."

Goebbels was, in a way, right. He was a writer of considerable talent (and an orator of brilliance), but his mistake was to consider himself a literary figure. His talent lay in the ability to invent advertising slogans, and in the expression of political hysteria. Even his literary efforts show that. In the year of his graduation, he wrote a novel called *Michael*, the diary of a heroic soldier, lover, and revolutionary, which was rejected by the great Jewish-owned publishing houses of Ullstein and Mosse and did not appear until 1929, under the auspices of a Nazi firm. The very first sentences, which are ludicrous in a novel, provide a prophetic example of the shrill prose style that was to make Goebbels a master of Nazi propaganda:

"No longer is the stallion neighing under my thighs; no longer am I hunched over a gun or tramping through the muddy clay of neglected trenches.

"How long it is since I walked the vast Russian plain or the shell-ridden French countryside!

"A thing of the past!

"Like a phoenix rising from the ashes of war and destruction.

"Peace!

"The very word is like balm on a wound still trembling and bleeding."

Michael, despite its peculiar style, is in many ways the standard first novel. The hero returns from the war and goes to a university and meets a girl. They have long talks about the meaning of life. He meets another student who introduces him to the works of Dostoyevsky. He resolves to write about Christ (Goebbels himself wrote a play in verse about Christ, entitled *The Wanderer*). At the end, he dies, young and tragic.

One reads the novel now only to hunt for truffles among the roots of Nazism. One inevitably finds a ferocious tirade (perhaps inserted later) against those who had rejected the young author: "Jews make me physically sick; the mere sight of them does this. I cannot even hate the Jew. I can merely despise him. He has raped our people, soiled our ideals, weakened the strength of the nation, corrupted morals. He is the poisonous eczema on the body of our sick nation. That has nothing to do with religion. Either he destroys us or we destroy him."

Somewhat more unusual is the scene in which Michael goes to hear a speech by an unnamed political orator. This, then, is presumably Goebbels' account of the first time he ever heard Adolf Hitler:

"I sit in a hall I have never been in before. Among utter strangers. Poor and threadbare people most of them . . . I hardly notice how the man up there begins to speak, slowly, hesitatingly at first.

"But then, all of a sudden, the flow of his speech is unleashed. It's like a light shining above him. I listen. I am captivated. Honor! Work! The flag! Are there still such things in this people from whom God has taken his blessing hand?

"The audience is aglow. Hope shines on gray faces. Someone clenches his fist. . . .

"And the man up there speaks on, and whatever was budding in me falls into shape.

"A miracle!

"Among the ruins is someone who shows us the flag.

"Those around me are no longer strangers. They are brothers.

"I go up to the rostrum and look in the man's face.

"No orator he! A prophet!

"Sweat is pouring down him. A pair of eyes glow in the pale face. His fists are clenched.

"And like the Last Judgment word after word is thundering on, and phrase after phrase.

"I know not what I do. I seem demented.

"I shout 'Hurrah.' And no one seems astonished.

"He on the rostrum glances at me for a moment. Those blue eyes sear me like a flame. That is an order!

"I feel as if I were newly born.

"I know now whither my path leads me."

We who remember the Hitler years may all have been brainwashed by wartime propaganda, but it is still difficult to imagine the effect that Hitler's oratory had on his listeners. Recordings of those speeches confirm one's recollections: Hitler's voice was coarse, shrill, hysterical, basically repulsive, and the content of his speeches was nothing but rhetoric, a sequence of slogans about "struggle" and "rebirth" and "Fatherland."

They reflected the man himself. We know now that he was a monster, half-insane, but we also know now that he was the most unimpressive of men. He was short, ugly, slightly flabby. We see him always with that ludicrous little mustache of the Austrian civil servant, and if we try to imagine the face without the mustache, we see nothing at all. He was grossly uneducated, unable even to speak or write German without the errors of illiteracy, and so untalented in his chosen field of art that he could not pass the rudimentary exams for entrance into art school. Above all, he was essentially boring, not only in that he had no ideas worth hearing but in that his whole concept of the good life consisted of sitting around the lunch table, eating sweet pastries and conducting monologues on his war experiences or the loyalty of dogs. In the evenings—and, as Albert Speer has informed us, this remained true even after he came to power—he liked nothing better than to watch movie operettas, often two at a time, and then, when the screening was over, to resume his monologue about his war experiences and the loyalty of dogs.

As a political leader, he was not only ignorant and lazy but strangely indecisive. He was a thoroughly frightened man, frightened of every occasion for action, frightened of the quarrels among his associates, frightened, even, perhaps, of what he saw inside himself. And yet, like many frightened men, he had an immense cunning, an immense talent for letting his stronger enemies destroy themselves through their own mistakes, an immense, intuitive skill at waiting for a situation to ripen, waiting for the precise moment when something *must* be done, and then, right or wrong, plunging ahead. It was this capacity for last-minute decisions, and his vehement insistence that every such decision was inevitable, incontestable, or, as he liked to say, "historic," that somehow convinced people that he, Adolf Hitler, knew and possessed the path to the future.

Perhaps there was something in the eyes that we cannot see in photographs, something in the voice that we do not hear in the old recordings, something that persuaded people to regard him as a hero. Not everyone was so impressed, of course. President Hindenburg, for example, loathed the little man on sight, and Kurt Tucholsky said there was no point even in criticizing the Nazis, because "Satire . . . has a lower limit. In Germany it is the fascist forces. It doesn't pay—you can't shoot that low." But there were others who were deeply moved, particularly women and young people. Frau Hélène Bechstein, for instance, the wife of the piano manufacturer, offered Hitler a home in her Berlin apartment, donated money to his cause, held his head on her lap and called him her "little wolf." Winifred Wagner, the daughter-in-law of the composer, welcomed him with equal warmth to the shrine at Bayreuth and apparently had hopes of becoming his wife. And the youthful crowds that gathered whenever the Führer spoke seemed to feel, as Goebbels indicated, that they had found a Messiah.

It is not clear whether Goebbels really did hear Hitler as early as 1922—that whole scene in *Michael* may also have been inserted later—but a friend in the Nazi movement began taking him to meetings during the winter of 1923–24. Toward the end of 1924, Goebbels approached the Nazi Gauleiter of the Rhine-Ruhr district, Karl Kaufmann, and asked for a job. Kaufmann discussed the case with his superior, Gregor Strasser, and Strasser was interested. And so began a relationship that was to end, ten years later, with Geobbels in the seat of power and Strasser bleeding to death in a prison cell. Strasser was a burly man, not very intelligent but a skilled organizer and leader. He had started as a druggist in a suburb of Munich; after falling under the spell of Hitler, he sold his drugstore and dedicated both his money and his energy to the fledgling movement.

When Hitler emerged from prison at the end of 1924, he had to start organizing his shattered party all over again. He assigned Strasser, who had also served a prison term for his part in the Munich Putsch, to lead the party in northern Germany, where Hitler himself was forbidden to appear. Strasser took charge with great fervor. He wanted, among other things, to start a weekly Nazi paper, to be edited by his brother Otto, and the Strassers thought they might use the young Goebbels as a secretary and assistant.

The applicant appeared for his interview with Otto Strasser in a threadbare gray suit, and, despite the winter cold, no overcoat, but he spoke with manic enthusiasm. "We are going to win the German working man for National Socialism," he said. "We are going to destroy Marxism! As for the bourgeois refuse, we shall sweep that away into the dustbin!" Otto Strasser was impressed. His brother's previous assistant, a peculiar Bavarian poultry farmer named Heinrich Himmler, had proved so inefficient that he had to be fired. In the gaunt young man with the soulful voice and the glowing brown eyes, Strasser thought he had found an admirable replacement, at $65 a month.

For the better part of a year, Goebbels served as the devoted lieutenant of the Strasser brothers, not Hitler. He was tireless. He made innumerable speeches, and wrote innumerable articles for the Strassers' *Berliner Arbeiter Zeitung* (*Berlin Worker Newspaper*), all attacking "the system" of the Weimar Republic. And he worried about himself. On his twenty-eighth birthday, he wrote in his diary: "I'm getting old. It makes me shudder to notice it. My hair is beginning to fall out. On the way to getting bald. But in my heart I want to remain young for ever and ever." And he worshiped his boss. "Strasser is quite a man!" he wrote. "What a wonderful Bavarian type he is. I am very fond of him."

Despite the Strassers' energetic organizing, there was a basic contradiction in the very name of the National Socialist Party. To the conservatives, particularly at Hitler's headquarters in Munich, the party's mission was to fight against Communism. To the left-wingers, notably the Strassers and Goebbels, who had to do their recruiting among the factory workers of northern Germany, Nazism was a genuine Socialist movement, dedicated to attacking monopoly capitalism. "I am the most radical," Goebbels wrote, but only in his private diary. "Almost the new type. Man as revolutionary." And again: "In the last analysis better go down with Bolshevism than live in eternal capitalist servitude."

The confrontation between the two wings of the party came early in 1926, over a now-forgotten issue that was then dividing all of Germany: Should the former royal families of the various states surrender their lands to the government, and, if so, should they be paid for them? The general feeling among the working classes of the north was that the estates belonged to the people, but Hitler, who was then receiving most of his personal income as a dole of $400 a month from the Duchess of Sachsen-Anhalt, sided with the royal families. Gregor Strasser called his northern Gauleiters together at a conference in Hannover, where everyone supported his views. And when the small delegation from Munich argued feebly that Hitler's views should be made a matter of party loyalty, Joseph Goebbels rose to his feet and shouted: "In these circumstances I demand that the petty bourgeois Adolf Hitler be expelled from the National Socialist Party." (Or so say the standard histories. The provable facts are less certain. Goebbels himself never mentioned such a statement in his diaries, and some of his biographers attribute the astonishing outburst to another one of Strasser's protégés.)

Hitler, threatened with a north-south split within his party, called a rival conference in the Bavarian city of Bamberg. He convoked the meeting on a weekday, which made it difficult for the penniless Gauleiters of the north to travel such a distance, and, in fact, only Gregor Strasser and Goebbels were able to make the trip. Outnumbered in the day-long debate, which ranged over every aspect of Nazi policy, the forces of the Socialist north gave in. Goebbels, it is said, got up once again and announced that he and Strasser had been wrong, and that everyone should unite behind Hitler. (This, at least, is the embittered Otto Strasser's version of the affair, though, once again, accounts vary. Goebbels himself makes no mention of such a confession, but his diary gives a somewhat more plausible account of silent cowardice under pressure: "Hitler speaks for two hours. I am almost beaten. What kind of Hitler? A reactionary?

Amazingly clumsy and uncertain . . . [He says] it is our job to smash Bolshevism. Bolshevism is a Jewish creation . . . ! Strasser speaks. Hesitant, trembling, clumsy, good honest Strasser; Lord, what a poor match we are for those pigs down there . . . ! I cannot say a word! I am stunned. By car to the station. Strasser is quite beside himself! Waving and *heil*. My heart aches . . . ! I can no longer believe in Hitler absolutely. That is terrible: I have lost my inner support. I am only half myself.")

Hitler must have realized that the need for hero worship was essential to Goebbels, and so, while he offered Gregor Strasser only material profits for remaining loyal—"Listen, Strasser," he said, "you really mustn't go on living like a wretched official. . . . Draw on the party funds and set yourself up as a man of your worth should"— he offered Goebbels something far more precious, himself. He knew that Goebbels had seen and despised Strasser's weakness in the crisis, and now he invited the little cripple to bask among the victors. He even presented him with red roses. Goebbels' diaries show the results: "*April 13* [1926] . . . Hitler . . . speaks for three hours. Brilliant . . . We are moving closer. We ask. He gives brilliant replies. I love him. . . . I am reassured all round. . . . He is a man. With his sparkling mind he can be my leader. I bow to his greatness, his political genius . . . ! *April 19* . . . Hitler sees me and embraces me. I believe he has taken me to his heart like no one else. . . . Sunday . . . we celebrate Hitler's birthday. He is thirty-seven. . . . Adolf Hitler, I love you, because you are both great and simple. A genius . . . *June 16* . . . Hitler is the same dear comrade. You cannot help liking him as a man. And on top of it that overriding mind . . . *July 12* . . . I am looking out of the window of a wonderful guest-house in Berchtesgaden [Hitler's retreat in the Alps]. . . . It is almost miraculous . . . ! *July 23* . . . Hurray! The chief has arrived. . . . We meet like friends. Then he begins to talk. . . . Yes, you can serve under this man. The creator of the Third Reich . . . And now to bed! Surrounded by friends and pleasures! Bliss! *July 24* . . . The chief talks about race questions. It is impossible to reproduce what he said. It must be experienced. He is a genius. The natural, creative instrument of a fate determined by God. I am deeply moved. He is like a child: kind, good, merciful. Like a cat: cunning, clever, agile. Like a lion: roaring and great and gigantic. A fellow, a man . . . Up in the skies a white cloud takes on the shape of a swastika. There is a blinking light that cannot be a star. A sign of fate? *July 25* . . . [Hitler] spoils me like a child. The kind friend and master! . . . These days have signposted my road. A star shines leading me from deep misery! I am his to the end. My last doubts have disappeared. Germany will live! *Heil Hitler!*"

Hitler no longer trusted the Strasser brothers. He thought, not without reason, that they wanted to take over the party. As for the Strassers, they were somewhat less than pleased about the defection of their protégé. Goebbels, having had his vision on the road to Damascus, complained bitterly in his diary that the Strassers were accusing him of exactly that. "The latest story: in the eyes of the movement I have met my Damascus. . . . I have already called them [the Strassers] to account . . . in personal letters. . . . I shall teach that gang how to behave." To counter the ambitions of the Strassers, Hitler obviously needed a new man in Berlin, someone intensely loyal to him, someone who, as he later said, "possesses the two attributes without which no one could master the conditions in Berlin: intelligence and the gift of oratory." Someone, in fact, like Joseph Goebbels.

Shortly after the seduction in the mountains, Hitler indicated that he wanted Goebbels to become the Gauleiter in Berlin. Goebbels, just beginning to enjoy the pleasures of the Führer's favor, was dismayed at the prospect of having to move to "that stony desert" and to fight the Strassers on their own territory. "Sent a semi-refusal to Munich regarding Berlin," he noted on August 28. "I do not want to kneel in muck." The diary does not disclose what happened next, but Hitler eventually had his way, for Goebbels noted six weeks later: "On Nov. 1 I really go to Berlin. . . . After all, Berlin is the center. For us, too." And two weeks later: "Letter from Hitler there, Berlin signed and sealed. Hurray!"

"Berlin needs its sensations," Goebbels wrote, "as a fish needs water." It was true, as it is true of every metropolis. And in the year of the young Gauleiter's arrival in Babylon, one of the greatest sensations was the singing and dancing of a young Negro girl from St. Louis.

Josephine Baker had already become a star in Paris, where she delighted the audiences at the Folies Bergère by swirling through the Charleston in nothing but a ring of bananas around her waist.

She lives in France to this day, a heavy and angry woman in her sixties, trying to maintain a home for some two dozen orphans, but she was once a figure of carefree exoticism, and in old recordings of songs like "Madiana" and *La Petite Tonkinoise*," we can still hear a voice of both sensuality and immense charm. The jaded nightclub audiences of Berlin knew next to nothing about Negroes. They considered them strange, primitive, barbaric, and therefore fascinating. But they loved the new music called jazz, which they pronounced "Yats," and so Josephine Baker became a phenomenon, after which, according to one survivor, "the women of Berlin were never the same again."

Count Kessler was, as always, part of the festivities. One evening, after he had bade farewell to his guests at a dinner party, he received a telephone call at one in the morning from Max Reinhardt, the theatrical producer. "Josephine Baker was there and the fun was starting." Kessler drove to an apartment on the Pariser Platz and found a party in full flight. The men were in evening dress, and the girls were naked. "Miss Baker was also naked except for a pink muslin apron," he noted afterward, "and the little Landshoff girl . . . was dressed up as a boy in a dinner-jacket. Miss Baker was dancing a solo with brilliant artistic mimicry and purity of style, like an ancient Egyptian or other archaic figure performing an intricate series of movements without ever losing the basic pattern. This is how their dancers must have danced for Solomon and Tutankhamen. Apparently she does this for hours on end, without tiring and continually inventing new figures like a child, a happy child, at play. She never even gets hot, her skin remains fresh, cool, dry. A bewitching creature, but quite unerotic. Watching her inspires as little sexual excitement as does the sight of a beautiful beast of prey. The naked girls lay or skipped about among the four or five men in dinner-jackets. The Landshoff girl, really looking like a dazzlingly handsome boy, jazzed with Miss Baker to gramophone tunes. . . .

"By this time Miss Baker and the Landshoff girl were lying in each other's arms, like a rosy pair of lovers, between us males who stood around. I said I would write a dumb show for them on the theme of the *Song of Solomon*, with Miss Baker as the Shulamite and the Landshoff girl as Solomon or the Shulamite's young lover. Miss Baker would be dressed (or not dressed) on the lines of Oriental Antiquity while Solomon would be in a dinner-jacket, the whole thing an entirely arbitrary fantasy of ancient and modern set to music, half jazz and half Oriental, to be composed perhaps by Richard Strauss.

"Reinhardt was enchanted with the idea. . . . We fixed on the twenty-fourth of this month for dinner at my apartment to discuss the matter. . . ."

Once Dr. Goebbels had his little party reorganized, he decided it was time to attack. The days of hiding in obscurity were over; now he wanted publicity. "The Berliners may insult us, slander us, fight us, beat us up," he said to a party meeting, "but they must talk about us." And again: "Whoever can conquer the streets can conquer the masses, and whoever conquers the masses thereby conquers the state."

Goebbels announced as his target "the Marxists," by which he meant both the Social Democrats and the Communists, both the Weimar system and its chief critics—in short, everyone who claimed the support of the working people of Berlin.

The gigantic Socialist organization generally ignored the newcomer, which was just as well, since Goebbels preferred to concentrate on the Communists, and the Communists alone were a Goliath. In the previous year's presidential campaign, they had polled nearly two million votes, as against 280,000 for the Nazis, and in the streets of "Red Berlin" the ratio stood even more strongly in favor of the uniformed Red Front Fighters League. Like a half-sleeping dragon, the Communists took note, two months after Goebbels' arrival in Berlin, that a small but annoying enemy had appeared in their midst. The next time Goebbels called a meeting in his suburban citadel of Spandau, the Communists sent agitators to heckle him, and, for good measure, they beat up several of the Nazis on their way home from the meeting.

"Now we had two possibilities," said Goebbels, "either to give up, and thus to lose forever the party's political appeal to the proletariat, or to strike out with renewed and redoubled force . . . to challenge Marxism to a showdown." Goebbels promptly ordered a new series of blood-red posters pasted up on billboards all over Berlin. "The bourgeois state is coming to an end," the posters said. "A new Germany must be forged." The posters invited the poor and the discontented to come to the Pharus Hall, in the North Berlin district of

Wedding, to hear Goebbels speak on "the breakdown of the bourgeois class state."

In all of Berlin, there was no area more solidly Communist than Wedding, a bleak jumble of brown stucco tenements, and in all of Wedding there was no single building more totally identified with Communism than the Pharus Hall. It was a shabby little place on the Müllerstrasse, next to a beer hall, but for the Communists, it was practically a party headquarters. They held their meetings there every week. So Goebbels, in effect, was leading his little band, waving their swastika flags, on an invasion to the very heart of enemy territory. "This was indeed a provocation," Goebbels wrote happily, "such as nobody had ever before seen in Berlin. . . . It was the start of open warfare. So meant by us and so understood by the opposition."

The Communists were quite ready for the invasion. "At about eight o'clock," Goebbels wrote, "we drove in an old, rickety car from our headquarters to Wedding. A cold, gray fog filled the sky. . . . As soon as we got to the Müllerstrasse, we knew that this evening would not bring good things. On every streetcorner, groups of ominous figures were lounging around. . . . In front of the Pharus Hall stood dark masses of people shouting loud and insolent threats. The SS leader forced his way through to us and informed us that the hall had been barricaded by the police since quarter past seven and was now two-thirds filled by Red Front Fighters. That was exactly what we wanted. Here the showdown must come. One way or the other . . .

"At the doorway of the hall, we were struck by the hot, stifling atmosphere of beer and tobacco. The air was hot enough to explode. A crazy, babbling uproar filled the room. People were sitting all over the place, and it was difficult to force one's way through to the podium. As soon as I was recognized, I was threatened by a howl of rage and vengeance from several hundred voices. 'Bloodhound!' 'Murderer of the workers!' Those were the mildest curses that people shouted after me. . . . The SA leader [Kurt Daluege] stood tall as a tree in front of the podium and raised his arm to ask for silence. . . . Scornful laughter was the answer. Insults flew from every corner of the room toward the podium. . . .

"When the chairman [Daluege] announced the opening of the meeting, a dark individual got up on a chair and shouted, 'The meeting will come to order!' And hundreds of voices immediately took up the cry. . . . When every move I made to call the meeting to order proved unsuccessful, I called the SS leader to my side, and his men immediately started marching into the Communist crowd. . . . They dragged the agitator off his chair. . . . Then a beer glass flew through the air and smashed to bits on the floor. That was the signal for our first big brawl. Chairs were smashed apart, legs were torn off tables, batteries of glasses and bottles were quickly lined up as weapons, and then it started. For ten minutes the battle raged to and fro. Glasses, bottles and table legs flew through the air. There was a deafening uproar."

According to Goebbels' account, which may be greatly exaggerated, the SA men gave way—"It seemed at first that we were all lost"—but then boldly counterattacked and drove the Communists from the hall. In actual fact, the police, who had surrounded the hall before the meeting even began, intervened to restore some semblance of order. Goebbels thus emerged, through no particular heroism of his own, victorious. The hall was by now a shambles of splintered furniture and shattered glass. The Gauleiter was euphoric. He had ten of the injured Nazis carried to the podium, where they lay groaning in pools of blood while he delivered an impassioned oration to the survivors of the battle. Pointing to the casualties on the stage, he spoke of the heroism of "the unknown SA man" and vowed vengeance against "the Red mob." (He was so pleased with this dramatic effect, in fact, that he subsequently took to having perfectly healthy SA men swathed in bandages so that they could be displayed on stretchers at party meetings.)

The next day brought Goebbels all the headlines he wanted. He, Goebbels, had challenged the enemy on its own territory. He, Goebbels, had begun the battle for the streets of Berlin. "Making noise," he said, "is an effective means of opposition." And when one of the more partisan newspapers referred to him as a bandit, Goebbels cheerfully put up new posters announcing new meetings and referring to himself as "the chief bandit."

"Sure, I used to fight in those days," says Peter Wallenberg. He is a short, stout man, just past sixty, with bright blue eyes and a fringe of white hair. For the past fifteen years, he has been the United Nations correspondent for the New York *Daily News*, but now he is tired of it, so he is moving to Florida, and in his little house on Long Island, there is an atmosphere of things being rooted up. In the living room, there are several shelves of toy animals and other bric-a-brac that he is hoping to sell. All this is part of his past. His father was one of the Ullsteins' chief executives, editor of the *Berliner Zeitung am Mittag* and also of an afternoon tabloid called *Tempo*. Wallenberg was fourteen when he joined the youth group of the Socialist Reichsbanner "without the approval, or even the knowledge, of my parents."

"It was very glamorous," he says. "You got an arm band with the colors of the Republic—black, red, and gold. You got a blue uniform, and a blue cap, and those—what do you call them? You know, those bands that cross over your chest, like the people who direct the traffic outside the schools here."

"Who paid for all that?" one asks.

"Well, you had to pay for it yourself," Wallenberg says, "but it wasn't much. So I—well, I took some books from my father's library—he had a lot of books—and I sold them to get the money. And then you not only got the uniform but also what they used to call a *Gummiknüppel*, which was a sort of nightstick, about so long, a foot long. Some of our people had brass knuckles too, and even guns, but I never had a gun, just the *Gummiknüppel*. Of course, all these weapons were illegal, but you could get them at headquarters without too much trouble. The uniforms you bought openly, and the weapons under the counter, and then you'd carry them like this— inside your shirt."

"How much ideology was there in all this marching?"

"Not very much, really, but I felt that we were right, and everybody else was wrong. I mean, the other youth groups, the Nazis and the Communists, were organized in pretty much the same way, but the big difference was that we were on the side of the government. We were the good guys."

"So then what happened? How did the fights start?"

"Well, we'd start on our marches, any time there was a holiday or anything like that, and I used to cut school to join in. We'd start outside the *Vorwärts* newspaper offices, near the Hallesche Tor, and then we'd start out for—well, different places—the Lustgarten or Unter den Linden or some other place. And pretty soon, at some intersection, the Communist youth groups would join in and start marching along next to us, and then the Nazis would join in too, so we'd all be marching along. We'd be in the middle of the street, and the Communists on the left side of us and the Nazis on the right side of us. Sooner or later, one of them would say something, some insult, and then you'd have to answer back, and then the fighting started, and the police would try to break it up."

"Did anybody ever get killed?"

"I never saw anybody killed—that came later—but there were plenty of bloody noses, that kind of thing. But there were lots of us on the side of the Republic in those days, so we could—you know —take care of ourselves pretty well."

On the higher levels of political power in Berlin, the election of President Hindenburg had brought a number of subtle changes. Although the field marshal scrupulously adhered to the republican Constitution he had sworn to uphold, everyone knew that he was a conservative and a monarchist, and so the still-unfinished process of liberalizing the civil service, the judiciary, and the educational system came to a halt. The apparatus of the Imperial regime, which had quietly resisted change during seven years of Friedrich Ebert's rule, now settled back into the old ways.

Even more significant, the old question of the army's loyalty simply vanished. The army now was loyal to Hindenburg. And because of that, General Hans von Seeckt, who had once said, "The army stands behind me," became politically obsolete. He was unnecessary, and therefore expendable.

The crisis came in the fall of 1926, when word leaked to the press that Seeckt had approved the idea of the Kaiser's eldest grandson taking part in the army's annual maneuvers. It seems, in retrospect, like a trivial subject for controversy, but there was considerable speculation in the Berlin press about the army plotting to restore the Hohenzollerns to the throne. And Seeckt had made all the mistakes of the proud. He had failed to inform his civilian superior, Defense Minister Otto Gessler, of the step. He had also failed to realize that one of his ambitious subordinates—namely, Colonel Kurt von Schleicher—might overthrow him by leaking just such a story to the press. And finally, he had failed to foresee that an uproar in the press—mere scribblers, mere civilians—might lead to his own ruin. His reaction was one of surprise, then bewilderment, then dismay, then anger. Then he resigned.

Despite his love of power and his awe of physical force, and despite his considerable personal courage in leading the Storm Troopers into enemy territory, Joseph Goebbels was not by nature a street fighter. ("My foot troubles me badly," he noted in his diary. "I am conscious of it all the time.") He wanted to dominate the crowds by his oratory, by his mind and his personal authority.

Like many Germans, baffled by the collapse of the Imperial Army in 1918, he attributed the loss of the war partly to British propaganda—to those impressive legends of Belgian children having their hands cut off, and to the repeated promises that the Germans would not be punished if they laid down their arms. "The most modern of all political methods is propaganda," Goebbels wrote. "It is also basically the most dangerous weapon that a political movement can put to use. Against all other methods, there is a counter-method; only propaganda becomes, as it works, unstoppable."

Propaganda, to Goebbels, had little to do with ideology, much less with truth. "The propaganda which produces the desired results is good and all other propaganda is bad," he said. "Therefore, it is beside the point to say your propaganda is too crude, too mean, too brutal, or too unfair, for all this does not matter. . . . Propaganda is always a means to an end." Propaganda was thus a matter of technical skill, and the first skill that Goebbels insisted on was that of oratory. "Did [Jesus Christ] write books or did he preach? And what about Mohammed? Did he write sophisticated essays or did he go out to the people and tell them what he wanted . . . ? Look at our own century. Was Mussolini a scribbler or was he a great speaker? When Lenin went from Zurich to St. Petersburg, did he rush from the station into his study to write a book or did he speak before a multitude?"

Whatever the theoretical merits of this argument—for it might be said that Lenin's writing was more influential than his speaking, or indeed that Karl Marx never spoke at all—it provided the basis for Goebbels' almost intuitive grasp of a technological revolution that was just beginning. Today, we take it for granted that no politician can achieve national importance without a mastery of television; in the thirties and forties, it was radio that contributed substantially to the power of Roosevelt, Churchill, and Hitler; in the twenties, radio was still a largely unknown force—the first radio station in Berlin opened only in 1923. But Goebbels understood its power. "Radio! Radio!" he noted in his diary. "Radio in the house!

The German with his radio will forget about his occupation and his Fatherland! Radio!"

Before the Nazis could master the techniques of radio, however, they had to master the techniques of oratory, and Goebbels himself trained like a prizefighter for his speeches. He had—as though nature were compensating for the curse of deformity—an exceptionally powerful and resonant voice. He wrote out every important speech, marking the manuscript with various colored pencils to indicate different kinds of tone and emphasis. Then he practiced in front of a large, three-sided mirror in the living room of the apartment where he stayed. He even rehearsed his gestures—the hand on the hip, or both arms rising.

When he was ready to speak, finally, he turned each appearance into a theatrical event. There were parades beforehand, and bands played marches. Goebbels himself often arrived late, limping to the podium in the midst of an honor guard of Storm Troopers. After one of his very first meetings, when Otto Strasser criticized him both for keeping people waiting and for the extravagance of using a taxi, Goebbels retorted: "You don't know much about propaganda. Taxi be damned. I should have taken two, not one. The other for my briefcase. Don't forget, you've got to impress people. And as for being late, I did that deliberately. I always do. You've got to keep them in suspense."

Goebbels' only superior as an orator was Hitler, but Hitler was banned from making public speeches anywhere in Prussia. To circumvent the ban, Goebbels rented a large Berlin dance hall named the Clou for a "private" meeting of the party. The Social Democratic municipal authorities, finally going into action against Goebbels' persistent provocations, responded four days later by outlawing the Nazi Party throughout Greater Berlin. "We National Socialists refuse to accept the ban," Goebbels cried. He turned the Storm Troopers into a series of sports clubs—the Good Wood Bowling Club, the Good Wet Swimming Club, and, as he put it, "similar fantastic enterprises"—and if they could not wear their brown shirts, then they would all appear in white. The Prussian authorities consequently forbade Goebbels to address any public meeting of any kind. Goebbels tried to evade that by getting up at various public meetings and asking long "questions." On each occasion, the police summoned him to the central courts in Moabit and had him fined.

Goebbels decided that he could fight back only by starting his own newspaper. "I remember vividly to this day how we sat around together, brooding about a name for the paper. Suddenly, I had an inspiration: There could be only one name for our paper: *Der Angriff* [*The Attack*]. The name would be effective as propaganda, and it covered everything we wanted and aimed for. . . . Our goal was not to inform but to goad, to inflame, to drive forward."

Once again, Goebbels sent his Storm Troopers out with posters and glue. The first announcement, in bright red, said only:

The Attack

?

A second series of posters announced: "The attack begins on July 4." Only with a third series of posters did the baffled Berliners learn that the attack was to be a weekly event staged by Dr. Goebbels. "Why attack?" he demanded in the first issue of his paper. He answered by denouncing all rival parties, who "make money out of the funeral of our nation. . . . Away with these lamentable organizations and men. . . . Put the German future into German hands!"

Goebbels' first target was Dr. Bernhard Weiss, Berlin's deputy police commissioner, whom Goebbels blamed for the "persecution" of the Nazis. Weiss was a very respectable democrat, but in the surviving photographs of the victim, with his horn-rimmed glasses, his little mustache, and his starched wing collar, we also see the face of bureaucracy incarnate. Weiss was a Jew—of course, that was why Goebbels singled him out—and so *Der Angriff* invariably referred to him as "Isidor," which the Germans apparently consider an insulting name for Jews. Goebbels made up endless stories about the police official; he accused him of associating with loose women; he published cartoons showing him with horns sprouting from his forehead, or as the toga-clad Nero of decadent Berlin. Only much later did he admit that it had all been a game. "How grand it was," he said, "to transform Isidor . . . into the most brutal bailiff of the Weimar Republic . . . [when he] was actually only a harmless fool."

Goebbels was simply using Dr. Weiss, of course, as a symbol of "the system." He was no less impudent in his attacks on more important figures. He described Foreign Minister Gustav Stresemann, for instance, as "a bit corpulent, a bit yellow, a bit artful, with an intolerable provocative smile on his lips, with his small cunning eyes carefully bedded in a cushion of fat." As for the system itself,

Goebbels sounded as though he were trying to become a modern Savanarola: "Who once made Germany the proudest and happiest country of the world? Who sacrificed two million of our best far away on the battle fields? Who fought and starved and suffered during the war? It was us Germans. . . . Who has besmirched [our] honor and . . . stolen our money? Who owns our mines and railways today? Who has made a profit out of our misery while we starved and suffered? It was our enemies, Jews and serfs of Jews."

Despite the thunderous tone, it is worth remembering that *Der Angriff*, like Goebbels himself, was not much more than a tiny nuisance in the great metropolis of Berlin. The Nazi Party was now banned and generally ignored. There were four million people in the city, and the powerful dailies of Ullstein and Mosse sold hundreds of thousands of copies; *Der Angriff* had a weekly circulation of only two thousand, and those few readers came from the little knots of the converted. Even Otto Strasser's *Berliner Arbeiter Zeitung* was considerably larger, as was the main Nazi organ in Munich, *Der Völkischer Beobachter*, but Goebbels was determined to keep his debt-ridden paper going. He raged against the ban, against the "tactics of silence" that were withering his movement. He demanded that his Storm Troopers sell subscriptions, and paste up announcements, and hound shopkeepers for advertising, and slowly *Der Angriff* began to grow (it finally started making money in 1929). And like all revolutionaries, Goebbels paid special attention to the destruction of his closest rivals. The Storm Troopers not only worked for *Der Angriff* but worked against Strasser's *Arbeiter Zeitung*.

"One morning in the spring of 1928," Otto Strasser recalled later. "I was at work in my enormous study . . . when Hitler burst in unannounced. . . .

" 'This can't go on [Hitler said]. . . . Your incessant quarrels with my people . . .'

" 'Quite so [Strasser said]. But you should tell that to Goebbels. He came here after I did, and he founded his paper after mine. I am within my rights.'

"Hitler gave a dry little laugh.

" 'It's not a question of right but of might. What will you do when ten of Herr Goebbels' Storm Troopers attack you in your office?'

"I slowly took my big revolver from my drawer and placed it beside me.

" 'I have eight shots, Herr Hitler. That will be eight Storm Troopers less.'

"Hitler stiffened.

" 'I know you are mad enough to shoot,' he barked. 'But nevertheless you can't kill my Storm Troopers.'

" 'Yours or Herr Goebbels'? If they are yours, I advise you not to send them. If they are Herr Goebbels', it's up to you to stop them from coming. As for me, I shall shoot anyone who attacks me.'

" 'Otto,' said Hitler suddenly, for the first and last time calling me by my Christian name, 'be reasonable. Think it over for your brother's sake.' He had seized my hands. I remained unmoved. The tearful eyes, the trembling voice, the whole studied performance was wasted on me.

" 'You think it over, Herr Hitler. I'll do the same.' "

Goebbels was not the only prophet haranguing the people of Berlin, nor was he by any means the most unusual. In the same year that the new Gauleiter arrived in the capital, there also appeared a seventy-one-year-old faith healer and hypnotist named Weissenberg. A short, fat figure with a white beard, who regularly wore a blue suit and a peaked cap, Weissenberg had been a shepherd, a coach driver, and an innkeeper. He had undertaken the last of these professions, he said, "because Jesus Christ ordered it." Now he set up headquarters on the Gleimstrasse in the slums of northern Berlin and established what he called "The Evangelical Church of the Manifestation of St. John." He held meetings in a rented hall near the Hallesche Market, and there a series of marvels occurred.

The meetings began quietly enough, with Weissenberg preaching from the podium, while two women sat at a nearby table. In due time, the elder of the two, a heavy-set matron who called herself Sister Grete Müller, would suddenly fall into a trance. From her lips, strange voices spoke, most notably that of the late Chancellor, Otto von Bismarck. Weissenberg then proceeded into the audience, where a number of the devout were also crying out and falling into trances. After a laying on of hands, Weissenberg and the second woman led selected parishioners to the podium to join in the seance. Through their lips, too, came the voices of historical personages, mainly those from the period of Kaiser Wilhelm I—Prince Friedrich Karl or Generals Moltke and Roon. The voices expressed various patriotic sentiments to the audience, but they also urged everyone to donate money to Weissenberg's building fund.

With the money he raised, Weissenberg proceeded to develop a commune he had founded in some hills about an hour's drive south of Berlin. It was a huge establishment, laid out on sixteen hundred acres that Weissenberg had bought as early as 1919. He called it, variously, "Peace City" or "The New Jerusalem Living Community," or, taking the name of a little group he had organized back in 1900, "The Union of Investigators from Here to the Beyond." By this time, Weissenberg had already lured four hundred people to the commune, which included two rows of houses, an administration building, a garage, a laundry, and a large Hall of Devotion. His hope was to increase the population to about fifteen hundred.

For a time, the Berlin authorities looked benignly at Weissenberg's operation, since there was no law against evoking the spirit of Bismarck or persuading people to move to an exurban housing development. They were less indulgent, however, toward Weissenberg's claims of being able to heal the sick, and even, so he said, to raise the dead. Weissenberg's only cure, apart from prayer, was to prescribe cottage cheese. In one case, a child with an inflammation of the eyes, treated with prayer and cheese, went blind; a druggist with diabetes received the same treatment and died. The police arrested the bearded old prophet on a charge of medical malpractice, and a court sentenced him to six months in prison. Weissenberg's followers did not desert him; they considered him a martyr. The court of appeals reversed the conviction, and then there was a new trial.

"Where did you receive your medical training?" the judge asked.

"I work only according to the directions of the Holy Scriptures," said the prophet.

"But there's nothing about cottage cheese in the Bible," said the judge.

"Even I," said the prophet, "cannot help a man who has no faith."

The judge gave up. Weissenberg was set free. And only his death ended the construction of the community of the New Jerusalem.

"God Does Not Play at Dice" 1927

> The political and military horrors and the complete breakdown of
> ethics which I have witnessed during my lifetime may be . . . a
> necessary consequence of the rise of science. . . . if this is so, there will
> be an end to man as a free, responsible being.
>
> MAX BORN

AT THE END OF WORLD WAR II, the Allies rounded up Germany's
leading physicists and began interrogating them on their knowledge
of nuclear weapons. To their surprise—for the specter of a Nazi
atom bomb had inspired the Americans to organize the whole Manhattan Project—they found that their prisoners knew virtually nothing. Perhaps because of the German scientists' hostility to Hitler,
perhaps simply because of their lack of imagination, they had made
no effort at all to develop an atom bomb. The Allied authorities were
somewhat puzzled, therefore, about what to do with their distinguished captives, but since they were still maintaining the closest
secrecy over the plan to attack Hiroshima, and since they feared
that the German physicists might somehow learn of the plan, they
shipped them all to the luxurious confinement of an eighteenth-
century brick mansion called Farm Hall, in the countryside some
twenty-five miles from Cambridge, England.

The ten prisoners, three of whom had won the Nobel Prize, were
even more bewildered than their guardians. Nobody interrogated
them any more, but they were totally isolated from the outside
world, and so they occupied themselves as best they could. Carl
Friedrich von Weizsäcker began tending the roses in the garden.

Max von Laue walked fifty times around the rose garden every day, a total of six miles, keeping track of his progress with chalk marks on the garden wall. Werner Heisenberg, foraging through the Farm Hall library, decided to spend his time reading the collected works of Anthony Trollope. In the evenings, they all gathered for discussions of nuclear physics, which the British secretly tapped and recorded.

On the afternoon of August 6, 1945, one of the physicists was listening to the radio and heard that an atomic bomb had been dropped on Hiroshima. "At first I refused to believe it," Heisenberg said later. "I was convinced that the construction of atom bombs involved enormous technical efforts. . . . I also found it psychologically implausible that scientists whom I knew so well should have thrown their full weight behind such a project." As later broadcasts cleared away the Germans' skepticism, however, one of the prisoners, Otto Hahn, began to feel a terrible sense of guilt. "Hahn withdrew to his room, visibly shaken and deeply disturbed," according to Heisenberg, "and all of us were afraid that he might do himself some injury." Another one of the captives wrote in his diary two days later: "Poor Professor Hahn! He told us that when he first learned of the terrible consequences which atomic fission could have, he had been unable to sleep for several nights and contemplated suicide."

There is no evidence that Hahn or any of the other physicists felt any particular guilt as Germans, for what Germany had done. Hahn's sense of guilt was that of a physicist, for what the Americans had done. And it was as a physicist that he must have looked back to those extraordinary days just before Christmas of 1938, when he had read a report from Paris saying that Frédéric and Irène Joliot-Curie had succeeded, by bombarding uranium with neutrons, in creating a new substance that closely resembled lanthanum. And when he had repeated the experiment in Berlin and discovered that the new substance was not lanthanum but barium, which had just half the atomic weight of uranium. And when he had sent a report of his findings to his chief colleague, Lise Meitner—who had worked with him for years in a basement at Berlin University because no woman could be allowed into the laboratories, and who had now been forced to flee to Sweden because she was a Jew—Lise Meitner had received the report in the frozen Baltic resort of Kungalv, where her nephew had taken her on a skiing vacation, and the nephew, who just wanted a rest from physics, set out on skis with his aunt trotting along behind him, talking about Otto Hahn's mysterious discovery, and as they struggled along through the snow, Lise Meitner suddenly realized what Otto Hahn had done. He had split the atom.

In the beginning, when science was relatively innocent, there was Max Planck. He was a gaunt, bony man, quite bald, with steel-rimmed spectacles, a physicist of the classical school, and a highly respected professor at the University of Berlin. He specialized in the study of heat radiation. In the last few years of the 1890's, engineers developed new spectroscopic equipment that could analyze radiation with unprecedented accuracy, and as Planck studied the results, he saw that the new measurements did not conform to the traditional rules governing waves of energy. These waves of energy were not continuous, as, by definition, waves must be. All through the summer of 1900, he puzzled over the problem, and once he even took his son out for a walk in the Grunewald Forest and tried to explain the solution he had devised. A conservative by nature, he hardly believed in the solution himself, but he told his son that he thought it might represent one of the greatest discoveries since the time of Newton. On December 14, 1900, at a meeting of the German Physical Society, Planck outlined what was to become known as the Quantum Theory. Light and energy, he said, do not move in continuous waves but in a flow of tiny particles. These particles, or quanta, vary in size according to wavelength, and the energy can be measured according to the formula $E = hf$—f being the frequency of the wave and h being the so-called Planck constant, which is .00000000000000000000000000655.

Planck himself was bewildered by the idea of measuring light in terms of particles, but it fascinated the young Albert Einstein, whom Planck was to bring to Berlin, and Einstein's investigations led quite naturally to the idea that light has mass. Hence the famous astronomical experiment of 1919, and the proof that light rays bend when they pass near the gravity of the sun. And by one of those paradoxes of twentieth-century publicity, Einstein suddenly became famous precisely because nobody could understand his new theories of Relativity. It was alleged in the newspapers that only twelve people in the world—or perhaps seven, or perhaps only three—had truly mastered the concept of curved space, or of time as a fourth dimension. If the theory was incomprehensible, however, then the press paid all the more attention to the man who had created it. Reporters pursued him everywhere, interrogating him on anything from the speed of light to his views of women. The *Times* of London asked him to write a short autobiographical statement, and Einstein, looking back on his mysteriously tormented youth, when he had been left in school in Munich while his family migrated to Italy, and when he finally had migrated to Zurich by himself, sent back a tart answer: "Today I am described in Germany as a German savant and in England as a Swiss Jew. Should it ever become my fate to be represented as a bête noire, I should, on the contrary, become a Swiss Jew for the Germans and a German savant for the English."

The answer was typical of Einstein. It expressed his celebrated dislike of personal publicity but also his Garbo-like talent for creating publicity. It expressed his inherent dislike of nationalism but also his sense of how to make use of national interests (like Bert Brecht, he skillfully calculated the advantages of traveling on an alien passport in his own land, and, though an ardent Zionist, he never lived in Israel). Above all, it expressed Einstein's enigmatic personality, ironic but not hostile, acute but detached, self-deprecating but not at all without pride. And in the turmoil of postwar Berlin, these qualities were not widely appreciated. To the Nationalists, indeed, Einstein epitomized everything contemptible—he was a Jew, a liberal, an internationalist, a pacifist, a skeptic, an innovator, and a scientist whose work baffled the average intelligence.

Some of these Nationalists took to waiting for Einstein outside his apartment on the Haberlandstrasse, or his office in the Prussian Academy of Science, and shouting denunciations of "Jewish science" as soon as the familiar figure appeared. Others filled his mailbox with obscene and threatening letters. On one occasion, a gang of right-wing students disrupted Einstein's lecture at the Berlin University, and one of them shouted, "I'm going to cut the throat of that dirty Jew." An anti-Semitic demagogue named Rudolph Leibus was arrested—and fined the trivial sum of sixteen dollars—for offering a reward to anyone who would assassinate the hated scientist. A right-wing group called the Working Committee of German Natural Philosophers rented the Berlin Philharmonic Hall for a series of lectures against the "Einstein hoax." Einstein himself took a box and attended the meeting, greeting the attacks against him with bursts of laughter and applause. In private, however, he was less defiant. "The yellow press and other half-wits are at my heels to the point where I can scarcely draw breath," he told an associate, "let alone do any really decent work."

Einstein's admirers were almost as much of a nuisance as his enemies, and despite his professed dislike of publicity, he repeatedly succumbed to suggestions that he should use his celebrity for good causes. He accompanied the Zionist leader Chaim Weizmann on a fund-raising tour of America, giving, in every city, various answers to the inevitable request for a simple explanation of Relativity. He won the Nobel Prize. He toured the Orient. He visited Palestine and wrote an article about "the magic of such amazing achievements and of such superhuman devotion." He became a leading member of the Committee on Intellectual Cooperation, under the League of Nations, and he took part in joint meetings of French and German pacifists. All of this activity further infuriated the Nationalists. There were rumors that Einstein had been definitely marked for assassination, like his friend Walther Rathenau, and his wife arranged for him to be accompanied by a bodyguard, without his knowing about it.

But during this whole period of Einstein's sudden celebrity, the rapidly evolving study of nuclear physics began to move on without him. The nature of the atom had never been Einstein's primary concern, of course—he was more interested in the laws of the universe —but the young physicists who had gathered in Germany, most notably at the University of Göttingen, were becoming convinced that the nature of the universe could best be studied in the structure of its essential unit, the atom. The Danish genius, Niels Bohr, had applied Planck's Quantum Theory to the problems of atomic structure and shown that the atom's electrons, too, give off energy only in terms of specific quanta. But other experiments showed that atomic energy could also be measured purely in terms of waves, which seemed to violate the theory of quantum particles. Still other experiments on the whirling flight of the electron demonstrated that an observer could determine either the position of the electron or its velocity, but never both.

Bohr formulated a new theory, which he called "complementarity," which argued that two contradictory methods of measuring energy were not necessarily contradictory but simply complementary means of observing the same phenomenon. But that hardly satisfied anyone. The young Werner Heisenberg spent several vacations at Bohr's house, and, as he recalled later, "discussions . . . went through many hours till very late at night and ended almost in despair; and when at the end of the discussion I went alone for a walk in the neighboring park I repeated to myself again and again the question: Can nature possibly be as absurd as it seems to us in these atomic experiments?"

In February of 1927, Bohr wearied of all the talk and decided to go skiing in Norway. Heisenberg was "quite glad to be left behind in Denmark, where I could think about these hopelessly complicated problems undisturbed. . . . It must have been one evening after midnight when I suddenly remembered my conversation with Einstein and particularly his statement, 'It is the theory which decides what we can observe.' " It had, indeed, been an extraordinary conversation. Heisenberg had spent a good deal of time trying to compute the orbits of electrons, and he was troubled by the possibility that electrons might not spin in orbit at all. After all, who had ever seen them do so? In a lecture at the University of Berlin, he suggested a return to the old-fashioned theory that nothing could be considered as scientific evidence unless it could be scientifically observed. Einstein, one of his listeners, was dismayed. And not without reason, since most of atomic theory was still a matter of theory, and the structure of the universe, which so fascinated Einstein, was even less subject to the traditional laboratory tests.

"You don't seriously believe," Einstein argued after Heisenberg's Berlin lecture, "that none but observable magnitudes must go into a physical theory?"

"Isn't that precisely what you have done with relativity?" Heisenberg answered, according to his own account of the meeting. "After all, you did stress the fact that it is impossible to speak of absolute time, simply because absolute time cannot be observed."

"Possibly I did use this kind of reasoning," Einstein said, "but it is nonsense all the same. . . . On principle, it is quite wrong to try founding a theory on observable magnitudes alone. In reality the very opposite happens. It is the theory which decides what we can observe."

At the time, Heisenberg was impressed but not persuaded. Yet now, Einstein's argument struck him as "the key to the gate that had been closed for so long." Heisenberg, a vigorous young man, still in his early twenties, devoted to skiing and mountain-climbing, set off into the darkness. "I decided to go on a nocturnal walk through Faelled Park and to think further about the matter. We had always said so glibly that the path of the electron in the cloud chamber could be observed. But perhaps what we really observed was something much less. Perhaps we merely saw a series of discrete and ill-defined spots through which the electron had passed."

The result of Heisenberg's reflections, announced later in 1927, was the celebrated Principle of Indeterminacy (or Uncertainty). It abolished, to state it simply, the whole idea of exact observation. There was no longer any such thing as a "scientific fact." The most that one could determine, according to Heisenberg, was that a certain observer, at a certain point in space and time, had seen certain phenomena which he believed to represent the possibility of thus-and-such. The implications of Heisenberg's Indeterminacy Principle were as fundamental and as radical as those of Einstein's Relativity Theory. If, basically, Einstein taught that all facts are relative, Heisenberg taught that all facts are purely momentary perceptions of possibilities. There was no real difference between what we think of as laws of cause and effect and what we think of as random events or pure chance. Or, to put it another way, Karl Barth was right in arguing that all we can know about God is our own lack of knowledge. Or, to put it still another way, Hans Arp was indeed recreating reality when he dropped some pieces of paper to the floor and glued them where they fell, for the whole universe is a Dada universe.

The most passionate opponent of Heisenberg's theory was, oddly enough, Albert Einstein, who clung to the belief that the scientist's purpose was to discover the laws of God's creation. In answer to the idea that any such laws were unknowable, Einstein repeatedly said, "God does not play at dice." The two men clashed that year at a conference of physicists in Brussels. Einstein, according to Heisenberg, "had no objections against probability statements whenever a particular system was not known in every last detail. . . . However, Einstein would not admit that it was impossible, even in principle, to discover all the partial facts needed for the complete description of a physical process. . . . He refused point-blank to accept the uncertainty principle, and tried to think up cases in which the principle would not hold."

Every morning, according to Heisenberg, Einstein would arrive at the breakfast table, in the hotel where the physicists were all staying, with an imaginary experiment that would prove the existence of a fact, and thus of a law. All day, the physicists would argue over Einstein's challenge, and by suppertime, Niels Bohr would offer a refutation. The next morning, at breakfast, Einstein would arrive with a new problem to be solved. "Einstein, I am ashamed of you," one of the physicists said, but the master continued to raise objections. "Einstein had devoted his life," said Heisenberg, "to probing into that objective world of physical processes which runs its course in space and time, independent of us, according to firm laws. . . . Now it was being asserted that, on the atomic scale, this objective world of time and space did not even exist and that the mathematical symbols of theoretical physics referred to possibilities rather than facts. Einstein was not prepared to let us do what, to him, amounted to pulling the ground from under his feet. . . . 'God does not throw dice' was his unshakable principle, one that he would not allow anybody to challenge. To which Bohr could only counter with: 'Nor is it our business to prescribe to God how He should run the world.'"

Albert Einstein went his own way. His own way took him, among other places, to the Philharmonic Hall, where the thirteen-year-old Yehudi Menuhin was making his Berlin debut by playing the concerti of Bach, Beethoven, and Brahms. After the concert, the fifty-year-old physicist, his thick hair and mustache by now quite gray, hurried backstage to shake the hand of the prodigy, who seemed supernaturally capable of performing feats that the amateur violinist had struggled all his life to achieve. "Today, Yehudi," Einstein said, "you have once again proved to me that there is a God in heaven."

Einstein's God was not the God of all men, nor even of all Jews. The Vatican newspaper *Osservatore Romano* criticized him for "cutting off faith in God from human life. . . . This is authentic atheism even if it is camouflaged as cosmic pantheism." A New York rabbi sent Einstein a cable demanding to know whether he believed in God at all, and Einstein promptly sent back his answer: "I believe in Spinoza's God who reveals himself in the harmony of all that exists, not in a God who concerns himself with the fate and actions of men."

In search of this harmony, Einstein began an effort to devise formulas that would unite the laws governing the two basic forces in the universe, gravity and electromagnetism. The idea was already obsessing him when he went to Switzerland early in 1928 to lecture on physics to the tuberculosis patients in Davos. There, almost exactly like the hero of Thomas Mann's *Magic Mountain*, he fell seriously ill, though not from tuberculosis but rather from an enlargement of the heart. His wife came to fetch him back to Berlin, and he lay in bed for months, fretting over the formulas that were to become known as the Unified Field Theory.

When it was finally published on January 30, 1929, it was just six pages of wholly unprovable and wholly incomprehensible equations, but the international press greeted it as the greatest scientific event since the furor over the tomb of King Tut. The Berlin correspondent of the New York *Herald Tribune*, for example, cabled the entire text verbatim back to New York, where a team of physicists from Columbia University did their best to decipher it. Other correspondents clustered outside Einstein's door for interviews, but Einstein would consent to see only the *New York Times* (whose managing editor had once impressed Einstein by correcting a mathematical error Einstein had made). Einstein affected bewilderment at all the excitement, and when the *Times* man said that the whole world was waiting for the explanation of his new theory, Einstein put his hands to his head and cried, "My God!"

To the new physicists, however, Einstein's theory was unconvincing. He had made no attempt to reconcile his theories of gravitational fields with the new discoveries in atomic physics; in fact, he completely ignored the whole area of quantum mechanics. In time, Einstein was to realize that his Unified Field Theory of 1929 was wrong. The equations didn't work. And he was to spend the rest of his life in an equally unsuccessful attempt to revise and correct his formula for God's universe. But the younger physicists were already following a different road. "Many of us regard this as a tragedy," said one of Einstein's most brilliant colleagues, Max Born, "both for him, as he gropes his way in loneliness, and for us, who miss our leader and standard-bearer."

The young physicists who gathered in Berlin and Göttingen in the 1920's—the Hahns and Heisenbergs, the foreign wanderers like Oppenheimer and Teller—were probably as brilliant a group as ever gathered anywhere. Most of the young Germans of this period were not physicists, however, and most of them were somewhat less intellectual. It was the children of the 1920's, in fact, who marched in Hitler's torchlight parades of the 1930's, and operated both the tanks and the gas chambers of the 1940's, and finally turned up, in the 1950's, as pudgy, middle-aged fugitives in places like Cairo and São Paulo.

When a whole generation of children has been corrupted, then, one begins to wonder who was in charge of raising and educating them. Or, to put it another way, was there a connection between the fact that Lise Meitner, as a highly gifted young physicist, could not even set foot in the laboratories of the University of Berlin, because she was a woman, and the fact that in her middle age, more than thirty years later, she had to flee into exile because she was a Jew? One must beware of easy analogies—discrimination and persecution are not the same, and Harvard College never hired a woman as a professor until 1948—but yes, there probably was some connection, and it probably can be found at the very core of the German school system.

Albert Einstein, who hated his own schooldays, hated the whole German process of education. "To me," he wrote some years later, "the worst thing seems to be for a school principally to work with methods of fear, force, and artificial authority. Such treatment produces . . . the submissive subject. It is no wonder that such schools are the rule in Germany and Russia." But that was, of course, a way of life. "You must remember that the basic questions were not intellectual questions," says another elderly German as he reflects on his youth. "The basic questions involved the development of character. I remember, for example, one day when we got a barrel of apples, and our governess always made us eat the bad ones first, the wormy ones, so that no apples would be wasted. And since we were only allowed to eat one apple a day, the good apples went bad while we ate the bad ones, and so most of the apples we ate had worms in them. But that was supposed to develop the character. And I remember that when I went to have my tonsils out, there was no talk of anesthetic or anything like that. The doctor just stared at me for a long time, and then he said, 'Are you a brave German boy or are you a coward who cries because of a little pain?' Of course, I had to say I was a brave German boy, and not a coward, and so he took his long shears and reached into my mouth and cut out my tonsils. And I didn't cry."

The system by which such boys were educated was this: At the age of six, all children started in a *Volksschule* (people's school) or *Grundschule* (elementary school); at the age of ten, the upper-class students, accompanied by a few nervous scholarship winners from the lower orders, began attending a *Gymnasium,* which emphasized Greek, Latin, and the humanities. Or the *Realschule,* which was somewhat more practical, since it offered more science and modern languages—and therefore had less status (Berlin had 110 of these, as compared to 30 *Gymnasia*). At the end of eight or nine years (requirements varied), the student won a diploma called the *Abitur,* and then was ready to enter a university, or, more often, to join some institute of applied learning, or, still more often, to go and look for a job. And when, in 1927, the Prussian Student Organization took a poll of its members on the question of whether Jews should be allowed to join, fully 77 percent of the young intelligentsia voted in the negative, indicating, or perhaps simply confirming, that there was something radically wrong with the German students. They were, far more than their parents, not just anti-Semitic but pro-Nazi—60 percent by actual count—and ready for violence.

How had such a perversion of the young taken place? Even today, a surprising number of old Berliners still remember the day the Kaiser fled to Holland as the day on which they discovered the abyss that separated them from the generation of their parents. "I remember my father burst into tears when we heard the newspaper boys shouting that the Kaiser had abdicated," says Friedrich Luft, now a portly, gray-haired man, one of the most prominent theatre critics in Berlin. We are sitting in, of all places, the coffee shop of the Berlin Hilton Hotel, sharing a pot of tea. "Being a teacher, he was a conservative, and a Nationalist—and I had never seen him cry before. . . .

"The school I went to then—the Friedenau Gymnasium—was completely nationalistic," Luft goes on. "When I think of it now, it's a scandal. We lived in a republic, after all. The headmaster was a member of the Prussian parliament, and a Nationalist, of course. On August 11, the day when the Weimar Constitution was created, the headmaster had orders from the government that we should all go to school for a short time and hear a short lecture on the Constitution, and then have some little festivity. He said, 'I won't do it.' So all the children were instructed to go to another school to have the ceremony there. The headmaster announced, 'I have heard that you are expected to go to another school to hear ceremonies on August 11. I expect all of you to get ill on the evening of August 10, and I don't wish to hear that any of you have been to these ceremonies.' I went anyway, but I was one of the few who did. Most people stayed home."

"The atmosphere in a Gymnasium was rather special," says Dr. Heinz Pachter, now a professor of history in New York, a tall, well-tanned man of sixty-three, with a mass of wavy gray hair. "The one I went to had no children of workers, for example. It wasn't a matter of money—forty marks for a semester—but the workers generally thought there wouldn't be much point in having their children learn Greek and Latin and then go back to being workers. I remember, though, there was one student who was the son of a coachman, and the teacher made his life miserable. Every time this boy made a mistake, the teacher said, 'Well, that's about all one could expect from the son of a coachman.' And after about a year, the boy left school and didn't come back.

"So in my graduating class in the Gymnasium, there were twelve boys, all about eighteen. Two were marching with the SA, the Storm Troopers, and one was a strong sympathizer. Two were sons of converted Jews, and they were very Nationalist, but they were not allowed to be Nazis. One was a Christian Scientist, conservative but nonpolitical. Two were Nationalist. And the rest were members of the Youth Movement, which generally didn't accept Jews, so they were sympathetic to the Nationalist cause."

"Was the Youth Movement really serious? Was it comparable to the radicalism of American students?"

"Frighteningly comparable," says Dr. Pachter.

"But the students are mostly left-wing nowadays, whereas they all seem to have been right-wing in the twenties."

"Right-wing, left-wing, it doesn't make that much difference," Dr. Pachter says with a shrug. "The Nazi youth talked of 'liberation.' They were also in rebellion against their parents, and against 'the system.' The left today—they just want power, and the worship of power is Fascist."

"You cannot understand anything about Germany," says Professor Richard Lowenthal, "unless you realize that a majority of the professional classes were right-wing all the way up until 1945. Professors of law, schoolteachers, doctors, lawyers, there was an enormous majority on the right. Democracy was not intellectually respectable. The basic intellectual mood was that the Weimar government was contemptible. This was true on both left and right, but more true on the right."

Professor Lowenthal is a small, wispy man in his sixties. His head is rather bald, with a bit of gray hair growing out of it. He has long sideburns. He wears a gray suit and a necktie that hangs below his belt. He lives in a sunny villa in Grunewald, and he sits in a Louis XV chair, pink, and he pours coffee for his visitor, and he recalls that he was once a Communist.

"What were the elements of Berlin in the 1920's?" he asks aloud. "First, Marxism and pacifism; then psychoanalysis—here we really lived with Freud; then theatre, music, art, and so on; and radical educational experiments. . . . When I started at the University of Berlin in 1926, I was already a member of the Communist Party. In 1928, I was the national leader of the Communist student group. And in 1929, I was expelled, for what they called 'right-wing deviation.'"

"What did that involve?"

"I was against splitting the trade-union movement, and I was against treating the Social Democrats as 'Social Fascists,' as the others called them. I still had some common sense."

Professor Lowenthal takes a sip from his cup of coffee and then says "Um." The conversation is not going quite the way he wanted it to go. He has a point to make.

"The creative intellectuals—Brecht, for example—never really understood what was happening," he says. "In fact, one of the most striking things about the whole Weimar period, and perhaps this is where I should have started, is the *gulf* between the small minority of intellectuals and the general mood of the country."

There are always gulfs, of course, between generations and classes, between the intellectuals and the workers, the peasants and the urban masses. But the isolation of each group is not necessarily total, and there are often elite groups that exert a wide influence over those who wish they could become part of the elite. And so it was with the German Youth Movement. It had begun most inconspicuously in 1896, in Steglitz, then a staid middle-class suburb just south of Berlin. There, a twenty-one-year-old youth named Hermann Hoffmann, a student at Berlin University, organized a little group dedicated to self-improvement through the practice of shorthand.

When their studies finished, they would go hiking together in the nearby Grunewald Forest. Hoffmann soon faded away, off on a trip to Turkey, but ten of his associates gathered at a Steglitz tavern, drew up a constitution for their hiking society, and named themselves the Wandervögel (roughly, birds of passage). They saluted each other with the word *"Heil!"*

That was in 1901. Within a dozen years, the movement had spread all over Germany, and the Wandervögel hiked by the tens of thousands to a convocation on the Hohe Meissner, a rain-swept mountain south of Kassel. They lit bonfires, sang songs, recited Goethe, listened to speeches on the German spirit, and generally behaved with the traditional solemnity of youth. The Wandervögel were not originally a political movement—except to the extent that the wandering youths already shared certain political views, ranging from an emotional patriotism to an equally emotional mistrust of Jews (and girls). With their banners and songbooks, therefore, they marched off to the slaughter in the trenches of France. "O holy fortune," one of them wrote of the heroic spirit of 1914, "to be young today!"

Those who survived, and there were not that many, returned to find, as often happens, that the new leaders of the Youth Movement considered them old and irrelevant (there were periodic resolutions to expel everyone over the age of twenty-five, or thirty, resolutions that the aging Wandervögel resisted for dear life). The returning veterans discovered, too, that the Youth Movement had inevitably become a political force, divided by the same political passions that divided the nation as a whole. Not entirely, of course. There were some who had just found out about Rudolf Steiner's anthroposophic movement, and others who had gone beyond that to discover, once again, the Wisdom of the East: Zen Buddhism, Taoism, and the preachings of Rabindranath Tagore. Then there were the militant idealists, like the Christian Socialists who called themselves "The Brotherhood," who established a commune to live off the land (and survived emigrations to England, Paraguay, and finally back to post-Hitler Germany). But to be nonpolitical, as George Orwell once wrote, is itself a political act.

The first major conflict divided the pro-Communist youths from those who supported the new Weimar government. The battleground was the major left-wing student group, the Free German Youth, which had been founded in 1913 as a haven for those who had grown too old for the Wandervögel. At a series of conventions, the students wrangled so fiercely with one another that the group divided forever, splintered, and by the end of 1923, it was dead. At that, the Youth Movement gradually came under the control of various right-wing groups that called themselves *Bünde*. These *Bünde* were far more political than the old Wandervögel, dedicated to the idea of renovating German society rather than simply escaping from it. The hierarchy was more strictly organized, and the restrictions on Jews (and girls) were more sternly enforced. This was, after all, the era of Stefan George.

It has been said that all young Germans of the 1920's were influenced by Stefan George "whether or not they had ever heard his name or read a single line he had written." This is, if true, an odd commentary on any nation, for George seems never to have wanted to convert anyone outside his little circle of worshiping students (a circle to which, we recall, the young Joseph Goebbels was not admitted). He did, to be sure, use a swastika as the symbol of his magazine, *Blätter für die Kunst* (*Papers for Art*), which repeatedly advocated the mystical concepts of brotherhood in service under the rule of a true leader. But George himself, though rather overtly homosexual, was scarcely a Storm Trooper. He was a votary of Greece, which he had never seen, and of the Mediterranean spirit. He hated the violence of the war, and when the Nazis finally offered him a high office in the cultural hierarchy of the new Third Reich, the aged poet fled to Switzerland, where he died.

As one considers the various patrons of German youth during the 1920's, one finds figures far stranger than George. For example: John Hargrave, who had been "commissioner for camping and woodcraft" in the Boy Scouts of Britain. He left the Scouts in 1920 to form his own group, "Kibbo Kift, the Woodcraft Kindred," which sponsored the building of wigwams, the playing of tom-toms, and other manifestations of frontier skills in the wilds of Europe. This may seem rather exotic, but Hargrave's movement won the support not only of German frontiersmen but of D. H. Lawrence, Anatole France, and Maurice Maeterlinck. How far is it, then, to Martin Voelkel, a pastor in Berlin, and his belief in "the holy, divine Reich of the German vision, which is everywhere and nowhere," and his genuflections before the "German trinity," which was apparently to be defined as God, the I, and the weapon?

In a decade of argument, the German Youth Movement never achieved either unity or mass power. There were a dozen major *Bünde,* and many minor ones, and the total membership of the independent bunds totaled about sixty thousand (much larger numbers of Germans went on hikes with the youth groups of their churches and labor unions and other established organizations). But the elite groups did have their effect. Youth hostels spread across the country, and many of the older Wandervögel went on to become teachers, spreading the gospel among their new pupils. And as the 1920's passed, the Youth Movement, like the country itself, seemed to become more and more nationalistic. One group called the "Artamans," for example, worked on the farms of eastern Germany to prevent them from being desecrated by migrant workers from Poland; among these Artamans, in a minor official capacity, was Heinrich Himmler. Other factions, like the Order of Young Germans, concentrated on military training, gunplay, and parades. Prussian traditions were too mild, according to one of the militant leaders; every youth group must become a garrison, every youth a soldier, dedicated to the principles of the Japanese samurai, which he described as "demonic, knightly masculinity."

It is tempting to draw a line connecting the Wandervögel on their mountaintop to the cheering ranks of the uniformed Hitler Youth, but the connection is not so simple. The Hitler Youth was relatively weak throughout the 1920's, as was Hitler himself, and indeed the Führer used the term "Wandervögel" as an insult. When he came to power, he disbanded the *Bünde* and threw a number of their leaders into prison. Are we justified, then, in indicting the prisoners for the misdeeds of their jailer? Perhaps we are, to some extent, for the evidence indicates that it was Hitler, the necromancer of the lower orders, who rejected these hero-worshiping students, and not they who rejected him. And although many prim and stiff-collared teachers had perverted the whole process of education, the history of the Youth Movement suggests that the young were quite capable, without any teachers, of miseducating each other.

After more than a decade of drill and discipline, then, the young German was ready to confront the uncertain winds of the university. But by now, he was indeed ready. "In a big-city university like Berlin, about two-thirds of the students were already committed to the right," says Professor Lowenthal. "Only 20 or 25 percent were liberal or Social Democrats. That left us, the radicals, about 5 percent, at the most. And we were not really very radical at all. It would never have occurred to us to interrupt a lecture, or insult a professor, the way they do nowadays. The only ones who did that were the Nazis."

"Did you fight them?" asks a visitor, leaning back on one of the Louis XV chairs. Outside Professor Lowenthal's living room, the wood thrushes are singing.

"Yes, but we were always beaten. I remember once I had to jump out a window. We were in a corner, against the walls, and this gang of Nazis was much bigger than we were, so we went out the window. But it was only a first-floor window, not very exciting."

"How was it that the Nazis could appeal so strongly to young students, when one usually thinks of young people as idealistic?"

"Because the Nazis were idealistic too," says Professor Lowenthal, former leader of the Communist youth movement, sipping coffee. "They promised national unity and national resurrection. And there was that basic German romanticism—you know—you know the difference between *Gemeinschaft* and *Gesellschaft?* The first is a medieval concept, a society in which everyone works for the common good; the other is the modern, materialistic idea, a society in which everyone competes against the others for his own good. There was a widespread feeling that this was un-German, that it had been imposed by foreigners. There was some truth to this too. Capitalism did come from outside because Germany was so backward, and democracy was brought in by the armies of Napoleon. The whole German romantic movement was a criticism of that, and this is still true for the young radicals of today.

"So the Nazis promised an alternative to what they called the corrupt plutocratic system. And everybody wanted to believe."

The University of Berlin, Friedrich Wilhelm University, was originally a palace, a tomb of gray stone, built in the best eighteenth-century manner for the brother of Frederick the Great. Today, it still stands proudly across from the Opera on Unter den Linden. It calls itself Humboldt University, and the statues of the Humboldt brothers, Alexander and Wilhelm, the two scientists who converted the palace into a university a century and a half ago, guard the gates. In the courtyard, there is also a tree that was planted during the Humboldts' lifetime, a ginkgo tree.

The men who taught here were among the greatest figures of their times—Fichte and Hegel, the Grimm brothers, Helmholtz, Ranke and Mommsen. Mark Twain, for one, was captivated by the sight of a whole roomful of Berlin students raising their sabers and lurching to their feet in honor of the entry of the historian of the Roman Republic. "There was an excited whisper at our table —'Mommsen!' and the whole house rose. Rose and shouted and stamped and clapped and banged the beer-mugs. . . . Then the little man with his long hair and Emersonian face edged his way past us and took his seat. I could have touched him with my hands— Mommsen!—think of it!"

Now a huge poster of Walter Ulbricht, the bearded bureaucrat of East German Communism, hangs over the classic doorway of Berlin University. And everywhere, red banners proclaim the slogans of Ulbricht's regime: "*Unsere Liebe, Unsere Kunst—Unserem Sozialistichen Vaterland*" ("Our love, our art—to our Socialist Fatherland"). The degradation is not so extreme as it may appear, however, for the tradition at Berlin University is authoritarian. The great Mommsen, for example, hated and despised the Kaiser's Reich but was afraid to state his criticisms except as a posthumous indictment. During the war, Albert Einstein was almost the only faculty member who declined to sign a manifesto supporting the army's cause. And when Walther Rathenau was murdered in Grunewald, the University of Berlin was one of the very few public institutions in the capital that refused, giving a variety of technical excuses, to shut down.

A few months after Rathenau's death, the government asked the university—which was, after all, a public institution—to organize a festivity for the sixtieth birthday of that theatrical relic of the previous century, Gerhart Hauptmann. The worthies of the university considered themselves insulted. "The most memorable point about the celebration," according to Count Kessler, who watched the proceedings with a mixture of irritation and sorrow, "was the grotesquely narrow-minded behaviour of the students and professors. The students' union solemnly resolved (by a majority, I believe, of four to two) not to participate in the event, as Gerhart Hauptmann, having admitted to republican sympathies, has evinced himself as being no longer a staunch German!"

The reluctant chairman of the event was Professor Julius Petersen, an expert on the works of Schiller, who had formally asked that President Ebert not be invited to the ceremony, on the grounds that, according to Kessler, "it would be disagreeable for the University to have the republican head of state appear within its walls." When this proposal was rejected, Petersen asked that the university at least be permitted to bar Paul Löbe, the chairman of the Reichstag, since the professors felt that "to put up with two Social Democrats simultaneously was a bit much!"

"At the end of the celebration [Eugen] d'Albert gave a magnificent rendering of the *Appassionata*," Kessler concluded. "Whereupon another of the professors in my row distinguished himself by growling bad-temperedly to his neighbour, 'That was of course a composition by the pianist himself, wasn't it?' "

To older Germans, the problem of youth was not a matter of politics but of morality, and they found all their anxieties justified when they read about the great scandal of 1927, the case of Paul Krantz.

It was a re-enactment of every Expressionist melodrama. Paul Krantz and Günter Scheller were both eighteen, classmates in the Mariendorfer Gymnasium, and Scheller had a younger sister, Hildegarde, aged sixteen, and the Scheller parents went off on a trip to Denmark, leaving their adolescents in Berlin to take care of themselves. One June evening, Paul Krantz went to bed with Hilde Scheller, and there, according to Hilde's subsequent testimony, they exchanged "sinful kisses." Krantz's description was equally Victorian: "Impure caresses . . . but not definitive."

Krantz reappeared on the following evening for more of these adventures, but he found to his chagrin that Hilde had invited another boy, an apprentice cook named Hans Stephan, to spend the night with her. While Hans and Hilde settled down in a locked bedroom of the Schellers' apartment, Krantz and his friend Günter sat in the kitchen, drinking apple brandy and arguing about how to punish the sinners in the bedroom. At some point during that night of intoxication, they agreed to a suicide pact, in which Scheller would kill Stephan and himself, while Krantz would deal with the faithless Hilde. They even wrote out their plan in a letter to posterity, in which Krantz, who liked to dabble in morbid poetry, declared that he had been "murdered by Life."

All this might have passed as a minor absurdity except for the fact that Krantz did have a revolver, which had been entrusted to him by a youth group called the Order of Young Germany, which he and his various schoolmates had taken turns in carrying around, and which he now turned over to Günter Scheller. Drunk and hysterical, Scheller fired a practice shot in the kitchen and nearly killed Krantz. At that point, according to his testimony, Krantz changed his mind about the whole project. He tried to get the gun back, but Scheller now accused him of cowardice.

As dawn broke, Hilde decided to bluff her way out of the trap. First she told her companion to hide in a niche next to the clothes cupboard, and then she sauntered out to accost her brother. "Hilde . . . joined us, fully dressed, as though she had just got up and prepared for school," according to Krantz's account. "She whispered softly to me, 'Hans isn't here any more.' . . . As for Günter . . . she told him that it was only his drunkenness that had made him think he had heard or seen someone; nobody had been in her room. She had also left her door ostentatiously open, and she seemed completely at ease. . . . Günter appeared to accept the situation. He had a strange look, however, a look both deceived and disbelieving. Günter went into the adjoining room, slowly, and with an indifferent air—apparently, I thought, to convince himself that nobody had lied to him. But in that room, Hilde had hidden her friend behind a curtain attached from the clothes cupboard to the wall. Almost immediately, several shots rang out. . . . We ran into the room and found two corpses."

The police were soon there, and the press soon after, and every question seemed to lead to further complications and further scandals. Why, for example, did Günter Scheller feel such homicidal rage against the apprentice cook? His schoolmates began testifying that Scheller was the founder of a suicide society, mysteriously named Fä-Hu, a society in which a score of youths had vowed to kill themselves, taking with them, in each case, "a rival." This made splendid headlines for a time, but further investigation indicated that the secret society was largely a creation of schoolboy imagination. But even if the suicide society was imaginary, why would Scheller consider the apprentice cook his "rival"? A matter of incest? Possibly, but there were also witnesses who testified that Scheller and Stephan had both, at one time, been protégés of an elderly homosexual, who made a practice of escorting young Berlin students on sightseeing tours of Paris—and that Stephan had recently become the favorite not only of Scheller's sister but of his patron.

Confronted with two corpses, no culprit, and an aroused press, the Berlin police promptly arrested Krantz. Indeed, the Scheller parents, returning from Denmark, formally accused Krantz of murdering both boys, but the ballistic evidence contradicted such a charge. The police therefore brought him to trial as an accomplice, for providing the gun, for signing the suicide letter, and for not preventing the murder. These were capital charges, in the 1920's, and when the eighteen-year-old student went on trial for his life, it was one of the grand events of the Berlin season. Reporters flocked in from all over Europe, and from America, and there was even a delegation of visiting jurists from Japan.

Judge Dust of the Second Circuit Court in Moabit seemed to feel, as many German judges did under such circumstances, that it was his duty to question witnesses as sternly as any prosecutor. Specifically, he singled out Hilde Scheller as the cause of the entire tragedy and subjected her to an elaborate public interrogation on her sexual relations with Krantz, Stephan, and her contemporaries in general. On the witness stand, Hilde wept and babbled and lied and called for her parents and finally fainted dead away. The judge's inquisition caused a public outcry, for the middle-aged spectators wanted to ogle and cluck at the misdeeds of their children, but they didn't want them persecuted and humiliated by even the most righteous of judges. Krantz's family, in the meantime, had hired one of the best defense lawyers in Germany, an elegant gentleman named Erich Frey, who liked to sport a monocle and bow tie, and Frey soon cut the prosecution's rather feeble case to pieces. There were endless quarrels between Frey and Judge Dust, and Frey offered several spectacular resignations, but the case finally lurched to the obvious conclusion: Krantz was acquitted.

He was, according to the photographs of the time, a rather unpleasant-looking young man, pale, with thick lips, and his hair parted high on the head and then glued down to either side. Not long after the trial, he left Berlin, and then went to Paris, and changed his name, and started writing novels, and then emigrated to the United States. We pick up the trail in Who's Who in America, under the name of Ernst Erich Noth, educator. Arriving in America in 1941, he worked for the National Broadcasting Company for seven years, then moved into the comparative tranquillity of the academic life, first at the University of Oklahoma, then at Marquette, where he became chairman of the department of classical and modern languages.

Such revelations might seem an invasion of privacy, but for the fact that Noth, now a portly gentleman with a bald head and a gray mustache, has finally written his memoirs and recalled both his trial and his liberation. "After my acquittal, the police had a hard time clearing a way for me through the crowd that cheered me at the doorway. Those shrill cries, I hear them even today. But perhaps, at that moment, I still heard the cries of hatred that had greeted me eight months earlier. . . . I ran into a nearby bar, and threw up. And then my face appeared before me in the washroom mirror. My eyes were haggard, my skin pale, my features soft as wax."

During the trial of Paul Krantz, the defense had brought in several "experts" to testify to the youth's artistic talent, mental competence, and sexual "normality." In the latter categories, the most unusual witness was a small, fat man with flabby hands and owl-like eyes. "His enemies," according to Krantz's account, "spread legends about his penchants, [which] were not, unfortunately, without foundation."

Dr. Magnus Hirschfeld was his name. He had been one of the ten original members of the Berlin Psychoanalytic Association, when it was founded in 1910, and he cajoled Freud into contributing to his *Journal for Sexual Knowledge*. Hirschfeld resigned from the movement the following year, however, and though the reasons are obscure, they may be surmised. Hirschfeld was primarily interested not in psychoanalysis but in the amassing of evidence of sexual peculiarities. His specialty was homosexuality, which he also practiced, but his interests in this field were eclectic, and he ultimately published a multivolume illustrated encyclopedia of sex. It contained page after repellent page of passport-style photographs—mournful-looking hermaphrodites, castrati exhibiting their scars, mustachioed rapists staring out through prison bars, and every other variety of sexual misfit. There is no evidence that Hirschfeld's work ever accomplished any notable goal, and nobody takes it very seriously today, but it was, in its time, a classic of pseudo-scientific pornography.

In the Imperial era, such studies were not officially encouraged. With the coming of the Republic, however, there came the time of "sexual reform," and anyone who professed to be a scientific investigator of sexual practices might anticipate not only a flock of disciples but governmental patronage. "The sexual reformers were a varied lot, for or against almost anything possible," according to one chronicler, "for nudism . . . for the toleration of homosexuality . . . or, if that didn't work, for the punishment of Lesbians . . . for voluntary sterilization . . . for the sexual education of schoolchildren . . . for cosmetic surgery, and for psychoanalytic therapy in free clinics." Dr. Magnus Hirschfeld, seizing the opportunities of the moment, won a government subsidy to build himself an Institute of Sexual Research at the edge of the Tiergarten. From that fortress, he preached in the daily newspapers on the need for a civilized toleration of all sexual irregularities. He was, in fact, one of the city's most vociferous celebrities.

Hirschfeld invited the newly liberated Paul Krantz, by now a confused and rootless nineteen-year-old, to become his pupil. "I visited him several times in his luxurious institute," Krantz recalled, "and attended several of his private courses and seminars, which were all a bit beyond me. I was not exactly a pillar of the church, but I never succeeded in seeing every bell-tower as a phallic symbol."

Krantz duly went his way to Paris, and he did not see Dr. Magnus Hirschfeld again until the spring of 1933, not long after Joseph Goebbels, in the course of burning the books of his enemies, ordered a bust of Dr. Hirschfeld fetched from the padlocked Institute of Sexual Research and had it thrown onto the bonfire. Dr. Hirschfeld managed to escape from Berlin to Switzerland, and now he was spending his days in long automobile rides through the beautiful hills around Ascona, together with a Chinese companion. "He still feared for his life, even after having succeeded in fleeing Germany," Krantz said. "He was pursuing his work, but nobody could pretend that it had achieved any exceptional success. . . . Even today, one shudders with a certain embarrassment at the simple mention of his name."

Sexual research is a relatively harmless form of science, and government subsidies in such a field represent a relatively modest waste of money. The real danger in that gap between what C. P. Snow has called "the two cultures," that gap between the arrogant scientist and the ignorant humanist, is that the government, any government, always subsidizes those who will serve its own interests. And to the extent that all government represents a system for the application of force, then government's basic interest in science is an interest in developing the technology of war.

One of the few factors that helps to save us from devastation, however, is the ignorance of both politicians and generals of the horrors that science is capable of inflicting. Nor are scientists determined to do their worst. In times of peace, at least, they concentrate on relatively abstract problems, and it was only the threat of disaster—the threat of Otto Hahn's discovery of nuclear fission leading to a Nazi atomic bomb—that could prompt so peaceful a man as Albert Einstein to propose to President Roosevelt that the United States start its own nuclear weapons program. Most of the time, though, the military technicians go on demanding money for the perpetuation of the technology of the past. And so, when the German authorities decided in the late 1920's to rearm themselves through technology, they concentrated much of their effort on a weapon that was virtually obsolete before it was ever built, the so-called "pocket battleship."

The German generals, to be sure, had never accepted the principle of disarmament or the restrictions of the Versailles Treaty, which limited them to a force of 100,000 men, without either tanks or airplanes. They had watched helplessly while the French invaded the Rhineland, and they seemed genuinely concerned about an attack by the Poles. To prevent that, General Seeckt had organized the secret "Black Reichswehr" as a defensive force in the East; he had sent his officers to Russia for training in mobile warfare; he had arranged deals for the construction of German weapons in neutral countries like Sweden and Spain.

As a justification, the generals argued that the Versailles Treaty called for a general disarmament in Europe, and that none of Germany's neighbors showed any sign of reducing its own armed forces. Foreign Minister Gustav Stresemann covered up for the generals by repeatedly assuring the Allies that Germany wanted only peace, and in time his assurances had their effect. When the Germans applied for admission to the League of Nations in 1926, they also asked for the abolition of the Allied Control Commission, which had been created to supervise German disarmament. In its last report, the Control Commission declared that Germany "had never disarmed [and] had never had the intention of disarming," but Stresemann's diplomacy was victorious, and the Allies agreed to abolish their Control Commission.

The German generals' secret adventures cost money, however, and their financial demands on the government seemed insatiable. From 1924 to 1928, the military budget almost doubled (from 490 million marks to 827 million). Beyond that, the generals got money from other ministries for military-support costs; beyond even that, they started phantom projects under various civilian disguises, which brought them, according to one estimate, a secret fund averaging 400 million marks a year. But as the military budget became increasingly a creation of fancy, even these routine deceptions proved insufficient. The generals wanted not just a few secret funds but more and more of them. They therefore devised a plan to make quiet investments in various commercial enterprises, including even the movie business. The War Ministry's gullible financial strategists singled out the Phoebus Film Company as a project deserving a loan of three million marks, and when Phoebus went bankrupt in 1927, just like any other mismanaged corporation, the court proceedings brought to light the War Ministry's peculiar investment practices. In the subsequent uproar, Defense Minister Otto Gessler, an able and basically democratic figure who had run the ministry ever since the fall of Gustav Noske, had to resign.

To replace him, President Hindenburg summoned out of retirement his old deputy, General Wilhelm Gröner, and Gröner began by announcing an end to all the Byzantine financial manœuvers in the War Ministry. If Germany was to evade the restrictions of the Versailles Treaty, then let it be done openly, by exploiting possibilities that Allied officials had not foreseen and could no longer control. Hence, the pocket battleship. The treaty permitted Germany to build warships of up to ten thousand tons' displacement, and German technicians had devised a plan to equip armored cruisers with eleven-inch guns, thus creating a ship which, according to its advocates, "could outrun anything that could defeat it and could defeat anything that could overtake it."

In Gröner's first budget, therefore, he requested nine million marks to start the building of the pocket battleship. The Socialists promptly turned the plan into a successful election slogan—"We want food for children, not pocket battleships"—but President Hindenburg took a personal interest in the program and imposed it on each succeeding Chancellor. Through all the financial crises that were to come, through bank closings and unemployment, every Chancellor kept demanding more money for the pocket battleships, which, when finally sent into combat in World War II, proved nearly worthless.

Dr. Walter Dornberger, now living near Buffalo, New York, as a retired vice president of the Bell Aerosystems Company, took a more imaginative view of the possibilities of military technology. "The Treaty of Versailles restricted Germany in all branches of armament," he wrote many years later, echoing the familiar complaint, and then, in a series of imperatives and inevitabilities that illustrate the military-technological mind at work, he went on to explain the results: "The consequence, logically enough, was that the Army Weapons Department began to look for new developments in armament which would increase the fighting power of the few existing troops. . . . Neither industry nor the technical colleges were paying any attention to the development of high-powered rocket propulsion. There were only individual inventors who played about. . . . The Army Weapons Department was forced to get in touch with the individual inventors, support them financially. . . . No progress was being made. . . . There was also the danger that thoughtless chatter might result in the department's becoming known as the financial backer of rocket development. We had therefore to take other steps. . . . There was nothing left to do but to set up our own experimental station for liquid-propellant rockets at the department's proving ground in Kummersdorf near Berlin. . . . We were tired of imaginative projects concerning space travel."

It was these "imaginative projects," though, that prompted a group of young Berliners to found, in 1927, an organization called the Society for Space Travel. They gathered in an abandoned arsenal in the northern suburb of Reinickendorf, named its three-hundred-acre field the "Rocket Airport," and fired their miniature missiles at the moon. One of their most eager members was an eighteen-year-old student, Wernher von Braun, now a top official at the National Aeronautics and Space Administration in Washington. He had been converted to the cause by an article in a magazine. "I don't remember the name of the magazine or the author," Von Braun recalled later, "but the article described an imaginary trip to the moon. It filled me with a romantic urge. Interplanetary travel! Here was a task worth dedicating one's life to! Not just to stare through a telescope at the moon and the planets but to soar through the heavens and actually explore the mysterious universe! I knew how Columbus had felt."

The members of the Society for Space Travel had little money for their experiments, but they managed to talk various manufacturers into providing materials at low cost, and they got workmen to help out in exchange for free housing in the arsenal. News of their experiments duly reached the army, and one day a black sedan drove out to the Rocket Airport, bearing Walter Dornberger, who was ultimately to become a major general in command of Hitler's missile program, and two of his assistants. "They were in mufti, but mufti or not, it was the army," according to Wernher von Braun. "That was the beginning. The Versailles Treaty hadn't placed any restrictions on rockets, and the army was desperate to get back on its feet. We didn't care much about that, one way or the other, but we needed money, and the army seemed willing to help us. In 1932, the idea of war seemed to us an absurdity. The Nazis weren't yet in power. We felt no moral scruples about the possible future abuse of our brainchild. We were interested solely in exploring outer space. It was simply a question with us of how the golden cow would be milked most successfully."

Dornberger was impressed, he said, "by the energy and shrewdness with which this tall, fair, young student with the broad massive chin went to work, and by his astonishing theoretical knowledge." In the fall of 1932, before Hitler, before any sign of war, Dornberger hired Von Braun to design rockets for the German Army. "It was not easy at first," Dornberger recalled, "to get my young collaborators away from their space dreams and make them settle down quietly to hard research and development work. We began with the development of a rocket motor with a thrust of 650 pounds."

The first rocket fired at Kummersdorf, a mere clearing in the pine forests some seventeen miles south of Berlin, rose about a hundred feet into the air and then crashed in the woods. By the end of that year, 1932, Dornberger had built a new concrete launching platform and was ready to try again. Von Braun used a twelve-foot rod, with a can of gasoline at the end, as a kind of giant match to start the rocket, and everything blew up. "Clouds of smoke rose," according to Dornberger. "A single flame darted briefly upward and then vanished. Cables, boards, metal sheeting, fragments of steel and aluminum flew whistling through the air. . . . Steam hissed. Cables were on fire in a hundred places. Thick, black stinging fumes of burning rubber filled the air. Von Braun and I stared at each other wide-eyed."

A month later, Dornberger and Von Braun were carrying on their experiments under a new commander-in-chief, Adolf Hitler, but the change seems to have had very little effect on them—Dornberger's account does not even mention the Nazis coming to power. Two more years passed before the German Army successfully fired its first rocket to a height of 1.4 miles, thus forging the weapon that maintains today's intercontinental balance of terror. "We had made," Dornberger said, "a beginning."

To the musical world of Berlin, which loved Einstein as a violinist but knew very little about either Heisenberg or Von Braun, the year 1927 marked the one hundredth anniversary of the death of Beethoven, and so Artur Schnabel became the first pianist ever to play the cycle of all thirty-two Beethoven sonatas. He performed them in a series of seven consecutive Sundays, and it was characteristic of Schnabel, in his dislike of display, that he played the cycle at the Volksbühne (People's Theatre) in Berlin's working-class district. The pianist himself wore only a plain business suit as he sat down to start with the gentle opening theme of the Pastoral Sonata.

Among the two thousand Berliners gathered in the auditorium, Sunday after Sunday, was Käthe Kollwitz, the artist, who represented, as much as any one person could, those Germans who wanted neither rockets nor the victories that rockets might bring. Just the year before, she had made a pilgrimage to the Belgian village of Roggevelde, where, less than three months after the start of the war, her eighteen-year-old son Peter had been killed. She found the entrance to the cemetery blocked by barbed wire, but a villager helped her through the barricade. "What an impression: cross upon cross," she wrote to her surviving son back in Berlin. "We found our grave. . . . We cut three tiny roses from a flowering wild briar and placed them on the ground beside the cross. All that is left of him lies there in a row-grave. Here and there relatives have planted flowers, mostly wild roses, which are lovely because they arch over the grave and reach out to the adjoining graves which no one tends, for to the right and left at least half the graves bear the inscription *allemand inconnu*. . . . In this place alone the Germans are said to have lost 200,000 men in the course of the four years. . . .

"Tonight," Käthe Kollwitz wrote her son, "I dreamed there would be another war; another was threatening to break out. And in the dream I imagined that if I dropped other work entirely and together with others devoted all my strength to speaking against the war, we could prevent it."

She was wrong, of course. The war was more than a decade away, and when its time came, no group of artists could prevent it. Art never stops war, after all, any more than satire does, or armies of women marching with banners of protest. The only thing that stops war is defeat, not necessarily defeat on the battlefield but defeat in the sense of a recognition that too much money is being lost, and, almost incidentally, too much blood. But if art does not stop wars, it may yet convince the survivors that military victory or military defeat need not be our basic standards. "The function of literature," as Ezra Pound said, ". . . is . . . that it does incite humanity to continue living."

So here, in the Volksbühne, on a Sunday afternoon in 1927, long before Hitler came to power, Käthe Kollwitz found herself "stirred through and through" by Schnabel's performance of the Hammerklavier, and even more moved by his closing work, the Opus 111. "The strange, glittering tones shot flames—a translation into the spheres," she wrote in her diary. "The heavens opened almost as in the Ninth. Then a return. But a return after Heaven has been assured. Clear—consoling—good—that is what this music is. Thank you, Schnabel!"

"The Show Can Begin" 1928

The theatre must in short remain something entirely superfluous, though this also means that it is the superfluous for which we live. Nothing needs less justification than pleasures.

BERTOLT BRECHT

IN ONE OF THE MOST CELEBRATED DRAMAS of the Expressionist the-atre, Georg Kaiser's *From Morning to Midnight,* a nameless antihero called the Bank Cashier suddenly falls in love with a glamorous client at his bank and tries to win her favor by absconding with sixty thousand marks. When the lady rejects him, the Cashier starts wandering through the city and throwing away the stolen money in a kind of suicidal revelry. His wanderings soon lead him to one of Berlin's great spectacles, the six-day bicycle races.

"Childish, this sport," says the Cashier, who has never seen such a circus before. But he quickly recognizes the emotions that have been aroused in the balcony.

"Look up, I say!" he cries. "It's there, among the crowds, that the magic works. The wine ferments in this vast barrel of spectators. The frothing is least at the bottom, among the well-bred public in the stalls. . . . One row higher the bodies sway and vibrate, the limbs begin to dance, a few cries are heard. Your respectable middle class!— Higher still all veils are dropped. A wild fanatic shout, a bellowing nakedness, a gallery of passions!"

"Yes, only Berlin had such wonderful—incredible—events as the six-day bicycle races," says Michael Josselson, the refugee Russian businessman, the one who knew the young Vladimir Nabokov on

241

the tennis courts, and who now sits on a sofa in Geneva and reflects on his past. "We used to queue up for hours to get tickets for the upper tier. We stayed up all night and then slept during the day. What was so wonderful was the *Stimmung*—the atmosphere—it was a kind of popular festival. There was an invalid who walked on crutches—*Krucke*, he was called—and he would cheer the racers on, in a voice that carried all through the Sportpalast, and we would all cheer with him.

"You've never seen a bicycle race?" Josselson says, surprised. "Well, here's how it worked. There were teams, two men on each team. You'd have twelve teams in a race. One of the two had to keep riding all the time. They would cruise along at about twenty miles an hour. Then there were times when one rider would try to steal a lap on the others, and they'd all have to start sprinting. That was the exciting part—we'd all start cheering—and that could last for half an hour or more.

"Every six hours, you had sprints for points. The one who won the sprint got five points, and so on. Most of the races were won on points, because it was so hard to steal a lap. It was rather dangerous too. I know because I tried the tracks myself as an amateur racer, and it's very easy to fall. The curves are very steep, and when you're going very fast, thirty or forty miles an hour, you have spills all the time. And collisions. Not deliberately, just accidents.

"In the mornings, there was a period of 'neutralization' for six hours. Nothing would happen. The bicyclists would just pedal along, very slowly. This was generally from 6 A.M. until noon. They used this time to clean up the stadium, and that's when we all went home to sleep. I would come home absolutely hoarse from cheering—for the Americans. McNamara and Hogan were their names."

At about this time, the *Literarische Welt* sponsored an event of a sort that was once quite popular, a poetry contest, to be judged by one of Germany's most brilliant young writers. The contest ended in recrimination and confusion, however, for the poet-judge rejected all five hundred entries and publicly denounced them as imitations of Rilke and Stefan George, as works of "sentimentality, insincerity, and unworldliness." He recommended that the prize be given to a poem that hadn't been submitted at all, a piece of newspaper doggerel with an English title, "He, He, the Iron Man," which extolled the hero of the bicycle races:

> There's a legend abroad
> That his arms, legs and hands
> Are made of wrought iron. . . .
> He's a miracle man—this Reggie McNamara.

More conventional commentators naturally denounced this bizarre judgment by the young poet, and one of them accused him of "dismal rowdiness," but the poet did not mind in the least. He delighted in provocation and turmoil.

"I, Bertolt Brecht, come from the black forests," he had written.

> My mother took me to the cities while I lay
> Inside her. And the coldness of the forests
> Will be with me till my dying day.
> The asphalt cities are my home. From the very first
> They supplied me with every last sacrament.

And he added, prophetically, for this was written in 1921:

> Of these cities will remain that which blew through them,
>   the wind. . . .
> We know we're only temporary and after us will follow
> Nothing worth talking about.

The young Brecht was a small, slight figure, gangling and awkward, but with the shrewdly watchful eyes of a raccoon. A Russian friend remarked that he "resembles a note blown through a very slender clarinet." He had been born on February 10, 1898 (an Aquarian), into the petty bourgeoisie—his father was a minor official in a minor paper factory in the minor Bavarian city of Augsburg—and he had been christened Eugen Berthold Friedrich Brecht. Even as a youth, though, he had an image of himself as a public figure. He knew that Eugen was no name for a poet, and neither was Berthold. Bertolt, although pronounced in almost the same way, looked better and reverberated more strongly.

Strength—a pseudo-proletarian masculinity, rather aggressively asserted—formed the core of Brecht's carefully contrived image. He almost invariably wore a truck driver's cap and a black leather jacket (with a soft white shirt hidden underneath). His hair, combed forward over the skull, was clipped short around the neck and ears, and he generally had a two-day growth of stubble. (More than twenty years later, in fact, when Brecht was still affecting the appearance of a Berlin truck driver among the dyed and manicured grandees of Hollywood, someone remarked that the celebrated exile mysteriously managed "always to appear with two days' growth of beard; never clean-shaven, but never a three days' growth either.") He took a certain pride in having bad teeth, too, and he was often grimy, at least in these early days, since grime was partly a matter of economy and partly a matter of proletarian solidarity. And he was never without his cheap cigars, which he puffed and waved and gnawed at and left behind in forgotten ashtrays.

The public image—which is scarcely an accurate portrait of this rather wary and very vulnerable poet—may seem unappetizing, but it achieved its effect on the theatrical world of Berlin, and on the many women Brecht encountered in that world. From his youth in Augsburg, there was already an illegitimate son; in the years to come, there were to be two wives, and mistresses beyond all reckoning. "It was a queer thing that he should be so popular with women," observed one of the characters in a novel by Brecht's first patron, Lion Feuchtwanger. "The man literally reeked of sweat . . . and he smelled unmistakably of revolution. Obviously it must be his vulgar ballads that fascinated them. Whenever he sang them in his roaring voice, the women were swept out of themselves." It was, in other words, not just the Brechtian character that Brecht had created for himself but also his vivid talent that attracted and fascinated so many people. "Whenever he took up the guitar," recalled the young playwright Carl Zuckmayer, "the babble of conversation stopped; the footbeat of the tango dancers shuffling around in murky corners came to a halt, and everyone gathered around him as if in a spell. . . . He was an expert on the instrument and loved complicated chords. . . . His singing was raw and abrasive, often with the crudity of a street-singer or music-hall minstrel. . . . You could say of his voice what Herbert Ihering had written about the diction of his early works: 'It is brutally sensual and melancholically delicate. There is vulgarity in it, and abysses of sadness, savage wit, and plaintive lyricism.' "

"*Als im weissen Mutterschosse aufwuchs Baal,*" began one of the young poet's favorite songs,

> *War der Himmel schon so gross und still und fahl. . . .*
> *Jung und nackt und ungeheuer wundersam*
> *Wie ihn Baal dann liebte, als Baal kam.*

Poetry is always difficult to translate, and Brecht's is more difficult than most. Two of his chief acolytes, Eric Bentley and Martin Esslin, have labored over the "Chorale of the Great Baal" and produced the following:

> When inside the white maternal womb grew Baal
> Large already was the sky and still and pale
> Young and naked and almost miraculous
> As Baal loved it when Baal came to us.

Even in the stilted English, a certain energy survives, and one can imagine the interest that the twenty-one-year-old poet aroused in Feuchtwanger and the other literary figures of postwar Munich. Feuchtwanger remembered him as "thin, ill-shaven, unkempt" when he first brought the manuscript of a play, *Spartakus*, which he said he had written solely to make money. Feuchtwanger scolded him for such a base ambition, and Brecht then said he had "another play, which was really good, and he would bring it along. . . . It was called *Baal*."

The play Brecht had written to make money was in fact the first to be produced, under the title of *Drums in the Night*. It was of that popular category known as "homecoming plays," in which various war veterans returned to their various fates. Brecht's hero, Kragler, comes back to find his fiancée pregnant by another man, and his prospective in-laws raging against the Spartakist revolt taking place out in the streets. The rebels appeal to Kragler to join them, but—an odd decision in view of Brecht's subsequent theories —Kragler refuses. "The bagpipes play," he says, "the poor die among newspapers, houses fall down on them, morning dawns, they lie like drowned cats on the pavement. I'm a pig and the pig is going home." Seeing a choice•between revolt and sensuality, Kragler chooses sensuality. "Now for bed," he says to the faithless Anna, "the big, white, wide bed. Come!"

The play opened in Munich in 1922, and the critic Herbert Ihering is noted to this day for having journeyed from Berlin to the premiere and then written: "The twenty-four-year-old poet Brecht has changed the literary complexion of Germany overnight. With Bert Brecht a new tone, a new melody, a new vision has come into our time. . . . He lets the naked human being speak, but in a language we have not heard in years. And with the very first words of the play we become aware: *Tragedy has begun*." With that triumph behind him, Brecht got two of his plays produced the following year—*Baal*, the extravagant and quasi-autobiographical chronicle of a poet searching after the pleasures of life, and *In the Jungle of the Cities*, an even more bizarre story of two men struggling to dominate one another.

It would be a mistake to make too much of Brecht's early works. They are by no means good plays; on the contrary, they are rather sloppy and shapeless, poorly planned and carelessly executed (according to one account, Brecht wrote *Baal* in four days, on a bet). And although avant-garde German audiences of the early 1920's may have admired Brecht's plays because of the vigor of his poetry—*Baal* set off another notable riot when it opened in Berlin—we read them today mainly to observe the antecedents of *The Threepenny Opera* and *Mahagonny* and *Mother Courage*.

In the Jungle of the Cities introduces us, though, to one of the most marvelous creations of the German imagination of the 1920's, that fabulous land of Chicago gangsters, Negro prizefighters, *der Charleston*, and Karl May's invincible cowboy, "Old Shatterhand"; that land where Franz Kafka, too, had set the most baffling of his baffling novels: *Amerika*. Brecht's play is subtitled, "A Boxing Match between Two Men in the Giant City of Chicago," and it begins with a confrontation between the most Brechtian of Chicagoans: a Malayan lumber dealer named Shlink (whose henchmen are known as Skinny, the Baboon, and the Worm) and young George Garga, who works in a rental library. For no apparent reason, Shlink wants to pay Garga fifty dollars for his opinion of a book, and Garga refuses to cooperate. Out of that modest beginning arise the most extraordinary conflicts. In the struggle for "possession of the soul," Shlink gives Garga his entire business but also assaults Garga's sister and fiancée; Garga, on the other hand, uses Shlink's business in a fraud that will lead his antagonist to prison, or, better yet, to a lynching. Shlink defeats him by committing suicide; Garga sets the business on fire.

America? Like Kafka, Brecht not only made no attempt at accuracy but rejected the whole idea of accuracy. "Incorrectness," he said, "[is] hardly or not at all disturbing, so long as the incorrectness [has] a certain consistency." The New York or Chicago that rose on the horizon of the German imagination was a city much like Berlin, but a Berlin of the future, a little like the Los Angeles that exists in the mind of the New Yorker, a place in which all present possibilities are exaggerated and intensified. *Amerika* was the land of extremes of wealth and poverty, extremes of cruelty and violence, but also extremes of hope and freedom and self-fulfillment. "I hear it said," Brecht wrote in one of his poems,

He speaks of America,
And doesn't understand a thing about it.
Why he wasn't even there!
But believe me:
They understand me very well when I speak of America.
The best thing about America is that we understand it.

Brecht's real goal, though, was Berlin, the capital, the metropolis, where, for a young playwright, the Kurfürstendamm offered the same lure, the same sense of theatrical destiny, as Broadway. Brecht finally moved to Berlin in 1924 to take a job as *Dramaturg* at Max Reinhardt's Deutsches Theater (a *Dramaturg* in a German repertory theatre is a playwright who is assigned the responsibility for the company's repertoire, which he can write himself, adapt, commission, or select—an admirable idea unknown in New York), and he found an apartment on the Spichernstrasse, a few blocks south of the Kurfürstendamm. "One had to climb five stories," according to one of his friends, "and balance oneself on a breakneck staircase, push open a massive iron door, walk through a wide corridor to reach his garret. From the large windows one could look down on Berlin. This ocean of roofs Brecht kept constantly in view, as he planned the conquest of the capital."

"But the great things, we haven't yet talked about!" says Professor Fritz Bamberger. "The literature, the theatre! Max Reinhardt's Shakespeare!"

"Max Reinhardt's *Fledermaus!*" says Yehudi Menuhin. "Ah! *Fledermaus!* I walked on air for three days afterward. I loved *Fledermaus.*"

"And the theatre was not *peripheral*," says Rabbi Joachim Prinz. "A new Hamlet would be discussed at breakfast tables all over Berlin. And the biting reviews of Alfred Kerr—they made a *difference* to people."

"Look here—you see—she has kept everything," says Dr. Fred

Grubel. He is the director of a New York research institute dedicated entirely to the preservation of the records of German Jewry, and he is displaying two giant scrapbooks that have just been presented to him by his receptionist, a small, frizzy-haired lady who guards the institute's main door against roving drug addicts. "She's a typical Berliner," says Dr. Grubel, "and so even though she didn't have much money, she went to the theatre every week, even two and three times a week. See—Elisabeth Bergner in *Romeo and Juliet* —Fritz Kortner as Shylock—and Josephine Baker—and she saved all the tickets and all the programs and all the reviews in these scrapbooks, from 1913 to 1933. That's when it ends."

The Germans' relationship to their theatre is quite unlike the Americans' distant view of Broadway. The German drama is not simply a series of box-office hits in a far-off metropolis but part of a nationwide tradition. A young American who wants to write is likely to write a novel; a young German is likely to write a play, quite probably in verse. That is because Goethe and Schiller— unlike, say, Melville—wrote dramas in verse. If Melville actually had written a verse drama, as a matter of fact, it is safe to assume that nobody would ever produce it on Broadway nowadays, but the works of Schiller are redesigned and restaged every year. And not just in Berlin, with its thirty-odd theatres; Germany's regional capitals also have a stage tradition, which derives from their former court theatres, and as a result, it is still easier to see Shakespeare in Munich or Frankfurt than in Chicago.

This kind of theatrical tradition naturally stimulates writers to create new plays, but it stimulates even more the rise of producers and directors who achieve their celebrity by spectacular recreations of the classics. One of the most noted of these was Leopold Jessner, who arrived in Berlin in 1919 to become head of the Prussian State Theatre and opened his season with an Expressionist version of Schiller's *William Tell*. The centerpiece on stage was a device that Jessner made famous—a huge stairway, creating a series of platforms from which the actors could declaim, meditate, or fall. He also dressed up Fritz Kortner, playing the tyrant Gessler, with a uniform and medals much like those of a Prussian Junker, and for good measure, he had Kortner's cheeks rouged bright red. The audience responded with the first of Berlin's great theatre riots of the 1920's. There was shouting and whistling and blowing of trumpets and intermittent fist-fighting, and everyone had a grand time.

Of all these impresarios, the master impresario was Max Reinhardt. A Viennese by origin, and trained as an actor, Reinhardt was short and stocky and rather handsome, with wavy hair and bright blue eyes. He had arrived in Berlin in 1894, at the age of twenty-one, as an actor in Otto Brahm's repertory company at the Deutsches Theater, and eleven years later, when he succeeded Brahm as head of the company, he set out to revolutionize the fundamental techniques of the stage. "The theatre is neither a moral nor a literary institution," said Reinhardt. To him, it was a place for display, spectacle, magic. The revolving stage was his specialty, and so were the mysterious lighting effects that nobody else could duplicate. Reinhardt abolished the walls of conventional theatre sets; he abolished footlights and curtains; his actors moved out into the audience and made it part of the spectacle.

Reinhardt was already famous before the war for his grandiose productions of *Oedipus Rex* and *As You Like It* and *Turandot*, but during the 1920's, he became an international institution. Next to the Grecian façade of his Deutsches Theater, he organized a Chamber Theatre for the production of experimental work, and not far away, he founded a Max Reinhardt School for the training of young actors and actresses in diction and elocution and Dalcroze's rhythmic dancing (one of his pupils was a pudgy girl named Maria Magdalena Dietrich). As his passion for extravagance grew, Reinhardt also acquired a former Berlin circus, the Great Theatre, seating three thousand people, which he reopened with a gigantic production of Aeschylus' *Oresteia*. And he created a new version of *Everyman*, which he staged in front of the cathedral at the Salzburg Festival. And he took his various productions on tours of England and France and the United States.

All the financial details came under the scrutiny of Reinhardt's brother, Edward, a man of great skill and shrewdness, who apparently lived only for the fulfillment of Reinhardt's ambitions. As for other details, Reinhardt acquired a large staff of assistants and experts and sycophants. Salka Viertel, who played a Trojan slave in that *Oresteia*, saw the great director only from a great distance. "Reinhardt himself was invisible in the dark auditorium. Only his voice penetrated it from time to time. [Two assistants] were transmitting Reinhardt's instructions to the chorus and the huge masses of extras through a megaphone. . . . Whenever I saw him passing me in the vestibule, he was surrounded by such an impenetrable wall of satellites and society women that to make him notice me I would have had to faint at his feet, as more enterprising actresses frequently did."

"Reinhardt didn't pay too much attention to his theatrical school," says Walter Slezak, puffing on a cigar as he basks on the balcony of a villa overlooking Lugano. "He left all that to one of his assistants. But you could always tell a Reinhardt actor, by the emotion. You know, the hand to the heart. *Oh, Schmerz!* Pain! And then Reinhardt would tone them down during the rehearsals. It's always easier to have an actor so full of emotion that he has to be toned down rather than have someone so dead that he has to be toned up. Reinhardt never worried much about the minor details of his productions either. He didn't even come to the theatre until the sixth rehearsal. Then he would sit there for four days without saying a word, which made everybody very nervous. Then suddenly, he would say, 'You should move this way instead of that way,' or 'You should say these lines so and so.' And suddenly he had taken charge of everything. And that was the way it always was, even in Hollywood. He didn't do too well there because he wasn't really a movie man, he didn't *see* the way movie men do, but that production of *Midsummer Night's Dream* in the Hollywood Bowl, with Mickey Rooney as Puck, and that wedding march for Titania, with people coming down out of the mountains with torches, and the fire department hidden behind every tree—marvelous!"

Reinhardt, who was already in his mid-forties when the Kaiser's regime collapsed, helped to organize the postwar theatrical revolution by founding a group called "Young Germany," but the members of the group were considerably more radical, and more innocently idealistic, than Reinhardt himself. During a metalworkers' strike shortly after the war, for instance, they marched to the picket lines and presented the half-frozen strikers with their readings of contemporary poetry. Among the most radical and most idealistic of all these theatrical visionaries was a twenty-five-year-old Bavarian actor, son and grandson of a long line of Calvinist ministers, named Erwin Piscator. He had produced a number of plays for his fellow soldiers during the war, then directed a radical theatre group in Königsberg, which went proudly bankrupt, and then arrived in Berlin to found what he called the Proletarian Theatre.

Piscator's Proletarian Theatre expressed the guileless belief that the drama was a medium of revolution. The director favored radical authors like Gorki and Upton Sinclair, and his actors were, at the beginning, not professional performers but unemployed workmen. Once his productions were ready, Piscator ignored the theatres of the Kurfürstendamm and took his little repertory troupe out into the beer halls of the Berlin slums. The stage facilities were primitive, of course, but Piscator found that an interesting challenge. "Styles are born out of necessity," he said.

Early in 1920—on January 15, to be exact—Piscator experienced a kind of revelation. He had brought his troupe to the Kliens Festsaal in the South Berlin working-class district of Neukölln, where he planned to direct and star in a play called *The Cripple*. He had commissioned a young designer, John Heartsfield, to create the sets, and though Heartsfield was notorious for dawdling, Piscator found himself on opening night with a restless audience, no sets at all, and no news of what might have become of Heartsfield. He decided simply to begin, with nothing but a black curtain, a bare stage, and a few props, collected more or less at random. Everything went smoothly until the first act was almost over. At this point Heartsfield suddenly burst into the theatre, carrying huge rolls of painted backdrops under his arm, and shouting for his right to array them onstage.

The performance came to an abrupt halt. Piscator objected that Heartsfield himself was to blame for the lack of sets. Heartsfield retorted that it was Piscator's fault for not having sent a car. When Heartsfield had appeared at the streetcar stop with his rolls of painted backdrops, a series of conductors had refused to let him board their streetcars. Even after Heartsfield had found a conductor who gave in to his pleas, he had had to stand on the swaying back platform of the streetcar, clutching his stage settings as best he could.

"I turned to the audience," Piscator recalled later, "and asked what we should do—whether we should go on with the performance or first place this piece of scenery. The overwhelming majority decided we should first put the scenery into place. . . . We began all over again." And from this moment, Piscator dated his own concept of what came to be known as Bertolt Brecht's "Epic Theatre." It was not—as it sometimes later seemed to be—a matter of the bare stage. Nor was it the artificial decoration of the bare stage, nor the fact that the decorator had interrupted the play in mid-course. No, it was the fact that the audience had decided to put the sets in place and start the play over again. "We had suddenly and definitely broken with the old course of theatre," Piscator said. "Audience and stage were united in one desire."

Epic Theatre, according to Piscator's widow, Maria, consisted of these basic elements: political (and implicitly radical) texts; the abolition of all Aristotelian unities and all naturalistic devices; the introduction of technological innovations ("elevators, treadmills, platforms . . ."). But the basic idea was Piscator's decree: "The purpose of Epic Theatre is to learn how to think rather than how to feel." The first question, though, was whether anyone wanted to watch Epic Theatre. The workers in those neighborhood beer halls, draped with fading flags and smelling of overboiled cabbage, apparently did not. Lacking bread, they wanted circuses—escapism, festivity, and frivolity. "The proletarians," as Mrs. Piscator observed, "did not care for the Proletarian Theatre. . . . [It] died without mourning in April of 1921."

During the next ten years, Piscator's career provided an interesting sequence of radical pronouncements and conservative compromises. For in spite of all theory, the theatre cannot escape from its own economic necessities. It really is not a vehicle for revolution—it does not even have the potentialities of such mass media as television or the movies—but simply an expensive form of middle-class entertainment. In 1923, Erwin Piscator learned that he could lease the Central Theatre for three million marks a year. This was the year of the inflation, so he paid one million in cash and then produced the other two million by ripping out the theatre's heating pipes and selling them to a junk dealer. Once installed there, however, he found that he could draw audiences only with relatively conventional plays—Tolstoy and Romain Rolland, for example—and even then, at the end of the year, he lost his theatre.

The next step took him to the Volksbühne, that extraordinary labor-union creation of the 1890's, which, by recruiting thousands of subscribers for only one-half mark per ticket, had helped to achieve the triumph of the new Naturalists like Ibsen and Gerhart Hauptmann. Now, thirty years later, the Volksbühne organization owned one of the best theatres in Berlin, with a sign over the door that said "Art for the People," and a huge production fund supplied by thirty thousand members—but it was still producing Ibsen. Piscator determined to radicalize this musty institution. His first production there was a play called *The Flags*, about the anarchist riots in Chicago, and then came *Storm over Gothland*, a historical drama which Piscator turned into a pro-Bolshevik account of the Russian Revolution. That was too much for the cautiously conservative directors of the "People's Theatre," and Piscator once again parted with his backers.

The next time—it is now 1927, and we can watch the whole decade roll past as the once-proletarian director searches for the true technique of proletarian theatre—Piscator acquired a baroque institution on the Nollendorfplatz, that shabby traffic circle, partly proletarian, partly just decrepit and run-down, which Christopher Isherwood was later to make the center of his Berlin stories. Piscator proudly renamed his new headquarters the Piscator Theatre. Here, according to his widow, "the plays he proposed to do were . . . plays of active protest, a deliberate *J'Accuse*; a reportage and montage; a warning, history marching on; political satire, morality plays and court trials, purposefully shocking."

Piscator's opening production on the Nollendorfplatz was characteristic. *Hoppla, Wir Leben (Hey, We're Alive)* featured that familiar hero of the German drama, in the splendid tradition of Wozzeck and Doctor Caligari, the madman who shows the sane world to be insane. This version of the familiar paradox was strikingly realistic, however, for its author was Ernst Toller, a distinguished young poet who had just served five years in prison for his leading part in the Bavarian revolutionary regime of 1920. Emerging into the prosperous and bourgeois Germany of 1925, Toller had good reason to make his half-mad hero, Karl Thomas, cry out against the complacency that he saw everywhere around him. "The faces in the street . . ." he remarks at one point. "I've never noticed before how few people have faces. Lumps of flesh, most of them, blown up with worry and conceit." And again, inevitably: "Perhaps there's no distinction between the world and a madhouse nowadays. Yes, yes . . . really . . . the same men as are here under observation as lunatics are strutting about outside as normal, trampling down the others." Karl Thomas finds that one of his former comrades is now a cabinet minister ("What are the masses?" says the betrayer. "Could they do any work in the old days? Nothing! Spout catch phrases and smash things up!"). Karl Thomas vows to assassinate the minister, but a right-wing student, obviously modeled on the youths who killed Rathenau, steps in and does the actual shooting. Karl Thomas is arrested for the murder, however, and, like so many German stage heroes, commits suicide. "There are only two choices left—" according to the closing lines of the play, "to hang oneself or to change the world." At which point, various enthusiasts in the audience began singing the "Internationale."

To Piscator, Toller's manuscript was a perfect medium for all the devices of Epic Theatre. At the very beginning, movie projectors showed newsreels of the marching revolutionaries—a Piscator trademark—and actors paraded around with signs and placards—another trademark. A huge framework of metal bars contained the various levels of the stage, and there was even a screen that showed the heartbeats of an aviator crossing the Atlantic. There were no self-contained "acts" but rather a series of scenes, for, as one commentator put it, "Piscator [had] found his style, a theatre between narrative and drama." And this was only the first of many scandalous successes on the Nollendorfplatz. Piscator's staging of Alexei Tolstoy's *Rasputin* provoked a lawsuit from the exiled Kaiser Wilhelm, and George Grosz's sets for Piscator's version of *The Good Soldier Schweik* (partly rewritten by Brecht) led to an official charge of criminal blasphemy. But there was something fundamentally artificial in this belated triumph of the left-wing theatre. Piscator's annual production budget of a half-million marks had been guaranteed by a famous actress, who had married a rich art collector, and who, in due time, got a choice role in one of Piscator's productions. And when Piscator's widow describes the director's new success on the Nollendorfplatz, she writes, without any sense of irony, that "the bejeweled *nouveaux riches* paid unheard-of fees to ticket agents to acquire their first-night seats."

By this time, though, Piscator had still bigger dreams. He began negotiating to buy a large plot of land near the Hallesche Tor, that site of the fierce fighting during Spartakus Week, and he commissioned Walter Gropius to design what they both called a Total Theatre. The plans still exist. The auditorium is oval, a circle of seats supported on twelve columns. At one end, there is a three-part stage, designed as a kind of triptych. In front of that, there is a circular proscenium stage that protrudes out among the orchestra seats. But

—and this is what makes the Gropius-Piscator Total Theatre so total —the circular proscenium stage is itself part of a larger circle (including a lot of orchestra seats), which can be rotated in mid-performance so that the nearby seats turn backward, and the circular proscenium stage spins out into the very center of the theatre. In addition to this mechanical legerdemain, there were to be movie screens at various points in the theatre, for Piscator's multimedia displays. There was also to be a kind of tunnel leading from the three-part stage around the whole amphitheatre, so that a chorus could march out and surround the audience. The purpose of all this, according to Gropius, was the "mobilization of all three-dimensional means to shake off the audience's intellectually directed apathy, to overwhelm them, to stun them, and to force them to participate in experiencing the play."

The term "Total Theatre" became popular, just like "Epic Theatre." Piscator, by now thirty-five, was a celebrity. We can only wonder whether he remembered, as he studied Gropius' plans for this Disneyland structure, how far he had come in the decade since those amateur productions by the Proletarian Theatre in the evil-smelling beer halls of the Berlin slums. Capitalism, too, has its rules, however, and Piscator never succeeded in raising enough money to build the spectacular showplace that he and Gropius had designed.

Bert Brecht's view of the ideal theatre was somewhat different. This was not a matter of physical production so much as of tone and style. He was convinced, for instance, that the lights in the auditorium should stay on, and that people should wander around, and that everyone should be free to smoke cigars. What he called the *Verfremdungseffekt* (generally translated as "alienation effect") required that the audience remain aware that it was in a theatre, watching a spectacle, not participating in a simulation of reality— but not involved in the mechanisms of Total Theatre either. In anticipation of Marshall McLuhan, Brecht wanted the drama to remain "cool." The actors, instead of representing characters in a play, should simply "present" them, without emotion. Nor was his view without precedents. Hadn't the Globe Theatre produced Shakespeare's tragedies in the light of midafternoon, and with girls selling oranges in the aisles? "In the disconnectedness of [Shakespeare's] scenes," said Brecht, "one recognizes the disconnectedness of human fate." Brecht wanted the theatre to become once again a festival, like the circus, or the races, or, above all, the prizefights.

We are a bit sated, nowadays, with prizefighting. We know the heavyweight contenders, and a middleweight or two, and we have forgotten that boxing once was banned by law, and not so long ago, and that it therefore had all the glamour of the forbidden. George Bernard Shaw devoted an early novel to the struggle of a prize-fighter, and Ernest Hemingway wrote with great feeling about two prostitutes arguing over which one had slept with the great Stanley Ketchel. And Bertolt Brecht, when he came to listing the various vices in *Mahagonny*, placed boxing near the top of his list of sensual indulgences. The fight in *Mahagonny* is not a matter of skill either, but of brute force. "Let's go!" cry the men in the audience. "It's fixed! Bull! He's getting it! Careful! Don't fall! Below the belt! No holding! That one hit home! Doesn't matter! . . . Moses, make some mincemeat! Beat him to a pulp!" Trinity-Moses soon knocks out his smaller opponent, and the referee begins counting: "One—two—three—four! The man's dead!" And the onlookers just drift away, saying, "A knockout is a knockout. He couldn't take it."

Prizefighting appears to have been almost unknown in Berlin before World War I—the Germans tended to prefer more abstract forms of mortification, like running and swimming and gymnastics—and it was popularized by war veterans who had learned it in British prison camps on the Isle of Man. But once the regular fights started, the combination of skill and violence, nicely regulated and confined within a spotlit square, proved immensely popular. First at the Busch Circus, behind the cathedral, and then at the new Sportpalast, prizefights became not just spectacles for the plebeians but sparkling social events. The Crown Prince attended regularly, along with flocks of actors and debutantes. And when Alfred Flechtheim, the king of Berlin's art dealers, opened a new show, he liked to have a boxer or two in attendance. Hans Breitensträter, who was once a promising young middleweight, still remembers Flechtheim saying, at his first showing of Picassos, "Hännschen, buy one of these paintings yourself and just keep it, and you will be rich."

This was, of course, the era of Jack Dempsey and Gene Tunney, and Berlin, limited to heroes like Breitensträter, was very far from the center of action. There was, indeed, a certain amount of small-town fraud and artifice in the arenas of Berlin. One youth named

Sally Mayer, for example, achieved a mild notoriety under the name of Sabri Mahir, alias the Terrible Turk, by fighting against four carefully selected opponents in one evening. After a number of opponents proved to have been selected without sufficient care, the Terrible Turk retired from active combat and opened a gymnasium just off the Tauentzienstrasse, where aging bankers, sales executives, and an occasional movie star liked to come for workouts, massages, and a touch of lower-class glamour.

Then there was Dixie Kid, an American Negro who had been world welterweight champion between 1904 and 1906 and who now had come to find refuge among the boxing enthusiasts of the German capital. Dixie Kid was long past his prime, but he fascinated the Berliners. When he smiled, he displayed a number of gold teeth, and some of them had diamonds embedded in them. Dixie Kid could still outwit and outbox the local heavyweights, even though he gave away fifty pounds or more to his younger opponents. He also staged exhibitions in which he threw a handkerchief onto the floor of the ring and then fought the entire bout with one foot on the handkerchief. But when the exhibitions were over, the middle-aged Dixie Kid wandered back to his quarters and surrendered to his poison. He was desperately addicted to cocaine.

Not all of Berlin sport was provincial melodrama, however. "Carraciola," says Walter Slezak, savoring the mellifluous sound of the name. "He was the great Mercedes driver, he made Mercedes famous as a racing car, and I still remember seeing him race on the Avus. Now they're building a museum for him in Indianapolis, and his widow, who lives right near here, is going there for the opening. And I remember Max Schmeling when he was still a middleweight. I saw him win the middleweight title at Luna Park in Berlin. We all thought he was a good middleweight, but none of us ever dreamed that he would go to America and become heavyweight champion of the world."

"Berlin had spruced up its façades and done some repainting. . . . There was a new Kurfürstendamm society whose parties were more elaborate and select than those of the good old sharks of 1920 and who felt themselves entitled to an even crasser display of snobbish cynicism. At one such affair that I attended in February of 1924 the walls were festooned with such maxims as 'Love is the foolish overestimation of the minimal difference between one sexual object and another.' The girls hired to serve drinks went about naked, except for transparent panties embroidered with a silk fig leaf. They were not, like the 'bunnies' in modern American nightclubs, there just for looks, but could be freely handled—that had been included in their pay."

The mildly cynical voice is that of Carl Zuckmayer, who had just returned to the capital. "Brecht said we had to go to Berlin," according to Zuckmayer. "That was where the theatrical battles were being fought, he said." Both of the two young playwrights became *Dramaturgs* at Max Reinhardt's Deutsches Theater, but Brecht, according to Zuckmayer, "did not even make a pretense of working. Occasionally he turned up in the theatre and demanded dictatorial powers. Above all he wanted the 'German Theatre' to be renamed the 'Epic Smoking Theatre,' with the whole operation devoted exclusively to his plays. . . . When all these suggestions were turned down and he was . . . not allowed to direct a Shakespeare performance, he vanished again and thereafter limited himself to coming in punctually to collect his salary."

Zuckmayer, however, devoted himself to working in Reinhardt's theatre, learning all the elements of how plays were staged (and stealing coal from his office stove). This was the year in which Reinhardt produced Shaw's *St. Joan*, starring Elisabeth Bergner, even before it opened in London, and for good measure, he offered the premiere of Pirandello's *Six Characters in Search of an Author*. The young playwright watched Reinhardt dictate long notes on how every scene, almost every sentence, should be presented—and then he watched Reinhardt discard all his own notes in order to pursue the actors' "natural reactions." And while Brecht's plays appeared and disappeared at various theatres, Zuckmayer was working toward a different goal, the commercial hit. He had a chance to spend a summer with a rich cousin in a villa on the Wannsee, and there he began writing a comedy called *The Merry Vineyard*. "I laughed with every sentence I wrote," he recalled later. To the rich cousin, he had to pretend that he was highly prosperous, on the verge of leaving for a vacation in the Alps, but from the cousin's butler, he had to borrow streetcar fare, and even used razor blades.

Zuckmayer finished his play in the fall of 1925, and fumed at having it rejected by all the major Berlin theatres, but it finally fell into the hands of a gray-haired entrepreneur named Julius Elias, who promised him, "Your play will make millions! Millions!" Elias found a producer, and a few weeks later, before the play had even opened, Zuckmayer won the Kleist Prize, the most important award for a young dramatist. The prize was worth fifteen hundred marks in cash, and as soon as Zuckmayer heard of his triumph, he took his new wife, Alice, and her daughter on a grand shopping spree. "We went from shop to shop. We needed shoes, socks, stockings, coats. Michaela received a dress and toys. . . . That we were running through all the money in a single day seemed to us perfectly natural. Those fifteen hundred marks were a gift from heaven, not destined to be doled out thriftily." By the end of the day, Zuckmayer had only enough money left to buy a lavish dinner at a theatrical restaurant called Hacker's, and to pay off the debts he owed from previous meals there. He ordered venison; he ordered the finest wines. When the feast was over, he asked for the bill, and for an accounting of all his past debts. The waiter went to Herr Hacker himself, and Herr Hacker appeared at Zuckmayer's table. "A man who wins the Kleist Prize has no debts here," said Herr Hacker, tearing up every bill that Zuckmayer had ever signed.

The Merry Vineyard opened in Berlin in December of 1925, to roars of applause and rave reviews. It was soon leased to other theatres all over Germany. It made Zuckmayer rich. It also inspired, because of its mockery of the Nationalists, and particularly Nationalist students, no less than sixty-three different riots. For Germany was approaching the time when a riot was the measure of theatrical success.

The German word for the tropical tree is "*Mahagoni*," which both is and isn't relevant to Brecht's invention of the term "Mahagonny." He started using it as early as 1923, applying it to both Berlin and Munich, and there seems to have been a connection between the brown wood of the tree and the spectacle of Hitler's new Storm Troopers. Brecht himself never defined the connection, but one of his friends has recorded that Mahagonny originally stood for "masses of petit-bourgeois, wooden figures in brown shirts," and that it also represented a "utopia of the philistine," a "cynical, stupid beer-hall state."

"If Mahagonny comes," Brecht said at one point, "I go."

Eventually, in 1930, Brecht moved his mythical "City of Nets" to his mythical America, apparently on the west coast of Florida, not far from Pensacola, but Brecht's geography was always subject to his love of exotic names—Pensacola, Alabama, these are not places but, like Soho and Cooch Behar, a series of vowel sounds. ("Incorrectness . . . [is] not at all disturbing. . . .") And in the legendary America of vast wealth and total materialism, Mahagonny represented, like Berlin, a state of mind. "Here we'll offer fun," says the founder of Mahagonny, the Widow Begbick,

> For it is the delight of all men
> not to suffer and to be allowed to do anything.

Just before a hurricane threatens to destroy the city of Mahagonny at the end of Act I, the hero, Jimmy Mahoney, asserts Widow Begbick's philosophy in even more extreme terms:

> Do everything tonight that is forbidden.
> When the hurricane comes, it'll do exactly the same.

Throughout most of the 1920's, then, Brecht gestated the slowly changing concept of Mahagonny. In its original form, the work was a series of five songs, which he published in his brilliant collection of poems, *Die Hauspostille* (*Manual of Piety*) (1927). Of these five, two were written in Brecht's strange English, including the chorus of whores singing the marvelous "Alabama Song":

> Oh! Moon of Alabama
> We now must say good-bye
> We've lost our good old mamma
> And must have whisky
> Oh! You know why.

Brecht, with his guitar, had sung these songs all over Berlin, and *Die Hauspostille* provided his own music, including a crude version of the "Alabama Song." But he was too much of a professional not to realize that he needed an equally professional collaborator. What was strange was that he chose for this collaboration a shy, bespectacled, wholly untheatrical composer, a pupil of the great Busoni, a creator of atonal chamber music, several unsuccessful one-act operas, and a rather unpopular concerto for violin and winds—Kurt Weill.

It is not certain exactly how Brecht and Weill discovered each other. Weill apparently made the first approach, impressed by some of Brecht's poems, and discontented with the sterility of academic composition. "What do you want to become, a Verdi of the poor?" asked Busoni. "Is that so bad?" Weill replied. It is also uncertain why Brecht's collaborations with Weill were so much more subtle and sophisticated than anything he had written until then, or why Weill, in turn, changed from a composer of string quartets into the man who ultimately wrote *Lady in the Dark*. Such relationships always involve a series of interactions, but the general view is that Brecht dominated the partnership, not only because he was an immensely gifted poet and an exceptionally musical poet, but because he was Bert Brecht, who ultimately dominated everyone around him. "Brecht was much the stronger of the two," says Nicholas Nabokov, the composer, a tall, white-haired man, cousin of the novelist, and also a pupil of Busoni. He is standing serenely, with his elbow propped on a mantelpiece, in the midst of a cocktail party on Long Island, and remembering. "Brecht had to *force* Weill to write differently," says Nabokov, "to make the music go like—like this. . . ." Standing there, amidst the noise of the party, Nabokov starts to hum in the slightly syncopated beat that can be recognized instantly as the Berlin jazz of the 1920's.

John Gutman, an assistant director of the New York Metropolitan Opera, a sad-eyed, somewhat wrinkled man, with a collection of twenty-two toy elephants on his desk, recalls the change vividly. "Weill started out as an *academic* revolutionary. His early works, the violin concerto, and an opera called *The Czar Has His Picture Taken*, they were all atonal. Nobody will ever want to hear them unless he's writing a dissertation on Weill. But Brecht wasn't interested in that kind of thing."

Gutman was a young music critic in those days, on the *Börsen-Courier*, and he wrote some reviews on the side for a music magazine produced by Brecht's publisher, Gustav Kiepenheuer. "He told me that Brecht had written some beautiful songs for a new play. Brecht performed them on the guitar, but he couldn't write them down, so Kiepenheuer sent me to see whether I could do something about the problem. I went to Brecht's place on the Spichernstrasse—that's spelled S-p-i-c-h-e-r-n-strasse—I don't know why I remember that, but I do—and it was nothing but what you'd call a pad nowadays. No rugs, no curtains. I remember, there was a broken-down sofa in

one corner, and Brecht said, 'Look at that—it's not even good enough
to make love on.' Then he sat down—he was wearing the leather
jacket, and chewing on a cigar, and he played his guitar and sang
these songs, which later appeared as Weill's works. . . . No, not
The Threepenny Opera. These were the first of the *Mahagonny*
songs. I remember there was one that went,

> Auf nach Mahagonny
> Das Schiff wird losgeseilt
> Die Zi-zi-zi-zivilis
> Die wird uns dort geheilt.

That means, 'Off to Mahagonny, the sails are set, and there the
tse-tse-tse'—well, '*Zivilis*' is a sort-of made-up word that sounds like
both civilization and syphilis— 'and there *Zivilis* will be cured.' That
was in maybe 1925 or 1926, and of course he eventually got Weill
to work on the music, to turn it into theatre music, not academic
music. I can just imagine him saying, 'If you want to work with me,
then forget that shit stuff'—that's the way he talked, he was the most
vulgar man—'forget that shit stuff you've been writing and write
some *songs*.'"

Lotte Lenya, Weill's widow, naturally remembers the collaboration somewhat differently. A two-room apartment on the Louisen-
platz, and Weill working away with a large black piano. . . . "It was
the spring of 1927, and Kurt had just finished setting to music the
five Mahagonny songs from Brecht's book of poems, *Hauspostille*.
Now Brecht had linked the songs with a narrative into a completely
new kind of song-sketch, and the work was to be performed at the
Baden-Baden Kammermusik Festival that summer. Kurt had written
the 'Alabama Song' for my completely untrained voice—I had begun
as a dancer, then turned to acting—and insisted that I must sing it in
Baden-Baden; so this was to be my audition for Brecht, also my first
meeting with him. . . . [Brecht] listened with that deep courtesy
and patience that I was to learn never failed him with women and
actors. 'Not quite so Egyptian,' he said, turning my palm upward,
extending my arm outward in direct appeal to the moon of Alabama.
'Now let's really work. . . .'"

The Baden-Baden festival was one of those heavily subsidized
affairs at which modern music traditionally receives its ceremonial
premieres and instant interments. First came Darius Milhaud's *Rape*

of Europa, described as a series of "spoofs on Greek legends," then Ernst Toch's *The Princess and the Pea,* then Paul Hindemith's *There and Back,* which proceeded from a beginning to a middle and then, exactly and literally, backward from the middle to the beginning. Then, according to Miss Lenya, "the sophisticated international audience stared in bewilderment when the stagehands began to set up a boxing ring on the stage. . . . And *Mahagonny* began—with a real, an unmistakable *tune!* The demonstration began as we were singing the last song, and waving placards—mine said, 'FOR WEILL'— with the whole audience on its feet cheering and booing and whistling. Brecht had thoughtfully provided us with whistles of our own . . . so we stood there whistling defiantly back. . . .

"Kurt and Brecht, on our return to Berlin, at once set to work on the full-length *Mahagonny,* taking a few months off in 1928 to finish something commissioned by producer Ernst-Josef Aufricht *Die Dreigroschenoper,* no less, and its story belongs elsewhere."

"Aufricht, yes," says Salka Viertel. "He was the pretty son of a very rich man. In coal or wood or something like that. He was a little actor in Dresden, and he didn't have the slightest idea of how to act. We used to make fun of him, mimic him. I tried to give him some diction lessons. When my husband founded *Die Truppe* as a repertory company in Berlin, Aufricht's father gave him some money to put in it—maybe a thousand dollars—I don't remember the exact sum, but it was a good sum in those days, though not really a lot. He had no real influence on us, but he was pleasant and amusing."

Five years later, in 1928, Aufricht was still determined to make his way as a theatrical entrepreneur, and he rented the century-old Theater am Schiffbauerdamm, a tower-topped relic ornamented with alabaster tritons and dolphins and assorted nymphs and muses, which still stands on the quay where Berlin's shipbuilders once worked. Here, Aufricht vowed to stage a play, if he could just find one. He telephoned publishers and agents, and he even announced, according to one account, that he would commit suicide if he couldn't get a play on stage for the opening of the theatre season. Finally, in a Berlin café named Schlichter's, he encountered Brecht, who said he was busy on *Mahagonny* but had sketched six scenes of an adaptation of an old English musical play. Brecht had a secretary called Elisabeth Hauptmann, and she, knowing English somewhat better than the master, made it her business to provide him with ideas and partial translations from works being produced in England and the United States. In London, from 1920 to 1923, there had been a highly successful revival of John Gay's eighteenth-century drama, *The Beggar's Opera*. Miss Hauptmann urged Brecht to read it. She also translated a few scenes, and Brecht, recognizing a work that expressed many of his own views, began sketching a modernized version.

On the day after Aufricht encountered Brecht—a rainy day, as it happened—the producer sent a maid to Brecht's apartment to get the manuscript, and she returned with a few pages, soaking wet. Aufricht read them and decided immediately that he would buy them, commission the play, and produce it that same August. He didn't even know, at first, that there would be new music involved, and when he heard that the music would be provided by a relatively obscure avant-garde composer named Weill, he secretly hired a young technician to work over the original songs by Johann Christoph Pepusch, so that he would have an alternate score available. Brecht and Weill decided, meanwhile, that they could finish the work only by getting out of Berlin. They rented a house on the French Riviera for themselves, their wives, and Brecht's young son, Stefan. "The two men wrote and rewrote furiously, night and day, with only hurried swims in between," according to Lotte Lenya. "I recall Brecht wading out, pants rolled up, cap on head, stogie in mouth. . . ."

"No, I don't remember any of that," says Stefan Brecht. He is a thin, frail man with a thin, frail voice, deeply sunken eyes, and thick, bushy hair. Now in his mid-forties, he lives in a house in Greenwich Village and wears a turtleneck sweater and gray suede boots. He is writing a book about Karl Marx. He is acting in a small theatre, Off-Off-Broadway, in which he plays the role of a hermaphrodite who marries himself. Like his father, he constantly puffs on a cigar, but he shrugs off any suggestion that he is keeping up any traditions. "I am not an expert on Brecht," says Stefan Brecht.

The conversation drifts into the question of Brecht's political ambiguities—the ambiguity, for example, of a Marxist trying to earn his living in Hollywood ("Every morning, to earn my bread,/I go to the market, where lies are bought," Brecht had written. "Hopefully/

I join the ranks of the sellers.") And of a Marxist cooperating docilely with the House Un-American Activities Committee, supposedly investigating Communism in Hollywood. ("Have you ever made application to join the Communist Party?" asked the attorney for the committee, and Brecht said, "No, no, no, no, no, never." And Ring Lardner, Jr., one of the so-called "Hollywood Ten" who went to prison for refusing to cooperate with the committee, recalls that Brecht was very apologetic after the hearing but said he had to testify because he had to get back to Germany. And when asked whether Brecht hadn't been a little too—well, perhaps a little groveling, Lardner indignantly says, "No, he was *not*, he was *not* groveling.") And of the famous libertarian finally returning, with an Austrian passport, a Swiss bank account, and a West German publishing contract, to his own state-subsidized theatre in Stalin's colony of East Germany. ("We know," wrote Günter Grass, in his accusing drama, *The Plebeians Rehearse the Uprising*, "that while the revolt in East Berlin [in 1953] . . . was going on, Brecht did not interrupt his rehearsals. . . . We know that Bertolt Brecht took an attitude of wait-and-see. . . . In my play the construction workers, who interrupt the Boss's rehearsals, [believe] that he is somebody whom the government supports and tolerates as a display of cultural property, or as a kind of privileged court jester.")

And of that strange Brechtian story, which is fundamental to Brecht's view of life, and to such great creations as *Mother Courage* and *Galileo*, of the man who said no. There once was a little man who lived peacefully in a little house, and one day a powerful official came to his door and said, "Will you serve me?" The little man did not say a word, but he let the official into his house, and for seven years, he bowed down to the official, and fed him, and served him. Finally, the official grew so fat and indolent that he died. The little man quietly wrapped the official's body in a blanket and threw it out of the house. "Then he washed the bedstead, whitewashed the walls, breathed a sigh of relief and answered: 'No.' "

"Yes, I think I understand that," says Stefan Brecht, putting his feet on the desk, with the gray suede boots raised high. "It's about hypocrisy, the hypocrisy of thinking no but doing yes. So many people do that. You're wearing a white shirt and a tie—that's doing yes.

"But although I feel I understand the story," says Stefan Brecht, smiling vaguely, "that might be compatible with not understanding. Perhaps the story is just humorous, a kind of game. Perhaps it's not supposed to have any meaning. One function of a poem is simply to express a complexity. These are Hegelian situations, concerning opposites that relate to one another."

"Let's go back to the specific example, though. When your father went back to Germany after the war, why did he pick the East rather than the West?"

"Was there any choice?"

"Well, yes."

"I don't think so at all."

"Why not?"

"There's never a choice. When people think they have a choice, they're mistaken."

"But there are always alternatives, and you can always pick one or the other."

"That's all metaphysics," says Stefan Brecht, heatedly, "and I'm talking about experience. If you can't understand what I'm saying, there's nothing I can do about it."

Down in the kitchen, Mrs. Brecht is cooking supper, roast lamb and fried onions and kidneys with lots of butter and herbs, and two small children are wandering about, concocting a dessert that contains what they call a secret ingredient. There is a noise offstage, and Mrs. Brecht disappears for a moment and then returns with an enormous goose in her arms, not a toy goose but a real goose, its long white neck swaying to and fro in stoical bewilderment. Mrs. Brecht takes the goose to the kitchen door and then dumps it outside. "The children got it in school when it was very small," Stefan Brecht explains, "and it just kept growing."

Two centuries before Brecht, John Gay was a Brechtian. As a youth, he served a disagreeable apprenticeship to a London silk merchant. Trying to make his living as a poet, he became an unsuccessful supplicant to various aristocratic patrons. He invested his savings in a South Seas stock swindle, and the subsequent bankruptcy brought him to physical collapse. On his grave is inscribed one of his own couplets:

> Life is a jest, and all things show it.
> I thought so once, and now I know it.

His *Beggar's Opera,* produced in 1728, was intended as a satire on the corrupt administration of Sir Robert Walpole (and also as a parody on the stately operas of Handel). Its central figure is Mr. Peachum, the organizer and ruler of London's thieves, who starts with a very Brechtian ballad:

> Through all the Employments of Life
> Each Neighbour abuses his Brother;
> Whore and Rogue they call Husband and Wife:
> All Professions be-rogue one another.

(And Pepusch's melody for this song was appropriated by Kurt Weill for "Mr. Peachum's Morning Chorale.") The basic plot is all in the original version: Peachum is furious because his daughter has fallen in love with a highwayman, Captain Macheath. Peachum gets his revenge by informing on Macheath and having him arrested. But Macheath has also seduced the jailkeeper's daughter, who helps him escape. Macheath repeatedly visits a brothel, however, and so he is caught once again. Doomed to execution, he is saved by theatrical decree. A two-part chorus appears on stage, and the "player" announces that "an Opera must end happily." It is left to a beggar to complain that there is now no moral, because "it is difficult to determine whether (in the fashionable Vices) the fine Gentlemen imitate the Gentlemen of the Road, or the Gentlemen of the Road the fine Gentlemen."

Brecht had always been a radical, but by the time he set to work on his adaptation of the *Beggar's Opera,* he had evolved from a purely emotional radical into a convinced Marxist. When other playwrights brought him their manuscripts, he presented them with copies of *The Communist Manifesto* and told them to reconsider their work in terms of "scientific socialism." He even spent a good deal of time trying to convert the *Manifesto* into hexameters. And he wrote: "When I read *Das Kapital* of Marx, I understood my own pieces. . . . This Karl Marx was the only spectator of my pieces I have ever seen." But although Brecht determined to turn the *Beggar's Opera* into an illustration of class conflict, he could not resist the temptation to strengthen Gay's rather stilted work with his own sense of drama (the surprise ending, to cite only one example, is announced by a royal messenger on horseback). And so Mac the Knife began to grow, from the rather minor highwayman in Gay's work into the nihilistic hero of *The Threepenny Opera.*

Gay had already endowed Macheath with a violent character and a curious ambiguity toward women. ("I must have women," he says at one point, but later, after being betrayed to the police, he cries out, "Women are Decoy Ducks; who can trust them! Beasts, Jades, Jilts, Harpies, Furies, Whores!") Brecht added a new element of betrayal, then, by creating the character of Tiger Brown, the police commissioner, to whom Mac the Knife betrays his own followers. "Betrayal," as one critic has observed, "is almost a structural element of the play, because the action succeeds through a complicated series of double-crosses. . . . Mackie, therefore, functions in two distinct ways, being both the agent of the author's rebellion and the thing rebelled against." As a rebel, Mac the Knife often talks like today's most vehement radicals—"What is the burgling of a bank to the founding of a bank?" he demands—but Brecht insisted that his hero must not be heroic. "The gangster Macheath should be presented by the actor as a bourgeois phenomenon," Brecht declared. "The original English drawings for *The Beggar's Opera* show a squat but thickset man in his forties, with a head like a radish, already somewhat bald."

Despite all of Brecht's theories, however, the character of Macheath escaped from his control, and so did that of Jenny Diver, who was originally only one of Macheath's many girls. This loss of control occurred partly because Brecht infused more vitality into his characters than into his theories, but also because the musical theatre has needs of its own. It is quite possible that Brecht believed that any musical collaborator would simply amplify and orchestrate a few melodies that Brecht whistled for him, providing a few musical interludes to ornament the text of the play. If so, he was quite mistaken, for music always tends to dominate text. Kurt Weill knew that perfectly well. And in his quiet way, he began turning Brecht's play into his own opera.

He did not need or want an overpowering orchestra. He used only eight instruments, including harmonium and banjo. But he did need a hero, and a crotchety old man like Mr. Peachum wouldn't do. The songs he wrote for Peachum were humorous, and short. In following his own theatrical instinct, Weill wrote the big songs for Macheath—"The Cannon Song," "The Ballad of the Easy Life," "The Procurer's Ballad," and "What Keeps a Man Alive?"—the last with that powerful declaration of Brechtian ethics: "What keeps a man alive? He lives on others. He likes to beat them, cheat them, eat them whole if he can." And that famous, untranslatable Brechtian line: *"Erst kommt das Fressen, dann kommt die Moral"* (roughly: "Feed us before you preach to us").

Musical theatre needs not just a heroic hero but also a heroic heroine, and Polly Peachum was too mild and bland for that. Like most of Brecht's early heroines, she was somewhat thin and passive, a victim of various circumstances. The songs Weill wrote for her are mostly parodies of love songs; they make her, like her parents, a somewhat ridiculous figure. Weill's own idea for a heroine required someone tougher and more earthy, and so it was the raucous voice of Jenny Diver that he combined with Mac the Knife in the great tango ("The Procurer's Ballad") and in "What Keeps a Man Alive?" As for solo songs, Brecht had written for Polly Peachum the dramatic "Pirate Jenny," the vengeful fantasy of a kitchen maid who becomes commander of a mysterious pirate ship and decides which prisoners to kill: "All of them." Weill's passionate song was no longer assigned to Polly, however, but to Jenny Diver. And it is not entirely coincidental that the role of Jenny had been assigned, from the beginning, to Weill's wife, Lotte Lenya.

She was and is one of the phenomena of the musical theatre, now past seventy, but still singing and still fascinating audiences with a talent that defies description. She has, according to one critic, " a face like a clock without a second hand." According to another, "she has a rasping voice that could sandpaper sandpaper, and half the time she does not even attempt to sing, but she can put into a song an intensity that is almost terrifying." She was born in the slums of Vienna, daughter of a coachman and a laundress, and she still remembers that, at the age of four, she walked the tightrope with an umbrella at a neighborhood circus. She came to Berlin as a dancer, and played a few minor roles in Shakespeare and Molière. The playwright Georg Kaiser took a fancy to her and invited her to stay with his family in their lakeside villa. One Sunday, the Kaisers asked her to take a rowboat and meet a young composer they were expecting. "I took the rowboat and went to the station and there was this funny-looking little man in great thick glasses and a little blue suit. 'Would you mind entering our transportation?' I asked him. Our eyes met. We lived together for two years, and then I married Kurt Weill."

As the opening of *The Threepenny Opera* approached, according to Miss Lenya, "all the big Berlin producers said it would be a 'smash flop.' When Weill suggested me for the role of Jenny the prostitute, they didn't want me. I was nobody. The producers said, 'We'll give her three days out of courtesy to the composer, then fire her.'" The Lenya problem was only one of many. The original Polly Peachum, a great friend of Brecht's, walked out—either because she wanted to be with her ailing husband or—accounts vary—because she resented the cuts in her part. Brecht's wife, Helene Weigl, who was to play the role of the brothel madam, suddenly came down with appendicitis. Peter Lorre, the original Mr. Peachum, also fell ill and had to be replaced. And Harald Paulsen, who was to play Macheath, insisted on wearing a blue bow tie that everyone else hated. He also insisted that his own role should be strengthened. Why begin, he argued, with Mr. Peachum singing his gloomy "Morning Chorale"? Why not begin with a song about him, the highwayman, with his blue bow tie? Brecht agreed, at the last minute, and wrote, literally overnight, the "*Morität*" that is now known as "Mac the Knife." And Weill, also in one night, wrote the haunting melody that achieved the final triumph of his music over Brecht's play.

The dress rehearsal, the night before the opening, lasted until six o'clock in the morning, and everyone seemed to agree that the play was much too long. "Everyone was completely distraught, shouting and swearing," according to Miss Lenya. "The brothel scene was torn apart, begun over—and still didn't work. It was after five when I began singing my 'Solomon Song'—which was interrupted by the cry, 'Stop! Stop!' So that was cut. . . . We heard that Aufricht was asking people out front if they knew where he could find a new play in a hurry." Aufricht's recollections are different. According to his account, the actors and stage hands were finally sent home, and he stayed on with Brecht, Weill, and the director, Erich Engel, cutting and patching the manuscript. At noon, the cast straggled back to the theatre for a final rehearsal. When the last-minute changes were announced to the cast, according to still another account, "the actor who was to play Peachum announced that he was leaving town on the afternoon train. Aufricht told him with what little voice he had left that he had a wife, several children, and a birthday. The actor stayed."

Finally, at the last minute, Kurt Weill cracked. Miss Lenya again: "It was late in the afternoon when suddenly a new voice was heard shouting in wild fury. It was Kurt, who had just discovered that my name had inadvertently been omitted from the program. For the first and last time in his whole theatre career Kurt completely lost control. . . . 'I won't let you go on,' [he] said. 'Darling,' I said, 'I've waited so long for this break; they'll know who I am tomorrow.' And they did, they did."

The street singer's performance of "Mac the Knife" made a good beginning, but the theatre was full of skeptics, waiting. Miss Lenya: "Up to the stable scene the audience seemed cold and apathetic, as though convinced in advance that it had come to a certain flop. Then after the *Cannon Song*, an unbelievable roar went up, and from that point it was wonderfully, intoxicatingly clear that the public was with us. . . ."

That opening night was, of course, a legendary triumph, and of every ten Berliners alive today, at least three claim to have been in the cheering audience. But the success was not without its ironies. One was that the "proletarian" creators, Brecht and Weill, became rich. Another, more significant, was that the sleek and the wealthy flocked to the Schiffbauerdamm to hear themselves derided and denounced. "I was at the opening night," says one of the many who make that claim, "and when I heard the howling applause, I said to my wife, 'This makes me think of the first performance of Beaumarchais' *Marriage of Figaro* three years before the Revolution.' That music—'Pirate Jenny'—I still remember it. But if somebody said that this was 'Cultural Bolshevism,' I really couldn't say that it wasn't."

The greatest irony of all, though, was that in this year of 1928, when Brecht and the other radicals were denouncing the sins of the Weimar Republic, the Germans were actually enjoying the greatest degree of both freedom and prosperity that they had known during this entire decade. In this same year, Chancellor Wilhelm Marx, relatively confident of the Republic's authority, lifted the ban on the half-suppressed Nazis and permitted them to offer candidates in the national elections. The results, inconclusive as ever, brought a mild shift to the left, and the Social Democrats returned to power for the last time, under the chancellorship of Hermann Müller. As for the Nazis, they won just twelve seats in a Reichstag of some five hundred members.

One of those twelve was the irrepressible Joseph Goebbels, who announced that his election meant to him the start of a new kind of drama. He did not consider himself a representative of anything, he said, and his election meant only that he was now the possessor of a free railway pass for his speech-making forays and the possessor of parliamentary immunity against prosecution. Such a campaigner, said Goebbels, in words that strangely echo those of Bert Brecht, "is a man who may speak the truth from time to time even in this democratic republic. He distinguishes himself from other mortals by being permitted to think aloud. He can call a dung heap a dung heap and needn't beat about the bush by calling it a state. . . . This is but a prelude. You're going to have a lot of fun with us. The show can begin."

But this was largely braggadocio. The Nazi were still pitifully weak, and to the world at large, they scarcely seemed much of a threat. In this same year, the former British Ambassador to Berlin, Viscount D'Abernon, finished his memoirs, *The Diary of an Ambassador*. To elucidate obscure points, "historical notes" were added by Maurice Alfred Gerothwohl, diplomatic correspondent of the London *Daily Telegraph*. When Lord D'Abernon made a reference to "Herr Hitler," therefore, Dr. Gerothwohl added a footnote to identify the man in question: "HITLER, Adolf . . . Rose to notoriety in 1922 shortly before the Mussolini coup d'état in Italy by founding the so-called German National Socialist Workmen's Party. Concentrated on exploiting the Semitic and Bolshevik bogies. . . . In the autumn of 1923 he joined with General von Ludendorff in leading the insurrection in Bavaria, but after a temporary escape, was arrested. . . . He was finally released after six months and bound over for the rest of his sentence, thereafter fading into oblivion."

"Things Would Never Be So Good Again" 1929

People discussed Berlin . . . as if the city were a highly desirable woman. . . . We called her proud, snobbish, *nouveau riche*, uncultured, crude. But secretly everyone looked upon her as the goal of his desires. Some saw her as hefty, full-breasted, in lace underwear, others as a mere wisp of a thing, with boyish legs in black silk stockings. The daring saw both aspects, and her very reputation for cruelty made them the more aggressive. To conquer Berlin was to conquer the world.

CARL ZUCKMAYER

JOSEF VON STERNBERG, born Jo Sternberg, recalled that it was a pleasant day in August of 1929 when he arrived at the Zoo Station to direct his first film in Berlin. Among the group of movie-makers who had come to the station to welcome him was his star, Emil Jannings. After their last movie together in Hollywood, *The Last Command*, the temperamental director and the temperamental actor had become so furious at one another that each had sworn he would never work with the other again. Sternberg, specifically, had "told [Jannings] in plain language that I would not do another film with him were he the last remaining actor on earth."

But two years had passed since then, and Jannings, in terror at the prospect of his first sound film, had cabled Sternberg and asked him to direct it, and Sternberg, flattered, had agreed. The thirty-five-year-old director had not asked, however, what the film was to be, and it was only after he arrived in Berlin that he learned that he was

273

expected to do the story of Rasputin. He immediately rejected the idea, for reasons that he never made quite clear, and announced that he was returning to the United States. Jannings and the others protested vehemently and promised that they would find another story for him. As for his own behavior, the actor vowed that everything would be "different this time."

Outside the archives of film history, the name of Emil Jannings does not figure very prominently today. For anyone who has seen him, however, as Louis XV in Ernst Lubitsch's *Du Barry* or as Mephistopheles in F. W. Murnau's version of *Faust*, he remains in the memory as one of the very greatest actors of this century. And although the chronicles of the 1920's favor the celebrity of a Charlie Chaplin or a Greta Garbo, Jannings was also among the greatest of stars. When Paramount brought him to Hollywood in 1926, it not only paid him the extraordinary salary of $400,000 a year but provided him with a huge house, free servants, and all the other perquisites that he felt he needed. He surrounded himself with expatriated admirers and staged nightly feasts of German roast pork and chocolate pastries and champagne. He won the first Oscar ever awarded to an actor, for his role in *The Way of All Flesh*, but he soon became one of the major victims of the arrival of talking movies, not because his voice was inadequate to the new technology but because he couldn't or wouldn't learn English. He returned home, instead, and surrounded himself once again with admirers, and in due time he fell prey to the last self-indulgence. He became a Nazi, not an ideological Nazi but a victim of vanity and official flattery, an "Aryan" artist, even a figurehead official of the Third Reich. After the war, nobody believed his simple-minded excuses, and when he died, very few mourned.

Now, however, his only passion was to placate the celebrated director whom he had lured from Hollywood to Berlin. "One morning, not a week later," Sternberg recalled, "Jannings called at my hotel in great excitement, and with a show of enviable enthusiasm brought a book which had been published in 1905 and had kicked around in film circles for the last ten years. It was entitled *Professor Unrat*." It was a strange story of an elderly schoolteacher in the provincial Baltic Sea port of Lübeck, where the author, Heinrich Mann, and his more celebrated younger brother, Thomas, had grown up. The schoolteacher, a lumbering burlesque of middle-class respectability, becomes outraged at the discovery that some of his wayward pupils are visiting a cabaret that features a tawdry singer named Rosa Fröhlich. Pursuing his pupils to the cabaret, the schoolteacher becomes infatuated with the singer and falls into disgrace. By joining forces with the singer, however, he eventually starts a gambling establishment that lures the respectable burghers of the city to their own disgrace.

Sternberg liked the idea but not the ending. He had other plans, which he explained to Mann, and Mann approved. Then he began dictating a scenario. The UFA studio provided a series of scriptwriters, including Carl Zuckmayer (who still declares that he "wrote the scenario," although, according to Sternberg, the playwright's contributions "are not worth mentioning"). One of Berlin's most skillful song writers, Friedrich Holländer, was hired to produce incidental music. The best UFA technicians began designing sets and costumes. The only thing that was missing was an actress to play the role of the cabaret singer, whom Sternberg, inspired by Frank Wedekind's famous play about an elemental female called Lulu, had determined to name Lola.

Sternberg interviewed everyone. At one point, some UFA officials informed him that Heinrich Mann's novel was autobiographical, and that the real Lola still existed, and "one stately and dignified elderly German lady, thought to be the original, [was] presented to me as a prospect for the part of the alluring female. . . . And as I proceeded to dictate the scenario, everyone's inamorata was ushered into the office to unveil charms. . . . As the deadline for starting the film approached, the uneasiness made itself felt. A rumor began to circulate that the woman was not on earth. In turning over the pages of a trade catalogue that contained a photograph of every actress in Germany, I had paused at a flat and uninteresting portrait of a Fräulein Dietrich, and, asking my assistant about her as I had asked about many others, saw him shrug his shoulders while saying, 'Der Popo ist nicht schlecht, aber brauchen wir nicht auch ein Gesicht?' (Not at all bad from the rear, but don't we also need a face?). So she was promptly relegated to the others and forgotten until, by accident, I attended a play by Georg Kaiser called Zwei Kravatten [Two Neckties], in which members of my cast already chosen were performing. It was in that play that I saw Fräulein Dietrich in the flesh, if that it can be called, for she had wrapped herself up to conceal every part of her body. . . . Here was the face I had sought."

"I do not wish to be known as a movie star," Marlene Dietrich said not long ago, "because, quite simply, I am *not* a movie star. . . . I am an international theatre star now. It's so boring, all that talk about the legendary Marlene and the legendary films of von Sternberg. That's why I loved Russia so. There was nobody crying in their beer there about *The Blue Angel* because *The Blue Angel* never played there. They've never seen it. Those films are all right, but keep them in their place. Don't make them that important. I do not like to be interviewed any more by pansy film-fan writers."

She still is a legend, though, a legend created by the artifices of the cinema. In real life, at the age of nearly seventy, she is not easy to recognize, a short, rather stocky figure with thick makeup and thickly sprayed hair. Emerging from a party on New York's Upper West Side, she stands alone for a long moment, trying to hail a cab, then offers to share it with anyone going across town. Inside the cab, there is an awkward silence, since nobody quite knows what to say to a legend. Finally, as the cab swerves and careens through the darkness of Central Park, someone has an idea.

"Who is your astrologer, Miss Dietrich?"

"Carroll Righter," says the legend, starting to talk, then, about the supernatural forces in her life. . . .

Before she was a legend, before she was a movie star, she was, throughout most of the 1920's, an ambitious and rather unsuccessful starlet. She had been born (apparently in 1901, although accounts vary) into one of those sternly upright families of the Prussian middle class. Her father was a police official, who died when she was a child; her stepfather a Grenadier lieutenant who was killed on the Russian front; her mother the daughter of a jewelry store owner. She hoped to become a concert violinist and won admission to the Berlin School of Music, but her fierce practicing caused the formation of a ganglion on the primary nerve of her left wrist, and her doctor insisted that she give up the instrument forever. She compressed her name from Maria Magdalena into Marlene and tried to enroll in Max Reinhardt's acting school, but the great impresario told her she was not ready. She got a job as a chorus girl in a touring revue. The next year, she applied again at the Reinhardt school and finally gained admission. That led to a bit part in Reinhardt's production of *The Taming of the Shrew* and the role of Hippolyta in *A Midsummer Night's Dream*. She married a young director, Rudolf Sieber, and they had a daughter, Maria. She retired from show business for a while, then returned to try again. She got a bit part in G. W. Pabst's splendid film, *Street Without Joy*, in which she, along with Greta Garbo, stood in line outside the shop of a black-market butcher. And eleventh billing in *Manon Lescaut*. And three scenes in Alexander Korda's *A Modern Du Barry*. There were seventeen such movies in all, as well as a number of musical comedies. In 1928, the year of *The Threepenny Opera*, the biggest hit in Berlin was a now-forgotten musical by Mischa Spoliansky called *It's in the Air*, and one of its four stars was Marlene Dietrich. Spoliansky also wrote the music for Georg Kaiser's *Two Neckties*, and Reinhardt produced it, and although Marlene Dietrich's part was not very large, she made a stunning effect on the Hollywood director sitting out in the orchestra.

Over the protests of various assistants, who insisted that Marlene Dietrich couldn't act, Sternberg summoned her to his office the next day. She came, but by now she had apparently erected an elaborate set of defenses against disappointment. Her display of indifference interested the director. "She made not the slightest effort," he re-called later. "She was seated in a corner of a sofa facing my desk, her eyes downcast, a study in apathy. . . . Clad in a heliotrope win-ter suit, with hat and gloves to match, and furs, she appeared to have come to visit me to take a much-needed rest. . . . Erich Pommer [the producer], flanked by a jovial Jannings, entered and with ad-mirable directness asked her to take off her bonnet and walk up and down. This was the usual ceremony of interviewing an actress to determine at once whether she was bald or had a limp. She complied by strolling through the small room with a bovine listlessness, not seeming to look where she was going. . . . Her eyes were completely veiled. The two experts exchanged telling glances and, one clearing his throat while the other delicately scratched his ear, left the room after a couple of limp handshakes that were meant to give me their opinion."

Marlene Dietrich regarded them, according to Sternberg, "with a look of deep contempt." Sternberg nonetheless sat down with her and told her what he had in mind. The actress, expecting another minor role, appeared surprised and not particularly pleased. "She came out of her shell long enough to inform me that she could not act," said Sternberg, "that it was impossible for anyone to photograph her to look like herself, that she had been treated badly by the press and, to my surprise, she also revealed that she had been featured in three films in which she had not been good. . . . Apparently everyone in Berlin had 'discovered' her long before I came along."

In order to persuade his disapproving colleagues, Sternberg decided to make a film test. First, though, he screened several of her previous movies, all of which he disliked. Miss Dietrich told him that the test would be a waste of time, and Sternberg agreed, since he had already decided to use her. Nonetheless, he proceeded with the ritual. "I sent her to the wardrobe to discard her street clothes and to change into something with spangles, and she returned with a costume roomy enough to contain a hippopotamus. I pinned the dress to fit her somehow and asked her to sing something she knew in German and to follow it with an English song if possible. I then . . . blended her image to correspond with mine, and, pouring lights on her until the alchemy was complete, proceeded with the test. She came to life and responded to my instructions with an ease that I had never before encountered."

In Berlin, as in most of the Western world, 1929 was the year of euphoric prosperity. "The snow of twenty-nine wasn't real snow," as Scott Fitzgerald wrote. "If you didn't want it to be snow, you just paid some money." Headwaiters in New York were making paper fortunes by playing the stock market on margin, and in such times of easy money and easy credit, the Germans were no more frugal than anyone else.

Ever since Gustav Stresemann's regime had stabilized the mark back in 1923, Germany had become a prime field for foreign investment. But what the investor thinks of as an investment is, to the recipient, simply a debt. German corporations borrowed money to build new factories and assembly lines, which brought them a growth rate far higher than that of England. State and city governments floated loans to subsidize parks and theatres, and churches borrowed in order to build more churches. And if Mies van der Rohe wanted to build the German Pavilion at the 1929 World's Fair out of travertine marble and onyx and chromium-plated columns, no bookkeepers ever mentioned the fact that his creation was destined to be dismantled within a few months. The national government even used American loans to pay back reparations to the French. By the end of 1928, therefore, German wages had risen almost 20 percent over the 1925 figures, and so had retail sales. Unemployment stood at a negligible 650,000. But in this era of artificial prosperity, Germany's foreign debt soared to some $7 billion, much of it in short-term high-interest loans, and the German government complained that it could not continue to carry the burden of war reparations.

As Foreign Minister, Stresemann succeeded in convoking another international conference on the problem, and so this complex and tedious question of reparations, which bedeviled European diplomacy throughout the twenties, entered a new phase. Since 1924, the Germans and their creditors had been operating under the so-called Dawes Plan, which never specified any total of reparations due but required the Germans to pay the Allies 2.5 billion marks (about $600 million) every year, indefinitely. To make sure that the payments were made, the Allies acquired partial control of the German railroads plus the tax revenues on tobacco, sugar, beer, and alcohol. Now, in 1929, at The Hague, the Germans and their former enemies negotiated a new and theoretically final settlement. According to a formula worked out by an American banker, Owen D. Young, the German annual payments were to be reduced from 2.5 billion marks to 2 billion, and the Germans were to reacquire full control over their own economic machinery, but they were also to commit themselves to continue these payments for another fifty-nine years.

These events made headlines in the Berlin newspapers, but international economic conferences rarely have much effect in the streets and on the beaches. To the ordinary Berliners, the new prosperity meant jobs, and a little extra money after all the years of privation. They could sit on the sunny terrace of an outdoor café and enjoy a glass of the favorite local brew, a semifermented beer known as a "Weisse," spiked with a shot of raspberry syrup. Or they could hike out into the Brandenburg woods for a picnic of cake and coffee along the shores of the Müggelsee. Or, if they wanted more excitement, they could race along the new Avus speedway, which ran for more than eleven miles without a curve from the Kurfürstendamm almost all the way to Potsdam.

Speed fascinated the Berliners, as it fascinated many people in 1929. Speed, and the new technology, the triumph of the machine age. The transatlantic flight by Charles Lindbergh had become a symbol of the whole era, and Bert Brecht even wrote a radio play about it, with music by both Weill and Hindemith. ("Our steel innocence/rose up in the air,/showing the possible, without letting us forget/the Unattainable.") And as they looked upward and marveled, nothing fascinated the Berliners more than the exploits of Dr. Hugo Eckener and his Zeppelins.

It has become customary to deride the Zeppelin because of the ghastly crash of the *Hindenburg* at Lakehurst, New Jersey, in 1937. There were photographers on the scene, and their unforgettable pictures of the inferno were promptly shown before horrified newsreel audiences all over America, with such effect that no paying passenger has ever again flown on a Zeppelin. In actual fact, however, only thirty-five of the ninety-seven passengers and crewmen aboard the *Hindenburg* died in the fire—a figure that seems almost Utopian when compared to the toll in one of today's jet crashes— and the thirteen passengers who died were the first and only ones ever killed in a Zeppelin accident. In its time, in other words, the Zeppelin was an aeronautical marvel, and there were many who considered it far superior to heavier-than-air craft—bigger, longer-ranged, cheaper, more comfortable, and, as far as one could tell, safer. During World War I, while rickety little Spads and Fokkers battled a few hundred feet above the trenches, the Zeppelins soared all the way to London and dropped bombs on the amazed city.

When peace came, the Allies demanded the Zeppelins as reparations, but the Germans destroyed them. The Allies thereupon banned the construction of any new ones. The Zeppelin Company (the old Count Zeppelin had died in 1917) was reduced to manufacturing aluminum pots. Zeppelin's technological heir, Hugo Eckener, would not give up, however. He negotiated an agreement with Washington to build a new Zeppelin for delivery to the U.S. Navy, and in 1924, he piloted his new LZ-126 on a four-day cruise from Germany to New Jersey. America welcomed him with feverish enthusiasm. Eckener, a sternly bearded figure, waved his way through a ticker-tape parade on Wall Street, surveyed an Army-Navy game at the Polo Grounds, and ended his trip as President Coolidge's guest in Washington.

The following year, the Allies lifted their ban on Zeppelin production, and Eckener began working toward his dream of transatlantic passenger service. Since the Weimar government had no money to subsidize him, Eckener appealed to the German people for contributions and managed to scrape together enough money to build his LZ-127, the *Graf Zeppelin*. It was a huge ship, more than twice the length of a football field, and Eckener himself stood at the controls as he set off with twenty paying passengers and a load of 66,000 pieces of mail.

The flight almost ended in disaster. In mid-Atlantic, the *Graf Zeppelin* ran into a squall, and an inexperienced helmsman turned the ship in the wrong direction, nearly making it capsize. When the ship had been righted, Eckener found that some fabric had torn off the port fin, which meant that the ship could not be steered. In a driving rain, he shut off the motors, drifted down to three hundred feet over the ocean and called for volunteers to climb onto the outside of the ship to repair the fin. Four men volunteered, one of them Eckener's own son, Knud. And while they crawled out into the storm, the ship kept dropping down nearer to the waves. A few minutes before the Zeppelin's destruction, Eckener's son managed to repair the fin, and the ship soared up out of the storm.

The narrow escape did not deter Eckener. On the contrary, he announced in 1929 that he would fly his Zeppelin around the world. And indeed he did, carrying not just a full load of passengers but a cargo that included a gorilla named Susie, several cages of canaries, and a grand piano. Cruising at an average speed of more than seventy miles an hour, Eckener made the tour in twenty-one days and landed in New Jersey to receive another ticker-tape parade and another summons from the White House. Mayor Jimmy Walker of New York saluted him as "one of the greatest living men," and back in Germany he was seriously considered as a candidate to run against Hindenburg for the presidency of the Reich.

We know now that Zeppelins can fly in complete safety when filled with helium, but there was something symptomatic about the heedless optimism with which the Germans of 1929 set off around the world in a giant gas bag filled with highly inflammable hydrogen. There was nothing secret about the danger, after all, since British technicians had developed incendiary bullets to shoot at Zeppelins during the war, and when incendiary bullets hit a Zeppelin, there were generally no survivors. But the Germans were awed by the sheer size of the *Graf Zeppelin* (a record 775 feet, framed by ten miles of girders), and by its sequence of successes, all of which seemed to defy the laws of probability.

And so, in the field of international finance, it seemed quite possible for the German government to pay billions of dollars in war reparations to the Western Allies by borrowing even more billions from those same Allies. And to promise that reparations (and presumably borrowing) would continue for another sixty years. The man who made this seem plausible, who made almost anything seem plausible, was Gustav Stresemann, the portly ex-merchant, who, as Germany's apparently permanent Foreign Minister, had served in every cabinet since his own brief chancellorship in 1923. Once an extreme Nationalist, an ally and protégé of General Ludendorff, Stresemann had devoted these last years to ending the old conflicts with France. He spoke—and he was an outstanding orator—for the good Germans, for the Germany of peace and democracy. Stresemann was not without his critics, of course, both then and now. On the left, it has been alleged that he knew and ignored the German generals' secret rearmament in the East; on the right, he was accused of selling out German interests to foreign powers. If a rapprochement between Germany and France was important, however, then Stresemann dedicated his efforts to a good cause. Between him and the French Foreign Minister, Aristide Briand, there developed a trust and friendship that benefited both nations, and in 1926, the two of them shared the Nobel Peace Prize.

Now, however, in the midst of the debate over the Young Plan, Stresemann began to falter. He had a kidney disease, which compelled him to take sick leave in Switzerland, but as the right-wing opposition to the Young Plan developed, he defied his doctor's orders and returned to Berlin in the fall of 1929 to fight for the agreements he had negotiated. "His last coffee hour with the foreign press of Berlin . . . was a sorrowful experience," according to Louis Lochner, who was then head of the Associated Press bureau in the capital. "As he approached the extremely long, rectangular table at the center of which he usually took his seat, all of us were aghast. '*Er ist vom Tode gezeichnet* ['The mark of death is upon him'], [another correspondent] remarked to me later. . . . Dr. Stresemann motioned to me to sit beside him. He tried to tell me how very much better he felt, but his words came with difficulty. I felt under compulsion to pretend that I thought he looked well and rested, yet I knew in my heart that I was being merely kind, but not truthful. With a supreme effort Dr. Stresemann finally proceeded to say a few words—it would have been tactless for any one of us to ask this sick man a leading question. The 'few words' lengthened into a heart-gripping restatement of his philosophy of international reconciliation coupled with a fervent expression of his unshakable faith that reason and law would soon prevail in international relations. Sitting next to him, I could not help noticing how the sweat broke out on his brow, how he turned alternately deathly pale and flushed, how his breathing came harder as his farewell address— for this it proved to be—continued for about twenty minutes. Exhausted, he ended and was quitely ushered out of the room by members of his staff. He had, as it were, given us his political testament."

Five days later, Stresemann was dead. There was an elaborate funeral, and many speeches of mourning and loss, but the campaign against his policies continued. The chief force of opposition was the Nationalist Party, which, in the previous year, had come under the leadership of Alfred Hugenberg. At sixty-three, Hugenberg was a thin, glum-looking man with a drooping mustache, but despite his appearance, he intimidated people by his blustering manner. Once a director of the Krupp armaments empire, he had become rich during the inflation and had invested much of his new wealth in publishing and propaganda. He acquired the Scherl chain of newspapers, which included the mass-circulation *Berlin Lokal-Anzeiger*; he bought a controlling interest in UFA, the biggest German film company; he also controlled the ALA publicity firm, which dominated German advertising; he even had a news service to distribute right-wing news stories to anyone who would print them. As a result of all these powers, Hugenberg had access to large sums of money through his contacts with Germany's biggest businessmen, notably Albert Voegler, general director of the United Steel Works, and Hjalmar Schacht, president of the Reichsbank.

Like many of his business associates, Hugenberg was still fiercely opposed to the Versailles Treaty, to any attempt at reconciliation with the Allies, and to any payment of reparations. Unable to stop the new reparations agreement in the Reichstag, Hugenberg determined to fight it by means of a public referendum. For this, he had money, and power, and a propaganda machine, but he needed an orator who could go out into the streets and cry for votes. At the Deutsche Orden club in Berlin, an intermediary finally brought Hugenberg together with a magnetic young (he was now forty) orator from Bavaria. Hugenberg proposed that they join forces, and Adolf Hitler was interested. He demanded full financial support from Hugenberg, and complete autonomy for his own campaign, but the two men finally agreed on a draft of a "Law against the En-slavement of the German People," which would, among other things, repudiate all reparations.

In a month of fierce campaigning, Hitler helped to get the neces-sary 10 percent of the electorate to request that this private bill be placed before the Reichstag. There, of course, it was rejected. Hugenberg and Hitler then organized a campaign for a national ref-erendum against the Young Plan. If they could get more than half of the forty million German voters to approve their "Freedom Law," the result would have overridden the Reichstag. The referendum brought them only six million, however, and early in March of 1930, the Young Plan legislation was finally passed by the Reichstag and signed by President Hindenburg. ("Is Hindenburg still alive?" Goebbels cried out in his paper, *Der Angriff*.) The failure of the referendum was a defeat for Hugenberg, who had staked a good deal of money and prestige on the campaign, but it was scarcely a defeat for Hitler. Through the propaganda of the Hugenberg press, he had become, for the first time, a figure in national politics. And through Hugenberg's contacts, he had made a strong impression on the militant leaders of big business. Having achieved these goals, Hitler blamed Hugenberg for the failure of the campaign and broke off their alliance. He wanted to pursue his own course.

Even now, though, very few Berliners took the little Austrian seriously. Very few, in fact, paid much attention to politics. They wanted to enjoy themselves, and the rituals of self-enjoyment be-came almost a religion of narcissistic self-indulgence. To various foreigners who drifted to Berlin during this last year of prosperity, it seemed bizarre that the Germans, supposedly so grim and stolid, appeared to have become a nation of nudists. Stephen Spender, for one, thought that the young Germans' preoccupation with sunbath-ing represented a purgation of bourgeois standards. "The sun— symbol of the great wealth of nature within the poverty of man— was a primary social force in this Germany," he wrote. "Thousands of people went to the open-air swimming baths or lay down on the shores of the rivers and lakes, almost nude, and sometimes quite nude. . . . The sun healed their bodies of the years of war, and made them conscious of the quivering, fluttering life of blood and muscles covering their exhausted spirits like the pelt of an animal: and their minds were filled with an abstraction of the sun, a huge circle of fire, an intense whiteness blotting out the sharp outlines of all other forms of consciousness, burning out even the sense of time."

And the young Vladimir Nabokov, despite his distaste for the more elderly sunbathers, with their paunches and boils and red knees, joined in the Berliners' hegira to the beaches of the Grune-wald. "I felt myself an athlete, a Tarzan, an Adam, anything you like, only not a naked town-dweller," says Fyodor, the autobiographical hero of *The Gift*. "The sun bore down. The sun licked me all over with its big, smooth tongue. I gradually felt that I was becoming moltenly transparent, that I was permeated with flame and existed only insular as it did. . . . My personal I , . . had somehow disintegrated and dissolved. . . . It was now assimilated to the shimmering of the summer forest with its satiny pine needles and heavenly-green leaves . . . with its birds, smells, hot breath of nettles and spermy odor of sun-warmed grass."

All is not narcissism and self-indulgence, however. On returning from a swim in the Havel, Fyodor finds that another sunbather has stolen all his clothing except for one sneaker, in which the thief has left a scrap of newspaper with the scribbled notation, "*Vielen Dank*" ("Many thanks"). Emerging, then, onto one of the boulevards back to central Berlin, he encounters a policeman who informs him, "Whether you've been robbed or not, you can't go about the streets naked." A police sergeant is more understanding, however, and there are always taxis. . . .

And from Paris came Count Harry Kessler, bringing with him the seventy-year-old Aristide Maillol, who was fleeing from his jealous wife and taking a German vacation with a young model. The sculptor's wife was so jealous, in fact, that he had to base many of his sculptures on pictures in magazines, but now that he had reached the land of the sunbathers, the model in his company seemed less unique. "Maillol was in raptures about the unabashed nudity," according to Kessler's diary. "He continually drew my attention to the splendid bodies of girls, young men and boys. '*Si j'habitais à Frankfurt, je passerais mes journées ici à dessiner.*' ['If I lived in Frankfurt, I would spend my days here, drawing.']" Kessler, like a number of others, seemed to think that this outburst of nudity had a philosophical importance. "I explained to him that this is indicative of only a part of a new vitality, a fresh outlook on life. . . . People want to really *live* in the sense of enjoying light, the sun, happiness, and the health of their bodies. It is . . . a mass movement which has stirred all of German youth."

And again: "Went with Maillol and Mlle Passavant [the model] to see the School for Physical Culture in Grunewald. In the magnificent grounds and glorious sunshine the sight of almost naked young people performing athletic exercises was reminiscent of ancient Greece . . . Maillol asked me to photograph two youngsters who were '*beaux comme des dieux antiques.*' Unfortunately Mlle Passavant moped the whole time, somewhat spoiling our pleasure." The sculptor's concentration on bodies was total. The next day, at a luncheon in his honor, he was introduced to Albert Einstein and later observed, "Yes, a beautiful head; is he a poet?" Kessler added: "I had to explain to him who Einstein was; he had evidently never heard of him."

Despite Kessler's theories and Nabokov's rhapsodies, the Berlin cult of nakedness was not entirely inspired by the sun. There was, in fact, a nudist group which rented a lake for its rituals all year long. In the summer, the members flocked to the beach to swim, but they were determined to prove that their ideas also applied to harsher seasons. And so, in December, when the lake froze solid, they gathered there for nude skating parties. The only compromise they made with the raw Berlin winter was that they wore boots on their skates. And some of them, according to one chronicler, wore earmuffs.

The Blue Angel has become so famous as a Marlene Dietrich film that one can overlook the fact that the most important figures in the project were Sternberg, the director, and Jannings, the star. And because the decadent eroticism of the film seems to express so perfectly the mood of Berlin in the late 1920's, it is surprising to hear Sternberg declare, with some vehemence, that "most of the story of the film and its details existed only in my imagination, that I knew very little about Germany before I began it, that then I had not seen anyone resembling a Nazi, and that the entire stimulation to make the film came from a book that was written by Heinrich Mann in the good old days before 1905."

Mann was an ardent liberal, and his story of the decline and recovery of Professor Unrat was a rather ponderous attack on the hypocrisy of the middle class. Sternberg was not interested in class conflicts, however. In his scenario (there never was an official shooting script, and much of the dialogue was improvised, scene by scene), Sternberg changed the basic idea from the downfall of an autocrat to the downfall of a puritan, a victim not of social forces but of infatuation. And there is no recovery. The teacher's degradation continues inexorably toward the harrowing scene in which he is forced to totter on stage at Lola's cabaret and to crow like a chicken while an egg is broken over his head.

It was a role made for Jannings, and his performance is one of the greatest ever filmed, but the struggle to evoke that performance was a melodrama in itself. Sternberg has portrayed his antagonist with a mixture of admiration and malice: "Fat and ungainly, with a complete memory for his own tricks, shifty like a pellet of quicksilver, agile in his repertoire of misbehaviour, he was the perfect actor. His forte was to portray the zenith of personal misfortune; his limpid eyes brimming with misery, he could picture debasement in the most abject terms. To be humiliated was for him ecstasy." Sternberg himself was not without flaws, of course, and if Jannings loved to be humiliated, Sternberg showed no aversion to inflicting humiliations. Many of his actors hated him, and people outside the movie business believed that he had brought from Hollywood an arrogance worthy of the exiled Kaiser. George Grosz, for one, encountered him at a dinner party at the home of Alfred Flechtheim, the art dealer, and reported that the director had "shocked" the other guests by boasting of his salary: "I don't really earn so much —at most, perhaps, three times as much as the President of the United States."

When the two antagonists met, then, on what Sternberg called "a typical morning," the sadomasochistic conflict provoked extraordinary scenes. "I would knock on his door, enter, and inquire as to the state of his health. If I had failed to do this, he would have been wounded to the extent of sending word to the stage that he was desperately ill and wanted me to call an ambulance immediately. He had arrived promptly at seven to take his place in front of a triptych of mirrors in order to don his mask of the old professor, building the beard with precision, hair by hair, studying each hair for shade and length, coaxing it to join the others until the beard became part of him. My greetings were received with a deep look of reproach, which he checked with his ever-present man servant, König, whose face would pale at this look. . . . Then Jannings lit a cigarette, exhaling the smoke as if his soul went with it, cleared his throat, and bared his teeth so as not to interfere with the pyramid of hair he had built, and followed this by casually mentioning that I no longer loved him. I would counter this by assuring him of my undying affection and then ask him to show his love for me by assisting me to make a few more feet of film. Jannings would then extinguish the cigarette as if to grind me to ashes, and view me through the mirror with his limpid eyes filled with the usual self-induced torment, a prerequisite to winding himself up to be his masochistic self in order to be able to act, and would say, as if never before had he made so horrendous an accusation, 'You did not lunch with me yesterday.'

". . . I knew there could be no reprieve from what was coming. He would go on to tell me, looking up to the ceiling with the innocence of a new-born baby, that he had heard through the grapevine that Frau Dietrich had risen at dawn to prepare my lunch. . . . 'You prefer to eat with a female, don't you, rather than to eat with me?'. . . . A short and tricky exchange . . . ended with a threat that he was leaving for good. This ultimatum persuaded me to promise him that I would have lunch with him and him alone. But Jannings had not yet whipped himself into the proper mood. 'I don't believe you.' And with that, while König swooned, he would rip off the beard on which he had worked for two hours. . . . 'You were going to lunch with that Dietrich woman, weren't you?' Knowing what was certain to follow, I turned to leave. And now the inevitable, each time worse than the one before. He would hurl himself to the floor so that the whole room shook, weep, scream, and shout that his heart had stopped, and I would pick him up, which was not easy as his playful resistance accounted for more kilos than he boasted, then kiss him on the mouth, moist with tears and sticky with glue, and return him somehow to his mirrors, where he would plead to be forgiven."

The image we still have of Marlene Dietrich in *The Blue Angel* is the image of her lounging on the cabaret stage and singing. Her air of nonchalant hedonism seemed, and still seems, to express a whole era, but the songs themselves were grand ones, for Sternberg had made a superb choice in hiring Friedrich Holländer to write Miss Dietrich's music:

> My name is naughty Lola
> The favorite of the gang
> I have a pianola
> At home with lots of tang. . . .

And, of course:

> Falling in love again
> Never wanted to . . .
> What am I to do?
> Can't help it
> Love's always been my game
> Play it how I may
> I was made that way
> Can't help it
> Men cluster to me . . .
> Like moths around a flame.

The songs of the 1920's sound marvelously evocative, on scratchy old gramophone records, but do Broadway tunes like "Night and Day" or "Somebody Loves Me" really reflect the years of Teapot Dome and the Sacco-Vanzetti case any more than "I Want to Hold Your Hand" or "Raindrops Keep Falling on My Head" reflect a war in Vietnam? Probably not. Song writers just keep writing songs, and ever since the age of radio and recording began in the 1920's, the biggest hits have become international phenomena, more or less remote from the social problems of their audiences. Just as many rock-'n'-roll lyrics make very little sense, and just as one of the big successes during World II was a nonsense ditty called Mairzy Doats, one of the triumphs of the early 1920's was "Yes, We Have No Bananas." In Berlin, where it was sung everywhere under the mysteriously literal title of *"Ausgerechnet Bananen,"* it irritated a song writer named Hermann Frey to such an extent that he wrote a burlesque of it under the title: "My Parrot Doesn't Eat Hard-boiled Eggs." To his dismay, it became one of the year's biggest hits, even leading to a court case in which a Berlin matron prosecuted her maid because the girl, trying to test the accuracy of the song, had fed hard-boiled eggs to the family's aged parrot, whereupon it died.

If popular songs do not really express the social spirit of an age, however, they do express something no less fundamental, a sense of feeling—artificial, perhaps, and certainly commercialized—about the cherished banalities of life. These songs, unlike the big international hits, are strongly rooted in their time and place. And if the songs are to be believed, the Berliners, like all big-city cynics, have a broad streak of sentimentality, mainly about themselves. "Give my regards to Broadway," runs a famous song of the period, "remember me to Herald Square. . . ." For the Berliners, every aspect of their city was equally worthy of commemoration. They sang of romance by the shores of the Krumme Lanke, and a whole revue was entitled *We Who Live Around the Memorial Church*. Sometimes it seems that a song writer needed only to evoke the magic name of the city to become a celebrity in the cafés of the Kurfürstendamm. "The Prettiest Legs in Berlin" was a hit, and so was "That's the Berlin Air" and "What Does It Take to Make a Berliner Happy?" The answer, apparently, was that a Berliner could be happy only in his own city. "I keep a suitcase in Berlin," Marlene Dietrich sang in one of her most popular numbers, going on to explain that, wherever she traveled, the suitcase justified her returning home from time to time. If all this seems a bit parochial, the Berliners were only emulating the example that came from across the Atlantic. In one song, indeed, a deservedly forgotten group who called themselves "Die Drei Travellers" made the connection in a boop-a-doop number that goes, "The Kurfürstendamm and the Tauentzi [meaning the Tauentzienstrasse]—that's the Broadway of Berlin."

The popular music of Berlin, which reached its greatest flowering in the cabaret songs of Brecht and Tucholsky, evolved during the Imperial era out of a mixture of street fairs, wandering minstrel troupes, and, particularly, the circus. Throughout most of the nineteenth century, when the theatre was under the control of various German courts, the circus was banned as a vulgarity, but it flourished in Italy, moved to America, and finally reached Berlin in the 1870's. First at the Schumann Circus on the Schiffbauerdamm, and then at the Busch Circus a few blocks to the east, a whole new generation of clowns and acrobats introduced such feats as "the American water act." In this number, a variation of a standard *commedia dell' arte* drama known as "the abduction of the bride," the captive maiden fled by horseback to the roof of the circus, where she could escape her pursuers only by guiding her horse into and then down a waterfall that plunged into a miniature lake at the center of the ring.

For a time, the Berliners packed the circus every night, but they eventually tired of pure spectacle, and the circus began to give way to vaudeville. Now the crowds flocked to the Winter Garden, on the Friedrichstrasse, where Negroes in gold braid held open the doors, and the customers not only could watch trapeze artists swinging across a star-flecked blue ceiling but could eat sausages and drink beer and smoke cigars (all of which were forbidden at the circus) while they watched. And there were singers and dancers—La Belle Otero came from Paris to perform at the Winter Garden, and another one of the stars was a young dancer named Mata Hari.

Berlin vaudeville, in which the circus stunt men still played a part, gave way, in turn, to the purely musical shows of the 1920s. There were still clowns and an occasional acrobat, but the Friedrichstrasse's newer theatres like the Apollo and the Metropol, put the emphasis on a local art form known as the "Berlin Revue." In one typical production, the curtain would rise on a statue of Neptune standing outside the Royal Palace, and, in due course, the statue would come to life, sing a song, and then start on a tour of the city, observing a pair of strolling lovers (a chance for a duet or a trio), wandering into a criminal dive (here perhaps a chorus), and so on. During the course of such a tour, the management rarely failed to provide a tableau in which the wandering hero encountered a group of topless dancers.

As long as Berliners kept buying tickets—and they did—the opportunities for variations on the basic themes were limitless. At the upper level, where middle-class matrons flocked to the kind of show that had artistic pretensions, the Luxus Theater regularly featured Richard Tauber, a onetime operatic tenor, in an immensely popular series of musicals by Franz Lehar—*Paganini, Tsarevitch, Frederica,* and *Land of Smiles.* And for the matrons' husbands, Laurence Tilly imported from England a regiment of "Empire Girls" who danced and kicked in unison at the Admiralspalast. At the lower levels, where the theatres were small and smoky, there were cabarets like the White Mouse, which acquired its name because it started across the Friedrichstrasse from an earlier cabaret called the Black Cat. It was one of many—the Catacombs, the Cabaret of Comedians,

Tingeltangel—all celebrated for the sharp wit of the master of ceremonies, a type known as "the *conferencier*," who would gibe at the
politicians of the day and then introduce the various performers.

The White Mouse was somewhat different from the others,
though, because its featured dancer was a girl named Anita Berber,
who, unlike most cabaret dancers, performed without any clothes
or costumes at all. Nobody remembers her now, but in her time, she
seemed to epitomize the spirit of the Berlin cabaret. The daughter
of a violinist in the Leipzig orchestra, and originally a serious student
of ballet, she took several husbands and many lovers; she was also
a Lesbian. She was an alcoholic, and addicted to both morphine and
cocaine. She appeared at every major prizefight and bicycle race,
often accompanied by a band of thugs. "She was always surrounded
by scandal," according to one old Berliner. "Occasionally, she would
answer the protests of the public with an obscene gesture. . . . The
last time I saw her was on the night of Mardi Gras, in front of the
house of Alfred Flechtheim. He was giving a private masked ball
for his friends . . . and Anita had not been allowed in. She was
shouting, in vain, all up and down the Tiergartenstrasse." Not long
afterward, she was dancing in Munich when she collapsed from a
mixture of drugs, alcohol, and tuberculosis. She was penniless, but
she refused to end her life in the southern provinces, and she somehow managed to drag herself back to Berlin, where, at the age of
twenty-nine, she died.

The cabaret songs of Berlin may well have expressed the spirit
of the 1920's, or at least part of that spirit, the spirit of cynicism and
nihilism. But there was a vast audience, both in Berlin and in the
rest of Germany, that rarely went to cabarets. This audience wanted
entertainment too, but of another sort. It wanted to be beguiled
and amused, to be told that everything was all right, and it found
its satisfaction in the great new medium of the pre-radio, pre-tele-
vision era: the movies.

There were a number of distinguished artists working in the UFA
studios in Berlin, and film experts have written exhaustively on the
camera angles and architectural masses in Fritz Lang's monumental
treatment of the *Nibelungen*, on the symbolism of the revolving door
in F. W. Murnau's *Last Laugh*, on the sense of physical detail in G.
W. Pabst's *Street Without Joy*. But these artistic analyses have very

little to do with most of the films that the Germans flocked to see. These were not, in general, the expressions of their creators' artistic visions but rather, like American Westerns, the expressions of a national mythology.

The hero of one such myth was an otherwise obscure actor named Otto Gebühr, who represented, to a whole generation, the splendid figure of Frederick the Great. He appeared first in an UFA film of 1922, entitled *Fridericus Rex*, which dealt with the epic conflict between the young Frederick and his father, King Frederick William I. The father was an ogre, determined that his son should become a Spartan drillmaster like himself; the son preferred to read French and play the flute. The father, disappointed and vengeful, repeatedly degraded the son; the son decided to run away. It was a theme that fascinated the Germans—indeed, it has fascinated all people—and during the Expressionist era, a number of young playwrights produced dramas in which rebellious youth finally overthrows paternal tyranny. In Arnolt Bronnen's *Parricide*, for instance, the son stabs his father, then turns against his Jocasta-like mother:

> I've had enough of you.
> I've had enough of everything.
> Go bury your husband, you are old,
> I am young however,
> I know you not,
> I am free.

The true history of Frederick the Great was somewhat different. Frederick William discovered his son's plan to escape from the Prussian court. He had his son arrested, along with an accomplice named Lieutenant Katte, and then forced the eighteen-year-old prince to watch Katte being beheaded. The prince finally bowed down to his father and devoted the next ten years to his military and governmental apprenticeship. This apprenticeship ended, according to the movie version, with the old king dying in the knowledge that his son would be a worthy ruler.

The audiences loved it. Hostile critics have argued that the submission of the prince represented a political or psychological yearning to submit before a higher authority, and perhaps this is true. But Frederick the Great has always been a folk hero—a combination of the triumphant warrior and the sophisticated intellectual

—and perhaps the success of the film might more naturally be attributed to the desire of a shamed and shattered people to revere one of the great figures of the past. In any case, *Fridericus Rex* was so successful that the magnates at UFA promptly commissioned a sequel, and so, throughout the 1920's, the Berliners watched Frederick the Great leading his armies against the Austrians, Frederick the Great chatting with Voltaire, Frederick the Great playing his flute. The films, long forgotten now, had names like *The Mill of Sans Souci* and *The Chorale of Leuthen,* and in all but one of them, Otto Gebühr made a career out of playing the young king on his white horse, the middle-aged king playing chess, the old king hobbling about on a crutch.

The popular movies were not all so stern, of course. On the contrary, the German mythology, the Germans' view of themselves, includes many legends that may seem turgid to an outsider but still fill the middle-class German moviegoer with a sense of warmth and satisfaction. One of the most enduring of these legends is that of the happy student life, for which Walter Slezak has provided a splendid all-purpose scenario:

"Young student, usually called Hans-Heinz or Horst-Juergen, scion of prominent, wealthy family, arrives at Heidelberg University, rents room—always overlooking the Neckar River—meets daughter (Elfrieda or Jutta, lovely young blonde curls) of landlady (impoverished kindly widow of heroic German officer who lies in eternal sleep in French soil). Romance begins, breath-taking outdoor shots, young couple boating on the Neckar, hiking, climbing vineyards, holding hands and sipping wine at picturesque inn (comedy shot of someone at next table eating pig's knuckles and sauerkraut). They are joined by other student-landlady's daughter combinations. Some jerk has brought a lute hung with gay ribbons, so they sing German student songs, linking arms and swaying in unison. Hans-Heinz or Horst-Juergen is pledged into fraternity and proudly wears *couleur* ribbon and cap. Obnoxious student—unpleasantly drunk —stares at Elfrieda-Jutta. A duel! Hans-Heinz-Horst-Juergen is wounded; prominent wealthy parents thus discover romance. Accuse landlady of trying to snag rich son-in-law. She proudly rejects young scion as suitor for her daughter. Young scion moves to other rented room, also overlooking Neckar. He's heart-broken (close-up of him: *not* smiling). He decides life without those long blonde curls not worth living. Leaves farewell note, goes to top of Heidelberg Castle, where he is spotted by kindly old professor who talks him out of jumping. Professor informs parents—stern father would rather have his son dead—but mother, having herself been daughter of impoverished heroic German officer's widow, accepts Elfrieda-Jutta. Final tableau of picturesque inn where they are joined by the creep with the lute. They sing 'Gaudeamus igitur. . . .' This story I played in twenty-three variations and under twenty-three different titles."

It is difficult to determine whether such rubbish represents a purely commercial policy of producing whatever the public will pay to see or whether, as some politically minded critics have argued, the production of rubbish is a form of propaganda. One might ask, similarly, whether the old-fashioned Hollywood Westerns are simply a series of commercial products or whether they express a feeling of racism, violence, and various other disreputable emotions. Perhaps both, but one does not need to be a cynic to suspect that commercialism is the governing force. As an industry, however, the German movie business of the 1920's was somewhat different from Hollywood. In contrast to the California studios, founded and fostered by a bizarre assortment of nickelodeon operators, the German film industry began as a government propaganda service, under the aegis of General Ludendorff, and it never completely freed itself from the influence of national politics.

The economics of German film-making were unique. Shortly after the war, when the Social Democrats decided to liquidate the government's one-third interest in the film combine known as UFA, the Deutsche Bank stepped in and became a controlling owner. The bank considered UFA a promising investment, and rightly so, but the returns on the investment soon fell under the influence of the inflation. While Germans flocked to the new movie theatres that sprang up everywhere, they brought only their increasingly worthless paper marks to buy their tickets. As a result the whole German revenue on an average film netted only 10 percent of the cost of making it, whereas exports proved to be a bonanza—the Swiss rights alone generally paid for the entire production.

After the stabilization of the mark in 1924, then, the entire situation reversed itself. The German audiences once again became a valuable market, and the authorities at UFA, instead of having to fight for exports, had to fight against imports. Hollywood films began pouring into Germany, and the Hollywood studios even bought and built theatres to show their pictures. And throughout these years, Hollywood drained off some of the best talent in Berlin, not only stars like Pola Negri and Greta Garbo and directors like Ernst Lubitsch and F. W. Murnau but a whole army of cameramen, film cutters, and other indispensable technicians.

UFA, the centerpiece of the German movie business, struggled in vain against the competition from Hollywood, and finally, in 1927, it was tottering on the edge of bankruptcy. Its losses were running at a rate of $12 million a year, its creditors were crying for a solution, and it became clear that the whole concern was up for sale. The liberal press empire founded by Rudolf Mosse had a chance to acquire UFA but rejected the offer. Instead, the creditors found their salvation in the Nationalist Party leader, Alfred Hugenberg. He had been dabbling in the movies as early as 1916, and he was fascinated with the prospect of adding UFA to his chain of news-papers, his news service, and his advertising agency. With the back-ing of the financiers of the Ruhr, he bought UFA in 1927, paid the debts, and took control. He did not, strikingly enough, turn UFA into an instrument of right-wing propaganda—he was too shrewd a businessman for that—but the film business that had once attracted such radicals as the authors of *Doctor Caligari* was never quite the same. The exodus to Hollywood continued. General Ludendorff had won.

After all the preparations, it took only six weeks to film *The Blue Angel*, but every week involved new arguments and confusions. Sternberg, determined to film a fantasy that he alone had envisioned, rejected all the usual attempts at documentary authenticity. He refused to visit either the schools where Professor Unrat might have taught or the cabarets where Lola might have sung. He refused to hire any "technical advisers." But although the director tried to isolate himself, Berlin's theatrical figures came flocking to the UFA studio to watch the making of the company's first talking film. "The stage of *The Blue Angel* was a public thoroughfare," Sternberg com-plained. "Not only representatives of the press, writers, actors, direc-tors, and even Max Reinhardt were present (his main concern was how a sibilant should be recorded), but sculptors and painters, among them George Grosz."

At the center of the uproar was the gigantic figure of Jannings, who, according to Sternberg, "opposed me every step of the way." Jannings persisted in declaiming his lines in the flowery Max Reinhardt manner; Sternberg constantly demanded more realism. They both worried over every detail, and as they approached the scene of Professor Unrat's final humiliation, Jannings insisted that the eggs to be broken over his head must be rotten; he even had Sternberg break a few on him beforehand so that his mood would be right.

If Jannings played the temperamental villain throughout the weeks of shooting, Marlene Dietrich played the all-healing heroine. Sternberg was fascinated by her irreverence and her air of indifference. "She was inclined to jeer at herself. . . . She was frank and outspoken to a degree that some might have considered tactless. . . . She attached no value . . . to anything . . . so far as I could ascertain, with the exception of her baby daughter, a musical saw, and some recordings by a singer called Jack Smith." On the other hand, she, in her own way, fought with Jannings for the director's favor. "Her attention was riveted to me," Sternberg recalled. "No property master could have been more alert. She behaved as if she were there as my servant, first to notice that I was looking about for a pencil, first to rush for a chair when I wanted to sit down. . . . Rarely did I have to take a scene more than once."

Even after the shooting was finally finished, Jennings continued his bizarre tantrums. First he came to Sternberg and announced to him, "I don't need to tell you that there is not enough money in the world to compel me to be in a film of yours again." But then, just before Sternberg was to leave Berlin, the actor knocked on his hotel door and said in a choked voice, "Whatever happens, Jo, I know that when I die you will weep, and that I will weep when you die." For Marlene Dietrich, on the other hand, the end of the adventure was more conventional. Sternberg showed rushes of *The Blue Angel* to Ben Schulberg, the head of Paramount, and Schulberg offered her a contract to come back to Hollywood and make another picture with Sternberg.

The day on which her train was to leave Berlin was the day on which *The Blue Angel* began its spectacular success in Berlin. "The railroad station was close to the Gloria Palast where the film opened," Sternberg said, "and as the boat train was not scheduled to leave until midnight, she had been persuaded to take a bow at the finish.

. . . It is pleasant to record that she was not attired as if she might have to sneak out of the stage door and run for the waiting train, but was festooned and garlanded in the flouncy tradition of a film star. She received a thunderous ovation. The beginning of the journey into the stratosphere had been nicely timed."

Despite the apparently carefree prosperity of 1929, there had been signs of trouble from the very start of the year. A new inflation was threatening, and in a fierce dispute over wages in the iron industry, the manufacturers abruptly closed their factories, locking out some 200,000 workers. And among the peasants, who had never benefited very much from the period of foreign loans, there was an increasing amount of poverty and unemployment. Indeed, unemployment throughout the country rose dangerously during the early spring of 1929. Still, most Berliners preferred to ignore the portents. They went on sunbathing and picnicking and drinking schnapps. In the newspapers, they heard of a sudden crash in the Wall Street stock market, but it was hard to believe that this distant event would soon ruin everything they now enjoyed. For the time being, they went their own ways.

To Dr. Fritz Bamberger, professor of philosophy at Berlin's Jewish Institute, the year 1929 represented the two hundredth anniversary of the birth of Moses Mendelssohn. He was not a philosopher of overwhelming significance, but he was an important figure in the evolution of the German Jewish community. A strong advocate of equality and assimilation, he translated the Pentateuch into German and wrote numerous works in favor of religious and political tolerance. Gotthold Lessing made Mendelssohn the hero of his famous play, *Nathan the Wise*, and, indeed, the philosopher was carrying a manuscript in praise of Lessing to his publisher when he caught cold and died.

"The anniversary was quite an event," says Dr. Bamberger, puffing slowly on his cigar. "We were putting out a complete edition of Mendelssohn's works, and every German state and city had some kind of a *Fest*. I gave a lot of lectures on Mendelssohn in various places. I made a fair amount of money from that, but I got very tired, so at the end of the year, I went to Saint Moritz for some skiing.

"I stayed at the Kulm Hotel, I remember. There were a lot of interesting people there. A man named Schwartzschild, Leopold

Schwartzschild, the editor of one of the best-known liberal magazines in Germany. And there were various rich people who liked to pick up the bills. There was a Swedish industrialist, and his mistress, a countess. And I remember that we sat around one evening, just about New Year's, and we were all pleasantly tired from the skiing in the mountains, and we all agreed that this was the high point. Things would never be so good again."

"Heads Will Roll" 1930

> We were simple because the people are simple. We thought in primitive terms because the people think in primitive terms. We were aggressive because the people are radical.

JOSEPH GOEBBELS

"WE ARE SEVENTY THOUSAND WORKERS in Lennox's packing plant and we/Cannot live a day longer on such wages," cried the chorus in Brecht's *Saint Joan of the Stockyards*. "Yesterday our pay was slashed again/And today the notice is up once more:/ANYONE NOT SATISFIED WITH OUR WAGES CAN GO/. . . But now by twelve hours' work a man can't even/Earn a loaf and/The Cheapest pair of pants. Now/A man might just as well go off and/Die like a beast."

Brecht set his play in the Chicago stockyards, but his unemployed workers were, of course, the workers of Berlin. Within a few months of the Wall Street crash of 1929, a world-wide depression had begun, and no nation was so vulnerable to the contraction of trade and credit as Germany. Foreign investors started calling in their loans and German capital began flowing out of the country; companies started laying off workers, or closing down entirely. During the one month of January, 1930, the number of German unemployed soared from 1.5 million to almost 2.5 million, and every month, the figure kept climbing. And these were only the official figures for the workmen who officially lost their jobs and went on relief, standing in long lines on the sidewalks outside the government employment offices and then getting a little stamp that entitled them to a dole of about seventeen dollars a month. Even those who still had jobs had to take pay cuts—the miners' average wages shrank from forty-seven dollars a month in 1930 to thirty-nine dollars the following year. And there are no figures for the millions who lost part-time jobs, or the farmers who could no longer sell their crops, or the students who reached their graduation and found no jobs to be filled.

The newspapers of 1930 began to report a wide variety of symptoms of the disaster. At the end of January, for example, Berlin's *Deutsche Allgemeine Zeitung* observed that the number of customers at the city's official pawnshops had doubled, and since all such customers had to state their occupations, the newspaper thought it noteworthy that the largest number of these customers (29.1 percent) were shopkeepers; the second-largest number (25 percent) were unemployed women. And the newspapers carried ads like this one: "Money available to anyone at 6 percent. Real estate or furniture required as security . . ." And stories like this: "The banker Max Cunow of Berlin was found dead in his bedroom Monday morning, shot through the head. The police announced that it was a suicide. A letter was found, citing financial difficulties. . . ." In one week alone, in Berlin alone, there were five cases of bankrupt businessmen committing suicide. And the unemployed, who could find nothing to do, huddled for warmth in various official "shelters." At one of them, on the Ackerstrasse, the crowd overflowed, and a fight started, and the police, in the dark phrase of one Berlin newspaper, "had to use their clubs."

"What was it really like for the unemployed?" Dr. Hans-Joachim Kausch repeats the question. He is a solid, gray-haired man of sixty-three, with a very white shirt and very large cufflinks, a public-relations director for the Springer press; once he was a Berlin correspondent for newspapers in Hamburg and Breslau. "They played cards. They demonstrated. Some became criminals. It was a sad time. You go to work, and hundreds of young men and young girls are standing around on the streets, just standing. In Berlin alone, a city of four million, there were 750,000 unemployed. They were drinking a little beer. They were walking in the forests. They were hungry."

In the forests that skirt Berlin, the unemployed drifted into a number of tent colonies, where they lived from spring until frost. Visitors marveled at the orderliness of these camps, and at the silence that hung over them. The tent camps had their own "mayors" and "town councils," their communal kitchens and cooperative garbage-collection teams. The streets were very straight, and they bore neat little nameplates. The women cooked turnips, the children played in special playgrounds, and the men sat in sullen despair. Not all of the unemployed were so docile, however. In the nearby fields, the peasants stood guard with rifles in an effort to prevent foraging bands of workmen from invading their domains and digging up the potatoes.

The economic crisis soon brought the coalition cabinet of Social Democratic Chancellor Hermann Müller to the point of collapse. Even by the most optimistic reckoning, the payment of unemployment benefits would reach a deficit of almost $100 million. The conservatives demanded a cut in payments; the left an increase in taxes on employers. The Catholic Center, now headed by Dr. Heinrich Brüning, worked out a compromise that provided for some sacrifices by both sides, but the Social Democrats felt that they could not compromise on so fundamental an issue. Chancellor Müller himself, one of the old Socialist stalwarts, was too weary and too sick to fight on. Ten years had passed since he had first served a brief term as Chancellor just after the Kapp Putsch, ten years of elections that always ended in a fragmented Reichstag, ten years of the deals and bargains that cynical politicians called *Kuhhandel*, or cattle-trading, and now, on learning that President Hindenburg wanted a new Chancellor, he resigned. And with his resignation, the last genuinely parliamentary government of the Weimar Republic fell.

Hermann Müller himself did not survive more than a year. The liver trouble that had plagued him during his chancellorship finally killed him the following spring, and the people of Berlin, somewhat inured by now to the deaths of their leaders, watched yet another parade of black-banded marchers.

"Come cast an eye at the funeral," said Clive, one of the hedonists in Christopher Isherwood's *Berlin Stories*.

" 'What funeral, darling?' Sally asked, patiently. . . .

" 'Why, say, haven't you noticed it?' Clive laughed. 'It's a most elegant funeral. It's been going past for the last hour.'

"We all three went out on to the balcony of Clive's room. Sure enough, the street below was full of people. They were burying Hermann Mueller. Ranks of pale steadfast clerks, government officials, trade union secretaries—the whole drab weary pageant of Prussian Social Democracy—trudged past under their banners towards the silhouetted arches of the Brandenburger Tor, from which the long black streamers stirred slowly in an evening breeze.

"'Say, who was this guy anyway?' asked Clive, looking down. 'I guess he must have been a big swell?'

"'God knows,' Sally answered, yawning. 'Look, Clive, darling, isn't it a marvelous sunset?' "

It is the improbable figure of Christopher Isherwood, novelist, playwright, onetime medical student, Vedanta enthusiast, who has created, more than any German writer, the image we have of Berlin in the 1920's. He achieved this in two autobiographical novelle, a thriller called *The Last of Mr. Norris* (1935) and a collection of character sketches called *Goodbye to Berlin* (1939). Or rather, he did not achieve it, for these two modest works (published together in America as *The Berlin Stories*) enjoyed only a modest success until 1951, when John Van Druten adapted them into a Broadway play, taking his title from one of Isherwood's opening sentences: "I am a camera with its shutter open, quite passive, recording, not thinking. Recording the man shaving at the window opposite and the woman in the kimono washing her hair. Some day, all this will have to be developed, carefully printed, fixed."

I Am a Camera then became a successful movie, and, with the addition of some rather undistinguished songs by John Kander and Fred Ebb, the vastly popular musical, *Cabaret*. In the course of these transformations, something odd happened. Isherwood had written a few simple portraits of people he had known, many of them living in a boardinghouse near the Nollendorfplatz, and most of them, like Isherwood himself, were outsiders, quite isolated from the life of the city. Sally Bowles, the wandering singer without either talent or morals, was no Berliner at all, and neither was Mr. Norris, the giggling and bewigged espionage agent. Even genuine Berliners like the Landauers lived apart, knowing that their wealth would never alter their position as Jews. "I wanted to call it *The Lost*," Isherwood recalls. "About people whom society regarded with horror. I also thought of calling it *The Rejected*."

The paradox is that Isherwood succeeded, precisely by focusing his camera on the lost and the rejected, in producing a matchless portrait of the city. But in transferring Isherwood's work to Broadway, the various creators of *Cabaret* decided that all the idiosyncratic characters of *The Berlin Stories* must become a series of types, and thus caricatures. Sally Bowles had to become a sprightly ingenue; Herr Issyvoo himself had to become a pink-cheeked American tenor named Clifford Bradshaw, and the tormented, self-destructive spirit of Berlin had to become a rousing chorus in which everyone sings, "Life is a cabaret."

The beginning had been almost accidental. W. H. Auden was the first of the young English poets to go to Berlin. "After I graduated from Oxford, my parents said I could spend a year abroad," says Auden, now a rather baggy figure with a deeply lined face, sitting before a table covered with five opened packs of Lucky Strikes and twenty books of matches. "Everybody else was going to Paris, and one thing I knew was that I didn't want that. So I went to Berlin. As a matter of fact, I arrived just in time to go to the opening night of *The Threepenny Opera*. Even though I knew no German."

Auden soon settled in and even began creating poems in German —using as his models "Rilke, Brecht, and cabaret songs"—and writing letters back to England to report that Berlin was a splendid place. "The climate," he still says, "is the best in the world. The clear air. When Hofmannsthal wanted to get work done, you know, he used to come to Berlin." Isherwood, an awestruck admirer of the young Auden's pronouncements, duly followed his friend to Berlin, but not just for the climate. He also wanted to check on the warnings proclaimed by one of his relatives, a Hamburg shipping executive whom he called Mr. Lancaster in *Down There on a Visit*. "I know Satanists when I see them," said Mr. Lancaster. "Christopher—in the whole of *The Thousand and One Nights*, in the most shameless rituals of the Tantras, in the carvings on the Black Pagoda, in the Japanese brothel pictures, in the vilest perversion of the Oriental mind, you couldn't find anything more nauseating than what goes on there [in Berlin], quite openly, every day. That city is doomed, more surely than Sodom ever was. These people don't even realize how low they have sunk. Evil doesn't know itself there. . . . You could never imagine such things."

"No—I'm sure I couldn't," Isherwood said meekly, adding, "And then and there I made a decision . . . that, no matter how, I would get to Berlin just as soon as ever I could."

The real Berlin was somewhat less orgiastic. At the age of twenty-five, Isherwood moved into a tenement room and tried to finish his second novel, *The Memorial*. He lived on the food of the poor, horse meat and lung soup, which generally cost only sixty pfennigs (about fifteen cents) for a meal. Stephen Spender visited him there and found the whole scene deeply depressing. "I would . . . walk past [the] grey houses whose façades seemed out of molds made for the pressing of enormous concrete biscuits. Then I would come to the Nollendorfplatz, an eyrie of concrete eagles, with verandas like breasts shedding stony flakes of whatever glory they once had into the grime of soot which caked the walls of this part of Berlin. The bridges, arches, stations and commanding noise of the overhead railway had taken possession of the square and the streets leading . . . eastward to the ever more sordid tenements which never yet quite lost some of their claim to represent the Prussian spirit, by virtue of their display of eagles, helmets, shields, and prodigious buttocks of armored babies. A peculiar and all-pervading smell of hopeless decay (rather like the smell of the inside of an old cardboard box) came out of the interiors of these grandiose houses now converted into pretentious slums."

When Spender finally reached the apartment of Fräulein Thurau (the Fräulein Schroeder of *The Berlin Stories*, alias Fräulein Schneider, alias Lotte Lenya, of *Cabaret*), he had to wait until this protectress "with pendulous jaws and hanging breasts" informed him that "Herr Issyvoo" was ready to see him. "Whilst I was waiting, one or another of the characters of his as yet unwritten novels would dart out of one of the rooms opening into this one. Perhaps Bobbi the bartender would shoot fish-like through this central tank and escape into another room, or perhaps Sally Bowles would appear, her clothes disheveled, her eyes large onyxes fringed by eyelashes like enameled wire, in a face of carved ivory."

They would go out, then, to one of those terrible lunches of lung soup—"a penance for Christopher to which he attached an unstated but disciplinary importance." Or, having saved money at lunch, they might wander northward to the Bahnhof am Zoo and splurge on caramel candy. "It may seem that there was an inconsistency about his extreme economies and the purchase of the sweets," Spender observed, "but I think that Christopher regarded the sweets as being in their way another penance, an excess ruining his teeth. What he would have regarded as inexcusable would have been a 'balanced diet.'"

After this ritual, the two young Englishmen would ride the

elevated railway out to Grunewald and talk about politics. "There was a sensation of doom to be felt in the Berlin streets," Spender recalled. The cabinet, he said, "had abandoned the attempt to govern through the yelling mob . . . which was the Reichstag (broadcasts of whose howling debates, punctuated by a tinkling bell, were a feature of the German wireless). . . . Every decree, accompanied by dissenting cries of 'dictatorship' . . . produced the impression of the . . . cabinet as a little boat manned by a hopeless crew, trying to navigate an unending storm. The feeling of unrest in Berlin went deeper than any crisis. It was a permanent unrest. . . . In this Berlin, the poverty, the agitation, the propaganda, witnessed by us in the streets and cafés, seemed more and more to represent the whole life of the town, as though there were almost no privacy behind doors. Berlin was the tension, the poverty, the anger, the prostitution, the hope and despair thrown out on to the streets. It was the blatant rich at the smart restaurants, the prostitutes in army top boots at corners, the grim, submerged-looking Communists in processions, and the violent youths who suddenly emerged from nowhere into the Wittenbergplatz and shouted: *'Deutschland Erwache!'* ['Germany, awake!']."

Today, in his late sixties, Isherwood looks back on Berlin, and the popularity of his stories, with a benign tranquillity. "I was the only one there," he says, by way of explanation, "the only English-speaking writer to write a book about that period. It was just one of those things. It wasn't a great success at first—there were good reviews, but the timing wasn't very good, just before the start of the war. I've never had a great success at first with anything I've written. I mean, nothing like a best-seller. But the stories created a world, and people like to read about other worlds, rather than just a narration of events. They like to be able to see people's whole lives, as though they were in a fishbowl."

Isherwood shapes a fishbowl in mid-air with his hands, then lets them drop. One notices a turquoise ring on his hand, which fits the different shades of the frayed blue shirt, the blue tweed jacket, and the bright blue eyes. With Isherwood, the pieces always seem to fit together. He is staying in a friend's apartment in South Kensington, where all the walls of all the rooms are white, and all the rugs are various shades of brown. Across from the chocolate-colored sofa in the living room, there is a small chair with gazelle antlers on top. Isherwood stands by the white fireplace and remembers.

"I understand that the original of Mr. Norris is still around," a visitor remarks. "Do you ever see him?"

"Oh, occasionally," Isherwood says. "His name is Gerald Hamilton. He's even written a book called *Mr. Norris and I.*"

"It must have had a strange effect on his life, to be famous but to exist only as the creation of someone else—"

"Don't let *him* hear you say that," Isherwood laughs. "He's written several other books, one about South Africa, as well as the books about Mr. Norris."

"Books? Are there several?"

"Three or four—at least three, I know. The last one was called *As Young as Sophocles.* Do I mean Sophocles or Socrates? Socrates. As young as Socrates. It's a poem. 'I'll bury life, and not grow old. . . .'"

Isherwood recites the whole poem, savoring every absurdity, and ending with a flourish, "To you, a Socrates, to freedom and to youth!" At the end of the recitation, he looks up for applause, and then laughs.

"What about the others? What ever became of Sally Bowles?"

"She lives in London. She has a daughter. She's my age, nearly seventy by now. The *Daily Mail* absolutely *nosed* her out, somehow. They kept calling me in Los Angeles to ask where she was, wasting a terrible lot of money, because they were absolutely determined to take her to *Cabaret* when it opened in London. When they finally found her, they called me up to ask if I had any comment, and I said, 'Well, I didn't want it to happen.'"

"And the others? The Landauers?"

"Well, that was Wilfrid Israel, of the Kaufhaus Israel, the department store. He got away to England, but then he was killed in a plane crash, on a flight from Lisbon to London, the same crash that killed Leslie Howard. There was a regular flight from Lisbon to London, and there was a sort of gentleman's agreement that it wouldn't be attacked, but this time the Germans intercepted it off the coast of France and shot it down. I don't know why. There's been some speculation that the Germans thought Churchill was aboard, but I don't think there's any basis for that."

"And the daughter? The one who took English lessons?"

"She wasn't really his daughter, not Israel's daughter. Her name was Giza Soloweichek, but I can't spell it. S-O-L-O-W-E-I-C-H-E-K.

It's something like that, but I can never get it right, so you're on your own. She went to Paris and married a nice boy. She's alive to this day, as far as I know, but I don't get to Paris very often."

"Have you ever been back to Berlin?"

"Just once, in 1952, to do one of those Berlin-revisited things for the *Observer*. Everything was very much smashed up. They'd simply pushed the rubble to the sides of the streets. I wonder what ever became of all that rubble. . . ."

(It did seem a mystery, but the answer came later. All the debris of Berlin of the 1920's—100 million tons of it—was carted off to form three giant hills at various points in the city. The biggest one, Teufelberg [Devil's Mountain], now rises 360 feet high in the Grunewald Forest. The Berliners have covered it with ten thousand trees and shrubs, plus a vineyard, and they have built a ski jump on one slope. At the top, the Americans operate a secret radar installation, which, the Berliners boast, can reach as far as the Urals.)

"Anyway, the spirit of Berlin was much the same. There was still the energy. Everybody was very brisk. They weren't moaning about things. After work, they'd volunteer for extra labor to clear away the mess. I remember, there was one big pile of rubble with a café built on top of it. And the incredible beauty of the girders of one of the railroad stations, which had been burned out, looking like the ribs of a whale.

"I went back to the Nollendorfstrasse. My old landlady was still there, in her seventies. The old building had been hit, so she was living next door. We thought it might be a shock if I just walked in, so some friends went ahead to prepare her. They said, 'You know, we hear that Herr Issyvoo might come to Berlin again.' She was amazed. '*Ach! Was Sie sagen!*' ['Oh, what are you saying!'] Then they said, 'He might already be in Berlin.' Then they said, 'He might even be quite near.' Then, when I went in, she gave a great *cry*. Like Tristan and Isolde.

"We talked. I said the air raids must have been ghastly. She said, 'Yes, we spent so many days in the cellar, and we prayed so much that I became quite religious.' Another thing. When the Russians came at the end of the war, they were sort of raping people. They were healthy young boys, and they pursued even old ladies like Fräulein Thurau. I think she was rather pleased at that. But she said, 'You know, I put a shawl over my head, and I went around with my face like this [here Isherwood, in his sixties, imitating Fräulein Thurau in her seventies, screws up his face into a hideous grimace], and then I looked just like an old hag, so they left me alone.' Anyway, that was the only time I saw her again, and now she's dead."

"How about your own feelings about *Cabaret?*" the visitor asks. "I read somewhere that you didn't like it."

"I've never seen it," Isherwood says. "I've read the script, and people have told me that there were some good things in it—the master of ceremonies and some of the choruses. But everybody warned me that I wouldn't like it."

"And curiosity didn't tempt you?"

"Oh, I've seen vulgarities so often. And then, they always manage to find out that you're in the theatre, and then there's the question of going backstage. Why pull a long face and be nasty and ungracious? It pays me money, so why fight the goose that lays the golden eggs?"

Since the divided Reichstag seemed unable to decide on either a new government or a program to combat the worsening economic crisis, the powers of state passed increasingly into the hands of President Paul von Hindenburg. And since Hindenburg was by now eighty-three years old, addicted to long naps and already suffering from intermittent mental lapses, the power of the presidency passed increasingly into the hands of his palace guard. This consisted of three key men—Hindenburg's corrupt and incompetent son, Oskar; the presidential state secretary, Otto Meissner, a factotum of such chameleon talent that he served in the same capacity under both Friedrich Ebert and Adolf Hitler; and, finally, the most powerful of all, the chief of the War Ministry Office, General Kurt von Schleicher.

Even before Chancellor Müller's downfall, Schleicher had decided on a candidate to succeed him: Dr. Heinrich Brüning. As the parliamentary leader of the Catholic Center Party, which never controlled even a fifth of the Reichstag, Brüning had little hope of winning the support of a legislative majority, but he had other qualities that won him the support of Schleicher and Hindenburg. A gaunt, skeletal man, who was then forty-four but looked considerably older, Brüning had been marked for life by the experience of commanding a machine-gun unit during the war. It had been a suicidal task. Brüning's little unit had been assigned to attack strongholds that couldn't be captured, and to defend outposts that couldn't be saved. In mowing down enemy forces, and in seeing his own men slaughtered, and in surviving, Brüning had acquired an almost unworldly sense of duty and sacrifice, of the transcendence of the national cause over merely human needs. "When talking with him," said one official, "I had noticed, from the beginning, a peculiarity which later became more pronounced. Not only did he always speak in a low voice; he kept looking around continuously like someone, who is afraid of being overheard." And now, if the poor and the unemployed were suffering, then the devout and rather mystical Dr. Brüning would suffer with them, for everyone must share in the national destiny. He soon became known as "The Chancellor of Hunger."

(And he was to spend the rest of his life fighting against that name. He taught for many years at Harvard, a dry, stiff, frigid old man with steel-rimmed spectacles and thin white hair, teaching a few courses and living by himself in a dark suite, the blinds always drawn, in one of the undergraduate dormitories. At the end, he retired to a country house near Hanover, New Hampshire, and worked at his memoirs, which would provide, posthumously, his version of the disaster. "He has an absolutely passionate desire to convince people that he wasn't responsible for the coming of Hitler," says one of his colleagues. "Which is a little absurd, because partly, of course, the coming of Hitler was a kind of tidal wave that nobody could have stopped. But partly, he *was* responsible.")

Brüning, taking over much of Müller's cabinet, put together a new government within three days, on March 30, 1930, and promptly warned the Reichstag that he was planning drastic measures: "This will be the *last* attempt to arrive at a solution with *this* Reichstag." The Socialists immediately proposed a vote of "no-confidence," but Brüning survived it. Then, with the unemployment deficit still climbing—now double what it had been at the start of the year— Brüning announced a program of austerity. Unemployment taxes were to be raised and unemployment benefits cut; income taxes were to rise, and government salaries were to be reduced.

When the Reichstag noisily rejected his program, Brüning resorted to the weapon that he had apparently planned to use from the beginning. Article 48 of the Weimar Constitution authorized the President to rule by decree whenever this was necessary for the maintenance of public order. Interpreting this article with unprecedented liberality, Brüning now produced Hindenburg's signature on a series of decrees that proclaimed his austerity program to be the law of the land. The Social Democrats in the Reichstag immediately answered with a motion to nullify the decrees. When this motion passed, Brüning responded with yet another decree, dissolving the Reichstag and calling for new elections.

There were wise advisers who told Brüning that his plan was suicidal, that he had no hope of winning votes with a program of austerity, and that any election in a time of mass unemployment could only result in a victory for extremists. "I implored the Chancellor not to take the fateful step of dissolution," said the Foreign Minister, Julius Curtius. But Brüning, he said, felt obligated "to protect the President's authority after it had been threatened by the nullification of the decrees."

It seems, in retrospect, an insufficient reason to call a general election in the midst of a terrible depression, but Brüning, the former machine-gunner, apparently felt a blind loyalty to his field marshal. And he did not schedule the new elections until the last permissible day, September 14, so he had that summer, at least, in which to perform some kind of miracle through the power of the presidential decree. He knew that the odds against him were great; as it turned out, they were even greater than he knew.

The slogan of Joseph Goebbels' newspaper, *Der Angriff*, had always been radical: "For the Oppressed. Against the Exploiters." And in a time of social breakdown, this kind of radicalism had an undeniable appeal. From a mere 17,000 members in 1926, the Nazi Party swelled to 120,000 in the summer of 1929, to 210,000 the following March. In the fall of 1930, Hitler claimed one million members. And as the party grew, it became increasingly interesting to Germany's fretful industrialists. Fritz Thyssen, the steel magnate, conservatively estimated the donations by heavy industry to the Nazis during the late 1920's at $500,000 a year; secret contributions were probably much larger.

One of the Nazi leaders whom Thyssen personally subsidized, paying for him to get a larger apartment and "to cut a better figure," was the onetime war hero, Hermann Goering. A fugitive in Sweden after the Munich Putsch of 1923, Goering had not dared to return to Germany until President Hindenburg declared a general political amnesty in the autumn of 1927. He turned up in Berlin, then, and became a kind of lobbyist for various aviation companies, including Heinkel, the Bavarian Motor Works, and, unofficially, Lufthansa. Having left his Swedish wife behind, he lived austerely, working late at night by candlelight in a small apartment decorated with a portrait of Napoleon and a medieval sword. When Thyssen's money began flowing in, however, Goering summoned his wife to Berlin and began entertaining handsomely at his new apartment on the Badensche Strasse. It was through him that one of the Kaiser's younger sons, Prince August, joined the Nazis in 1930 and became a featured speaker at party meetings. "Our house is so full of politicians," Carin Goering wrote back to Sweden, "that I would be driven mad if it were not so fascinating."

The Nazis remained split into left and right wings, as they had been from the beginning, and Adolf Hitler did his best to make both sides believe that they were his favorites. He equivocated, he avoided decisions, he lied, and he once said to a friend, "I shall go on my own way with the precision of a sleepwalker."

Joseph Goebbels, who belonged to the left wing of the party, resolved all contradictions by a worshipful adulation of Hitler himself. "You are like a meteor before our astonished eyes," he wrote at one point in an open letter to "Esteemed Herr Hitler." "And you have worked a miracle of enlightenment and belief in a world of skepticism and despair. . . . You personify the faith, and it suffices to your true modesty to be its first servant in the struggle for the mastery of the future." And again: "He [Hitler] alone has never deceived himself. He has always been right. . . . Like a servant of God he fulfills the task which was given to him and he does justice in its highest and best sense to his historical mission." Several years later, looking back on his career, Goebbels told an associate that he had helped the Nazi cause in four essential ways: by introducing Socialism into a middle-class group, by "winning Berlin," by working out the style of the party's public ceremonies, and by the "creation of the Führer myth. Hitler had been given the halo of infallibility."

There was considerable truth in these boasts, particularly the last one, for, as a series of elections soon demonstrated, millions of Germans began to believe that Adolf Hitler, a semiliterate incompetent, a failure in everything he had ever attempted, somehow had the skill and intelligence to solve all the nation's problems. One of the most willing believers in the "Führer myth" was, understandably enough, the nervous and uncertain Führer himself. When one of his supporters once told him, in the course of an argument, that he was mistaken, Hitler angrily answered, "I cannot be mistaken. What I do and say is historical."

His opponent in that argument was Goebbels' rival and onetime patron, Otto Strasser, who had never learned, as Goebbels had learned, that Nazi policy was whatever Hitler said it was. Strasser was a stubbornly independent man. A twice-wounded war veteran, he had once been a convinced Socialist, but after helping to organize the Berlin workers' resistance to the Kapp Putsch of 1920, he had broken with the Socialists on the grounds that they had failed to punish the Kapp conspirators. Strasser's views were always somewhat Utopian. Opposed to both Marxism and capitalism, he argued for a system that he called "state feudalism," under which the state would nationalize all land and lease it to various citizens. He had met and disliked Hitler as early as 1920, but when Hitler had assigned Strasser's older brother Gregor to organize the Nazi Party in northern Germany, Otto had joined in the struggle for Berlin by founding the *Kampfverlag (Combat Press)* and the city's first Nazi newspaper, the *Arbeiterzeitung (Worker Paper)*. And then Joseph Goebbels had arrived as Gauleiter of Berlin, and the two had started fighting.

Hitler, in the course of the argument, offered to make Strasser his press chief, but also threatened him with expulsion from the party. They argued about art, and about race, and about the relationship of the leader and the idea. Strasser believed that a political program was more important than its leader. Hitler scorned that. "With us, the Leader and the Idea are one," he said, "and every party member has to do what the Leader orders. The Leader incorporates the Idea and alone knows its ultimate goal. . . . I ask you: are you prepared to submit to this discipline or not?" Strasser accused Hitler of trying "to strangle the social revolution for the sake of . . . your new collaboration with the bourgeois parties of the right." Hitler rejected the charge. "I am a Socialist," he said. ". . . I was once an ordinary working-man. . . . What you understand by Socialism is nothing but

Marxism. Now look: the great mass of working-men want only bread and circuses. They have no understanding for ideals of any sort, and we can never hope to win the workers to any large extent by an appeal to ideals. We want to make a revolution. . . . What you preach is liberalism, nothing but liberalism. There are no revolutions except racial revolutions."

The argument ended in a stalemate, but Strasser was clearly no match for Goebbels in the struggle for control of the Nazi movement in Berlin. By the spring of 1930, Goebbels began systematically expelling Strasser's supporters from the organization. Strasser demanded a party meeting to argue over one of these expulsions. Goebbels agreed, but Strasser found himself barred at the door of the hall. Strasser then resigned from the party—his brother Gregor refused to join him, saying only, "Very well, [but] I must stay." Otto Strasser tried to organize a rival National Socialist group called the Black Front. But Goebbels by now controlled a private army.

One night in July of 1930, Strasser was leaving the first meeting of his Black Front, together with a disabled war veteran named Brehm. "We were suddenly attacked by a number of men dressed as hooligans," Strasser said, "and I was half-blinded by a handful of pepper which was thrown into my face. I wasted no time, but leapt into the road and gained the opposite pavement. My attackers' aim was poor, for I was left with one eye open. . . . I drew my revolver and shouted: 'The first man who moves is dead!' I then advanced toward my injured friend, helped him up and backed again towards the pavement, holding him up with one hand and keeping our assailants covered with my revolver. They were only armed with knives and bludgeons. Brehm was bleeding copiously and, with his wooden leg, it was not easy for us to get along. . . . 'I know them all. They're SA men,' Brehm . . . whispered in my ear. . . . We managed to reach the station, where my friend's injuries were attended to."

The case of the Barmat brothers, who had corrupted so many Social Democrats during the early 1920's, had a sequel. The Sklarek brothers operated a Berlin clothing factory, where they manufactured uniforms for policemen, firemen, and other city officials. The Sklareks prospered. The Sklareks bought race horses. The Sklareks entertained city officials. The Sklareks were friends of the Mayor of Berlin, Gustav Böss, a highly respected administrator who had reigned in

City Hall ever since 1921. The Sklareks provided Frau Böss with a fur coat. And to finance all their social activities, the Sklareks devised a system for turning in vouchers on uniforms that were never delivered. Their profit from this amounted to more than $2 million.

Mayor Böss was on a tour of the United States when the scandal broke. He returned to find himself welcomed at the station by a turbulent crowd of Nazis shouting denunciations of Jewish businessmen and corrupt officials. Mayor Böss promptly resigned, and even initiated a formal investigation of himself, which the Nationalists kept alive throughout most of 1930. Böss was eventually fined one month's pay, $750, and the Sklareks went bankrupt, but the political damage was irreparable. This, said Goebbels, was the kind of thing that the Nazis were determined to destroy: The System.

So the election campaign in that summer of 1930, which Dr. Brüning had started as a matter of high principle, would be fought, at least by Hitler, on the terms he stated to Strasser: "Not a matter of right, but of might." The economic crisis had provided Hitler with an ideal political climate of discontent and bitterness; it had also provided him with an equally basic ingredient for political success— manpower. Every week, thousands of men lost their jobs, their pay, and, no less important, their sense of self-respect. They stood in line for hours to get their semiweekly dole and then wandered through the streets or sat sullenly in some *Bierstube*. To these outcasts, Hitler now offered a sense of purpose and fraternity and the brown uniform of his SA, the *Sturmabteilung*, the Storm Troopers.

They gathered in their "storm centers," which were generally the back rooms of beer halls. "There sat the unemployed," according to one chronicler, "in their coarse brown breeches and discolored yellow shirts for many hours of the day over their half-empty beer mugs; at mealtimes they were fed for a few pfennigs from a great iron kettle that simmered in the laundry room. . . . But when the whistle blew . . . when the squad leader cried, 'Attention!' then these men rotting in inactivity sprang up, formed ranks, and stood at attention while a man in high boots and armed with a horsewhip shouted: 'Everyone listen! . . .' And they marched off. For wherever they might be marching, it could only be better." Day and night, the Storm Troopers tramped through the streets of Berlin, singing, shouting their slogans, looking for fights. The Communists, too, had their private armies, just as embittered and just as lawless, and whenever two rival gangs met, the fighting would start.

Joseph Goebbels, who had once swathed perfectly healthy Nazis in bandages so that he could have martyrs to show at his party meetings, now had no shortage of victims. There were not really that many—one man killed every week or so—but Goebbels turned each funeral into a state occasion. One of his staff members, Erich Maria Berger, recalled an occasion on which he accompanied Goebbels to a graveyard. Goebbels talked, during the drive to the cemetery, about various typographical changes he wanted made in his newspaper, *Der Angriff,* and he continued whispering instructions even while he walked past the ranks of Storm Troopers lining the path to the grave. Once he had reached the grave, he delivered an impassioned oration on the heroism of the dead man, vowing vengeance and revolution, but as soon as he got back to his car, he continued giving instructions to Berger, admitting that he couldn't even remember the name of the man he had just helped to bury.

Some of the SA formations could hardly be distinguished from professional gangsters. One troop in the tough North Berlin section of Wedding proudly called itself "The Robber Band," and one in Neukölln took the name "The Band of Rogues." Of all Goebbels' "martyrs," though, the most celebrated was a twenty-one-year-old student named Horst Wessel, the son of a Protestant military chaplain. Wessel had broken with his family and abandoned his studies. He lived in a Berlin slum with a prostitute, Erna Jännicke, and apparently supported himself by pimping. He was also an aggressive and successful leader of the Storm Troopers in his neighborhood. To help the cause, he wrote a three-stanza song entitled "Lift Up the Flag!" and filled with the standard Nazi rhetoric—"For the last time the call to arms rings out. . . . Soon the Hitler banners will fly over all the streets." One day in 1930, Horst Wessel received a visit from another pimp named Ali Höhler, who had formerly been Miss Jännicke's procurer and who had just emerged from a term in prison. There was some shouting and pushing, and then Wessel reached for his gun. Höhler got his own gun out first and shot Wessel.

For several days, while Wessel lay critically wounded in a Berlin hospital, Goebbels issued daily health bulletins on his new hero. And since Ali Höhler belonged to a Communist street gang, Goebbels portrayed the gun battle as an infamous act of political terrorism. The Gauleiter wrote an emotional account of his visit to the hospital, and he quoted from the hero's song: "Comrades shot dead by the Red front and Reaction march in spirit within our ranks!" When Horst Wessel finally died, Goebbels staged a tremendous funeral. "His song has made him immortal," Goebbels cried, and, echoing the line about the marching dead, he called out: "Horst Wessel!" And the assembled Storm Troopers shouted: "Present!" Goebbels affected to be inspired to new hyperbole. "A Christ and a Socialist!" he said of the dead youth. "One who calls through his deeds: Come to me: I will redeem you." Then everyone sang the "Horst Wessel Song," which, after Goebbels had produced enough pamphlets and posters, was to become the Nazis' official anthem.

(As for Ali Höhler, he was sentenced to life imprisonment, but that was not enough for the Nazis. After they came to power, the first head of the Gestapo, Rudolf Diels, a hard-drinking young man who liked to end his revels by literally chewing up beer glasses, fetched Höhler out of prison and drove him to a lonely Mecklenburg wood, where the car had the traditional breakdown. "What do you think we're going to do now?" Diels asked. "I guess you're going to knock me off," Höhler said. A few weeks later, a band of picnickers looking for mushrooms saw a hand sticking up out of the ground and found Höhler's half buried body.)

Throughout the first six months of 1930, the authorities took a number of steps to stop the street fighting. The Prussian government banned all parades and outdoor meetings throughout the state. The Reichstag passed a special Law for the Protection of the Republic to suppress political rioting. The Prussian authorities banned Nazi uniforms and emblems. The measures had all the effectiveness of an edict by King Canute. Forbidden to wear brown shirts, the Nazis all wore white. "And they took beer bottles," says one woman who remembers those days, "beer-bottle tops—you know those porcelain tops that used to clamp down on the bottle, and there was a little rubber ring around the top, and they would take that off and put it around a button on the front of their shirts, and then everybody knew who they were."

"Hate exploded suddenly, without warning, out of nowhere," Isherwood wrote in *The Berlin Stories*, "at street corners, in restaurants, cinemas, dance halls, swimming-baths; at midnight, after breakfast, in the middle of the afternoon. Knives were whipped out, blows were dealt with spiked rings, beer-mugs, chair-legs or leaded clubs; bullets slashed the advertisements on the poster-columns; in fifteen seconds it was all over and the assailants had disappeared." The impressionistic description comes easily from the newspapers of those days, but when one talks to the survivors, it is rare to find anyone who actually saw anything. The work of the metropolis went on from week to week, and the murders committed by the rival political gangs of Berlin were far fewer than those committed by outraged husbands and frightened holdup men in the New York of today. The city is simply so large that one rarely sees its violence. "It's the same here and in Berlin," says Dr. Margaret Muehsam, a stately lawyer with snow-white hair and two strings of pearls around her neck. "One may hear of fighting in Harlem, but one doesn't see it on Seventy-second Street."

Street demonstrations traditionally remained within certain frontiers. The Socialists and Communists marched through the working-class districts of East Berlin; the Nationalists and other right-wing groups paraded among the shopkeepers of the West. Occasionally there were collisions, but they were the exception. "We never marched in *their* districts," says Dr. Heinz Pachter, professor of history in New York; forty years ago, he was an official in the Socialist Youth Movement. "But the Nazis kept moving in, street by street. They would establish themselves in some café and start selling their newspapers on the corner. So we had to fight back. I must admit they were very brave, to show themselves in the working-class districts. I remember once they staged a march through Neukölln, a workers' district where they had absolutely no business. So we threw rocks at them."

Neukölln lies just east of Tempelhof airfield. It has been a slum for generations; it still is. It has always voted with the left, and it has always been violent. On May Day of 1929, the Communists announced a march through the district, the police banned the march, and the Communists marched anyway. Police opened fire on the crowd and killed thirty-one people.

"Did you ever see any of the fighting?" a visitor asks Dr. Fritz Bamberger, the philosophy professor, whose bookshelves are filled with leather-bound volumes of Spinoza.

"Oh, yes," says Dr. Bamberger. "In Neukölln."

"Tell me about it."

"Neukölln was strongly Communist, you know," says Dr. Bamberger. "They had terrible problems with poverty. But they were also doing interesting work with experimental education. I remember, a friend asked me out to visit a school there, the Karl Marx Schule, but it was a city school. The children could do whatever they wanted. There was no curriculum at all."

"How did that work?"

"It worked fantastically well in some areas, in areas that called for free expression. The children did wonderful pictures of the life they lived. They wrote stories, about whatever they wanted. There was one girl, with her hair in braids, tied with what they called *goldene Zigarrenband*—the gold paper that comes around a cigar—they used to put that on their hair sometimes. This child of eleven told a story of how she was sitting at home, taking care of her little sister, waiting for the mother to come home at seven. As the girl described it, she created quite a bit of tension—the children look at the clock, there are steps on the stairs, but it's somebody else. The little one starts to cry. There is nothing to eat, because the mother was going to buy food on the way home from work. Well, finally the mother comes home. She had to stay late at work to get her pay, something like that. That was all there was to it, but I have always remembered it.

"The father was never mentioned in the story," Dr. Bamberger goes on. "There often were no fathers in such stories. The children talked about their 'uncles'—meaning pimps. And the pictures they drew were very realistic. They drew the prostitutes, the girls of the district, exactly as they were, all with little umbrellas and with boots of various heights to show that they were specialists. The children didn't know what these things meant, but they saw everything quite clearly."

"But what about the street fighting?"

"Well—you know—" says Dr. Bamberger. "You went up to where you could see the barricades, and then you heard the 'knack-nack-nack' of rifles, so you didn't go any further."

"You didn't have to see any street fighting to know that things were going wrong," says Abram Chasins, the pianist. "People *knew* that there was a sort of Hitler underground, that the kids were being indoctrinated, that democratic teachers were getting fired, that the

Nazis were better organized than the newspapers ever told us. And there was a quality of political anger. Fierce arguments. We're beginning to have it in New York. If a foreigner were to come here now and just watch our television—the demonstrations, the fighting—that's the way it was in Berlin in 1930. I know we're not having a revolution here now—or are we? You laugh—see, that's the way it was then, just the way we're sitting here now. We laughed at the danger. And we didn't even *have* any television. But I *heard* about this meeting, that riot, somebody disappearing. I couldn't wait to get away. And I had been in love with Berlin."

Bertolt Brecht was visiting a friend, who lived on a third-floor apartment in the Koblanckstrasse, when fighting broke out in the street below. They stood at the window and watched. Brecht, according to the friend, "saw how the police dispersed and pursued the demonstrators. So far as we knew, they were unarmed. But the police did fire again and again. At first we thought they were only warning shots. But soon we saw a number of the demonstrators falling and then being carried off on stretchers. . . . When Brecht heard the shooting, and saw that human beings were being killed, he turned white, as I have never seen him before. . . . I believe it was this experience that was not least influential in bringing him closer and closer to the Communists."

It was at about this time that Brecht wrote his most devotedly Communist play, which is, surprisingly enough, one of his most moving, and, perhaps not so surprising, one that the Communists never approved of. It was called *The Measures Taken,* and it deals with a report by four "agitators" who voyage from Russia to China to organize the workers. Along the way, they meet a "Young Comrade," who looks to them for help.

"Our locomotives have broken down. Have you brought any new locomotives with you?"

"No."

". . . We have no way of putting our fields in order. Have you brought any seed?"

"No. . . ."

"Then you yourselves are going to help us?"

"No."

The four agitators, who are acting out all these scenes of their past experiences, took the Young Comrade with them on their mission to China, but first they all had to agree to "blot out our faces." The Party Leader tells them: "Then you are yourselves no longer. . . . You are nameless and motherless, blank pages on which the revolution writes its instructions." In a series of episodes, then, the Young Comrade repeatedly tries and repeatedly fails to carry out this oath of self-abnegation. When he sees coolies being mistreated, he tries to help them. When he starts to organize the factory workers, he cries for a strike. And when all his attempts to do good only jeopardize the agitators' mission, they decide to shoot him and dump his body in a lime pit. The Young Comrade himself agrees to his fate—"in the interests of Communism . . . saying Yes to the revolutionizing of the world"—and the "Control Chorus," to whom the four agitators have been telling their tale, praises the four murderers because

> Your work was successful
> You have spread
> The teachings. . . .
> In yet another country the revolution advances. . . .
> We agree to what you have done.

The Communists disliked Brecht's version of Communism, of course, for they could take no pleasure in the prophetic spectacle of the party killing its own members—and killing the best among them—but Brecht's play derived from the most fundamental of all his passions, a passion for nonpassion, a passion for nothingness. As early as the "Chorale of the Great Baal," which begins with the poet growing inside his mother's womb, the two basic images in Brecht's poetry are sky and water, and both represent the limitless space in which one can find peace. "You must not swim," he wrote in the *Manual of Piety,*

> no, you must be as if you
> Were a part of the earth like the gravel bed.
> You should look up at the sky and act as if
> A woman's womb still carried you: it fits:
> And without fuss like the Lord God of an evening
> When in His rivers He goes for a Swim.

In *Memory of Marie A.,* the poet cannot even remember the girl he kissed, but only the cloud overhead:

> Perhaps the plum trees still are there and blooming.
> Perhaps that woman has six children too.

But that white cloud bloomed only for a moment:
When I looked up, it vanished in the blue.

To surrender to these vast seas above and below is to die, but dying, from this viewpoint, is not a tragedy so much as a return to the state of nonbeing from which one emerged. Thus, in *The Berlin Requiem*:

She was drowned and was floating downstream
From the little brooks into the bigger rivers
The sky shone with a beautiful opaline light
As though to watch tenderly over the corpse. . . .

And in *Mahagonny*, when Brecht wanted to write a love duet, he created what Auden calls "one of the most beautiful pieces of lyric poetry ever written," entirely as a metaphor of the sky:

Look at those cranes sweeping wide
The clouds, which have been allotted to them
Accompanied them already when they flew from their nests
From one life into another life.

One suspects that Brecht was drawn to Communism not just because of the fighting in the streets, and not just because the radicals claimed to have a concrete program to deal with the economic crisis, but because Communism demanded the submission of the individual to the organization, and because many intellectuals seem to find a peculiar kind of satisfaction in the act of submission. From *The Jungle of the Cities* to *The Measures Taken*, and on to *Galileo* and *Mother Courage*, Brecht, the radical, dramatized not revolt but stoicism and surrender.

Officially, however, Brecht believed in the theories of Marxism, which require a somewhat more aggressive approach to the world, and as he surveyed the commercial triumph of *The Threepenny Opera*, he became more and more dissatisfied with it. Perhaps he came to realize that Weill's music had somewhat altered the tone of the play, or perhaps he simply resented rebukes like that of a left-wing critic who wrote that Brecht's work was actually less radical than John Gay's original play. In any case, when a movie company, Nero-Film, wanted to buy the screen rights, Brecht sold them for forty thousand marks, reserved the right to produce his own screen-play, for another fourteen thousand marks, and then proceeded to rewrite the whole work along more Marxist lines. Among other things, he decided to have the highwayman Macheath end as a successful banker. The film company, which simply wanted to transfer the stage success to the screen, argued for a time and then went ahead on its own, with G. W. Pabst as director and a lavish 800,000-mark budget. The company offered to pay Brecht off in full, but Brecht filed a suit to stop the movie.

The trial, in October of 1930, was a grand social event. Theatre and movie figures flocked to the Berlin courtroom to watch the famous author plead his cause, and Brecht responded with all the melodramatics they had expected. At one point, he turned down a settlement of 25,000 marks; at another, he stormed out of the courtroom. The movie company's lawyers successfully argued, however, that Brecht had actually done very little work on his script, had refused all compromises, and had even been hard to find. The court rejected Brecht's suit, which Brecht denounced as an example of capitalist coercion, but when the movie company offered still another payment (sixteen thousand marks) just to avoid any appeals to higher courts, Brecht followed his basic instincts and took the money. "The public," said Brecht, by way of explanation, "was entitled to our trying to obtain justice."

The election of September 14, 1930, was a disaster. The Nazis, who had held an insignificant 12 seats in the outgoing Reichstag, had hoped to gain perhaps 50 seats. Instead, they won 107, which suddenly made them the second-largest party in Germany. Their number of votes rose from 810,000 to 6.5 million. The Social Democrats were still the strongest party, with 143 seats out of a total of 577, but they had lost 10, and they now faced an increasingly strong challenge from the Communists, who had risen to 77. The moderate parties of the center all fared badly.

Like many Berliners, Bruno Walter, the conductor of the municipal opera, spent that evening listening to the radio. With him was the great cellist, Emanuel Feuermann. "Every few minutes," Walter said, "the triumphant voice of the announcer would tell us of the progress of the election. We knew at about three in the morning that Hitler had polled about 6,500,000 votes. . . . Feuermann, usually so gay, left us with the words: 'It's all over with Germany; all over with Europe.'"

In trying to analyze the disaster, some observers have blamed it on such technical causes as the German system of proportional representation. If Germany had used the American system of allotting each legislative seat to the candidate who wins the most votes within a specific district, the Nazis in 1930 would not have won more than about twenty seats. Still, it seems dubious to argue after the game that the rules should have been changed. The fact remains that 6.5 million Germans voted the Nazi ticket—and the figures were to get worse. Hitler had found a whole army of new supporters among a wide variety of discontented factions. The northern peasants of Schleswig-Holstein, traditionally liberal, had given him more than 25 percent of their votes. The unemployed, who now numbered more than three million, voted Nazi in large numbers. So did the traditional conservatives, no longer satisfied with Alfred Hugenberg's Nationalists, who lost heavily. So did the women, who generally give their votes to the right. Most important, perhaps, the younger generation, which is always the first to denounce a blundering establishment, now considered the Nazis a party of both youth and revolt. There were 4.6 million new voters in 1930—children during the war, adolescents during the upheavals of the 1920's, rootless, resentful, and now unemployed. To them, the forty-one-year-old Hitler stood for rejuvenation.

But was there some deeper reason, some half-hidden national belief in the Nazi creed of violence, even some prophetic instinct for collective self-destruction? Dr. Franz Alexander, the first pupil at the Berlin Psychoanalytic Institute and later the director of a similar institute in Chicago, thought he saw the answer in some of his patients: "The occasionally open, mostly hidden, scorn and contempt many of my German patients held for the [Weimar regime] was too obvious to be overlooked. . . . The national socialist movement—partially at least—was a rebellion . . . against the growing cosmopolitan, levelizing, super-national historical trend. . . . It was a neurotic defense against loss of identity on a national scale. The Weimar Constitution was felt as something superimposed on Germany by the Western Powers—which would make Germany like the rest of Western culture—something alien to German racial and national tradition . . . making it cosmopolitan and rational, something which was foreign to its history."

Other psychoanalysts, too, have tried in their various ways to explain the phenomenon. Erich Fromm, in *Escape from Freedom*, blamed the rise of Nazism on "the authoritarian personality," which he considered typical of Germany's lower middle class—"their love of the strong, hatred of the weak, their pettiness, hostility, thriftiness with feelings as well as with money, and essentially their asceticism." To Wilhelm Reich, on the other hand, it seemed absurd to blame Nazism on any one class or nation. In *The Mass Psychology of Fascism*, he argued that Hitler's movement was simply "the organized political expression of the structure of the average man's character. . . . There is not a single person who does not bear the elements of fascist feeling and thinking. . . . In its pure form fascism is the sum total of all the *irrational* reactions of the average human character."

Perhaps it is too easy, though, to psychoanalyze a whole people, and so one makes an appointment to see Dr. Sandor Rado, who has spent a long lifetime in analyzing the unconscious and the irrational. Dr. Rado was already the head of the Berlin Psychoanalytic Institute when Dr. Alexander came there as a pupil, and it was Rado who undertook to perform the training analysis on Reich. He is very old now—"Do you know how old I am?" he asks—eighty, to be exact, a small man with a fringe of white hair and a protruding lower jaw and a very shiny skin. He lives in New York in an expensive apartment building just off Fifth Avenue, and he likes to go walking every day in Central Park.

"Why did the Nazis come to power?" the interviewer asks Dr. Rado. "Why did so many Germans vote for them?"

There is a long silence. It is a sunny April afternoon, but Dr. Rado's rather cluttered library is dark. One notices that the backs of his hands are very freckled.

"That is not an easy question that you ask me," Dr. Rado says.

Another long silence. Dr. Rado stares into the dusk of his study, thinking. Finally, he decides on his answer. He speaks very slowly, very carefully.

"I don't know," says Dr. Rado.

The new Reichstag convened on October 13, 1930, and the Nazis immediately provided a demonstration of how they planned to use their victory. Thousands of party members, shouting their slogans, milled around the Reichstag building, where political demonstrations were traditionally forbidden. Inside the building, the Nazi delegates determined to show off their Storm Trooper uniforms. All party insignia had been banned by the Prussian authorities, so the Nazi delegates smuggled their brown uniforms into the building and then changed clothes in the washrooms. Once inside the legislature, the brown-shirted invaders enjoyed parliamentary immunity, and every subsequent debate became a scene of shouted insults, loud singing, and threats of violence. Outside, on that first day, when the police finally dispersed the crowd from the neutral zone around the Reichstag, the Nazi organizers led a parade over to the nearby Leipzigerstrasse, where they smashed the windows of department stores and attacked any bystander whom they took to be a Jew.

The victory was still only a partial victory, however, and the nearer the Nazis came to the rewards of power, the greater became the tensions within this riotous movement. Just before the elections, in fact, the whole Berlin SA had exploded. The unemployed Storm Troopers had become dissatisfied with their rations of beer and sausage. They wanted to be paid, and, in an outburst of rage, they wrecked their own headquarters. Gauleiter Goebbels, the tiny cripple, did not dare face his own soldiers. He called in the despised Berlin police to clear out the SA headquarters, and then he pleaded with Hitler to come and restore order. Hitler hurried to Berlin and spent one long night driving from beer hall to beer hall, shouting, occasionally bursting into tears, and promising the disgruntled troopers both money and power. He dismissed the head of the SA, an undistinguished ex-captain named Franz Felix von Salomon Pfeffer, and then summoned home his old ally, Captain Ernst Röhm, who, after the unsuccessful Munich Putsch, had wandered off to South America as a military adviser to the Bolivian Army. It was under Röhm that the SA became, in the next three years, the biggest military force in Germany.

A squat, ugly man, his red face scarred by bullet wounds, Röhm had no political views whatever. He considered himself a simple soldier, and, by all accounts, he was a good one, both shrewd and fearless. His ambition—and he was endlessly ambitious—was to turn the ragged troops of the SA into a private army and eventually to merge them with the regular Reichswehr, with himself in charge. He set up an SA general staff and even opened a school in Munich for the training of SA officers. Within nine months, SA membership multiplied from 70,000 to 170,000, almost twice the size of the Reichswehr. Under Röhm, the SA leadership acquired a rather special quality, however, for the crude and blustering *Oberster SA Führer* was also a fervent homosexual, and he liked to surround himself, in all the positions of command, with men of a similar persuasion. In Berlin, Röhm assigned the command of the SA to the dissolute Count Wolf von Helldorf, with another young homosexual, Karl Ernst, as his deputy.

The psychiatrist may take a clinical interest in this equation of violence and perversion, but Defense Minister Gröner and the rest of the Reichswehr generals were concerned primarily about the SA as a rival power, and Hitler, after the debacle of the Munich Putsch, was determined never again to oppose the army. Now that he saw the prospect of winning power through the electoral process, he insisted that he had no intention whatever of inciting his restless troops to rebellion against the Weimar Constitution.

The issue was joined during 1930 in the trial of three young lieutenants named Richard Scheringer, Hans Ludin, and Hans-Friedrich Wendt, on charges of spreading revolutionary Nazi propaganda, which the army had specifically forbidden. The defense lawyer, Hans Frank, who later won a kind of renown as Governor-General of occupied Poland, summoned Hitler as a defense witness, and Hitler testified, for the benefit of the generals, that "none of us [is] interested in replacing the army." On the contrary, he declared that "when we have come to power, out of the present Reichswehr a great German people's army shall arise." All this would be done legally, he insisted, and within the rules of the Weimar Constitution. Still, once he had achieved power, Hitler testified, "the November 1918 revolution will be avenged, and heads will roll." The three lieutenants were ultimately sentenced to eighteen months in prison, but the spectators at the Supreme Court in Leipzig greeted Hitler's prophecies with loud cheering. And the army heard them.

So the violence continued—petty violence, for the most part; self-righteous violence. The American film, *All Quiet on the Western Front*, opened in Berlin with the approval of the official censors, but the Nazis professed indignation at the portrait of weariness and defeatism among the soldiers in the Great War. Goebbels sent bands of Storm Troopers to the theatre to threaten and harass anyone who wanted to see the movie. When that failed to stop the film, the

Nazis invaded the theatre itself and started shouting and booing. They set off stink bombs. They even brought cartons of white mice and released them under the seats. President Hindenburg looked favorably on these commotions as an example of what he called "the indignation of nationalistic youth," and when a group of veterans organizations petitioned for a suspension of the movie, the Board of Film Review docilely reversed itself. It banned further showings on the grounds that the movie "would tend to endanger Germany's national prestige."

In this atmosphere, Brecht and Weill finally staged their opera, *Mahagonny*, that superb parable of the mythical "city of nets," the city in which everything is permitted so long as one has the money to pay the price, the city that illustrates, as one critic put it, "the failure of men to understand—and, ultimately, to deserve—freedom." Swarms of Berliners voyaged to Leipzig for the out-of-town premiere, and they found it a chilling experience. "We walked through crowds of Brown Shirts carrying banners and placards protesting the new work in ugly tones," said Hans Heinsheimer, the music publisher. "We had felt a new, never-before-sensed, ominous tension during the dress rehearsal the day before. On opening night, it was not long before demonstrations broke out in the auditorium. A little uneasiness first, a signal, perhaps, then noise, shouts, at last screams and roars of protest. Some of the actors stepped out of their parts, rushed to the apron of the stage, shouted back."

"The performance was well under way," according to Lotte Lenya, "before I was startled out of my absorption by the electric tension around us, something strange and ugly. As the opera swept toward its close, the demonstrations started, whistles and boos; by the time the last scene was reached, fist fights had broken out in the aisles, the theatre was a screaming mass of people; soon the riot had spread to the stage, panicky spectators were trying to claw their way out, and only the arrival of a large police force, finally, cleared the theatre. . . . The second performance was played with the house lights on and police lining the walls."

"It was in the last act that things got really violent," says John Gutman, who was covering the premiere for the Berlin *Börsen-Courier*. "That scene where God actually comes on stage, looking just like a German capitalist, you know, with a big fur coat, and a hat, and a cigar—that's when the booing and whistling got tremendous. And then God says, '*Gehet alle zur Hölle*'—'All of you, go down to hell!' They couldn't take that."

But Brecht had anticipated all this in the last lines of the closing chorus, which sum up not only an opera but an era:

> We cannot help ourselves or you or anyone!
> We cannot help ourselves or you or anyone!

CHAPTER XV

"I Couldn't Control Myself" 1931

And I was happy; the more I wallowed in filth and infamy, the more
my imagination burned with lust.

MARQUIS DE SADE

"ALWAYS . . . ALWAYS, there is this evil force inside me. . . . It's there
all the time, driving me out to wander through the streets. . . . It's
me, pursuing myself, because I want to escape . . . but it's impossible.
. . . I have to obey it. . . ."

No one who has ever seen Fritz Lang's powerful film *M* will ever
forget the closing scene in which the anonymous child murderer,
dragged before a court of his fellow criminals, shrieks and sobs his
explanation of why he feels compelled to kill young girls. "Who will
believe me? Who knows what it feels like to be me? How I'm forced
to act . . . *His eyes close in ecstasy.* . . . How I must . . . Don't want
to, but must . . . *He screams.* Must . . . Don't want to . . . must . . ."
The movie was one of the great hits of 1931, and it made a star out
of a pudgy little Hungarian actor named Peter Lorre, but it almost
failed to get into production at all.

Lang had announced to the press that his new movie was to
be called *Murderer Among Us,* and he soon began to receive threatening letters, warning him not to make the picture. Even more
curious, he was refused permission to use the big movie studio in
the Berlin suburb of Staaken. Lang demanded a meeting with the
studio manager, and the argument between them became quite
strenuous. Various people, the manager said enigmatically, were
opposed to Lang's project.

330

"But why this incomprehensible conspiracy," cried Lang, seizing the manager by the lapels of his coat, "against a film about the Düsseldorf child murderer Kürten?"

"*Ach*, I see," said the manager, smiling with relief.

Lang, too, had seen. On the inside of the manager's lapels, in the fold that many middle-class Nazis used in those days to keep their membership half-hidden, he had seen the small pin marked by the swastika. Now that the misunderstanding was resolved, now that it was clear that Lang's film was not a political venture, the manager willingly granted the use of the studio. "On that day," Lang said, "I came of age politically."

It was indeed a curious misunderstanding, but, in a way, it was not a misunderstanding at all, for some of the most horrifying Nazis of the coming decade were not the jackbooted brawlers of the SA but the Peter Lorre figures, neatly respectable, a little effeminate, and driven by uncontrollable demons. In the course of a few years, such men were to take power, and the Nazi regime was to reverse the very meaning of law and order. The criminals were to rule and the innocent were to be punished. And so it may be of some interest to consider the state of crime in Germany during the years before it became a way of life. Even under the Weimar Republic, the record of political and cultural justice was not without blemishes. While the right-wing assassins of the early 1920's had escaped almost unpunished, the authorities had seen fit to prosecute George Grosz, and Carl Zuckmayer, and even to ban the Arthur Schnitzler play that we know as *La Ronde*. But they did, unlike their successors, regard murder as murder.

Still, even apart from politics, not all murders are the same. The styles and methods vary from country to country, and from one period to another. It is tempting to infer too much from these variations in the basic human compulsion to violence, but it is nonetheless true that crime does provide a mirror image of society. And because murder is the most fundamental violation of law, the mirror that reveals the murderer provides the strangest image of all. In the Germany of the 1920's, a nation still scarred by the loss of two million dead in the war, it is not insignificant that the compulsive criminal was, in several notable instances, a mass murderer. Nor is it insignificant that, in these times of widespread hunger, the mass murderer sometimes implicated his neighbors in mass cannibalism.

Karl Denke, for instance, was a small shopkeeper in Münster-berg, near Breslau, a highly respected citizen who even performed minor functions in the local Lutheran church. Shortly before Christmas in 1924, the sounds of fighting in Denke's apartment brought in two neighbors, who found the shopkeeper fighting with a badly wounded young workman. Denke protested that the workman had attacked him, but police searched his house and found several barrels filled with smoked human flesh, a case full of bones, and a number of pots of human lard. During the years of famine, when the villagers had grown accustomed to eating roasted dogs and cats, Denke had done good business in the sale of "smoked pork," and now, while the villagers looked at one another in horror, Denke hanged himself, leaving behind a notebook that neatly recorded thirty murders, with the date of each killing, and the weight of each victim. The precision of his records, incidentally, helped to free another man who had already served sixteen years in prison for one of Denke's murders.

One such horror might be ascribed to a provincial lunatic, but there were more horrors to come. And besides, Germany was not a country in which the activities of provincial lunatics could be ignored. Once, the Germans had liked to call themselves a nation of *Denker und Dichter* (thinkers and poets), but during the 1920's, people began making puns on that old saying. According to Kurt Tucholsky, Germany now was a country of *Henker und Richter* (hangmen and judges). But Bertolt Brecht said, "I suggest replacing the word *'Denker'* in the formula by the word *'Denkes.'* Germany is the land of *'Denkes'*!" To his visitor, a Russian poet, Brecht went on to explain that he meant the mass murderer. "Denke is the name of a criminal who killed people in order to use their corpses. He canned the meat and made soap from the fat, buttons from the bones, and purses from the skins. He placed his business on a scientific footing and was extremely surprised when, after his apprehension, he was sentenced to be executed. . . . I contend that the best people of Germany, those who condemned Denke, failed to recognize the qualities of true German genius which the fellow displayed, namely: method, conscientiousness, cold-bloodedness, and the ability to base one's every act on a firm philosophical foundation. . . . They should have made him a Ph.D., with honors."

In Berlin itself, the figure of the mass murderer appeared in the form of Carl Wilhelm Grossmann. A heavy-set man in his early fifties, Grossmann had once been a butcher, but after the war, he tried to make a living as a door-to-door salesman, setting out every morning from his tenement apartment near the Schlesischer Bahnhof with a battered suitcase full of shoelaces, combs, mirrors, and hair-pins. In the evenings, he often went to the railroad station, which brought to Berlin a steady stream of peasant girls from the east, coming to the city in search of work. They were helpless and penni-less, for the most part, and Grossmann must have seemed a fatherly sort. He had no difficulty in hiring girls as housekeepers. Sometimes, he even took them out to a nearby *Rummelplatz*, a sort of fair, where he offered them rides on the merry-go-rounds. How many of these housekeepers he hired was never quite clear—occasionally one of them would run away, and then Grossmann would go to the local police station and file charges against the missing girl for having stolen money from him—but the total must have been in the dozens. Then came the moment when, as Grossmann later said, "I couldn't control myself."

One night, about an hour after Grossmann had brought home a new housekeeper, some neighbors named Iglitzki heard so much screaming that Frau Iglitzki sent her husband directly to the police of the Fiftieth Precinct. With a policeman leading the way, the Iglitzkis proceeded directly to Grossmann's apartment, pounded on the door, and then broke it open. What they saw was so extraor-dinary that Herr Iglitzki fainted dead away in the doorway. The housekeeper, Marie Nitsche, was lying on the bed, her hands tied behind her, her legs and thighs enmeshed in rope, her throat cut. Grossmann, his hands covered with blood, was standing over her, quite naked. The policeman beat Grossmann into submission and then searched the apartment. In the kitchen, he found a half-charred thorax and several hands and fingers. Through a crowd of shouting neighbors, who remembered that Grossmann used to carry packages into several local butcher shops, the policeman dragged Grossmann off to precinct headquarters, where the authorities subsequently accused him of murdering not just Fräulein Nitsche but also twenty-three other women, whose remains, in bits and pieces, were found in the nearby Luisenstädter Canal.

Grossmann refused to confess, however. He claimed that he had simply been trying to punish Fräulein Nitsche for stealing money from him. As for the remains of other women found in his kitchen, and in the canal, he showed neither interest nor remorse.

The only thing that seemed to affect him was the news that his pet bird, a siskin named Hänseken, was suffering from his absence. Grossmann told the police that he would talk if he could have his bird, and so, the next day, a detective brought in Hänseken in his cage. Grossmann's handcuffs were taken off, and he was given an hour to coo at his bird. The homicide detective then began to chat with Grossmann about the bird. He suggested that it might need some insect powder. Grossmann agreed, and a policeman was sent to fetch the powder. Then, once Hänseken had been treated and cared for and put back in his cage, Grossmann confessed. He completed the confession by hanging himself in his cell, with a twisted sheet tied to a nail.

Grossmann was not unique either. Perhaps even more characteristic of Berlin, since it all took place amid the gunfire of Spartakus Week, was the case of the mysterious Baron Winterfeld. A tall, thin man with a black beard, Baron Winterfeld had arrived just a month earlier, by taxi, at the most famous hotel on Unter den Linden, the Adlon. He seemed to know nobody in Berlin, but he did receive a special-delivery letter one day, and the mailman who brought it to his room was delighted to be tipped, in these times of hunger, with a ham sandwich and a cigar.

The mailman also brought a letter to Lorenz and Louis Adlon, owners of the hotel, warning them that the Spartakists intended to overthrow the government on January 4, and that all banks would be seized. Anyone with savings should have them returned to his home. Similar letters went to many rich Berliners, and one of them was even published in the newspaper *Berliner Zeitung am Mittag*, which also published an editorial warning that the letters sounded like some kind of criminal trick.

The day the Spartakus uprising began, the Adlon Hotel became a battleground, occupied in turn by Spartakists and Freikorps forces (both of whom paused to sample the hotel's famous wine cellar), but despite the bullets whistling up and down Unter den Linden, the city's mailmen dutifully continued on their rounds. The special-delivery mailmen were particularly conscientious. One of them, a fifty-year-old functionary named Lange, had been serving the Adlon for a decade, and when he arrived at the hotel with a letter for Baron Winterfeld, he declined the hall porter's effort to take it, because he remembered that the baron had once given him a ham sandwich.

As Lange walked up the stairs to the second floor, there was a burst of machine-gun fire outside the hotel, and nobody thought any more about the mailman until that afternoon, when the post office telephoned to ask what had become of him. He had been carrying forty-one special-delivery letters containing more than 270,000 marks. The detectives who came to the Adlon Hotel eventually found Lange's body, tied to a chair in a second-floor room and strangled with a curtain cord. His mailbag was empty, and Baron Winterfeld, who had occupied the adjoining room, was gone.

Three years passed before a man named Blume was arrested in Dresden for the attempted murder of a mailman, whom he had attacked with a hammer on the stairway of an apartment house. On investigating further, the police discovered that Blume had committed not only the Adlon murder but a similar murder of a mailman in the Berlin suburb of Spandau. There was perhaps nothing very surprising in this, since all criminals tend to repeat their crimes over and over, but there was something quite peculiar about the fact that the murderer turned out to be a playwright. Just a few months before his arrest, in fact, he had had a light comedy produced at Dresden's Neustädter Theater, and he had followed that success by submitting to the same theatre a manuscript entitled *The Curse of Retribution*, a melodrama about the murder of a mailman in the Adlon Hotel in Berlin.

"You really did write this, didn't you?" asked the Berlin police inspector in charge of his interrogation.

"Have you read it?" asked Blume, who was shortly, like so many of these multiple murderers, to commit suicide—in this case, with a razor blade. "Isn't it a wonderful play? All I hope is that it will be put on before my execution. If it is a success, I shall feel that I have not lived in vain."

Of all these mass murders, the case that reverberated most persistently throughout the 1920's was that of Georg Haarmann, a mild, soft-spoken man, who, prophetically, was an unofficial police agent, an informer on petty thieves. Like Grossmann, Haarmann liked to hang around in railroad stations, searching for his victims among the peasant youths coming to Hannover to look for work. Unlike Grossmann, he was looking only for boys. He would offer them sandwiches, beer, and help. Then, after taking one of his new friends home and putting him to bed, he would sexually attack the youth and finally tear out the victim's throat with his teeth. He never could remember the actual scene, Haarmann later told his lawyer. He would feel a kind of rage beginning to overwhelm him, he said, and then everything went blank until he woke up in the morning with another dead boy in his room.

Some children found a skull on the banks of the Leine River, and then, a few days later, a second skull washed ashore. When the police dredged the river, they found enough bones to represent between twenty-four and twenty-six victims, but nobody associated the bones with Haarmann until the mother of a missing boy recognized her son's jacket on another boy, who proved to be the son of Haarmann's landlady. Haarmann, it turned out, did a brisk business in used clothes. He also made use of the corpses. "He . . . would cleanly dismember the body," said Vicki Baum, the novelist, who was living in Hannover at the time, "and reduce it to nicely boiled, potted meat. Said meat, labeled pork or veal and attractively packaged, reached the Black Market, where it brought good prices. When . . . Haarmann made a full confession, there was much silent shock, frightened inspection of hidden larders, some discreet vomiting, and a general throwing-away of expensive potted-meat jars."

Haarmann's arrest and trial caused a national uproar. The mother of one of his victims tried to attack him, and Haarmann lived in dread of being lynched, but he seemed to have no feelings about either his crimes or his prospective execution. A local professor of psychiatry, Theodor Lessing, argued vehemently that Haarmann was insane and not responsible for his killings, but the court barred any psychiatric evidence and sentenced Haarmann to death. The execution itself then became an issue, which, according to Arthur Koestler, illustrated the growing power of the Nazis. "For years the Ullstein papers had waged a vigorous campaign against capital punishment," said Koestler, who was then working in Berlin as assistant editor of the Ullsteins' *Berliner Zeitung am Mittag*. "Owing to the strong current against capital punishment in the liberal strata of the public, no executions had been carried out in Weimar Germany for some years. Now, in 1931 . . . the Haarmann affair became a test case. . . . The managing director informed us that Haarmann was a disgusting character, and that to ask for commutation of his sentence would antagonize public opinion, 'which we could not afford to do in these times.' Already most of the editors felt so insecure in their posts that no protest was voiced. I remember that

I mumbled something about few murderers being attractive characters . . . and my muttering was passed over in polite and complete silence. Thus was abandoned, within an hour, a campaign which we had been waging with fervent conviction over a number of years. It was merely one in a series of capitulations, but all the more striking as it had no direct bearing on political issues. We capitulated before the rapidly increasing brutalization of the masses."

Haarmann was duly executed, and as the date drew near, the schoolchildren of Berlin took to singing a song about him. "I remember," says one of them, now a teacher in New York, "there was a hit song in those days that went, 'Just wait a while, be patient, and happiness will come to you too,' or something like that, but then everybody started singing a different version that went:

> Warte, warte nur ein Weilchen,
> Bald kommt Haarmann auch zu dir.
> Mit dem kleinen Hackelbeilchen
> Macht er Pökelfleisch aus dir.

"Which means, 'Wait, wait just a little while, and soon Haarmann will come to you. With his little hatchet, he'll make smoked meat out of you.'"

"Brutality is respected," said Adolf Hitler. "The people need wholesome fear. They want to fear something. They want someone to frighten them and make them shudderingly submissive. Haven't you seen everywhere that after the beer-hall battles those who have been beaten are the first to join the party as new members? Why babble about brutality and get indignant about tortures? The masses want them. They need something that will give them a thrill of horror."

"Gentlemen, the meeting can now begin," says Schränker, who is described in Thea von Harbou's script for M as "head of the underworld." He wears a chalk-stripe suit and black leather gloves. "According to the regulations, I confirm with pleasure that the leadership of every organization in our union is represented. I assume that you all have full powers . . . Medium closeup of the SAFE-BREAKER, who nods. Pan to the PICK-POCKET, who is cracking a nut; he nods too, then to the CON-MAN who, while lighting a

*cigarette, also nods. Finally, the BURGLAR, still bent over the bag,
also gives his assent. SCHRÄNKER off:* . . . authorizing you to vote
for your members. Good."

There is a kind of nihilistic irony in the way Fritz Lang mobilizes
both the police and the underworld to hunt for the murderer. "In-
genious cutting interweaves the milieus of the police and the underworld," as one critic observed. "While the gang leaders discuss their
plans, police experts, too, sit in conference, and these two meetings
are paralleled by constant shifts of scene which hinge on subtle
association." In other words, Lang, like Brecht in *The Threepenny
Opera*, portrays the organization of law-enforcers and law-breakers
as more or less the same. The juxtaposition of scenes provides a facile
sort of social commentary, but it seems hard to believe that official
unions of criminals represent anything more than a somewhat implausible cinematic device. The device is accurate, however. The
unions really did exist.

"Another writer and I founded a surrealistic restaurant in that
time," says Ludwig Wronkow, once a cartoonist and now executive
editor of the New York German-language newspaper, *Aufbau*. He
is a small, stout, and completely charming man of about seventy,
with wispy white hair, a blue bow tie and a blue cardigan. "It was
called the Topp Keller, in the Schwerinstrasse, near the Nollendorfplatz. It had Pop art all over the walls.

"What did we do there? Nonsense, always nonsense." He says
this dolefully, pronouncing the first "s" as though it were a "z." *Non-
zense.* "We made Dada," he says. "All the time. And there was
often trouble with the *Ringvereine*. You know what means *Verein?*
A group—a club—this was a club of people who had come out of
prison. I had to hire the waiters from this club."

"Why, what would they do if you refused?"

"Otherwise, they would all come in and drink the beverages, and
nobody would pay. You know?"

"Was there any one man who came in and told you he was in
charge?"

"No, not one—three—four—"

"When you hired a waiter from this gang, did the waiter work
then? Did he do the job?"

"Well—" Wronkow shrugs and stares out the window. The snow
has begun to fall on the bleak brick buildings of upper Broadway.

"The food was always very bad anyway, you know," Wronkow says with a smile. "It was fashionable to go to places like that, where the food was bad, where the waiters were—you know—"

"How long did you have this place?"

"Three months. Then some crazy man came along and wanted to buy it, so we sold it to him."

The *Ringvereine,* or gangs, began under government auspices, for the authorities permitted and even favored the formation of a group called the Reich's Union of Ex-Convicts. Before long, there were more than fifty such unions in Berlin—as well as in other cities —and they joined forces in larger groups called "Rings." Officially, these groups were supposed to dedicate themselves to the rehabilitation of criminals. They adopted splendid names like "German Strength" and "Forever Faithful," and their constitutions and bylaws spoke (like those of the SA during its period of interdiction) of sporting activities, credit unions, and social gatherings. "German Strength," for instance, held regular meetings at the Rheingold Restaurant on the Potsdamer Platz, with noted defense lawyers and police officials as guests of honor. (Once again, *The Threepenny Opera,* in which Police Chief Tiger Brown joins Mac the Knife in singing "The Cannon Song," is a more realistic portrait than one might think.) "The high point of the evening," according to one observer, "came when one of the police officials took the baton and conducted the orchestra."

The *Ringvereine* were rich. They charged their members stiff entrance fees and fined them for various infractions of the bylaws (such as gambling during a *Ringverein* funeral). In their headquarters, they displayed sports trophies and group photographs of assorted gangsters out on picnics in the Grunewald. Members wore special gold rings and pins, and they took pride in their club flags, some of which were made of silk and cost as much as $500. The bylaws were ambiguous, however. One of them, for example, declared: "Every member is entitled to help in the event of illness and other extraordinary circumstances." What this meant, in effect, was that if a member got arrested, the *Ringverein* would hire a lawyer, support the prisoner's family, and, on occasion, intimidate hostile witnesses. Throughout most of the 1920's, the Berlin police tolerated these gangster organizations on the theory that it was a good way to keep suspicious characters under surveillance. But the *Ring-*

vereine—under the influence, it is said, of gangster movies from America—got increasingly turbulent. On one occasion, a *Ringverein* officially condemned two disloyal members to death, sent a notice of the death sentence to their houses, and then shot them down in the street.

The most dramatic police counterattack came against a *Ringverein* that had established its summer headquarters in Schmöckwitz, a hilly peninsula where two rivers and two lakes come together in the southeastern corner of Berlin. The gangsters, who claimed that their organization was devoted to water sports, had established themselves in a cluster of boathouses surrounding an inn called Grosse Zug. The inn could be reached only by water, and the gangsters had thoughtfully bought control of all the motorboats that ferried people to and from the site. The police, trying to plan a raid with minimum casualties, created an organization of their own, a *Singverein,* or singing club, and sent a written announcement that they were planning to come to the Grosse Zug to give a choral concert. The gangsters were delighted to welcome such a cultural manifestation. When the plain-clothes police arrived in their special steamer, the gangsters greeted them warmly and gathered together to hear them sing. The police formed a long line, opened up their songbooks, and began their concert with an old favorite called "Who owns you, you beautiful forest?" Then, while the gangsters were still happily applauding, the police all pulled out their pistols, arrested everyone in sight, and hauled them back to headquarters on their steamboat.

Violence is commonplace in every city. In Berlin, it became an accepted part of day-to-day life. "There were always bodies being fished out of the Landwehr Canal," says Peter Wallenberg, the UN correspondent. "Who were they? I don't know. Just bodies. We even had a song about it."

He begins to sing, a robust, cheerful song, the kind of song that people sing when they march.

"That means, 'There lies a body in the Landwehr Canal. Bring it here. Bring it here. But don't hold it too tightly.' That's because— you know—they come apart."

He laughs, and offers another cup of coffee.

Carl Zuckmayer, the playwright, was penniless when he first came to Berlin, and so he took a job as a sidewalk hustler for one of the city's many after-hours clubs. "I would stand in front of the Trauben Casino or behind the Rheingold Restaurant," he recalled later, "and whisper, 'How about another nice little nightclub tonight? Intimate show, reasonable prices . . . ?' "

One wintry night, Zuckmayer's boss suddenly appeared on the sidewalk, took him in a taxi to the Tauentzienstrasse, and, once in the cab, loaded his coat pockets with packs of cigars and cigarettes as well as a number of squares of white paper, filled with white powder. He told Zuckmayer to wander up and down the Tauentzienstrasse, and to murmur at bypassers, always with a hissing "S," the offer of *"Tssigars, Tssigarettes?"* Prospective customers would answer with a snuffle, the boss said, and then Zuckmayer could sell them one of the squares of white paper. The young playwright asked what the papers contained, and the boss said, "Snow," which in those days meant not heroin but cocaine. But Zuckmayer wouldn't get into any serious trouble, the boss added, because the papers really contained only a mixture of cooking salt and aspirin. Then he jumped out of the taxi and disappeared.

The playwright tormented himself for a while about the ethics of selling *"Koks,"* or, perhaps, selling cooking salt disguised as cocaine, if the boss had really been telling the truth about the deception. Then he decided that he needed the money to survive. So he took up a position outside the shuttered windows of the giant department store called Kadewe (an abbreviation of Kaufhaus des Westens, or Department Store of the West) and began to whisper into the cold night, *"Tssigars, Tssigarettes."* The only response came from a thin, dark-haired Polish girl who swung her handbag as she asked, "What are you doing here?"

"What's that to you?" Zuckmayer retorted.

"Watch how you go, sonny boy," the Polish girl said. "The police are pretty sharp around here. I suppose you're new to the business?"

Zuckmayer turned away from the girl and started walking down the Tauentzienstrasse, only to note that a broad-shouldered plainclothes man in a heavy overcoat was starting to follow him. Zuckmayer began walking faster, zigzagging through clusters of people on the street, and seeing, over his shoulder, that the plainclothes man was gaining on him. He was starting to worry about how to get rid of the packets of cocaine when he suddenly realized that the Polish girl was at his side. "Take my arm," she said, "and act like you're one of my tricks."

Zuckmayer did as he was told, and the plain-clothes man let the two of them walk off in peace.

"You know," said the Polish girl after a few blocks, "you must be the biggest dope that ever walked. Did you really think you could get away with it?"

"I don't know what you mean," Zuckmayer said.

"That one over there knows," the Polish girl said. "He's from the plain-clothes squad. Nothing he can do to me because I'm registered. But he had his eye on you right away."

The Polish girl soon learned from Zuckmayer that he was selling cocaine, then learned the price, and then told him that she could sell the whole lot in a nearby bar called the Femina. Leaving him in a doorway, she returned half an hour later, smelling of cognac, and handed him the money. In her room, later, Zuckmayer found that she had kept a pack of the drug for herself.

"Don't you 'Coke'?" she asked him in surprise. Zuckmayer shook his head while the girl took a sniff from the packet.

"It's good," the Polish girl said. "It makes you forget everything. Try some."

"I don't want to forget anything," the playwright said.

Cocaine was the basic drug of Berlin in the 1920's, and it was everywhere. Girls pushed it in nightclubs, one-legged war veterans sold it on street corners, and if one were going on a trip, everybody knew of foreign contacts. "When I was going to Paris," says one old Berliner, "they told me before I left that you could get all you wanted right outside Maxim's. There was a man there who wore a yellow hat, and he could always provide it."

What was it like "to Coke"?

"It makes you feel *so* clever," says Walter Slezak. "*So* clever. You start talking a lot, and you think you are saying the cleverest things in the world, and then the next day people say, 'What was the matter with you last night? You were talking like an idiot.' "

Slezak, like many victims of the 1920's, got onto drugs through his doctor, for both cocaine and morphine were widely prescribed as pain-killers (Freud even published a paper in praise of cocaine). Slezak was trying to maintain a heavy schedule of film production when he fell ill with an infection known as "makeup poisoning," an infection that he described as "like lying on an anthill. Itching, crawling, prickling, creeping, stinging pains." To help him sleep at night, the studio doctor gave him Luminal, and when he accidentally took a slight overdose, the doctor revived him with cocaine. "After about five hours, the cocaine began to wear off," Slezak said, "so Dr. Hoellenreich, for that was the monster's name, gave me some more. He kept that up for the next five days, until my part was finished. He showed me the proper way to use the stuff. A little mound of that innocuous-looking white powder on the back of the hand, bring the hand up to your nose, two quick sniffs, and lick the hand so nothing goes to waste. As the days wore on, the intervals between sniffs became shorter. A few people warned me of the danger of becoming an addict, but I felt too good and too light to listen.

"Dr. Hoellenreich personally brought me to the railway station to see me off to Paris and handed me a small box with dope to carry me over my trip. . . . Shortly before the train arrived in Paris, two French nuns settled in my compartment and we fell into a conversation. In my talkativeness, I told them that I used cocaine—on doctor's orders—and related the whole story. They suggested that I go to a hospital to get my skin and my system cleansed. . . . 'Why don't you take one big sniff now,' one of them suggested, 'and then throw the rest of the stuff out the window?' I still don't know why, but that's what I did. They said they would pray for me. Their prayers must have been very powerful."

Morphine was even more dangerous than cocaine, and almost as widely used. When Hermann Goering was wounded during the Munich Putsch, for example, his infected hip filled with pus, and his doctors gave him so much morphine to kill the pain that he soon became a helpless prisoner of the drug. As a refugee in Sweden during the mid-twenties, he was certified as a dangerous addict. On one occasion, he attacked a nurse who refused to give him morphine, and the police then escorted him to the insane asylum at Langbro, where he was confined in the violent ward. He stayed there for three months and later made periodic returns when he found that he couldn't do without the drug. Even as Hitler's deputy and commander of the Luftwaffe, he never escaped his dependence on it.

"There was enormous addiction," says Salka Viertel, the actress, serving tea in the Swiss mountain resort of Klosters. "Cocaine. Morphine. I had one friend, a doctor, Dr. Joel, his name was. He had been a prisoner of war in England, and I think he got addicted there. Then he came to Berlin, and he and a friend, Dr. Frankel, started a hospital for addicts. He talked a lot about addiction, very frankly, answered questions about it. Then he committed suicide, and only after he died did we learn that he himself had been an addict. He was our own doctor. We had trusted him.

"Why were there so many addicts? Because of the horrible life. Just like now. Many of them had been soldiers, prisoners of war. They went through terrible things. Then there were other reasons, too, I guess. E—— was very successful, rich, beautiful, an actress. She was married to that pianist, and then to a baron. When she had morphine, she was quite normal. Without it, she was in a terrible state, terrible."

"What finally happened to her?"

"She killed herself. But you're not going to write about that, are you?"

Does any nation have an innate tendency toward violence? No, not really—but because of the Hitler era, we are still searching for clues to the reasons for what happened. Yehudi Menuhin, sitting in his New York hotel room, suggests a strange theory based on the tribe's most complex creation, its language.

"The German language is an abstraction. The language about music—I don't like it. Music is a living thing, but the German terms are always abstract. German has the words for philosophy and for romantic poetry, but not for music. The cultural words are all derived from Latin words—library: *Bibliothek*—*Eleganz*—everything civilized comes from Latin roots.

"And the grammar. When you start a sentence in German, you have to know at the beginning what the end will be. In English, you live the sentence through to its end. Emotion and thought go together. In German, they're divorced. Everything is abstract. That was how they made abstractions of Jews. They didn't kill them as individuals, the way we shot our Indians, but as an abstraction."

Even before the Nazis turned criminality into a system of government, there were instances of the Weimar authorities' turning the law against the law-abiding. In many ways the most significant "crime" of the year 1931 was the arrest and prosecution of Carl von Ossietzky, the editor of *Die Weltbühne*.

Ossietzsky was a strange, aloof, tormented man—unknowable, and yet demonstrating, in every act, a remarkable quality of spiritual courage. The photographs of the mid-1920's show a rather heavy-set young man with reflective eyes, a long, pointed nose, and a massive chin. Ten years later, a photograph taken inside the Oranienburg concentration camp shows a contemptuous, black-uniformed guard, with a hand holding his gloves on his hip, towering over a numb and frightened prisoner whose dark worksuit bears the number 562. Prisoner 562 was the former Carl von Ossietzky, and when he received the Nobel Peace Prize for 1935, the outraged Führer officially forbade any Germans to accept Nobel Prizes. The Nazis released Ossietzky just in time for him to die of tuberculosis in a private hospital in Berlin. But the authorities who had sent him to prison in the first place were those of the Weimar Republic.

Carl von Ossietzky was born in 1889 to a poor family of Polish descent. He once told a friend that the "von" in his name had come from an ancestor who served as a mercenary soldier in the seventeenth century under Frederick William, the "Great Elector" of Brandenburg, who, lacking money to pay his troops, rewarded them with aristocratic titles. Ossietzky's father, a stenographer, died when his son was two. Ossietzky failed to finish school, worked as a government clerk in Hamburg, served as a private on the western front. Even before the war, he was a pacifist, and, if not exactly a leftist, a believer in "social justice." He came to Berlin in 1919 as the secretary to Ludwig Quidde's German Peace Association. Then, tiring of the pacifists' interminable quarrels among themselves, he started writing for various liberal papers, the *Volkszeitung*, the *Tage-Buch*, and finally, the *Weltbühne*.

The *Weltbühne* was a tiny weekly, scarcely larger than the *Reader's Digest* and not nearly so fat. It never reached a circulation of more than twenty thousand, but, as the chief organ of Germany's intellectual left, it acquired—and still has, in memoriam—a reputation that extended far beyond its size. It was founded in 1904 by Siegfried Jacobsohn, an eccentric and impassioned theatre critic who had just been fired by his newspaper after being accused of plagiarism. Jacobsohn, who was then twenty-four, called his new theatre magazine *Die Schaubühne* (meaning, approximately, "a look at the stage"), but in 1918, he decided to broaden its political coverage and renamed it *Die Weltbühne* (*The World Stage*). Jacobsohn's *Weltbühne* was always a one-man magazine, and his fierce antipathies sometimes embroiled him in half a dozen libel suits at once, but he also attracted a whole generation of young writers— Arnold Zweig, Walter Mehring, Ernst Toller, and above all, Kurt Tucholsky, who alone provided more than a hundred articles, sketches, and poems a year. It was Tucholsky who contributed most to the raucous and combative tone of the *Weltbühne*. "We, the writers of the *Weltbühne*, are being reproached for always saying 'No,' for not being sufficiently constructive," Tucholsky wrote. "No, we cannot say 'Yes.' Not yet. We know only one thing: that we must sweep away with an iron broom all that is rotten in Germany. We will get nowhere if we wrap our heads in a black-white-and-red rag and whisper anxiously, 'Later, my good fellow, later!' " And again: "I proclaim, fully aware of the meaning of my words, that there is no secret of the Germany Army which I would not hand over readily to a foreign power, if this were warranted by the preservation of peace."

When Jacobsohn suddenly died in an epileptic fit in 1926, his widow persuaded Tucholsky to take over as editor, with the new editorial writer, Ossietzky, acting as his deputy. But Tucholsky, who had been living in Paris since 1924, didn't like either the chores of editing or the need to stay in Berlin. In less than a year, he turned the magazine over to Ossietzky and returned to Paris. Ossietzky was no less sharp a critic than his predecessor. "It is no cheap pessimism but a cogent recognition of facts to say at last in public: There is no republic in Germany!" Ossietzsky wrote. "One hears people say that this republic is without republicans. Unluckily, the situation is just the reverse: The republicans are without a republic." Unlike Tucholsky, Ossietzky was also a careful and skillful editor. He nearly doubled the magazine's circulation, which brought it a small profit, though at no great gain to himself. "While Tucholsky was living in Paris and writing for half the papers in Berlin," says a former member of the *Weltbühne* staff, "Ossietzky was the *poorest* man. He never had a clean shirt or a good suit. He lived on coffee, and sometimes a piece of cake."

Ossietzky devoted himself completely to the little magazine, and when he got a chance to expose Germany's secret rearmament, he did not hesitate to publish an article entitled "Windy Things in German Aviation." The author, Walter Kreiser, an aircraft designer and an official of the German pilots' union, disclosed, among other things, that a supposedly civilian institute of marine research named Severa was actually being subsidized by the Admiralty, and that an organization named Abteilung M, which supposedly tested planes at an airfield just outside Berlin, actually flew these planes out of the country for secret military training in Russia. Ossietzky toned down the ending of the article, deleting the reference to Russia and saying only: "Not all the airplanes are always in Germany."

The Reichswehr furiously demanded that both Ossietzky and Kreiser be prosecuted for "espionage and treason." "You must remember," says one of Ossietzky's associates, "that the Versailles Treaty was still the law, and the Versailles Treaty forbade Germany to have any military aircraft, and now Ossietzky was being prosecuted for giving away the secret that the German government itself was breaking the law." The prosecution did not deny the truth of the story—thanks in part to the Russian training program that General Seeckt had begun, Germany now had three fully prepared bomber squadrons, two fighter squadrons, and eight observation squadrons—but argued that this was precisely why the revelations were treasonous. And the judges agreed. "The Army Command, despite the Versailles treaty . . . considered itself obliged, from the point of an imperious necessity above the laws, to carry out this reorganization in the interests of national defense," the court ruled at the end of the closed trial. Ossietzky and Kreiser were sentenced to eighteen months in prison. Kreiser fled to Paris, and Ossietzky received word from General Schleicher himself that no obstacles would be placed against his leaving the country too. But Ossietzky refused to take that route. "Let us turn this movement of protest into a political campaign against the powerful forces of counter-revolution," he wrote. And again: "It is not out of loyalty [to the state] that I am going to prison but because by so doing I can become the more embarrassing. . . . I am remaining here: an inmate of a Prussian prison, a living symbol of protest."

"How the moon shines over this city," sighs Miss Battenberg as she walks arm in arm with her new friend, the hero of Erich Kästner's tart little novel of the 1920's, *Fabian.*

"Almost like being back home?" says Fabian. They are strolling along the Geisbergstrasse, just south of the Kurfürstendamm. "You're fooling yourself. The moonlight and the smell of flowers, the silence and the small-town kiss in the doorway—those are all illusions. Over there, on that square, is a café where Chinese, nothing but Chinese, are sitting with Berlin whores. Next to it is a bar where homosexual boys dance with elegant actors and Englishmen, and suggest their skills, and the price to be paid, and finally the whole price is paid by a dyed-blonde old woman, who's allowed to come along just for that. . . . In another street not far from here, there's a boarding-house where young schoolgirls sell themselves, to earn pocket-money. Just six months ago, there was a scandal, which wasn't easy to keep quiet. An elderly gentleman, who had rented a room for his pleasure, and who expected to find a naked sixteen-year-old girl waiting there for him, found that the waiting girl was unfortunately his daughter, which he hadn't expected. The better you know this huge city of stone, the more you think it's an insane asylum. In the east live the criminals; in the center, the swindlers. In the north, there's misery; in the west, it's prostitution. And in every direction under the sun, things are collapsing."

"And what comes after the collapse?" Miss Battenberg asked.

In the fall of 1931, a twenty-three-year-old girl named Geli Raubal died from a bullet wound in the heart. She was the niece of Adolf Hitler, and, as nearly as one can determine, the great love of his life.

Hitler's sister, Angela, had been keeping house for the Führer for a number of years. She seems to have been unaware that her older daughter, a large and cheerful blonde who had hopes of becoming a singer, was arousing the emotions of her "Uncle Alf." Early in 1929, Hitler wrote his niece a letter, in which he not only confessed his love but expressed it in terms of certain obscure per-versions. He never sent the letter to Geli, however, but left it lying around in his room, where it fell into the possession of the son of his landlady. After a series of complex negotiations, Hitler bought the letter back for a considerable sum of money, and the romance, now more tortuous than ever, continued.

Geli was a rambunctious girl, and Hitler a jealous uncle. When he learned that she had been out on a date with one of his hench-men, he locked her in the house. Geli finally decided to break with

Hitler and go to Vienna to study singing. Hitler forbade it. The last time they saw each other, he was starting out for Hamburg, and she shouted down from a window, "Then you won't let me go to Vienna?" Hitler shouted back, "No!" Geli spent the rest of the day making plans to visit her mother in Obersalzburg. She wandered around with a dead canary named Hansi, which she wanted to bury there. She started a letter to a friend in Linz. The next day, she was found dead.

Hitler was distraught. For a week, he seemed half-mad, and Gregor Strasser followed him around day and night for fear he might commit some violence. The official verdict on Geli's death was suicide, but there was no sign, during her last day, that she had any such plans. Her mother later hinted to a friend that Geli might have been murdered, or else forced to commit suicide, as a danger to the Nazi cause. The mother did not blame Hitler but rather Heinrich Himmler, the head of the SS. "Himmler's part in the matter can only be presumed," according to Hitler's first biographer, Konrad Heiden, who does so presume. "The mentality of this man and his entire circle justifies the most hideous speculations. Conceivably he thought it his duty to free his Führer from a dangerous woman. . . . We can see Himmler, calling at a late hour; explaining to Geli that she had betrayed the man who was her guardian, her lover, and her Führer in one. According to National Socialist conceptions, there was only one way of making good such a betrayal."

At about this same time, Klaus Mann, the son of the novelist, was sitting in the Carlton Tea Room in Munich. Across the street, in the Luitpold Café, bands of uniformed Storm Troopers were gorging themselves on pastry, but their leader was not among them. Apparently in search of peace and quiet, Adolf Hitler, too, was sitting in the Carlton Tea Room. He ate three strawberry tarts, one after another.

As the young writer watched the Führer picking at the remains of the strawberry tarts, he began to think that Hitler reminded him of someone, and it bothered him that he could not remember the other face, someone whose picture he had seen in the newspapers.

"There was nothing but dim, rosy light," Mann recalled later, "soft music and heaps of cookies; and in the midst of this sugary idyll, a moustached little man with veiled eyes and a stubborn forehead, chatting with some colorless henchmen. I caught fragments of their conversation. They discussed the cast of a musical farce scheduled for the same evening at the Kammerspiele. . . . While I called the waitress to pay for my cup of coffee, I suddenly remembered whom Herr Hitler resembled. It was that sex-murderer in Hannover, whose case had made such huge headlines. . . . His name was Haarmann. . . . The likeness between him and Hitler was striking. The sightless eyes, the moustache, the brutal and nervous mouth, even the unspeakable vulgarity of the fleshy nose; it was, indeed, precisely the same physiognomy. . . ."

"What Germany Needs Is a Strong Man" 1932

> We must go right through to the end in our misfortune; we need a chastisement compared to which the four years of war are nothing. . . . A dictatorship, resembling that of Napoleon, will be regarded universally as a salvation. But then blood must flow, the more the better. . . .
>
> OSWALD SPENGLER

"TONIGHT . . . IT IS VERY COLD," Christopher Isherwood wrote in *The Berlin Stories*. "The dead cold grips the town in utter silence, like the silence of intense midday summer heat. . . . Outside, in the night, beyond the last new-built blocks of concrete flats, where the streets end in frozen allotment gardens, are the Prussian plains. You can feel them all around you, to-night, creeping in upon the city, like an immense waste of unhomely ocean. . . . Berlin is a skeleton which aches in the cold: it is my own skeleton aching. I feel in my bones the sharp ache of the frost in the girders of the overhead railway, in the ironwork of balconies, in bridges, tramlines, lamp-standards, latrines. The iron throbs and shrinks, the stone and the bricks ache dully, the plaster is numb. . . ."

This was to be the last year of the Weimar Republic, the last year of Berlin's freedom. This was the year in which everything was attempted, and everything failed. This was the year in which Berliners talked of military dictatorship, and of a general strike,

351

and of civil war—but nothing happened. Arthur Koestler tried to describe the spirit of the time by telling the story of Wang Lun, who was the royal executioner during the Ming Dynasty. Wang Lun was famous for his speed in chopping off heads, but his ambition was to execute a man so skillfully that his severed head would remain on his neck. One day, Wang Lun carried out twelve executions, and at the end, he achieved his ambition. While the twelfth man was climbing to the scaffold, Wang Lun sliced through his neck so delicately that the man continued climbing the scaffold. At the top, he complained to Wang Lun, saying, "Why do you prolong my agony? You were mercifully quick with the others!" Wang Lun smiled at his triumph and said, "Just kindly nod, please."

This was the year in which General Kurt von Schleicher finally disposed of every rival but one. He became the head of the German Army. He named chancellors and overthrew chancellors. He even became Chancellor himself. But he could not figure out how to defeat his last rival, a mere ex-corporal. "Near the end," says Hans-Joachim Kausch, who was then a reporter on Berlin politics, "Schleicher received three journalists in the Reichschancellery, and I was one of them. Schleicher said that either he would—well, he used a very dirty word. I can't say it. You can't use it in a book. It means, to cut away someone's manhood. Either I will do that to Hitler, Schleicher said, or he will do it to me. And he was right. Hitler did it to him."

Kurt von Schleicher was a man of immense talent, intelligence, and charm, but he also had a serpentine quality that was implicit in his own name, which is the German word for "creeper" or "crawler." Born in 1882, Schleicher was a member of an old Brandenburg military family. He won his commission in 1900 as a lieutenant in the Third Foot Guards, which happened to be Hindenburg's old regiment. Schleicher made friends with a fellow officer, Oskar von Hindenburg, the son of the old general. When the elder Hindenburg retired in 1911, Schleicher often accompanied Oskar on visits to the general's home in Hannover. Schleicher was clever and amusing, and the old man took a great liking to him. But Schleicher's real patron—it seems to be one of the rules of military life that everyone needs a patron—was General Gröner, who was then an instructor at the War Academy and considered Schleicher one of his most brilliant pupils. When the war came, Schleicher served briefly on the eastern front, where he won an Iron Cross, but General Ludendorff didn't like him and shipped him off to the Limbo of press headquarters. After Ludendorff's fall, however, Gröner succeeded to his post and promptly summoned Major Schleicher to headquarters as his personal adjutant. He affectionately referred to Schleicher as his "adopted son." By then, the war was almost over, and though some of the combat commanders sneered at Schleicher as a "*Schreibtischoffizier*" (desk officer), it was precisely his talent for staff work and politics that made Schleicher indispensable to his commanders.

When Gröner voyaged from Spa to Berlin to negotiate with Ebert about the army's future, Schleicher was at his side, striding in full-dress uniform through crowds of angry Berlin workers. When Ebert telephoned military headquarters for help against the mutinous Marine Division, it was Schleicher who took the call and sent the troops. When the army began organizing the Freikorps forces, it was Schleicher who did much of the organizing. When General Seeckt, after Gröner's retirement, decided to negotiate a secret agreement with the Russian Army, Schleicher undertook the negotiations at his apartment in Berlin. When Gröner came out of retirement to take over the War Ministry in 1928, it was Schleicher who lobbied for the appointment and then became Gröner's chief political adviser.

Gröner created a special department for Schleicher, the *Ministeramt*, or Ministerial Service, which was to take charge of all liaison between the armed forces and civilian officials and political parties. From a small office in the massive gray Bendlerblock, overlooking the chestnut trees along the Landwehr Canal, Schleicher now supervised the most elaborate intelligence network in Berlin. He maintained spies in every ministry; he tapped telephones; he came to know every secret that was worth knowing. He also knew, from his days as a military information officer during the war, how to manipulate the press through leaks and insinuations and off-the-record briefings. Reporters found that Schleicher was a good source of information, and Schleicher told them only what he wanted them to know.

It is not clear to this day whether Schleicher deliberately sabotaged his superiors, but his career did resemble that of a modern

Macbeth, climbing over the bodies of all those who had stood between him and power. General Seeckt had to resign because the press created a great furor about a secret plan to have the Kaiser's eldest grandson take part in military maneuvers. Schleicher, it has been said, was the one who informed the press of that indiscretion. Defense Minister Otto Gessler suffered a similar fate—newspaper disclosures of the army's secret deals to finance German rearmament. Once again, there was a great uproar and a forced resignation, and once again there were rumors that Schleicher was the one who had leaked information to favored reporters. It is possible, of course, that Schleicher was acting for the best of reasons, subverting secret military adventures that should never have been undertaken. It is also possible that Schleicher never leaked the information at all, but, as with Macbeth, the systematic disappearance of Schleicher's superiors persuaded a number of people that the sly and witty general in the *Ministeramt* was, at the least, somebody to be treated with considerable caution.

In the political field, Schleicher was no less serpentine. The weary old Socialist, Hermann Müller, had been easy to sabotage, for President Hindenburg disliked Socialists anyway. He was pleased when Schleicher suggested as the new Chancellor a dedicated ex-soldier like Heinrich Brüning. But now, in the spring of 1932, Schleicher decided that Brüning, too, must go. The essential fact was that his policy of deflation and austerity had failed to bring any improvement in the economic crisis. Every month, the number of unemployed increased, from a little under three million at the time of Brüning's accession in 1930 to four million throughout most of 1931, and now to five million, and still climbing.

"Morning after morning," Isherwood wrote, "all over the immense, damp, dreary town and the packing-case colonies of huts in the suburb allotments, young men were waking up to another workless empty day to be spent as best they could contrive; selling bootlaces, begging, playing draughts in the hall of the Labour Exchange, hanging around urinals, opening the doors of cars, helping with crates in the markets, gossiping, lounging, stealing, overhearing racing tips, sharing stumps of cigarette-ends picked up in the gutter, singing folk-songs for groschen in courtyards and between stations in the carriages of the Underground Railway. After the New Year, the snow fell, but it did not lie; there was no money to be earned by sweeping it away. The shopkeepers rang all coins on the counter for fear of counterfeiters. [My landlady's] astrologer foretold the end of the world."

(For every variety of clairvoyant and soothsayer, in fact, this was a season of prosperity. The newsstands began to feature weekly magazines devoted entirely to astrology—*Germany's Future, New Germany, The Seer*. In a room over a tavern on the Friedrichstrasse, a medium who called herself Fatima offered advice day and night. In the commercial districts of western Berlin, the fortunetellers were more businesslike, with respectable offices and respectable business hours. The most celebrated of these was a short, swarthy Viennese named Herschel Steinschneider. A former journalist, who also dabbled in blackmail, he had once written several pamphlets exposing fortunetellers but then decided that there was more money to be made by joining them. He dyed his hair blond, proclaimed himself a Danish aristocrat, and took the name of Erik Jan Hanussen. He gave occasional displays of hypnotism and mind-reading in Berlin's variety theatres, but his headquarters was an impressive building on the Lietzenburger Strasse, which he called "The House of the Occult." He filled it not only with Hohenzollern furniture and dark draperies but also with microphones, which enabled him to listen to his subordinates gathering information from prospective clients. Among these clients was Count Wolf von Helldorf, the dissolute aristocrat who had become chief of the SA in Berlin. At Count Helldorf's lakeside villa on the Wannsee, according to Arthur Koestler's account, "Hanussen acted as master of ceremonies at nocturnal orgies, in the course of which he put pretty actresses into hypnotic trances and made them display the emotions experienced in a fictitious lover's embrace." Hanussen made the mistake, however, of loaning money to Count Helldorf and keeping the IOU's in his wallet as a kind of protective talisman. When the clairvoyant's bullet-riddled body was eventually found in the woods, all the IOU's had vanished.)

The effects of the economic depression were most visible among the unemployed, huddling in despair at tent camps like Kuhle Wampe on the outskirts of Berlin, but there was almost as much misery in the cold and threadbare apartments of the middle class. The shares in Fritz Thyssen's steel trust, for example, fell to one-third of their former value; city governments defaulted on their bonds;

small shopkeepers succumbed to the competition of the giant department stores. Over-all industrial production declined by one-third. And then the banks started closing. The bank crisis started in Austria, which had tried to join Germany in a customs union. The French, determined to prevent any unification of Germany and Austria, responded by withdrawing so much capital from Austria that the nation's biggest bank, the Kreditanstalt, soon had to announce its insolvency. As other bankers began calling in any loans that seemed uncertain, the series of bankruptcies spread northward. The North German Wool Mills in Bremen was the first to go under, owing $25 million. Almost half of that was owed to the Darmstadt National Bank, one of the four biggest banks in Germany, and now the indestructible Danat announced that it, too, was closing.

"Herr Issyvoo, what do you think!" cried Isherwood's landlady as she woke him up one morning. "They've shut the Darmstädter und National! There'll be thousands ruined, I shouldn't wonder! The milkman says we'll have civil war in a fortnight! Whatever do you say to that!"

Isherwood went out into the streets to see what was happening. "Sure enough, there was a crowd outside the branch bank on the Nollendorfplatz corner, a lot of men with leather satchels and women with stringbags. . . . The iron lattices were drawn down over the bank windows. Most of the people were staring intently and rather stupidly at the locked door. In the middle of the door was fixed a small notice, beautifully printed in Gothic type, like a page from a classic author. The notice said that the Reichspresident had guaranteed the deposits. Everything was quite all right. Only the bank wasn't going to open."

Brüning had to declare two "bank holidays." He also had to close down the German stock exchanges for more than a month. The Reichsbank increased its discount rate from 7 percent to 10 percent. Brüning issued decree after decree, taking control of foreign investments, tightening tax laws, even charging twenty-five dollars for any German who wanted to travel abroad. Nothing worked. The crisis went on, and got worse. "I place a major share of the blame against that man who died up in Vermont the other day, Brüning," says Professor Lowe, the economist who believes in Keynes. He starts drumming his fingers on his desk, angrily. "Like Rathenau, he had a thick front, but he was weak at the core. He was obsessed with being a *Kriegsteilnehmer* [a war veteran]—he had to *redeem* Germany from the Treaty of Versailles. But to insist on a deflationary policy the way he did—and he had the memos on his *desk,* telling him that it was a time for public *spending*—but his advisers didn't understand. And he also had a profound masochism. It was another case in which he felt he had to go through the valley of *death.* . . . And he got what he deserved—fired, like a second lieutenant."

General Schleicher had already decided by the start of 1932 that Brüning had to go, but there was one last mission for him to carry out. Hindenburg's seven-year term was expiring, and Hitler was preparing to run for the presidency, and the state of Germany was such that many political leaders expected Hitler to win. They could think of nobody to run against him except old Hindenburg himself. The field marshal was eighty-four years old by now, and his mind was fading into senility. He functioned for only a few hours a day. There had even been one period when he had gone totally blank for more than a week, but his aides had kept that secret. To save Hindenburg from the stress of a campaign, Brüning devised a plan to have the field marshal re-elected by the Reichstag. The rest of Brüning's plan, though it was never publicly announced, was to have Hindenburg serve as regent while Brüning negotiated a restoration of the monarchy under the Kaiser's grandson. Hindenburg wearily agreed, but the Nazis and the Nationalists did not, thus killing any chance for the necessary two-thirds majority in the Reichstag. The rejection angered the old field marshal so much that he agreed to run for re-election by popular vote.

Hindenburg's announcement filled Hitler with dread. He dared not avoid the presidential campaign, but he feared the prospect of defeat. For a whole month, he delayed and equivocated, and it was just three weeks before the election when Goebbels loudly announced in the Berlin Sportpalast: "Hitler will be the next President of the German Reich! . . . For when I say that he will be our candidate, then I know that he will be our President." The assembled Nazis stamped and cheered at the announcement. "A storm of deafening applause rages for nearly ten minutes," Goebbels noted in his diary. "Wild ovations for the Führer. The audience rises with shouts of joy. . . . People laugh and cry at the same time."

Goebbels (who had recently married a rich divorcée named Magda Quant) now launched the campaign he had been preparing for months—a campaign that was to last, with very little respite, through the five elections that were to be staged that year. Chancellor Brüning, leading the forces for Hindenburg, followed the strategy that was traditional in Germany—a series of sedate speeches on issues of the day. Hindenburg himself offered only one brief radio talk, saying, among other things, "Anybody who doesn't want to vote for me doesn't have to." But Goebbels' plan of battle was quite different—constant attack, with ceaseless noise, spread by every means that technology could devise.

Hitler himself raced from one mass meeting to another, shouting his emotional slogans to crowds as large as 100,000 at a time. "We stand at the turning point of Germany's destiny. . . . We fight today! We fight tomorrow!" Goebbels, who sneered at Hindenburg as "the candidate of the party of deserters" (i.e., the Social Democrats), not only made nineteen speeches in Berlin during the three-week campaign but also crisscrossed the country to address rallies in nine other cities. "Work has to be done standing, walking, driving, flying," Goebbels noted in his diary. "The most important conversations take place on the staircase, in the hall, at the door, while driving to the station. One hardly has time to think."

Wherever the Führer or his chief lieutenants could not appear in person, Goebbels relied on the new technology. He had films of Hitler's speeches shown in village meeting halls; he even had recordings shipped out in the mail by the thousands. (He also made mischievous use of a recording of one of Brüning's speeches. Since the Chancellor had refused to engage in public debate, Goebbels set up an empty chair at one of his mass meetings and then played the record, interrupting it repeatedly to offer his own rebuttals to the missing Chancellor.) In one week alone, Goebbels spent more than half a million dollars—the contributions of the Ruhr industrialists were beginning to have their effect—on these new forms of propaganda.

When the Germans voted on March 13, Hindenburg easily came in first, with 18.6 million ballots, but Hitler's 11.4 million meant that he had nearly doubled his strength since the Reichstag elections of 1930. And because of two minor candidates put forward by the Communists and Nationalists (not minor in "Red Berlin," where the Communist Ernst Thälmann won 29 percent of the vote to Hitler's 23 percent), Hindenburg failed by four-tenths of one percentage point to get the necessary majority. "The first election campaign is over, the second has begun today," Hitler announced. "I shall lead it."

For this runoff, Goebbels devised the strategy of sending the Führer all over the country in a rickety gray Junkers airplane—"Hitler over Germany," he called the campaign—and so he could reach twenty cities a week, addressing a quarter of a million people a day. This time, the polling on April 10 brought Hindenburg another 750,000 votes, enough to give him a 53 percent majority. But Hitler had gained more than two million additional votes, giving him a total of almost 37 percent, and he now had a powerful momentum. "The campaign for the Prussian state elections is prepared," Goebbels wrote in his diary the next day. "We go on without a breathing space."

President Hindenburg was pleased at his re-election, but he didn't like the way it had happened. He didn't like being called "the candidate of the party of deserters," not only because it was insulting but because he rather thought the Socialists *were* the "party of deserters." He didn't like being the candidate of the labor unions, and the Berlin press, and the Catholics, and the Jews, and he resented Bruning for having put together such a coalition to re-elect him. General Schleicher naturally fed these resentments during his frequent visits to the President, but before he gave the *coup de grâce* to Brüning, he wanted to get rid of Brüning's military chief, his old patron, War Minister Gröner. P 181 BRAMSTED

Gröner had decided that the violence of the Storm Troopers had gone on too long, and so he persuaded Brüning to persuade Hindenburg to decree their dissolution. Schleicher, however, was by now intoxicated with a theory that was to lead to his ultimate ruin. He was convinced that he, and he alone, could solve the Nazi problem— not by crushing the Nazis but by courting them, winning their favor, and finally splitting them apart. As early as the spring of 1931, Schleicher had begun a series of secret meetings with Captain Ernst Röhm, the beefy SA chief who had originally assigned the young Hitler to go and spy on the German Workers' Party in a Munich beer hall more than a decade ago. Röhm, restlessly ambitious, had long dreamed of merging his Storm Troopers into the regular army, and Schleicher, for his own reasons, encouraged that dream. Schleicher saw the Storm Troopers—now more than 300,000 strong—as a huge source of military manpower, and in his first meeting with Röhm, the two plotters agreed that in case of war, the SA would immediately come under army command.

Schleicher therefore lobbied against Gröner's decision to ban the SA, and when Gröner refused to budge, Schleicher went to Hindenburg and accused Gröner of favoring "left-wing" organizations against "nationalist" ones. He spread the same message among military commanders. There was also gossip all over Berlin that Gröner was in bad health. And there was laughter over the fact that the sixty-five-year-old War Minister had recently married for a second time, to a woman of inferior social position, who had borne him a son five months later (Schleicher told the scandalized Hindenburg that the hasty baby was known in the War Ministry as "Nurmi," after the celebrated Finnish runner).

The crisis came as soon as the Reichstag convened on May 10, when Hermann Goering made a fierce attack on Gröner for his ban on the SA. Gröner tried to defend himself, but he was not a good speaker, and the Nazi delegates greeted his efforts with catcalls and laughter. As soon as he left the chamber, Gröner encountered Schleicher, who informed him that he no longer had "the confidence of the army" and suggested that he take sick leave. Gröner held out for three days, but then, realizing that Schleicher had totally undermined his authority, he resigned. "Scorn and rage boil within me," he later wrote to Schleicher, "because I have been deceived in you, my old friend, disciple, adopted son; my hope for the people and the Fatherland."

Brüning told Schleicher that it was the general's duty to replace the man he had just overthrown. To this proposal that he himself become War Minister, Schleicher gave an arrogant answer: "I will, but not in your government." Schleicher had not only worked out a plan but had even told it to Hitler a week earlier at a meeting in Schleicher's home. Gröner would be forced out, then Brüning, and then Hindenburg would appoint a conservative "presidential" cabinet, which would dissolve the Reichstag and lift the ban on the SA. "How odd it seems that nobody as yet has the slightest prevision," Goebbels wrote in his diary, "least of all Brüning himself."

In the downfall of Brüning, there was another element that the Chancellor scarcely understood—the corruption of President Hindenburg himself. For years, the aristocratic landowners in the barren areas of eastern Prussia had been complaining of their difficulties, the decline in agricultural prices, the flight of peasants from the land, the increasing burden of debt on the old estates. During 1927 and 1928, the government approved a program known as *Osthilfe* (Help for the East), providing subsidies and cheap loans to the unhappy Junkers. According to a subsequent Reichstag investigation, a number of Prussian aristocrats had spent their *Osthilfe* loans on champagne and racing cars and trips to the Riviera. But the Reichstag investigation was kept secret, for by now the Junkers had figured out a splendid way to protect their interests. They started a fund-raising campaign to buy the estate of Neudeck, which had once belonged to the Hindenburg family, and to present it to the President on his eightieth birthday.

This million-mark venture, which connected Hindenburg's personal financial interests to those of the Junkers, was dubious enough it itself, but the fund-raisers went a step further by secretly making out the title deed to Hindenburg's son, Oskar, as a device to avoid the inevitable death taxes. It is uncertain how much the old man knew about this operation—and the newspapers that had once howled about Friedrich Ebert's tenuous connection to the Barmat brothers offered no criticisms now—but it may be supposed that he shared the average man's willingness to avoid the tax collector as much as possible. In any event, Hindenburg took to spending a good deal of time in Neudeck, where his neighboring landlords repeatedly informed him that Brüning lacked sympathy for the problems of Germany's noble old families—that, in fact, the government's plan to resettle some of the unemployed on Prussian estates was nothing less than "agrarian Bolshevism."

In his last few months of power, Brüning tried to save himself by negotiating some kind of diplomatic triumph—either the abolition of all reparations (which seemed implicit in President Hoover's proposal, in 1931, for a one-year moratorium) or some move toward the equalization of the German and French armed forces (Hindenburg and Brüning were still blindly determined to build pocket battleships). With a little more time, Brüning might have achieved at least one of these aims—"We are only one hundred yards from the goal," he declared—but General Schleicher was already letting it be known among Allied diplomats that there was little point in negotiating with Brüning because he would soon be replaced.

On May 29, Hindenburg returned from one of his visits to Neudeck and summoned his Chancellor for a meeting. Brüning arrived with a new list of emergency decrees that he wanted the President to sign, including a large program of public works to relieve unemployment. Hindenburg cut him short. "I request that you give me no more emergency decrees to sign," he said. Any new government programs, he went on, would have to go through the Reichstag. There, as both men perfectly well knew, Brüning did not have a majority behind him. Furthermore, the field marshal declared, he thought Brüning's government was too liberal. "I am informed that you have ministers with Bolshevist plans," he said. "That cannot go on." At this point, Hindenburg began reading from the inch-high letters on a piece of paper that somebody had prepared for him. Henceforth, he declared, the Chancellor's policy must be conservative in tone, labor-union leaders must be excluded from the government, and there must be no more "agrarian Bolshevism."

Brüning was aghast, not only at the President's demands but at his cold and peremptory tone—and perhaps at the realization that he was suffering a fate he had brought on himself. This, finally, was the end of the "presidential system" that Brüning had inaugurated two years earlier. At the beginning, it had seemed a splendid idea to override the quarreling factions of the Reichstag and to rule by decree in what appeared to be the national interest. But the presidential system meant that the national interest would be defined solely according to the whims and prejudices of the octogenarian President, or according to whatever his aides and advisers could persuade him to do.

Brüning had considered himself the President's most loyal adjutant, and now he could only ask whether the old man wanted him to resign. Hindenburg did not give a specific answer but said gruffly that his conscience forbade him to continue with a regime that had so little popular support. He suggested that Brüning might stay on as Foreign Minister under some other Chancellor. Brüning stiffly rejected the offer as an affront to his honor and reputation. "I, too, have a conscience," he said. The Chancellor then returned to his office, called a meeting of his cabinet, and proposed that everyone resign immediately. The cabinet agreed. Brüning called the President's office and asked for a new appointment in order to hand in his resignation. He was told that the President was busy until the next

day, at 10:30. The next day, the appointment was postponed, until
11:50. That gave Brüning only ten minutes in which to present his
resignation, for at noon, the Skagerrak Watch went on parade, and
the field marshal wanted nothing to interrupt his pleasure at review-
ing his guardsmen on the march.

During this same spring of 1932, the English military historian,
Sir John Wheeler-Bennett, was having dinner at the Königin Restaurant on the Kurfürstendamm. Suddenly the waiters began making
a place at the adjoining table for General Schleicher and a group of
his friends. "The general was resplendent in full uniform and in excellent spirits," Wheeler-Bennett said afterward. "His bald head
gleamed in the harsh light and he laughed a good deal. Suddenly the
dance-band stopped with the abruptness of syncopation and von
Schleicher, whose voice had been raised to be heard by his friends
above the music, was overheard declaiming: 'What Germany needs
to-day is a strong man;' and he tapped himself significantly on the
breast."

"When we were sitting at the Romanische Café," Stephen
Spender recalled, "Michael said to me one evening: 'There isn't a
girl sitting in this place who hasn't scars on her veins in an attempt
to commit suicide.' This was said in his statistical tone of voice, as
though to show that he retained the scientific spirit, but with a look
of dazed admiration as though at last he had really found something."

General Schleicher's candidate as the next Chancellor of Germany
was one of the most implausible characters on the Berlin political
scene. According to the French Ambassador, André François-Poncet,
he "enjoyed the peculiarity of being taken seriously by neither his
friends nor his enemies. . . . He was reputed to be superficial,
blundering, untrue, ambitious, vain, crafty and an intriguer." He
had managed to win a seat in the Prussian State Legislature, but he
was so unpopular with his own party, the Catholic Center, that he
could never even get into the Reichstag. Among those who strongly
opposed him was the party's septuagenarian honorary president, Carl
Herold, who, on being asked his reasons, said, "I am too old to have
to give reasons, but I will not have Franz von Papen in the Reichstag."

Papen, then fifty-three, had a narrow gray mustache and the long, bony face of a horse, which suited his social position as a former cavalry officer and an amateur racetrack rider of some eminence. He came from an aristocratic but impoverished Westphalian family, and he became rich by marrying the daughter of a Saar industrialist. He was a founder of the *Herrenklub* (Schleicher and Oskar von Hindenburg were also members), which, as the name somewhat crudely implies, considered itself a meeting place for the rulers of Berlin. His greatest celebrity, however, derived from his wartime service as military attaché in Washington, where he was expelled after being caught engaging in sabotage.

Papen was not totally without qualities, of course. He was lively and amusing, and he managed to ingratiate himself with Hindenburg. In fact, the old field marshal was quite captivated by his new Chancellor, whom he took to calling by the boyish diminutive of "Fränzchen." To General Schleicher, on the other hand, Papen's chief virtue was that he would do what he was told, or so Schleicher thought. When someone protested that Papen had no head for administration, Schleicher retorted, "He doesn't need to have a head, his job is to be a hat." And around this dapper Uhlan cavalryman, Schleicher assembled a crew of docile conservatives. "Now I can have a cabinet of my friends," said Hindenburg. Baron von Neurath became Foreign Minister, Baron von Gayl Minister of the Interior—seven of the nine ministers, in fact, came from the old aristocracy (four even came from the same regiment of Potsdam guards), and not one had any connection with the labor unions. General Schleicher, of course, became Minister of War.

Papen's first major step was to dismiss the Reichstag, where he had virtually no support at all, and to call for new elections. His second step was to lift the ban on the Storm Troopers. Both moves apparently had been promised to Hitler by Schleicher in exchange for Hitler's promise to "tolerate" the new regime, which the Berliners soon took to calling the "Cabinet of Barons." It is hard to imagine what Papen thought he could gain by new elections. Most likely, he simply succumbed, like Brüning before him, to the temptation of reigning for a time by presidential decree. He had, in fact, a plan for constitutional "reform," which would abolish equal suffrage and more or less abolish the Reichstag. In the meantime, he set off for Lausanne to take over Brüning's role at the international conference on reparations. The Allied statesmen did not think much of their new colleague— "The more I study the face of a Germany cavalry officer," French Premier Édouard Herriot remarked to British Foreign Minister Lord Simon, "the more I admire his horse"—but they had given up trying to collect reparations from their bankrupt enemies. Only three years after the Germans had signed the Young Plan, promising to pay two billion marks a year for fifty-nine years, they now won the Allies' agreement to a complete payment of only three billion marks, and not for three years. Three years later, with Hitler in power, they never paid at all.

Papen returned in a triumphant mood to Berlin and found the city in a state of near-collapse. Unemployment had risen to more than six million, about one-third of the work force, and street fights between uniformed gangs of Nazis and Communists broke out almost every day. Papen, having dissolved the Reichstag, now decided that he could best defend his unpopular regime by dissolving the government of Prussia as well. This was a move of unprecedented audacity, for the Prussian government represented the fortress of Social Democratic strength in Germany. There is a widespread myth that Prussia is a small, bleak province inhabited largely by generals with monocles. In actual fact, the Prussia of the 1920's extended from the feudal estates of the East to the factories of the Ruhr; it contained three-fifths of the area of Germany and two-thirds of its population. And while national cabinets came and went at the Chancellery, the Prussian government on the opposite side of the Wilhelmstrasse remained steadily under the control of the Social Democrats and their middle-of-the-road allies, the Center Party and the Democrats. Ever since 1920, a wise and able Socialist, Otto Braun, had ruled as Minister-President, and the Prussian police, under Carl Severing, remained a force not of "Prussian militarism" but of Social Democracy.

The Nazis knew the importance of capturing Prussia, and so, as soon as the presidential elections were over, they concentrated all their propaganda on the state elections. The results, on April 24, 1932, were stunning. The Nazis, who had held only 9 seats in the previous Prussian legislature, won 162 seats and became by far the largest single party. The Social Democrats sank from 137 to 94. The Nazis and the Communists immediately joined forces in a vote of "no-confidence" against Otto Braun, but since they could not agree on a successor, the Social Democrats patched together a caretaker regime. Otto Braun himself was sick of the struggle, however. He took a leave of absence "for reasons of health," feeling, as he later wrote, that he was a "finished man," with no desire "to expose myself to gutter cries of parliamentary rowdies, in a legislative chamber that has become no better than a den of thieves."

Carl Severing and the other ministers loyally carried on, but they, too, were weary and disillusioned. Chancellor Papen, with the support of Schleicher and Hitler, drafted a presidential decree to seize the Prussian government. All he needed was a pretext. It came on July 17, when the uniformed Nazis staged a flag-waving parade through the solidly Communist district of Altona, just outside Hamburg. The Prussian police, under the new rules that permitted SA demonstrations, did their best to protect the marching Storm Troopers from turbulent crowds lining the route of the parade, but the Communists refused to allow such an invasion of their traditional territory. Snipers opened fire from the rooftops. The parade turned into a brawl. At the end of the day, there were seventeen dead and several hundred wounded.

Three days later, Papen had his plan ready. He summoned the three chief Prussian officials, including Interior Minister Carl Severing, for a conference on "financial and agricultural matters." As soon as the three arrived at the Chancellery, Papen informed them that he was taking power as national commissioner for Prussia, to maintain law and order, and that he had appointed the Mayor of Essen, Franz Bracht, to take over Severing's Interior Ministry (and thus the police force). Severing and his two colleagues protested vehemently that Papen's coup was unconstitutional. The Prussian government was perfectly able to maintain order by itself, they said. Papen's answer was to ask whether they were willing to give way peacefully.

"We will yield only to force," said Severing.

Papen and Schleicher had prepared for that. They decreed a state of emergency and mobilized the troops of the Third Army District under General Gerd von Rundstedt. But the Prussian ministers were not ready to fight. They had already surveyed their forces and found them inadequate. Twelve years earlier, the workers of Berlin had defeated the Kapp Putsch by a paralyzing general strike, but the unions no longer believed they had the power to repeat such a triumph. In 1920, they had had President Ebert and his legal cabinet on their side, and the army had been divided; now, they would be facing, unarmed, both President Hindenburg and his army. And they themselves were divided. The Communists might well sabotage a strike, and in any case, there were more than six million unemployed workers ready to take any job that became available. The only force at hand, then, was the Prussian police, ninety thousand strong and under democratic leadership, but, as one survivor of that period says, "You just can't use the police against the army." Or, as the editor of the Socialist newspaper *Vorwärts* said to Carl Severing, "You have no right to be brave at your policemen's expense."

"I knew it was coming," says another survivor. Dr. Hans Herschfeld was an official in Severing's Interior Ministry; now he sits drinking coffee in the Berlin Press Club—a short, heavy man of about seventy, with a bald head and bushy gray eyebrows and deep pouches under his blue eyes. He fiddles with a green stapler on his desk as he recalls the day of his dismissal. "I was in Berlin when I heard about the Altona riot," he says. "Severing was in Kiel making a speech for the election, which was just two weeks off, so I telephoned him and told him that we were in a situation where Papen would appoint a commissioner to take over Prussia. I met him at the station the next day, and we got in touch with the trade unions, and the other state governments, and the Social Democratic Party. The Social Democrats said we should do nothing to hinder the general election, because Papen couldn't win, so he would use any excuse to cancel it. And all the other states said we should only act legally, not use force. And the workers had no arms. So we said to ourselves, 'What can we do? Nothing!'

"The night of Papen's announcement, at eight o'clock, the new police president of Berlin came to our office on the Leipzigerstrasse, with two of his men, and occupied Severing's office. For me, there was a letter from Dr. Bracht, Papen's assistant, forbidding me to do my work. We said, 'No.' They said, 'We'll use power.' So we went out. That was all there was to it."

The Prussian government took its case to the Supreme Court, which called for protracted arguments by both sides. In the meantime, the Prussians set up a sort of government-in-exile in the Welfare Ministry on the Potsdamer Platz, issuing bulletins and holding press conferences. Two months later, the court finally handed down an ambiguous ruling, declaring that Papen had been constitutionally entitled to make himself commissioner of Prussia, but rejecting most of his reasons for doing so, and giving the ousted regime the right to represent Prussia in the Senate. "But it was all over," Dr. Herschfeld says sadly. "That was the end, *Finis Germaniae*. Braun and Severing said, 'We cannot sacrifice thousands of policemen and workers for nothing.' But I think the decision was not right. I was not of the opinion that we should give in. I thought that we should go down fighting. But that is hindsight now, and I know that there were good men who had to decide, and good reasons for their de cision."

By the time the Supreme Court ruled on the coup against Prussia, Papen's own government was doomed, for the elections of July 31 had shown, once again, that every time the German people went to the polls, the Nazis gained strength. Democratic Germans had been horrified two years earlier when the Nazi delegation in the Reichstag jumped from 12 to 107; now it suddenly rose to 230, well over one-third of all the 608 seats in the chamber. The Nazis had become by far the largest party in parliament, almost twice as large as the second-ranking Social Democrats (133). Instead of trying to win power by either force or intrigue, therefore, Hitler could claim his right to become Chancellor by completely constitutional means.

Hitler promptly voyaged to Berlin for a talk with General Schleicher. He demanded that he be made Chancellor, and also Premier of Prussia. He vowed that he could win a majority in the new Reichstag. If that was true, Schleicher said enigmatically, then nobody could stand in his way. Hitler thought Schleicher had promised him the chancellorship. Röhm put his Storm Troopers in a state of alert. "The whole party has prepared itself to take power," Goebbels noted. But the summons to the chancellorship never came. Papen continued to rule by decree.

A week later, Röhm went to see Schleicher and find out what was going on. Schleicher said that the Reichstag would not convene for a month, and it remained to be seen whether Hitler could get the majority he claimed. If not, he should remember that he had promised to "tolerate" the Papen regime. Schleicher offered other lures—a Nazi vice chancellorship under Papen, perhaps the premiership of Prussia, other local offices. Röhm brought the message back to Hitler, and Hitler fumed. "All evening," Goebbels observed, "the Führer has been striding up and down the room and the terrace outside. . . . The decision which must be made tomorrow has immense implications." The decision, of course, was whether to accept Schleicher's offer of a share of power or to hold out for the chancellorship and run the risk of getting nothing.

The next day, Hitler and Röhm went to see Schleicher, who now had Papen with him. Hitler had decided to demand full power, and when it was denied him, he raged at his antagonists. He said it was his mission to destroy Marxism. He talked of a new St. Bartholomew's Night. He said that "the SA must have freedom of the streets," and he said he expected five thousand dead. His outburst may have been intended to frighten Papen and Schleicher—Hitler often staged such tantrums as a purely theatrical device—but it failed to do so. Schleicher later remarked that Hitler seemed to be insane.

Later that same day, President Hindenburg summoned the angry Führer to his office for an accounting. Hindenburg had met Hitler only a few times and had disliked him intensely. He had told Schleicher that he might appoint "that Bohemian corporal" as a postmaster, but never as Chancellor. Now he was displeased to see that Hitler had brought along Röhm, whom the President positively abhorred. The eighty-five-year-old field marshal did not even ask his visitors to sit down. He received them standing, leaning on a cane.

"Herr Hitler, I have only one question to address to you," Hindenburg said. "Are you prepared to offer me your collaboration in the Papen cabinet?"

Hitler said that he had already informed Papen and Schleicher, who were standing nearby, of his terms.

"So you want the whole power?" Hindenburg persisted.

Hitler said he wanted the same power that Mussolini had won in Italy.

Hindenburg "definitely rejected Herr Hitler's demands," according to the official communiqué that followed the meeting, "stating that his conscience and his duties to the Fatherland could not permit him to give the entire governing power exclusively to the National Socialist movement, which wished to make one-sided use of it."

Then, still leaning on his cane, the gigantic old man dressed down the little Führer as though he were an errant orderly. He accused him of lacking "chivalry" in his political campaigns, and he accused him of breaking his word. Or, as the communiqué publicly stated, he "regretted" that Hitler did not support "a national government appointed with the confidence of the Herr Reichspresident, as he had agreed to do."

After ten minutes, the President curtly dismissed his Nazi visitors, defeated and humiliated.

Hitler, blind with rage, was not without weapons, however. For a start, he took control of the Reichstag. It was traditional that the largest party named the presiding officer, and so the new parliamentary chairman, duly elected, was the corpulent ex-pilot who had been released only a few years earlier from a Swedish mental institution, Hermann Goering.

There followed one of the more preposterous scenes in the brief history of this hapless parliament. Chancellor Papen was bold enough to come before the hostile assembly to make a speech outlining his economic program—public works, reduced wages, and tax benefits to anyone who hired the unemployed. The Communists, who, like the Nazis, kept gaining in each election, and who now held 89 seats, promptly proposed a vote of "no-confidence" in Papen's "Cabinet of Barons." At that, Papen tried to wield the familiar weapon of dissolving the Reichstag by presidential decree. He had taken the precaution of having Hindenburg sign the decree before the newly elected Reichstag even opened, but, with his characteristic skill, he had forgotten to bring the decree with him to the Reichstag.

He managed to win a half-hour recess, during which he raced from the Reichstag to the Chancellery and back again, but when he returned, smiling happily, with the red dispatch case that traditionally contained dissolution orders, he found that Goering had different plans. The new Reichstag leader announced that the voting on the "no-confidence" motion was already under way, and, while the Chancellor shouted and waved for recognition, Goering pretended not to see him. Delegate after delegate voted "no-confidence" in the ignored Chancellor—the final tally was 512 to 42—and only at the end did Goering recognize the indignant Papen and receive his dissolution decree. Since the Reichstag had just voted overwhelmingly against Papen's regime, Goering declared that Papen was no longer Chancellor, and therefore the dissolution decree was invalid. "I am firmly resolved," said Goering, "to maintain . . . the rights of Germany's popular representatives to continue to exercise their proper constitutional functions."

Once the little game was played, however, the Nazis gave way to Hindenburg's decree of dissolution. Once again, elections were

called, this time for November 6. And once again, the battle for
power was waged in the streets. By this time, even Papen had grown
concerned about the weekly toll of dead and wounded, and he
decreed a special law imposing the death sentence on anyone who
committed homicide during a political brawl. The law had little
effect. In early August, in the Silesian town of Potempa, five Storm
Troopers broke into the house of a young Communist miner named
Konrad Pietrzuch and, while his mother screamed vainly for help,
kicked him to death. Two weeks later, the five murderers were condemned to death, and Hitler sent them a telegram saying: "My
comrades: in the face of this most monstrous and bloody sentence I
feel myself bound to you in limitless loyalty. From this moment, your
liberation is a question of our honor." A few days later, the murderers' sentence was commuted to life imprisonment, and no one
doubted that Hitler, once in power, would set them free.

Dr. Henry Lowenfeld, the psychoanalyst, working every day
with mental patients at the hospital in the district of Lankwitz,
noticed a strange change taking place during that year. "As the
threat of the Nazis coming to power became greater and greater,"
he says, "you could see its effect even on the mental patients. They
began to play at being Nazis themselves. Of course, a few really were
Nazis. But the others—they would pretend that they were Nazis
too. Some of them, when I came to talk to them, even tried to
threaten me."

The madness began to make people think about leaving their
homes. In Dessau, where the Social Democrats had sponsored the
Bauhaus, the local authorities now quivered at each new Nazi attack on the *Kulturbolschewismus* in their midst. Walter Gropius had
resigned as early as 1928, partly in the belief that the Bauhaus might
fare better under a less controversial director. His successor, the
Swiss architect Hannes Meyer, was of a practical mind, and he increased the production and income of the school's workshops for
furniture, weaving, and metalwork. The increases came not from a
desire for capitalist profits, however, but from a radical sense that, as
he put it, "building is a collective activity." Within two years, he had
reached such a state of conflict with the Dessau authorities that they
forced him to resign, whereupon he departed for Russia with several
of his best pupils.

At Meyer's urging, the Bauhaus students had become thoroughly involved in politics, and when Mies van der Rohe became the new director in 1930, he found a situation that any contemporary American college president might recognize. Bands of radical students gathered in the Bauhaus canteen, accused Mies of "formalism," and demanded that he stage an exhibit of his own work so that they could judge whether he was fit to run the Bauhaus. Mies received a delegation of radical students and told them: "You are here to work and learn. Anyone not present in his classes in the morning will be expelled." Ultimately, though, Mies called in the Dessau police, cleared out the radicals, and shut down the school for several weeks until order could be restored.

The real danger, however, resulted from the state elections in the spring of 1932. As in Prussia, the Nazis made large gains in the province of Anhalt, and the Nazi-dominated government of Dessau demanded that the Bauhaus close down, as of September 30. Mies van der Rohe, who lived in Berlin anyway, moved the remnants of the school to an abandoned telephone factory in the Berlin district of Steglitz, and there the celebrated Bauhaus began its last few months in Germany.

But even as the Bauhaus was moving into Berlin, a number of notable Berliners were beginning to leave. "I did not wait for the end," said Arthur Koestler. "I left Germany for Russia in July, 1932, a few days after the Social Democratic Government of Prussia was chased out of office by [a handful of] men acting on von Papen's orders." George Grosz had even better reasons for leaving. "I had received all kinds of warnings. I had been threatened with death, the destruction of my work, and so on." One night, Grosz had a nightmare about the coming disaster, and, trusting his intuition, he simply decided to pack up and go to the United States. "We had a rather large house on Trautenaustrasse, filled with lovely old furniture, [but] I wasn't really contented any more during those last few months in Germany." For theatrical people, the move was somewhat easier. Marlene Dietrich, already established in Hollywood, came back to her native Berlin in 1932, took a careful look at the state of political warfare, and then decided to return to America for good.

Albert Einstein, too, decided that the time had come for him to leave. Einstein, whom Max Planck had originally wooed to Berlin with such grand offers of money and position, had been treated somewhat differently in recent years. On the occasion of his fiftieth birthday, in 1929, the municipal council had voted to present him with a city-owned villa on the bank of the Havel, near the point where it flows into the Wannsee. Everyone seemed to think this was a splendid reward for the city's (indeed, the world's) most distinguished scientist, and the press published numerous pictures of the "Einstein House." When Mrs. Einstein went to see the place, however, she was surprised to find another family already living in it. The incumbent family was equally surprised, for when the city of Berlin had acquired the park area, it had guaranteed this family the right to remain in the house. The embarrassed City Council then decided to give Einstein a nearby plot of land and to let him build his own house there, at his own expense. Einstein agreed. But the family in the original "Einstein House" protested that the city had promised never to build another house obstructing the view of the water, so the City Council again reneged on its pledge to Einstein. The city then found another piece of land, not on the water but near it, but once again, after the presentation, it turned out that the city did not have the right to dispose of the land.

By this time, the affair was becoming a joke. A council delegate finally came to Einstein and said, "Please pick out a piece of land that suits you and is for sale. We will buy it." Einstein agreed, once more, and Mrs. Einstein finally discovered a beautiful lakeside plot in the suburb of Caputh, near Potsdam. Now, however, the council began to debate about whether to buy the land after all. The depression had begun, and the number of unemployed was rising every month. A Nationalist delegate argued that Einstein did not deserve such a gift of municipal funds. Einstein finally wrote an irritated letter to the Mayor, that unfortunate Gustav Böss who later resigned because of the fur coat that had been presented to his wife. His life was too short, Einstein wrote, for him to depend on the vagaries of the municipal council, and so, thanking the Mayor for his friendly intentions, but observing that his birthday was long past, he declined the gift.

It is hard to know whether this sequence of events represented anything more than official incompetence, though Einstein's biographer, Philipp Frank, insists that it was a conspiracy: "The officials of the city of Berlin carried out the orders of the municipal council in such a way as to result in failure and to make the republican administration look ridiculous." In any case, Einstein himself bought the land in Caputh and built a handsome villa there out of his own savings. "Now we have no money," said Mrs. Einstein, "but we have our land and property. This gives one a much better sense of security."

Einstein was less optimistic. He had gone to California in 1930 and 1931 to teach at Cal Tech, and each time he returned to Berlin, the political situation seemed more forbidding. The election results of 1932 filled him with despair, and as he left the villa in Caputh that fall for another semester at Cal Tech, he said to his wife, "Before you leave our villa this time, take a good look at it."

"Why?" his wife asked.

"You will never see it again," Einstein said.

Shortly before the new elections, scheduled for November 6, the city-owned Berlin Transit Corporation announced that it would have to cut wages. The Social Democratic labor union, with characteristic docility, agreed to negotiate on the problem, but the Communists called a strike, and the Nazis joined them. And so the two sworn enemies, who represented, together, the bitter nay-saying of a majority of the German population, finally united to paralyze the capital. "Not a single streetcar or subway train is operating in Berlin," Goebbels noted happily in his diary. "The general public is observing an admirable solidarity with the workers. . . . Berlin offers the portrait of a dead city. Naturally, our people have seized the direction of the strike in all parts of the city. That's the only way: if you're going to hit them, hit them hard!"

In this bewildering situation, the Germans once again went to the polls and produced the usual bewildering results. Chancellor Papen claimed a victory in the fact that the Nazis had finally slipped, losing two million votes and dropping from 230 seats to 196. (In Berlin, they got scarcely 25 percent of the vote.) But they were still by far the largest party in the new Reichstag, and the forces of Communist opposition on the left had risen from 89 seats to 100. Papen himself could count on the support of only about 60 delegates out of 584, and so, once again, the Germans had elected an ungovernable Reichstag. Hindenburg told Papen to negotiate with the party leaders to see if he could win more support. He failed totally. The Social Democrats passed a formal resolution rejecting even a meeting with the despised Chancellor. His own party, the Catholic Center, formally declared that "under the present political leadership" any prospect of a coalition government was "out of the question."

At this point, General Schleicher decided that it was time to dispose of Franz von Papen. Not only had he failed to solve the nation's economic and political crisis, not only had he failed to win any popular support for a conservative "presidential" regime, but he had showed more independence—incompetent independence, though it might be—than Schleicher had expected or desired. Worst of all, Papen's ability to charm the ancient President with his jokes and banter threatened Schleicher's own position as the unofficial leader of the presidential cabinet. After Papen had been turned away by all the major political parties, therefore, Schleicher artfully proposed on November 17 that the whole cabinet resign so that Hindenburg himself could recruit some support among the political leaders. Papen reluctantly agreed, and Hindenburg, with some distaste, summoned Hitler for a private conference. When Hitler still persisted in demanding full power for himself, rather than accepting the role of Hindenburg's assistant, the talks collapsed.

Papen stepped forward once again with his familiar remedy—he would resume the chancellorship and dissolve the Reichstag yet again, this time indefinitely. But now Schleicher presented a plan of his own. With a little persuasion, he thought he could split the Nazis apart by luring Gregor Strasser and perhaps one-third of the Nazi delegates into a conservative coalition. Papen tried to rally his cabinet behind him, but a number of ministers favored Schleicher's scheme, and so, when Hindenburg had to choose between Papen and Schleicher, he decided to give up his favorite, "Fränzchen." Papen later reported that "two great tears were rolling down [Hindenburg's] cheeks as I shook his hand and turned to go." As a souvenir of his six-month chancellorship, Hindenburg presented Papen with a photograph of himself, emotionally inscribed with the first words of the popular army song, *"Ich hatt' einen Kameraden"* ("I had a comrade").

And so, on December 2, Kurt von Schleicher finally became the last Chancellor of the Weimar Republic. Despite all his intrigues against other chancellors, he seems to have been genuinely reluctant to take the post himself. He proposed several other candidates to Hindenburg, including Hjalmar Schacht, former head of the Reichsbank, and he said of himself, "I am the last horse in your stable and would rather be kept dark." Hindenburg insisted, however, that Schleicher take the responsibility for his plan to divide the Nazis. On the following day, Schleicher called in Gregor Strasser, the Nazi Party secretary, and offered him the offices of Vice Chancellor and Premier of Prussia. If Strasser refused, Schleicher went on, he would again dissolve the Reichstag and put the Nazis through another expensive orgy of campaigning.

Strasser was tempted. He knew that the Nazis were by now virtually bankrupt. ("Nothing but debts and obligations," Goebbels complained in his diaries. "The financial situation of Gau Berlin is hopeless . . . God save us from having to go through with the next election campaign." The party's debts were estimated at between $3 and $5 million, and Goebbels even sent the Storm Troopers out into the streets with tin cups, which they rattled at pedestrians on street corners, begging contributions "for the wicked Nazis.") Besides, Strasser had always argued against the all-or-nothing policy of Hitler and Goebbels; he thought the Nazis should settle for a share of power and then work from inside the government. But now that Schleicher actually offered him the vice chancellorship, he could only answer that he would consult with his Führer.

The Führer was outraged. In a meeting at the Kaiserhof Hotel, he accused Strasser of betraying him and trying to divide the party; Strasser argued that he was trying to save the party from bankruptcy and ruin. They shouted at each other for several hours, and then Strasser stamped out and returned to his own hotel. Instead of fighting for power, he sat down and wrote Hitler an emotional letter, reciting a long list of grievances and resigning from the party leadership. When he had finished this outburst, he simply packed his suitcase and took a train home to Munich. Hitler was dumfounded. "The Führer is taking long strides up and down the hotel room," Goebbels noted. "You can see by his face that a great struggle is going on inside him. . . . Once he stops and says only: 'If the party falls apart, I'll put an end to it all in three minutes with a pistol.'" Hitler soon decided, however, simply to crush Strasser and all his supporters. He drafted a declaration of party unity, praising himself and condemning Strasser, and he had it signed by every party leader. Then he put his head on a table and wept. Goering wept. Goebbels wept. Afterward, Goebbels noted, Hitler "looked quite happy and exalted again."

General Schleicher's master plan was to construct a sort of national coalition that would cut across all the political parties in the Reichstag. On the right, he would bring the more reasonable Nazis into his government. On the left, he had also opened negotiations with Theodor Leipart, the white-bearded chairman of the General Labor Federation, and Leipart seemed quite interested in Schleicher's request for help in drawing up a social program. In the center, this coalition would be held together by the army, which Schleicher, like so many generals in so many centuries, considered the representative of a kind of suprapolitical national unity. It was, in a strange way, a revival of the plan that has been ascribed to the bunglers of the Kapp Putsch. In fact, it is an idea that continually attracts politically minded army officers, the Nassers and De Gaulles. Nor was it a bad idea, and if it had worked, General Schleicher might be praised to this day as the "strong man" who had saved Germany from Hitler.

But it was destined not to work—perhaps because Schleicher was too obscure and politically inexperienced to carry it out, perhaps simply because the breakdown of German society had become too advanced for any such plan. Hitler proved able to hold his party together. So did the Social Democrats, who summoned Leipart to a conference and informed him that "the party leaders opposed any form of collaboration with Schleicher, and that they expected the same attitude from him." But as the disastrous year 1932 ended, Schleicher had no idea that his plans were already doomed. "Hitler is no longer a problem," he said to one visitor. "It is yesterday's concern."

By now, it was nearly Christmas, and the Berliners, like most people, preferred shopping to politics. They celebrated the four Sundays of December by making Advent wreaths and adorning them with candles, lighting a new one each Sunday. Even in their poverty and hopelessness, they found ways to buy Christmas trees, and they gathered around for the traditional carols, "Stille Nacht" and "O Tannenbaum."

In the lull, President Hindenburg sent Schleicher a message on December 25, saying, "Christmas was never so peaceful before. I have to thank you for that, my young friend."

CHAPTER XVII

"The Great Miracle" 1933

No, said the men of Mahagonny . . .
You can't drag us into hell,
Because we always were in hell,
Because we always were in hell,
Because we always were in hell.

BERTOLT BRECHT

A MONTH BEFORE HIS VICTORY, not even Adolf Hitler could have guessed how quickly and easily that victory would come. General Schleicher appeared to be at the height of his power, supported by both the President and the army, and if Schleicher did not realize that his regime had already failed, neither did Hitler. On the contrary, the Nazis entered the new year in a state of virtual despair. Hitler had overcome the defection of Gregor Strasser, but the crisis left the party badly shaken—bankrupt and exhausted by a series of elections that had failed to bring them to power. President Hindenburg had declared repeatedly that he would never make Hitler Chancellor, and the last elections had proved that the Nazi tide could be stopped. "The future looks dark and gloomy," Goebbels wrote in his diary. "All chances and hopes have quite disappeared."

In the first week in January, everything changed. At the *Herrenklub* in Berlin, Papen had made a speech urging that the Nazis be taken into the cabinet, and though most of his listeners ignored his proposal—"The swan song of a poor loser," said one—a Cologne banker named Kurt von Schröder was greatly impressed. He subsequently invited both Papen and Hitler to meet at his house in

Cologne. Accounts of the meeting have varied widely, but if Schröder himself is to be believed, the two visitors soon found that they had a common interest in overthrowing Schleicher. Papen proposed that Nazis and Nationalists form a coalition with himself and Hitler as joint chancellors. Hitler insisted that he alone must become the leader, and that he must have full power to "restore order," which included the expulsion of all Socialists, Communists, and Jews from German public affairs. Papen did not agree with Hitler's plan, but he did agree that they would work together, and Schröder amiably agreed to see that the Nazis' campaign debts were taken care of. "If this coup succeeds," Goebbels noted, "then we shall not be far from total power."

The meeting was supposed to be very secret—Hitler arrived by way of Bonn, changing cars twice en route—but one of Schleicher's agents was stationed outside Schröder's house and took pictures of the visitors. The next day, the Berlin press was full of speculation about what had happened. Officially, though, the Nazis simply went on as before, trying to win power by winning votes. Hitler and Goebbels now put all their energies into a local campaign in the tiny state of Lippe. The total electorate consisted of only ninety thousand voters, but the Nazis' efforts brought them a gain of 17 percent and a symbolic victory, which Goebbels' propaganda machine began proclaiming as the renewal of the Nazis' political momentum. But the real danger, General Schleicher knew, was the possibility that Papen could convince Hindenburg to drop his opposition to Hitler's entry into the Chancellery. Schleicher formally asked that he be present any time Hindenburg received Papen, but Hindenburg rejected the request. Indeed, Hindenburg saw more of his Fränzchen than he did of the Chancellor, for Papen had taken an apartment near to the President's quarters, and the two of them often went for private walks in the President's garden.

Papen was not the only one engaged in persuading the old field marshal. In a Christmas Eve broadcast to the nation, Schleicher had said, among other things, that he planned to resettle thousands of the unemployed on 750,000 acres of "our thinly populated East," and now a delegation from the National Agrarian League called on their fellow landowner, Hindenburg, to raise anew the cry of "agrarian Bolshevism." And finally, there was a meeting between Hitler and Oskar von Hindenburg. Hitler offered bribes (Oskar subsequently was promoted to general, and five thousand acres were added to the Hindenburg estate), but he also threatened to expose the tax evasion involved in the original donation of the Neudeck estate. "In a taxi on the way back," according to Otto Meissner, the President's state secretary, "Oskar von Hindenburg was extremely silent, and the only remark he made was that it could not be helped —the Nazis had to be taken into the government."

Toward the end of January, Schleicher had to confess to Hindenburg that all his plans had failed. He had been unable to split the Nazis and unable to win a majority in the Reichstag. He could only propose, therefore, that the Reichstag be dissolved again. This meant that he could do no better than Papen, and if Hindenburg had to choose between Papen and Schleicher, he now preferred his Fränzchen. On January 28, when Hindenburg refused to let Schleicher dissolve the Reichstag that was to reconvene the following Monday, the general resigned. Hindenburg officially told Papen to undertake negotiations for a new cabinet.

Papen was delighted. He toyed with the idea of trying once again to persuade Hitler to form a joint chancellorship, but if that failed, he felt sure that he could neutralize Hitler's chancellorship by filling the cabinet with non-Nazis. And gradually a plan emerged —Hitler as Chancellor but Papen as Vice Chancellor and Minister-President of Prussia. Baron von Neurath would be summoned home from the German Embassy in London to resume the Foreign Ministry; Hugenberg would take charge of economic affairs. In a cabinet of eleven ministers, Hitler would have only two other Nazis— Wilhelm Frick, his long-time legal assistant, as Minister of Interior, and Goering as Interior Minister of Prussia. "In this way, we will box Hitler in," said Hugenberg.

The greatest uncertainty lay in the reaction of Schleicher and the army. All that weekend, Berlin was full of rumors of an army putsch. Hitler himself later claimed that he feared Schleicher might try to kidnap Hindenburg and proclaim martial law. To counter that danger, Hitler ordered Count Helldorf to put his Berlin Storm Troopers in a state of alert. In fact, however, Schleicher's only maneuver was to make one last, absurd bid for the support of the Nazis. He sent the army commander, General Kurt von Hammerstein-Equord, to call on Hitler and warn him that Papen might betray them all. He suggested that Hitler avoid this danger by joining forces with Schleicher. But Hitler now was gambling on the success of Papen's negotiations. He sent General Hammerstein away with a noncommittal answer.

It was essential to Papen's plan that Schleicher be dismissed from the War Ministry, and so General Werner von Blomberg, the army's third-ranking commander, was summoned to Berlin from Lausanne, where he had been serving as military adviser to the German delegation at the latest disarmament conference. Schleicher was not informed of the summons, but he inevitably learned of it through his network of spies. On the morning of January 30, he sent an officer to meet Blomberg at the Anhalter railroad station and order him to report immediately to the War Ministry. On the same railroad platform, however, stood Oskar von Hindenburg, with orders for Blomberg to report immediately to the presidential palace. Blomberg hesitated for a moment between the two conflicting orders, and then went with Hindenburg.

Only a week earlier, President Hindenburg had said to some officers, "Gentlemen, surely you do not think that I would appoint this Austrian corporal Chancellor of Germany!" But now he was weary of resisting. Papen assured him that Hitler could be kept under control, Blomberg assured him that the army was loyal, and nobody could deny that Hitler had repeatedly won more votes than any other political leader in Germany. The old man shrugged and gave in.

Hitler had stayed up all that night, accompanied by Goering and Goebbels, trying to figure out what Hindenburg would do. It was not until nearly 11 A.M. that Hitler received his summons to the President's office. He was welcomed in the anteroom by Papen, who, according to one witness, "greeted . . . Hitler as the new Chancellor." Hitler thanked him and promptly announced that now he himself would like to call a new election, with the Nazis in control of the machinery. Hugenberg promptly protested that there had been enough elections, and then, in the presidential antechamber, the plotters who had not yet even achieved power began squabbling over how they would run the country. Hitler promised Hugenberg that no matter how the elections came out, he, Hugenberg, could keep his place in the cabinet, but Hugenberg was still suspicious, and Papen was frantic. "Do you wish to endanger the alliance that took so much work to form?" Papen protested to Hugenberg. "Certainly you cannot question a German gentleman's word of honor."

At that point, State Secretary Otto Meissner came rushing in with his watch in his hand.

"Gentlemen, you were scheduled to take your oaths of office with the President at eleven o'clock," he cried. "It is now eleven-fifteen. You certainly cannot keep the President waiting any longer."

On the opposite side of the Wilhelmstrasse, in the Kaiserhof Hotel, Hitler's lieutenants were waiting, still uncertain of what was going on inside the President's office.

"In the street the crowd stands silently waiting between the Kaiserhof and the Chancellery," Goebbels noted. "What is happening there? We are torn between doubt, hope, joy and despair. We have been deceived too often to be able whole-heartedly to believe in the great miracle. Chief of Staff Röhm stands at the window the whole time, watching the door of the Chancellery from which the Führer must emerge. We shall be able to judge by his face if the interview was happy. Torturing hours of waiting. At last a car draws up in front of the entrance. The crowd cheers. They seem to feel that a great change . . . has already begun. . . .

"A few moments later he is with us. He says nothing, and we all remain silent also. His eyes are full of tears. It has come! The Führer is appointed Chancellor. He has already been sworn in by the President of the Reich. The final decision has been made. . . . All of us are dumb with emotion. Everyone clasps the Führer's hand. . . . Outside the Kaiserhof the masses are in a wild uproar. . . . The thousands soon become tens of thousands. And endless streams of people flood the Wilhelmstrasse. We set to work at once. . . ."

All day, the crowds gathered, and at 7 P.M., the great victory parade began. The marchers assembled under the trees of the Tiergarten and then tramped out onto the Charlottenburger Chaussee and eastward to the Brandenburg Gate, where the goddess of victory lashed her stone horses forward. The marchers waved their torches and sang with the lustful joy of a triumphant mob. At the Pariser Platz, just beyond the Brandenburg Gate, they swung to the right and trooped down the Wilhelmstrasse toward the Chancellery, where the forty-three-year-old Führer now reigned.

Hedda Adlon, wife of the owner of the great hotel, had the doors locked at 6 P.M. because every room was already filled with people who wanted to watch the parade. "Densely packed columns streamed out of the darkness," she recalled. "Bands marched between the columns, their big drums beating the rhythm while they played military and old Prussian marches. But as each band crossed the Pariser Platz, where the French Embassy was situated, they stopped whatever they had been playing and with a preliminary roll of drums broke into the tune of the challenging war-song, 'Siegreich wollen wir Frankreich schlagen'—'We mean to defeat France.' Many of the spectators on the crowded pavements were carried away with enthusiasm and burst into frenzied cheers at the playing of this song, but the members of the Embassy, watching from behind drawn curtains, listened with heavy hearts."

And so the exodus began. Not right away, for nobody could really believe that Hitler would be as demonic as he was. Among democratic Germans, the first reaction to his victory was surprise, then bewilderment, then fear. Still, people tried to reassure themselves that Hitler couldn't last, that the threat of dictatorship could be contained by the more respectable conservatives, by Hindenburg and the army. But Hitler moved too quickly to be contained. Through Frick and Goering, he had gained control of the police; through the docile General Blomberg, the army. Less than a month later, Goebbels organized a conspiracy by the Storm Troopers to set the Reichstag on fire and to blame the arson on the Communists. The next day, Hitler produced a presidential decree imposing "restrictions on personal liberty, on the right of free expression and opinion, including freedom of the press; on the rights of assembly and association." Only then, in March, did he stage his elections. He won 44 percent of the vote, the most he ever got, and though the election did not bring him a parliamentary majority, he achieved that by banning the Communist delegates and arresting most of their leaders. Then, with gangs of Storm Troopers bellowing threats outside the Kroll Opera where the legislature now assembled, Hitler demanded of the cowed delegates an "enabling act" that empowered him to rule by decree. After that, there was no need for any more elections.

Bertolt Brecht was among the first to leave. On the day after the Reichstag fire, he packed up and fled to Vienna. Kurt Weill and Lotte Lenya departed soon afterward for Paris. Others kept waiting a little longer, hoping. On April 7, Frick issued the first anti-Semitic decree, concerning the civil service and the educational system. "Officials of non-Aryan origin are to be retired," it said.

Arnold Schoenberg happened to be in Paris that spring, in the midst of his work on the opera *Moses and Aaron*, when he got a message from Berlin announcing that he had been dismissed as a professor at the Academy of Music, and that he had better not come back to Germany. He was stunned to learn, at the age of fifty-nine, that he no longer had either a job or a country. "After all, he was quite a famous guy, and very influential," says Virgil Thomson, the composer. "And now here he was stranded in Paris with a young wife and a baby. I used to go to his hotel on the Rue de Rivoli and take him out for walks. The French tried to be nice to him—particularly Milhaud—but he was very hard to be nice to just then. He didn't know what to do, under the shock of being pushed out of his own country." What he did, finally, was to go to the main synagogue of Paris and ask to see the rabbi. Though raised as a Catholic, Schoenberg now converted to Judaism.

That same April, Artur Schnabel was scheduled to repeat his cycle of the thirty-two Beethoven sonatas over the Berlin radio. He had completed the first four of the seven concerts when the Nazis abruptly cut him off the air. The last sonata to be broadcast, strangely, was the one in E flat, Opus 81A, known as *"Les Adieux."* Schnabel had also agreed to take part in a Berlin festival honoring the one hundredth anniversary of the birth of Brahms. A quartet consisting of Schnabel, Bronislaw Hubermann, Hindemith, and Piatigorsky was to play Brahms's complete chamber music for piano and strings, but now the city's cultural office began to equivocate. "This man telephoned me," Schnabel recalled, "and said: 'Mr. Schnabel, I have to tell you that I am no longer in charge of the Brahms festival and plans have been changed. If you want to negotiate with the new man in charge, it would be—' I interrupted him, saying, 'I expected that.' And I think these were about the last words I said in Germany: 'Though I may not be pure-blooded, I am fortunately cold-blooded. Good luck to you.'"

Rudolf Serkin and Adolf Busch were living in Switzerland at this time, but they were supposed to give a series of Beethoven recitals in Germany. "People told us not to go, many people," says Serkin, "but the people who were sponsoring the concerts wrote us that they expected us to come and play. And, you know, one did not want to be thought a coward. Busch said, 'We will go, and if any-one makes any trouble, I will break my violin over his head.' So we went, and he took a new violin, not his Stradivarius. In Stuttgart, a man stood up in the audience and gave the Hitler salute, and Busch stopped playing and shouted at him: 'Put your arm down!' So he put his arm down, and we went back to playing. Then in Hamburg, the Busch Quartet was going to give a concert, and the news came that Hitler was going to attend. The official in charge of this wrote a letter to Busch, telling him to get a different violist and a different cellist (he was not a Jew but married to a Jew). The letter ended with the words, 'Heil Hitler.' Busch wrote back, refusing to change his quartet and saying that he considered the words 'Heil Hitler' an insult to any decent German. So they took away his citizenship."

It is worth noting that these first moves were not directed against Jews as such—Jewish businessmen, for example, stayed in business for several years longer—but rather against the Jewish intelligentsia (or, as in the case of Busch, the independent-minded intelligentsia). One major reason is that this cultural purge was largely the work of Dr. Joseph Goebbels, who, though not a member of the original cabinet, got himself appointed in March as head of the new Ministry of Propaganda and Public Enlightenment. As such, he became the Gauleiter of German culture, and now it was time to repay that whole class of Jews and "Culture Bolsheviks" who had once rejected his articles and derided his novel.

On May 10, bands of Nazi youths broke into every main library and hauled out the works of the authors Goebbels hated. They brought them by the carload to Unter den Linden, where the Opera House on one side faces the university on the other, and there they set them afire. "*Brenne* [burn] Karl Marx! *Brenne* Sigmund Freud!" cried the young Storm Troopers as they danced wildly around the edges of the bonfire. They burned Walther Rathenau, and Heine, and Remarque, Mann, Zweig, Gide. . . . "This is a strong, great, and symbolic act," cried Goebbels. "Never, as today, have young men had the right to cry out; studies are thriving, spirits awakening, oh, century, it is a joy to live!" Somewhere in that pile of flaming debris, Heine had once written: "Wherever they burn books, sooner or later they will burn human beings also."

Goebbels was particularly attentive toward the press. At the *Berliner Tageblatt,* the Nazi "Labor Front" took over the editorial offices and changed Berlin's most noted liberal newspaper into a Nazi organ. The *Weltbühne* was closed, of course, and Carl von Ossietzky, who had been amnestied only a few months earlier, was rearrested. Kurt Tucholsky, an exile in Sweden, took poison, and on his gravestone, the inscription from Goethe reads: "Everything that passes is only a riddle."

The House of Ullstein, biggest of all German publishers, kept trying desperately to compromise with the new order. But Goebbels finally announced—this was in 1934—that the five Ullstein brothers would have to sell their firm to "Aryan" owners or have all their papers banned. Hermann Ullstein estimated the family's shares at $15 million; the best offer from an "Aryan" buyer was $1.5 million. Hermann Ullstein himself ended with $25,000, and, on trying to leave the country, he was told that he could not get a passport until he made "another sacrifice," namely a donation of $25,000 to the Berlin police. He went to England penniless.

Goebbels was also interested in art. In April, Storm Troopers raided and then closed down the Bauhaus on the grounds that it had supposedly printed Communist leaflets. For several months, Mies van der Rohe negotiated with the Nazi authorities to get the ban lifted, but when the Gestapo demanded the dismissal of Kandinsky and several other teachers, and their replacement by Nazis, Mies informed them that the Bauhaus was closing for good. Mies and Gropius and Albers and Breuer and Moholy-Nagy all went, eventually, to America.

And in the field of painting, too, Goebbels was an expert. The Berlin State Museum now took down from its walls the works of, among others, Van Gogh, Gris, Beckmann, Feininger, Grosz, Kandinsky, Kokoschka. Goebbels even put together a collection of such pictures, which he displayed under the title of *"Entartete Kunst,"* or "Degenerate Art." It proved to be quite popular. But the painters left—Grosz and Feininger to America, Beckmann to Holland, Kandinsky to Paris.

Goebbels' revenge was not always negative. He admired, for example, the films of Fritz Lang, and shortly after becoming the Minister of Public Enlightenment, he summoned the director to his office. "He told me that, many years before, he and the Führer had seen my picture *Metropolis* in a small town," Lang recalled, "and Hitler had said at that time that he wanted me to make Nazi pictures." Goebbels now proposed that Lang assume a prominent position in the movie productions of the new order. Lang answered by observing that he was partly Jewish. Goebbels said that this could be overlooked because of Lang's distinguished combat record in the war. Lang asked for twenty-four hours to consider the offer. Then he asked a friend to book him passage, under an assumed name, on the sleeper to Paris, and he fled Germany that same night.

And in Paris there was Count Harry Kessler, who had learned during a visit there that he would be arrested if he returned to Berlin. Kessler, who was to die in exile in 1937, now made his rounds among the refugees—Georg Bernhard, once the celebrated editor of the *Vossische Zeitung*, and old Ludwig Quidde, the head of the German Peace Movement, and Hugo Simon, the banker, and Rudolf Hilferding, the former Finance Minister, and Wieland Herzfelde, the publisher, and Alfred Flechtheim, the art dealer, and, finally, Heinrich Brüning. The Ex-Chancellor spoke bitterly of Hindenburg, repeated his plan of restoring the monarchy, and said that Hitler couldn't last. "My impression is that Brüning wants and hopes to attain power again," Kessler observed.

Hour after hour, the parade went on during that night of January 30. "Endlessly, endlessly," Goebbels observed with delight, "crowds march by the Chancellery. Storm troopers, Hitler-youths, civilians, men, women, fathers with their children held up high to see the Führer's window. Indescribable enthusiasm fills the streets. A few yards from the Chancellery, the President of the Reich stands at his window, a towering, dignified, heroic figure, invested with a touch of old-time marvel. Now and then with his cane he beats time to the military marches. Hundreds and thousands and hundreds of thousands march past our windows in never-ending uniform rhythm. The rising of a nation!"

The Berliners who left early were the lucky ones, or the wise ones, or simply the accidental survivors. "Heads will roll," Hitler had said, and so it was to be. From the day that Hitler came to power and Goering took control of the Prussian police, the Storm Troopers finally achieved their dream. In a score of abandoned warehouses and factory basements all over Berlin, they acquired, finally, the power not just to commit violence but the much more satisfying power to hit without being hit back. These places were called "concentration camps," but they were not the desolate barbed-wire fortresses that ultimately incriminated the whole German nation. That came later, beginning in the spring of 1934, when Goering demanded that the prison system be "normalized" under his Gestapo, and so the first true concentration camps were built, at Oranienburg, just north of Berlin, and Dachau, just outside Munich. In these early days, though, there were just the warehouses and cellars, where the Brown Shirts took anyone they disliked, and beat them with black-jacks and iron bars, or kicked them to death with their heavy boots. This was their nature and their vocation. "The SA man wants to fight," Goebbels had written, "and he has a right to it, to be led into a fight."

Röhm's Storm Troopers grew too big and too strong, however. They numbered more than 300,000, three times the size of the Reichswehr, and the generals became suspicious of Röhm's power. So did Heinrich Himmler, commander of the "elite" SS, and so did Goering, whose "legal" police forces included the Gestapo. All together, they convinced Hitler that Röhm, his old comrade, was plotting against him. And so, in June of 1934, Hitler unleashed his first great purge. Army and SS units routed Röhm out of his bed in the Hanselbauer Hotel in Wiessee, a lakeside resort not far from Munich, where, the authorities later claimed, the SA chief and his lieutenants had been engaging in a homosexual orgy. There is some evidence, however, that the SS fabricated this, just as they fabricated Röhm's supposed plan for a putsch. Two SS officers handed Röhm a pistol and left him alone in his cell to commit suicide. "If I am to be killed," said Röhm, "let Adolf Hitler do it himself." The two SS officers then shot him point-blank.

In Berlin, Goering and Goebbels decided that the SA leaders were not the only ones to be eliminated. One band of six plain-clothes SS men drove up to General Schleicher's villa on the Wannsee and shot down both the general and his wife. Another band arrested Gregor Strasser and brought him to Gestapo headquarters on the Prinz Albrechtstrasse. There, a police officer shot him through the bars of his cell, but succeeded only in wounding him. Strasser, a big, burly man, lay for several hours in a puddle of his own blood before he finally died. Still another band of assassins went to the office of Franz von Papen, shot down two of his assistants and smashed all the furniture, but Papen himself survived under house arrest. All in all, some 150 "enemies of the state" were rounded up in Berlin alone and taken before a firing squad at the Cadet School in Lichterfelde.

At the time, it seemed a shocking massacre, but as we look back past the massacres that were to follow, the most celebrated victims of the Röhm purge do not inspire great sorrow. One or two hundred murders were not many, according to the standard that Hitler himself set, and most of the victims were villainous characters. Röhm and his brown-shirted henchmen, Gregor Strasser, even General Schleicher, would have killed their enemies with just as little mercy as they received themselves. That is why we remember, among all the more celebrated victims, the case of Dr. Willi Schmidt, a music critic for a Munich newspaper, who was playing the cello in his apartment on that evening of June 30, while his wife cooked supper for their three children. Four SS men arrived at the door and took Dr. Willi Schmidt away, thinking he was another Willi Schmidt, an officer of the Storm Troopers. When Mrs. Schmidt got her husband's body back, the Nazis warned her not to look inside the coffin. They even paid her a pension and told her that her husband had been "a martyr for a great cause."

It was the innocent Willi Schmidt, and not those SA chiefs, who represented, in a way, all the innocent victims that were to come, the Anne Franks and the Dietrich Bonhoeffers and the millions of others whose names we have forgotten, or never known, the long rows of Jews pushed into the gas chambers at Treblinka and Sobibor, the Russian prisoners used for target practice, the fleeing women strafed by Messerschmitts on the highways of France, the children of the Warsaw ghetto, the Hungarian gypsies, and the mentally retarded, and the Seventh-Day Adventists, who refused to salute the swastika, and all the others—perhaps thirty million in all—who were to be bombed and shot and burned and starved for no reason at all except that Adolf Hitler willed it.

On into the night the people marched, waving their torches, singing, a river of fire and triumph through the dark center of Berlin. The masses, as Goebbels always called them, were jubilant.

"The treetops at the Wilhelmplatz in front of the Chancellery," Goebbels noted, "are swarming with boys who cheer the Führer in shrill ear-splitting chorus."

"But those weren't typical Germans," says a white-haired Berliner, a historian, who now lives in New York.

"Then who were they?"

"The Nazis—the Storm Troopers and people like that," he says.

"Weren't they Germans too?"

The professor shrugs. The good Germans like to say that Hitler never won a majority in a free election, but that is like saying that Jack Kennedy and Richard Nixon never won an absolute majority in an American presidential election. No, Hitler did come to power by the standard process of constitutional democracy. One can say that it was a terrible mistake, that nobody really knew how monstrous his rule would be, but one cannot say that it did not happen quite legally and quite democratically.

"Seldom has a nation so readily surrendered all its rights and liberties," according to Hans Gisevius, who, as a young lawyer, shared in the national illusion, "as did ours in those first hopeful, intoxicated months of the new millennium. . . . The lost war, continual unrest, the inflation, grave evidences of cultural decay, unemployment . . . all these things and a great deal more preyed upon the souls of sixty million people. And then it suddenly appeared that the pressure was relaxing. All distress of mind . . . all misery of body was to be exchanged for work, bread, and a good livelihood. . . .

"Abruptly men's spirits changed. A wild national jubilation broke out. Banners, garlands, testimonials, laudatory telegrams, worshipful orations, changes of street names, became as commonplace as parades and demonstrations. . . . The glorious sensation of a new fraternity overwhelmed all groups and classes. Professor and waitress, laborer and industrialist, servant girl and trader, clerks, peasants, soldiers and government workers—all of them suddenly learned what seemed to be the greatest discovery of the century—that they were comrades of one race, 'Volksgenossen.' Above all, youth, youth was getting its due."

And there were those who stayed, and went on about their daily lives, and lived through it all. Gisevius, for one, soon changed his mind and became a leader of the anti-Hitler underground. But that underground was never very large, for it took an exceptional degree of courage to run the risk of falling into the hands of the Gestapo. Even today, when one visits the whitewashed stone execution chamber in Berlin's Plötzensee Prison and sees the six meat hooks suspended from the ceiling (the nearby guillotine was taken away by the Russians) where the July 20 conspirators were hanged with piano wire and then filmed with movie cameras so that Hitler could watch their last twitches—even today, seeing this, one wonders how anyone ever had the courage to resist.

It took courage even to flee—courage and a certain amount of money, or friends abroad, or at least a sense that one did have the ability to make a new life for oneself and one's children in a foreign country. Flight also required a quality of despair, a conviction (true, as it turned out, but not wholly predictable) that things would never get better, and that the only alternative was death. Not everyone who fled did so as a matter of free choice, much less as a matter of democratic principle. And among those who stayed behind—to live or to die—there were all the usual reasons. Some, of course, were Nazis—though the number of these were probably smaller in Berlin than in any other German city—and some others stayed on to fight against the Nazis. But most people do not lead political lives; they do their best to avoid politics. And the reasons for staying or not staying were completely conventional—a job lost or a job that seemed worth clinging to, a divorce, a sick mother, a sense of adventure or of inertia.

The desire to live one's own life as best one can, to do one's own work and raise one's own children, is not a contemptible emotion. And to understand the ordinary Berliner in 1933, one can only try to imagine what one might do oneself in a similar situation.

For the Berliners of those early years, it must have seemed that Hitler not only achieved great successes but won the praise of the outside world. There was very little news from Dachau and Oranienburg, but everyone agreed to stage the 1936 Olympics in Berlin, and although Hitler may have been chagrined at the victories of Jesse Owens, he and his people could take pride in the fact that Germany won those Olympic games. When Hitler canceled all reparations, when Hitler marched troops into the Rhineland, when Hitler walked out of the League of Nations, when Hitler staged the *Anschluss* with Austria—which of the great powers of the world did anything to stop him? And what lessons should the ordinary Berliner have drawn from Hitler's triumphs?

Some of those who stayed "collaborated" with the Nazis—Wilhelm Furtwängler, for example, conducting Wagner at the party festivals in Nürnberg. Others did not—Käthe Kollwitz, for example, working beside her husband in his clinic for the workers of East Berlin, and continuing to produce her powerful portraits of the poor and the hungry. But most of the Berliners never had the freedom of choice that is available to famous artists. They stayed because they had nowhere else to go, and they lived as they always had, trying to earn their suppers and trying to survive. In the early days of the war, the Berliners probably profited, for the first and last time, for their acquiescence. There was more food in Berlin than in, say, Warsaw. But if this was a communal sin, the Berliners had to expiate it under the Allied bombings that began in 1943. For every extra egg they had eaten, they paid in fire.

The torchlit parade lasted until one o'clock in the morning, when, after six hours of singing and shouting, the last remnants of the faithful gathered outside the Chancellery in the hope of seeing their new Führer.

"Long after midnight," Goebbels recorded, "ten thousand people still stand in front of the Chancellery and sing the 'Horst Wessel Song.' I deliver a short address to the masses and close with three cheers for Hindenburg and the Führer. This miraculous night ends in a frenzy of enthusiasm.

"At length the square is empty. We close the windows and are surrounded by absolute silence. The Führer lays his hands on my shoulders in silence. . . .

"The German Revolution has begun!"

A Note on Sources

IT SEEMS ALMOST PRESUMPTUOUS to attempt a bibliography on Germany in the 1920's, for the subject has already been investigated so extensively that nobody can ever finish reading the available material. In the New York Public Library alone, the catalogue room has 47 drawers of cards of books on Germany. There also exists a *Berliner-Bibliographie*, published in 1965 under the auspices of West Berlin's Free University, which contains more than 1,000 pages simply listing works on various aspects of the city. The Wiener Library in London has published its own bibliographies in separate volumes—including *From Weimar to Hitler*, 269 pp., 1951, revised edition, 1964, and *German Jewry*, 279 pp., 1958.

Still, since I have avoided the apparatus of academic footnotes, I want to offer some accounting here of the material used in this book. (I shall cite, wherever possible, American editions rather than German ones, and recent works rather than old ones. I shall also omit, for the most part, novels and other works of the imagination, since they apply only indirectly to a history of the period.)

CHAPTER I. (PROLOGUE). Dr. Redslob's recollection of the Weimar eagle, like much of this chapter, comes from my own interviewing and observation. To differentiate this kind of material from quotations from published works, I have put all my own reporting, throughout the book, in the present tense. And as a matter of record, the present tense signifies the years 1969–70, when the interviewing was done.

For statistics on Berlin, the basic work is *Berlin-ABC*, an encyclopedia edited by Walter Krumholz and published in 1968 by the municipal authorities. See also *The Berliners: Their Saga and Their City*, by Walter Henry Nelson (N.Y., 1969).

The best social history of Berlin, and a splendid book, is *Berlin: Schicksal einer Weltstadt*, by Walter Kiaulehn (Munich, 1958). See also *Imperial Berlin*, by Gerhard Masur (N.Y., 1970). For the details of the destruction of Berlin during World War II, I have relied on *The Last Battle*, by Cornelius Ryan (N.Y., 1966).

CHAPTER II (1918). The best political history of Germany during the

1920's, in my judgment, is *A History of the Weimar Republic*, by Erich Eyck (Cambridge, Mass., 1962). I have used it repeatedly throughout my own work. For the revolutionary period, I have relied a good deal on Richard Watts' admirable book, *The Kings Depart: The Tragedy of Germany: Versailles and the German Revolution* (N.Y., 1968). I am also greatly indebted to Sir John Wheeler-Bennett's excellent study, *Nemesis of Power: The German Army in Politics, 1918–1945* (N.Y., 1964), and for his *Wooden Titan: Hindenburg in Twenty Years of German History, 1914–1934* (N.Y., 1936, revised edition, 1967). On Hindenburg's chief subordinate, see *Ludendorff: Genius of World War I*, by D. J. Goodspeed (Boston, 1966). For a short general summary, see also *History of Germany since 1789*, by Golo Mann (London, 1968). Also *Germany Tried Democracy: A Political History of the Reich from 1918 to 1933*, by S. William Halperin (N.Y., 1946).

As for specific material from other books: The account of how Berlin learned of the armistice comes from *The Rise and Fall of the House of Ullstein*, by Hermann Ullstein (N.Y., 1943). Friedrich Meinecke's account of how the war began comes from *The German Catastrophe: Reflections and Recollections* (Boston, 1950). Bertolt Brecht's story of his wartime experiences appears in a 1937 interview with the Russian poet Sergey Tretiakov, republished in *Brecht: A Collection of Critical Essays*, edited by Peter Demetz (Englewood Cliffs, N.J., 1962). The refutation of this story comes in Hugo Schmidt's notes to Brecht's *Manual of Piety* (N.Y., 1966). The quotations from Tucholsky are from *Kurt Tucholsky and the Ordeal of Germany, 1914–1935*, by Harold L. Poor (N.Y., 1968). Artur Schnabel's recollection of the revolution is in *My Life and Music* (N.Y., 1963), while Pola Negri's adventures are in *Memoirs of a Star* (N.Y., 1970). Ben Hecht's account of Liebknecht at the palace is in his autobiography, *A Child of the Century* (N.Y., 1954). The critic who denounces Ebert for his agreement with the army is William Shirer, in *The Rise and Fall of the Third Reich* (N.Y., 1960). The story of Goering's attack on the government comes from *Goering*, by Roger Manvell and Heinrich Fraenkel (N.Y., 1962).

The diaries of Count Harry Kessler, which I have cited repeatedly, were first published in Frankfurt-am-Main, Germany, in 1961, as *Tage Bücher, 1918–1937: Politik, Kunst, Gesellschaft der Zwanziger Jahre* (edited by Wolfgang Pfeiffer-Belli). A slightly condensed English translation appeared under the title *In the Twenties* (N.Y., 1971).

CHAPTER III (1919). The basic material on the Spartakus uprising is much the same as that for the revolution of 1918. I have followed, primarily, Eyck, Watts, and Wheeler-Bennett. From the large body of literature by and about Karl Liebknecht and Rosa Luxemburg, I have relied mainly on *Rosa Luxemburg*, by Peter Nettl (London, 1966). For a solid but rather partisan account of left-wing activity during the crisis, see *Stalin and German Communism*, by Ruth Fischer (Cambridge, Mass., 1948).

On Albert Einstein, who appears a number of times in this book, the best general biography is *Einstein: The Life and Times*, by Ronald W. Clark (N.Y. and Cleveland, 1971). See also *Einstein: His Life and Times*, by Philipp Frank

(N.Y., 1947). For nonscientific "popular" biographies, see *The Drama of Albert Einstein*, by Antonina Vallentin (N.Y., 1954), and *Einstein: Profile of the Man*, by Peter Michelmore (N.Y., 1962). Among the various attempts to explain Einstein's work, the best, I think, are *The Universe and Doctor Einstein*, by Lincoln Barnett (N.Y., 1948), and *Albert Einstein: His Work and Its Influence on Our World*, by Leopold Infeld (N.Y., 1950). Einstein himself published, apart from his scientific work, several collections of speeches and papers, notably *The World as I See It* (N.Y., 1934) and *Out of My Later Years* (N.Y., 1950).

George Grosz's memoirs, entitled *A Little Yes and a Big No*, appeared in New York in 1946.

CHAPTER IV (1920). The best book on the Freikorps is *Vanguard of Nazism: The Free Corps Movement in Postwar Germany, 1918–1923*, by Robert G. L. Waite (Cambridge, Mass., 1952). For an insider's version of the Kapp Putsch, see *The Political Education of Arnold Brecht: An Autobiography* (Princeton, N.J., 1970). On the life of Erzberger, the definitive work is *Matthias Erzberger and the Dilemma of German Democracy*, by Klaus Epstein (Princeton, N.J., 1959).

The story of the genesis of *Dr. Caligari* comes from Siegfried Kracauer's excellent book, *From Caligari to Hitler: A Psychological History of the German Film* (Princeton, N.J., 1947), which is still the basic history of the German movie industry. For the early years of Lubitsch, see also *The Lubitsch Touch*, by Herman G. Weinberg (N.Y., 1968), and the memoirs of Pola Negri. Ilya Ehrenburg's recollections are in *Memoires, 1921–1941* (Cleveland, 1964). The little book called *Caligari und Caligarismus* was edited by Walter Kaul and published by the Deutsche Kinemathek in Berlin in 1970.

The literature on the psychoanalytic movement is almost limitless. The basic work, aside from Freud's own writings, is *The Life and Work of Sigmund Freud*, by Ernest Jones (N.Y., 1957). See also *The History of Psychiatry: An Evaluation of Psychiatric Thought and Practice from Prehistoric Times to the Present*, by Franz Alexander and Sheldon Selesnick (N.Y., 1966). For more details on the movement in Berlin, see *Psychoanalytic Pioneers*, edited by Franz Alexander, Samuel Eisenstein, and Martin Grotjahn (N.Y., 1966), plus Alexander's semiautobiographical work, *The Western Mind in Transition: An Eyewitness Story* (N.Y., 1960). There also exists a short treatise devoted solely to the Berlin movement: *Zehn Jahre Berliner Psychoanalytisches Institut*, edited by Sandor Rado (Vienna, 1930). For an unusual view of politics, see *The Mass Psychology of Fascism*, by Wilhelm Reich (N.Y., 1946, reissued in 1969). See also *Escape from Freedom*, by Erich Fromm (N.Y., 1941, revised in 1965).

Kurt Tucholsky's description of the Nationalists comes from a recent anthology of his work, *What If—? Satirical Writings of Kurt Tucholsky*, translated and edited by Harry Zohn and Karl F. Ross (N.Y., 1967).

CHAPTER V (1921). The best general account of Russo-German relations is *Russia and Germany: A Century of Conflict*, by Walter Laqueur (Boston, 1965). Among the many recollections of individual Russians, I have quoted

Memoires, 1921–1941, by Ilya Ehrenburg; *Impresario: A Memoir,* by Sol Hurok (N.Y., 1946), and *Cellist,* by Gregor Piatigorsky (N.Y., 1965). The story of Horowitz's debut comes from *Speaking of Pianists,* by Abram Chasins (N.Y., 1957). The story of Pavlova comes from *A Part of Myself: Portrait of an Epoch,* by Carl Zuckmayer (N.Y., 1970).

There is no really comprehensive book on Vladimir Nabokov—least of all his own enigmatic *Speak, Memory: An Autobiography Revisited* (N.Y., 1966), a revision of *Conclusive Evidence,* published in 1951. Probably the best is *Nabokov: His Life in Art,* by Andrew Field (Boston, 1967). Mr. Field is now reported to be at work on a biography of Nabokov. But the basic material on Nabokov in Berlin is all in his novels—from *Mashenka (Mary),* originally published in 1924, to *Laughter in the Dark* (1938)—and after a long period in Limbo, they now are all newly translated and freely available.

On General Seeckt, I have relied mainly on Wheeler-Bennett. See also *History of the German General Staff, 1657–1945,* by Walter Goerlitz (N.Y., 1953).

CHAPTER VI (1922). The first biography of Rathenau, and still the best, is *Walther Rathenau: His Life and Work,* by Count Harry Kessler (N.Y., 1930). Kessler knew his subject well, and admired him, not without reservations. See also *Three Intellectuals in Politics: Blum, Rathenau, Marinetti,* by James Joll (N.Y., 1960).

For the story of Rathenau's killers, we must rely—warily—on the works of Ernst von Salomon, a member of the conspiracy. Salomon is scarcely objective, or even wholly reliable, but he was there. His first book on the case was a slightly fictionalized memoir entitled *The Outlaws* (London, 1931). He returned to the question in a postwar autobiography, *Fragebogen (The Questionnaire),* (Garden City, N.Y., 1955).

On the general history of the Jews in Germany, I mention again the Wiener Library bibliography, *German Jewry: Its History, Life and Culture,* edited by Ilse R. Wolff. Among the many works available, I found the following most immediately useful: *The Jews of Germany: A Story of Sixteen Centuries,* by Marvin Lowenthal (Philadelphia, 1936); *Before the Fury: Jews and Germans before Hitler,* by Emil Herz (N.Y., 1966); *Post-Mortem: The Jews in Germany Today,* by Leo Katcher (N.Y., 1968); *The Dilemma of the Modern Jew,* by Joachim Prinz (Boston, 1962); and the annual anthology called *The Leo Baeck Institute Yearbooks,* which began in London in 1956, under the editorship of Robert Weltsch, and now number more than a dozen volumes on many aspects of German-Jewish history and culture.

CHAPTER VII (1923). I know of no good economic history of Germany in the 1920's, so, for the story of the inflation, I have relied mainly on Eyck's *History.* For a prophetic analysis of the problem, see also *The Economic Consequences of the Peace,* by John Maynard Keynes (N.Y., 1920).

Everyone who lived through the inflation has his own stories to tell. I have quoted from *The Diary of an Ambassador,* by Viscount D'Abernon (New York, 1930); *The Kindness of Strangers,* by Salka Viertel (N.Y., 1969); *Exile's Return,* by Malcolm Cowley (N.Y., 1951); *Always the Unexpected,* by

Louis P. Lochner (N.Y., 1956); and the previously noted autobiographies of Artur Schnabel, George Grosz, and Hermann Ullstein.

The feverish sexuality of Berlin also appears in a great many memoirs. I have quoted from *The Turning Point: Thirty-Five Years in This Century*, by Klaus Mann (N.Y., 1942); *Fun in a Chinese Laundry*, by Josef von Sternberg (N.Y., 1965); *A Girl Like I*, by Anita Loos (N.Y., 1966); *The World of Yesterday: An Autobiography*, by Stefan Zweig (Lincoln, Neb., 1943); and *What Time's the Next Swan?*, by Walter Slezak (Garden City, N.Y., 1962).

The best general account of Hitler's rise to power, I think, is *Hitler: A Study in Tyranny*, by Alan Bullock (N.Y., 1952, revised, 1964). I have also relied a good deal on Konrad Heiden's fascinating but somewhat temperamental biography, *Der Führer: Hitler's Rise to Power* (Boston, 1944). See also William Shirer's *Rise and Fall of the Third Reich*. On Hitler's *Mein Kampf*, I have used the translation by Ralph Mannheim (Boston, 1943).

For a good survey of Stresemann's domestic policies, see *Stresemann and the Politics of the Weimar Republic*, by Henry Ashby Turner, Jr. (Princeton, N.J., 1963). On the curency reform, I have quoted Hjalmar Schacht's autobiography, *Confessions of 'The Old Wizard'* (Boston, 1956), but he is not the most reliable of witnesses.

CHAPTER VIII (1924). The best collection of documents on the Dada movement is *The Dada Painters and Poets*, edited by Robert Motherwell (N.Y., 1951), which contains the two basic statements by Richard Huelsenbeck, *En Avant Dada* (1920) and *Dada Lives* (1934). For another interesting memoir of the German Dada movement, see *Dada: Art and Anti-Art*, by Hans Richter (N.Y., 1965). The best American account of the movement as a whole is probably Malcolm Cowley's *Exile's Return*. See also *Dada, Surrealism, and Their Heritage*, by William S. Rubin (N.Y., 1968).

On the café life in Berlin, I have quoted both from Rubin and from *Life Among the Surrealists: A Memoir*, by Matthew Josephson (N.Y., 1962). See, also, *Das Romanische Café: Erscheinungen und Rander-Scheinungen rund um die Gedächtniskirche*, by Georg Zivier (Berlin, 1965). And, of course, George Grosz's *A Little Yes*, cited earlier.

The literature on Expressionism is very large. I have relied principally on *German Expressionist Painting*, by Peter Selz (Berkeley, Calif., 1957); *The German Expressionists: A Generation in Revolt*, by B. S. Meyers (N.Y., 1957); and *Voices of German Expressionism*, edited by Victor H. Miesel (Englewood Cliffs, N.J., 1970). The critic who denounced the New Objectivity is Siegfried Kracauer.

The basic collection of documents on the Bauhaus is *The Bauhaus— Weimar, Dessau, Berlin, Chicago*, edited by Hans M. Wingler (Cambridge, Mass., 1969). Basic is too mild a word for this gigantic 653-page volume; it is indispensable. For further details on various Bauhaus masters, I have found interesting material in the following: *The New Architecture and the Bauhaus*, by Walter Gropius (Cambridge, Mass., 1965); *Scope of Total Architecture*, by Walter Gropius (N.Y., 1962); *The Mind and Work of Paul Klee*, by Werner Haftmann (N.Y., 1967); *Pedagogical Sketchbook*, by Paul Klee (N.Y., 1953);

Moholy-Nagy, Experiment in Totality, by Sibyl Moholy-Nagy (Cambridge, Mass., 1950); *Wassily Kandinsky: Life and Work,* by Will Grohmann (N.Y., 1959); *Mies van der Rohe, Architecture and Structure,* by Peter Blake (N.Y., 1966); and *German Painting in the Twentieth Century,* by Franz Roh (Greenwich, Conn., 1968). For a curiously oblique view of Gropius, see also *And the Bridge Is Love,* by Alma Mahler Werfel (N.Y., 1958).

Several of these books deal with Berlin architecture, as distinct from the Bauhaus. The best book I have found on the work of Mendelsohn is *Eric Mendelsohn,* by Arnold Whittick (N.Y., 1940). See, also, *Letters of an Architect,* by Eric Mendelsohn (N.Y., 1967). In addition, I have made use of *Bauen Seit 1900,* edited by Rolf Rave and Hans Joachim Knöfel (Berlin, 1963), a collection of pictures and floor plans of every major modern building in Berlin. For various minor aspects of this story, like the building of Wertheim's department store, I am indebted once again to Kiaulehn's book, *Berlin: Schicksal einer Weltstadt.*

CHAPTER IX (1925). Friedrich Ebert never wrote his memoirs and never acquired a major biographer. In this section, I have relied again on Eyck, with contrary views from previously noted critics like Grosz and Tucholsky.

There is no comprehensive account of the musical scene in Berlin. On Busoni, I am indebted to Harold Schonberg's *The Great Pianists* (N.Y., 1963). On Schnabel, I have used not only his own memoirs but also *Artur Schnabel: A Biography,* by César Saerchinger (N.Y., 1957), and, again, Piatigorsky's admirable reminiscence, *Cellist.* See also *Theme and Variations: An Autobiography,* by Bruno Walter (N.Y., 1946), and *Fritz Kreisler,* by Louis P. Lochner (N.Y., 1950).

On the atonalists, I have relied primarily on *Arnold Schoenberg,* by H. H. Stuckenschmidt (London, 1959); *Arnold Schoenberg,* by Egon Wellesz (N.Y., 1969); *Schoenberg,* by Anthony Payne (London, 1968); *Alban Berg: The Man and His Music,* by H. F. Redlich (N.Y., 1957); and *Alban Berg,* by Willi Reich (N.Y., 1965). The effervescence of the new music, however, is best described in the memoirs of Hans Heinsheimer, *Best Regards to Aïda* (N.Y., 1968). See also *A Composer's World, Horizons and Limitations,* by Paul Hindemith (Cambridge, Mass., 1952).

The account of Hitler's plans to rebuild Berlin comes from *Inside the Third Reich: Memoirs,* by Albert Speer (N.Y., 1970).

CHAPTER X (1926). Joseph Goebbels is such an extraordinary creation of his own fantasy that I have tried, as much as possible, to let him tell his own story. He wrote tirelessly in his journals throughout his life, but, while unreliable in their original form, they were doctored and falsified even further before Goebbels published certain excerpts. The basic documents concerning the Weimar period are: *The Early Goebbels Diaries* (N.Y., 1963), covering the years 1925–26 and published posthumously; *Kampf um Berlin: Der Anfang,* by Joseph Goebbels (Munich, 1932), covering his early years as Gauleiter of Berlin; and *My Part in Germany's Fight,* by Joseph Goebbels (London, 1935) (originally: *Vom Kaiserhof zur Reichskanzlei*), covering the critical period of 1932–33.

The best general biography is *Dr. Goebbels: His Life and Death*, by Roger Manvell and Heinrich Fraenkel (N.Y., 1960). For a more detailed study of his methods, see *Goebbels and National Socialist Propaganda*, by Ernest K. Bramsted (Lansing, Mich., 1965). For vivid short profiles of Goebbels and his rivals, see *The Faces of the Third Reich: Portraits of the Nazi Leadership*, by Joachim C. Fest (N.Y., 1970).

Otto Strasser's version of history is about as reliable as that of Goebbels, but, once again, his personal involvement makes his story worth hearing. The basic version is *Hitler and I*, by Otto Strasser (Boston, 1940).

CHAPTER XI (1927). The central figure in the scientific world of Berlin in the 1920's is, of course, Einstein. I have already listed the basic works on this subject. The best general account of nuclear physics during this period is Robert Jungk's *Brighter than a Thousand Suns: A Personal History of the Atomic Scientists* (N.Y., 1958).

The best exponent of Werner Heisenberg's views is Heisenberg himself—*Physics and Philosophy: The Revolution in Modern Science* (N.Y., 1958) and *Physics and Beyond: Encounters and Conversations* (N.Y., 1971). Among the other memoirs of German scientists, I was particularly impressed by *My Life and Views*, by Max Born (N.Y., 1968), and *A Scientific Autobiography*, by Otto Hahn (N.Y., 1966).

General Dornberger has recounted his adventures with rockets in *V-2* (N.Y., 1954). Wernher von Braun's recollections appear in *The Man in the Thick Lead Suit*, by Daniel Lang (N.Y., 1954). For further details, see *The Birth of the Missile: The Secrets of Peenemünde*, by Ernst Klee and Otto Merk (N.Y., 1965), and *The Virus House: German Atomic Research and Allied Counter-Measures*, by David Irving (London, 1967).

On the German Youth Movement, the best work in English is *Young Germany*, by Walter Z. Laqueur (N.Y., 1962). On Stefan George, see also *The Mind of Germany: The Education of a Nation*, by Hans Kohn (N.Y., 1960). Paul Krantz's story was published in Paris in 1970 under the title *Memoires d'un Allemand*, by Ernst Erich Noth. Magnus Hirschfeld appears several times in Jones's biography of Freud. The quotation on sexual reformers comes from Kiaulehn.

The quotations from Käthe Kollwitz are from *Diaries and Letters of Kaethe Kollwitz* (Chicago, 1955).

CHAPTER XII (1928). The literature on the Berlin theatre is enormous. To start with Brecht, his sixty-odd plays are now available in German in a uniform edition published by Suhrkamp Verlag. The state of his work in America is less clear. We all owe a great debt to the pioneering and crusading of Brecht's American disciple, Eric Bentley, which resulted first in the notable collection, *Seven Plays by Bertolt Brecht* (N.Y., 1961), in the bilingual edition of *Manual of Piety* (N.Y., 1966), and in the series of Grove Press editions of Brecht's works (nineteen volumes have appeared in all). Bentley's translations are not entirely immune to criticism, however, and after a series of skirmishes over copyrights, Random House has begun the official publication of the collected works, under the general supervision of Ralph Mannheim and

John Willett. The first volume appeared in 1971, and the rest are expected to follow over the course of five years.

Bentley has never written a complete book on Brecht, but his introductions to the *Seven Plays* are full of ideas and insights. The first critical biography, and still one of the best, is *Brecht: The Man and His Work*, by Martin Esslin (N.Y., 1960). For pure biography, the best account is *Bertolt Brecht: His Life, His Art, and His Times*, by Frederic Ewen (N.Y., 1967). See also *Brecht: A Collection of Critical Essays*, edited by Peter Demetz; *Brecht on Theatre*, edited by John Willett (N.Y., 1964); *Bert Brecht*, by Willy Haas (N.Y., 1970); *Curtains*, by Kenneth Tynan (London, 1961); and *The Theatre of Revolt: An Approach to Modern Drama*, by Robert Brustein (Boston, 1964), from which I have quoted Brustein's analysis of *The Threepenny Opera*.

For details on the Berlin theatrical scene, I have relied once again on Zuckmayer's charming memoir, *A Part of Myself*. Also Salka Viertel's *The Kindness of Strangers*. My account of Piscator's struggles comes largely from *The Piscator Experiment: The Political Theatre*, by Maria Ley-Piscator (N.Y., 1967). For a survey of this whole period, see *Modern German Drama*, by H. F. Garten (London, 1959); for an entertaining memoir by one of its stars, see *Aller Tage Abend*, by Fritz Kortner (Munich, 1959).

The career of Kurt Weill is much less fully documented than that of Brecht, and for much of the detail, we must rely on the various statements by Lotte Lenya. Miss Lenya has declared that she is writing her memoirs, but no publication date has been announced. In the meantime, I have culled her recollections from the notes to her recordings of *The Threepenny Opera* and *Mahagonny;* from her introduction to the Grove Press edition of *Threepenny Opera* (originally published in *Theatre Arts* in 1956), and from a long interview with Rex Reed, republished in Reed's book, *Do You Sleep in the Nude?* (N.Y., 1968). I have also quoted again from Heinsheimer's *Best Regards to Aïda*.

Details on prizefighting come from Kiaulehn. For the story of Dixie Kid, and similar tales, I am indebted to Paul E. Marcus, who, under the name of Pem, wrote a memoir entitled *Heimweh nach dem Kurfürstendamm* (Berlin, 1962), and who still publishes an entertaining London newsletter called *Pem's Personal Bulletins*, recounting the latest doings of many German celebrities of the interwar period.

CHAPTER XIII (1929). On the making of *The Blue Angel*, I have relied primarily on Sternberg's *Fun in a Chinese Laundry*. It is not a book that one can trust without reservations, but it is by far the best account available. See also *Von Kopf bis Fuss: Mein Leben mit Text und Musik*, by Friedrich Holländer (Munich, 1965). Heinrich Mann's novel, *Professor Unrat*, was translated into English under the title of *Small-Town Tyrant* (N.Y., 1944), and the scenario for *The Blue Angel* was published in New York in 1968.

For the story of Marlene Dietrich, who is also said to be writing her memoirs, there is no biography that is even nearly adequate. As three currently available samples, see *Dietrich: The Story of a Star*, by Leslie Frewin (N.Y., 1967); *The Films of Marlene Dietrich*, by Homer Dickens (N.Y., 1968); and *Marlene Dietrich, Image and Legend*, by Richard Griffith (N.Y.,

1959). The quotations of Miss Dietrich criticizing her movies come from Rex Reed's *Do You Sleep in the Nude?*

On Zeppelins, I am indebted to *Ships in the Sky: The Story of the Great Dirigibles*, by John Toland (N.Y., 1957). See also *When Zeppelins Flew*, by Ken Dallison (N.Y., 1965). The account of the *Graf Zeppelin's* round-the-world flight is in Lochner's *Always the Unexpected*.

The various reports on the Berliners' self-indulgence come from *World Within World*, by Stephen Spender (N.Y., 1951), Nabokov's *The Gift* (N.Y., 1963), and the Kessler diaries. The story of the nude skaters comes from Kiaulehn.

And to Kiaulehn I owe thanks for the history of the popular theatre in Berlin, including the story of the girl who fed eggs to the parrot and the story of the water acts at the circus. The account of Anita Berber comes mostly from Pem's *Heimweh* and from *Berlin, Zwanziger Jahre*, by Herbert Pfeiffer (Berlin, 1961).

For the story of the movies on Frederick the Great, I return once again to Kracauer's *From Caligari to Hitler*, with a few borrowings from Peter Gay's *Weimar Culture* (N.Y., 1968). And for the scenario of the Heidelberg student, I must give full credit to Walter Slezak, in *What Time's the Next Swan?*

CHAPTER XIV (1930). As we return to political events, we return to the most reliable sources for the earlier chapters in this book—Eyck, Bullock, Heiden, and Wheeler-Bennett, plus the much less reliable memoirs of Goebbels and Strasser. For details of the effects of the economic crisis, I have quoted from an interesting anthology of contemporary documents, *Deutschland in der Weltwirtschafts Krise in Augenzeugen Berichten*, edited by Wilhelm Treue (Düsseldorf, 1967). See also *The Path to Dictatorship: Ten Essays by German Scholars*, by Theodor Eschenburg et al. (N.Y., 1966).

Brüning's posthumous autobiography has been published under the title *Memoiren, 1918–1934* (Stuttgart, 1970). For a cool view of the Chancellor, see also *The Education of Arnold Brecht*. The basic facts on Goering are in the previously cited biography by Manvell and Fraenkel. See also *I Paid Hitler*, by Fritz Thyssen (N.Y., 1941), a rather disingenuous confession by one of the most culpable of the Ruhr barons. For the details of the Horst Wessel case, see the memoirs of Hans Bernd Gisevius, *To the Bitter End* (Boston, 1947).

CHAPTER XV (1931). The effort to describe crime in Germany during the 1920's leads us in a number of curious directions. In 1933, for example, Geoffrey Gorer wrote a study of the Marquis de Sade, attempting to relate his ideas to those of the Nazis. He later changed his mind, however, and expunged virtually all references to Nazism from the revised edition of *The Life and Ideas of the Marquis de Sade* (N.Y., 1963). Gorer's work nonetheless remains an interesting commentary on the Nazi period. See also the previously cited works by Reich and Fromm.

Fritz Lang's account of his difficulties in filming *M* may be found in Kracauer's *From Caligari to Hitler*. Thea von Harbou's script of the movie itself was published in New York in 1968.

The stories of the various mass murderers have been pieced together from a variety of sources. Brecht's comments on the Denke case come from his previously cited interview with Tretiakov, republished in Demetz's anthology. On Haarmann, I have quoted *It Was All Quite Different*, by Vicki Baum (N.Y., 1964), and *Arrow in the Blue: An Autobiography*, by Arthur Koestler (N.Y., 1952). See also *Richter und Gerichtete*, by Sling (Paul Schlesinger), a collection of articles by the celebrated court reporter for the *Vossische Zeitung*, originally published in 1929 and republished in Munich in 1969; *Ich Beantrage Freispruch*, by Erich Frey, one of the leading defense attorneys of the period (Hamburg, 1959); and *Memoires d'un Allemand*, by Ernst Erich Noth.

The story of Baron Winterfeld comes from the entertaining memoir, *Hotel Adlon: The Life and Death of a Great Hotel*, by Hedda Adlon (N.Y., 1960). The story of the singing policemen comes, once again, from Kiaulehn.

For the story of Ossietzky and the *Weltbühne*, see *Weimar Germany's Left-Wing Intellectuals: A Political History of the Weltbühne and Its Circle*, by Istvan Deak (Berkeley, Calif., 1968); *Kurt Tucholsky*, by Harold Poor; and *Ossietzky, Ein Deutscher Patriot*, by Kurt R. Grossmann (Munich, 1963).

Konrad Heiden's speculations on the fate of Geli Raubal have not been generally accepted by other authorities, but they strike me as plausible, and so I cite them for what they may be worth. Klaus Mann's observations come from *The Turning Point*.

CHAPTER XVI (1932). There is, unfortunately, no good biography of Kurt von Schleicher, and I have relied mainly on the same sources as in Chapter XIV. The main new element is *Memoirs*, by Franz von Papen (N.Y., 1953), a work that strikes me as quite unreliable.

CHAPTER XVII (1933). The statement on 1932 is more or less true for the concluding chapter. But for some of the coming developments, see also *The Twelve-Year Reich: A Social History of Nazi Germany, 1933–1945*, by Richard Gruenberger (N.Y., 1971).

On completing this list, I find that I have omitted a number of books, which, while not quoted in any one chapter, have proved helpful for an understanding of the period as a whole.

First, the picture books, those splendid collections of photographs of long-dead personalities like Karl Liebknecht and Friedrich Ebert—and of personalities whom we think of as old men, who appear here in their youth, the young Max Reinhardt, the young Einstein—and finally of personalities who never became celebrities at all, who remain anonymous figures with umbrellas, scurrying through the rain on the Potsdamer Platz. Specifically, I am indebted to *Die Zwanziger Jahre*, by Bruno E. Werner (Munich, 1962); *Erlebnis Berlin, 300 Jahre Berlin im Spiegel seiner Kunst*, by Hans Ludwig (Berlin, 1960); *Kurfürstendamm Bummel durch ein Jahrhundert*, by Friedrich Wilhelm Lehmann (Berlin, 1964); *Berlin, So wie es war*, by Egon Jameson (Düsseldorf, 1969), and *Berlin als die Sirenen Schwiegen*, by Horst Cornelsen and Klaus Eschen (Hamburg, 1968).

Even then, there remain books of value and interest, which don't seem to fit into any category, but which should be included in any study of this period. I should like to list, in no particular order, the following:

Weimar Culture: The Outsider as Insider, by Peter Gay (N.Y., 1968).

The Origins of Totalitarianism, by Hannah Arendt (N.Y., 1950).

Behemoth: The Structure and Practice of National Socialism, 1933–1944, by Franz Neumann (N.Y., 1942, reissued in 1963).

Germany in the Twentieth Century: A Political and Cultural History of the Weimar Republic and the Third Reich, by Edmond Vermeil (N.Y., 1956).

Confessions of a European Intellectual, by Franz Schoenberner (N.Y., 1946).

A Sketch of My Life, by Thomas Mann (N.Y., 1960).

The Lost Library: The Autobiography of a Culture, by Walter Mehring (N.Y.–Indianapolis, 1951).

Language and Silence: Essays on Language, Literature, and the Inhuman, by George Steiner (N.Y., 1967).

The Intellectual Migration, Europe and America, 1930–1960, edited by Donald Fleming and Bernard Bailyn (Cambridge, Mass., 1969).

Illustrious Immigrants: The Intellectual Migration from Europe, 1930–1941, by Laura Fermi (Chicago, 1968).

In addition to some three hundred books that I have consulted in this work, I owe a special debt to the numerous people who have given up their time to offer an interviewer their recollections of Berlin in the 1920's. Specifically, I want to thank (in alphabetical order):

W. H. Auden, Fritz Bamberger, Stefan Brecht, Abram Chasins, Kurt R. Grossmann, John Gutman, Hans Hirschfeld, Sol Hurok, Christopher Isherwood, Helmut Jaeserich, Michael Josselson, Hans Joachim Kausch, Adolph Lowe, Mr. and Mrs. Henry Lowenfeld, Richard Lowenthal, Friedrich Luft, Yehudi Menuhin, Margaret Muehsam, Henry Pachter, Rabbi Joachim Prinz, Sandor Rado, Edwin Redslob, Franz Schoenberner, Rudolf Serkin, Walter Slezak, Rudi Springer, Hans Staudinger, Virgil Thomson, Salka Viertel, Hans Wallenberg, Peter Wallenberg, Hilde Walther, Otto Wolf, and Ludwig Wronkow.

In addition, I am indebted to a number of people who helped to arrange interviews, or provided ideas and insights. Specifically again in alphabetical order:

Gillon Aitken; Yakov Aviad, of the Israeli Consulate in New York; Heinz and Ingo Bondi; François Bondy; Erwin Böll, of the German Consulate in New York; Christopher Davis; Martin Feinstein, of the Sol Hurok office; Lou Gittler, of the German Information Office in New York; Fred Grubel, of the Leo Baeck Institute; Richard Hanser; Melvin Lasky, of *Encounter* magazine; Johanna Lenhardt; Karin Lenhardt; Paul E. Marcus (Pem); Martin Mayer; Peter Meriton; Paul Moor; Nicholas Nabokov; James P. O'Donnell; John Peet; Francis Robinson, of the Metropolitan Opera; Kenneth Tynan; Edgar Vincent; Tom Wallace; Peter Wyden; Mort Yarmon, of the American Jewish Committee; and, finally, a small army of my aunts and uncles, cousins, in-laws, and various other relatives here and in Germany.

I have consulted a number of libraries to gather research—specifically the New York Public Library, Widener Library at Harvard, the Wiener Library in London, the Hoover Library at Stanford, and the libraries of the New York

Psychoanalytical Institute, the American Jewish Committee, the Goethe House, and the New York Museum of Modern Art—but the greatest help has come from Helen Land and her staff at the Locust Valley Public Library, who exploited all the inter-library-loan resources of the New York State system on my behalf.

OTTO FRIEDRICH

Locust Valley, New York
June 10, 1971

Index

405

GREATER BERLIN
1972

TEGEL FOREST

SPANDAU FOREST

TEGEL
4

REINICKENDORF

PANKOW

TEGEL AIRPORT

Hohenzollern Canal

6
WEDDING

SPANDAU

5

PLÖTZENSEE

Spree River

WESTEND

MOABIT
TIERGARTEN
7

MITTE

19

PICHELSDORF

CHARLOTTENBURG

AREA OF CENTRAL BERLIN MAP

FRIE

3

WEST BERLIN

11 12

13

KURFÜRSTENDAMM

14

18

WILMERSDORF

15

Landwehr Ca

GRUNEWALD

KREUZBERG

GRUNEWALD FOREST

SCHÖNEBURG

NE
20

10

AVUS

TEMPELH
AIRPOF

8

DAHLEM

HAVEL

9

TEMPELHOF

16
STEGLITZ

2

LICHTERFELDE

MARIENDORF

ZEHLENDORF

Teltow Canal

WANNSEE

POTSDAM
1

| 0 | 1 | 2 | 3 | 4 | 5 KILOMETERS |

| 0 | 1 | 2 | 3 | 4 | 5 MILES |

J. P. TREMBLAY